LORENZO LORUSSO

EASTERN CATHOLICS AND LATIN PASTORS

Issues and Canonical Norms

English Edition

John D. Faris

© Copyright 2013 by the Canon Law Society of America

ISBN: 1-932208-35-6
SAN: 237-6296

Originally published as *Gli Orientali Cattolici e i Pastori Latini. Problematiche e norme canoniche.*
© 2003 - Pontificio Istituto Orientale

The Canon Law Society of America's programs and publications are designed solely to help canonists maintain their professional competence. In dealing with specific canonical matters, the canonist using Canon Law Society of America (CLSA) publications or orally conveyed information should also research original sources of authority.

The views and opinions expressed in this publication are those of the individual authors and do not represent the views of the CLSA, its Board of Governors, staff or members. The CLSA does not endorse the views or opinions expressed by the individual authors. The publisher and authors specifically disclaim any liability, loss or risk, personal or otherwise, which is incurred as consequence, directly or indirectly, of the use, reliance, or application of any of the contents of this publication.

Unless otherwise noted, all canons quoted are from the *Code of Canon Law, Latin-English Edition* (Washington, DC: Canon Law Society of America, 1999) and the *Code of Canons of the Eastern Churches, Latin-English Edition* (Washington, DC: Canon Law Society of America, 2002).

Printed in the United States of America.

Canon Law Society of America
Office of the Executive Coordinator
3025 Fourth Street, NE
The Hecker Center, Suite 111
Washington, DC 20017-1102

TABLE OF CONTENTS

ABBREVIATIONS..7

PREFACE TO THE ENGLISH EDITION..11

INTRODUCTION..13

CHAPTER I. THE TWO-FOLD LEGISLATION OF THE CATHOLIC CHURCH........18

I.1. Unity and Diversity in the Ecclesial Communion...........................19

I.2. Ecclesiological Notes of Vatican II regarding the Eastern Catholic Churches..22

I.3. Canon 1 of the Respective Codes of the Catholic Church..............30

    a. Prior Legislation..30

    b. Current Legislation..32

CHAPTER II. ASCRIPTION AND TRANSFER TO A CHURCH *SUI IURIS* IN THE TWO CODES..48

II.1. Criteria of Membership in a Church *sui iuris*..............................48

II.2. Membership in a Specific Church *sui iuris*..................................54

II.3. Parents Ascribed in Different Churches *sui iuris*........................57

II.4. Membership of Only One Parent in the Catholic Church............61

II.5. Child Born to Unmarried Parents..62

II.6. Child Born to Unknown Parents..63

II.7. Child Under the Age of Fourteen of Non-Baptized Parents........64

II.8. Child Under the Age of Fourteen of Baptized Non-Catholics.....65

II.9. Baptizing Persons at Least Fourteen Years Old.............................65

II.10. Transfer of a Spouse to the Church *sui iuris* of the Other Spouse..........66

II.11. Transfer of Parents or, in a Mixed Marriage, of the Catholic Spouse to Another Church *sui iuris*..69

II.12. Transfer to Another Church *sui iuris*..70

II.13. Baptized Non-Catholics..72

II.14. Final Observations..76

Chapter III. Ecclesiastical Hierarchy and the Pastoral Care of the *Christifideles*: Structures of Collaboration 79

    III.1. Apostolic Exarchates and Ordinariates for Eastern Faithful..........80

    III.2. Syncelli and Episcopal Vicars..........85

    III.3. Extra-Territorial Executive Power..........94

    III.4. Erection of Parishes..........96

    III.5. The Formation of Clerics..........101

    III.6. Ascription or Incardination of Clerics..........105

    III.7. Episcopal Conferences..........114

    III.8. Eastern Synods..........118

    III.9. Patriarchal and Eparchial Assembly..........120

    III.10. Inter-ecclesial Assemblies..........122

    III.11. Eastern Hierarchs and the College of Cardinals..........124

    III.12. Inter-ecclesial Associations..........126

    III.13. Evangelization of Peoples..........128

    III.14. Preaching of the Word of God..........130

    III.15. Catechetical Activity..........132

    III.16. Catholic Education..........132

    III.17. Pre-matrimonial Investigations..........133

    III.18. Ecumenism..........135

    III.19. Taxes..........137

    III.20. Penal Laws..........139

    III.21. Procedural Law..........146

    III.22. Ecclesiastical Dignities..........149

Chapter IV. Administration of the Sacraments..........150

    IV.1. Guiding Principles..........150

    IV.2. Christian Initiation..........158

    IV.3. Baptism..........161

        IV.3.1. Minister..........163

IV.3.2. Sponsors...167
IV.4. Chrismation with Holy Myron or Confirmation.......................170
    IV.4.1. Minister...173
    IV.4.2. Sponsor..178
IV.5. Eucharist...178
    IV.5.1. Obligations of the Faithful..179
    IV.5.2. Participation...180
    IV.5.3. Minister of Distribution...183
    IV.5.4. Concelebration...184
    IV.5.5. Offerings for the Divine Liturgy.....................................187
IV.6. Penance and Indulgences..188
IV.7. Anointing of the Sick..201
IV.8. Sacred Ordination...203
IV.9. Sacramentals...207

Chapter V. The Sacrament of Marriage.......................................212

V.1. Doctrine and Legislation..212
V.2. Laws that Regulate Marriage..215
V.3. Preparation...222
V.4. Impediments in General..225
    V.4.1. Competent Authority...225
    V.4.2. Temporary Prohibition..226
V.5. Dispensation..227
V.6. Specific Impediments...230
    V.6.1. Impediment of Age..230
    V.6.2. Impediment of Abduction...230
    V.6.3. Impediment of Affinity..231
    V.6.4. Impediment of Public Propriety.......................................233
    V.6.5. Impediment of Disparity of Worship..............................234
    V.6.6. Impediment of Spiritual Relationship............................234

  V.6.7. Impediment of a Vow..235

V.7. Mixed Marriages..235

V.8. Marriage under Condition..243

V.9. Canonical Form..245

V.10. Competent Minister..252

  V.10.1. Competence of the Minister by Reason of Office......................253

  V.10.2. Competence of the Minister by Reason of Territory.................254

  V.10.3. Competence of the minister in virtue of one of the parties belonging to his Church *sui iuris*..255

  V.10.4. Delegated Faculty..258

V.11. Personal Scope of Canonical Form..261

V.12. Secret Celebration of Marriage...262

CHAPTER VI. CONSECRATED LIFE..264

VI.1. Religious and Hierarchy..264

VI.2. Admission...267

VI.3. Transfer..272

VI.4. Inter-ecclesial Collaboration...275

CONCLUSION..278

APPENDICES..284

BIBLIOGRAPHY..328

Abbreviations

AA	*Apostolicam Actuositatem*, Vatican II, Decree on the Apostolate of the Laity, 18 November 1965.
AAS	*Acta Apostolicae Sedis: Commentarium Officiale*, 1909-
Acta Syn.	*Acta Synodalia Sacrosancti Concilii Œcumenici Vaticani Secundi*. Vatican City, 1970-1980.
AG	*Ad gentes*, Vatican II, Decree on the Church's Missionary Activity, 7 December 1965.
All	Allocution
Ap	Apostolic
Apcon	Apostolic Constitution
Aplet	Apostolic Letter
art./arts.	article/articles
ASS	*Acta Sanctæ Sedis*, 1865-1908.
c./cc.	canon/canons
CA	*Crebræ Allatæ*, 1949.
CCC	*Catechism of the Catholic Church*. Vatican City, 1992.
CCEC	*Code of Canons of the Eastern Churches*. Washington, 2001.
CCEO	*Codex Canonum Ecclesiarum Orientalium*, 1990.
CD	*Christus Dominus*, Vatican II, Decree on the Pastoral Office of Bishops, 28 October 1965.
CEI	Conferenza Episcopale Italiana
Ch.	Chapter
CIC	*Codex Iuris Canonici*, 1983.
CIC-17	*Codex Iuris Canonici*, 1917.
CL	*Christifideles Laici*, 1988.
CLD	*Canon Law Digest*
CollLac	*Acta et Decreta Sacrorum Conciliorum Recentiorum. Collectio Lacensis*. 7 vols. Frieburg I Br., 1870-1890.
CollPF	*Collectanea Sacræ Congregationis de Propaganda Fide, seu Decreta, instructiones, rescripta pro apostolicis missionibus ann. 1622-1906, vv. I et II*. Rome, 1907.
Comm.	*Communicationes*, 1969-
Const.	Constitution

CS	*Cleri Sanctitati*, 1957.
DEC	Tanner, N., ed. *Decrees of the Ecumenical Councils*. Washington, 1990.
Decr	Decree
Denz	Denzinger, H. and A. Schönmetzer, eds. *Enchiridion symbolorum, definitionum de rebus fidei et morum*. Bologna, 1995.
DH	*Dignitatis humanæ*, Vatican II, Declaration of Religious Freedom, 7 December 1965.
ECEI	*Enchiridion della Conferenza Episcopale Italiana*. Bologna, 1985-
ED	*Ecumenical Directory*, 1993.
Enc	Encyclical
Ep	Epistula
Ep Circ	Epistula circularis
EV	*Enchiridion Vaticanum. Documenti ufficiale della S. Sede*. Bologna, 1966-
Exh	Exhortation
ff.	and the following
Flannery	Flannery, A., ed. *Vatican Council II. The Conciliar and Post Conciliar Documents*. Northport, 1992.
GE	*Gravissimum Educationis*, Vatican II, Declaration on Christian Education, 28 October 1965.
GS	*Gaudium et spes*, Vatican II, Pastoral Constitution on the Church in the Modern World, 7 December 1965.
Guide	Nedungatt, G., ed. *A Guide to the Eastern Code*. Rome, 2002.
Ibid.	Ibidem
Id.	Idem
Incontro	Coppola, R., ed. *Incontro fra canoni d'oriente e d'occidente*, Atti del Congresso internazionale. 3 vols. Bari, 1994.
Instr.	*Instruction for Applying the Liturgical Prescriptions of the Code of Canons of the Eastern Churches*, 1996.
LG	*Lumen gentium*, Vatican II, Dogmatic Constitution on the Church, 21 November 1964.
Litt	Littera

Matrimonio	Gruppo Italiano di Docenti di Diritto Canonico, ed. *Matrimonio e disciplina ecclesiastica*, XXI Incontro Studio Passo della Mendola–Trento 4 luglio – 8 luglio 1994. Milan, 1996.
Mp	*Motu proprio*
n./nn.	number/numbers
Nuntia	*Nuntia*, 1975-1990. Official organ of the Pontifical Commission for the Revision of the Code of Eastern Canon Law.
OE	*Orientalium Ecclesiarum*, Vatican II, Decree on the Eastern Catholic Churches, 21 November 1964.
OT	*Optatum totius*, Vatican II, Decree on Priestly Formation, 28 October 1965.
PA	*Postquam Apostolicis*, 1952.
PB	*Pastor Bonus*, 1988.
PC	*Perfectæ Caritatis*, Vatican II, Decree on the Renewal of Religious Life, 18 October 1965.
PO	*Presbyterorum Ordinis*, Vatican II, Decree on the Life and Ministry of Priests, 7 December 1965.
q.	question
SC	*Sacrosanctum Concilium*, Vatican II. Constitution on the Sacred Liturgy, 4 December 1963.
Sess.	Session
S.I.C.O.	Servizio Informazione Chiese Orientali.
Suppl.	Supplement
S. Th.	St. Thomas Aquinas, *Summa Theologiæ*.
s.v.	sub voce
UR	*Unitatis redintegratio*, Vatican II, Decree on Ecumenism, 21 November 1964.
vol./vols.	volume/volumes

Preface to the English Language Edition

During a visit of officials of the Canon Law Society of America to the Congregation for the Eastern Churches, the secretary of the Congregation, Archbishop Cyril Vasil' suggested that it would be useful for the CLSA to publish an English translation of Lorenzo Lorusso's work *Gli Orientali Cattolici e i Pastori Latini. Problematiche e norme canoniche.* (Rome: Pontificio Istituto Orientale, 2003). The CLSA concurred that a study on the relationship of Eastern Catholic members of the Christian faithful to local Latin diocesan bishops and pastors would be useful, given the number of Eastern Catholics who now reside in the United States. The present work *Eastern Catholics and Latin Pastors: Issues and Canonical Norms* is the response to this suggestion.

The English edition contains updates and revisions to the original work that is now nearly ten years old. One notes that there are several references to the provisions of Italian civil law and the Italian Episcopal Conference (Conferenza Episcopale Italiana); as such, they are not directly relevant to the Anglophones, but have been retained because they provide examples of the response of one country to the pastoral needs of Eastern Catholic faithful.

The English translation of the 1917 *Codex Iuris Canonici* is taken from Edward N. Peters, *The 1917 Pio-Benedictine Code of Canon Law* (San Francisco: Ignatius Press, 2001). English translations of Vatican II documents are from Austin Flannery, *Vatican Council II. The Conciliar and Post Conciliar Documents* (Northport, NY: Costello Publishing Company, 1992). The English translation of the 1983 *Codex Iuris Canonici* is taken from *Code of Canon Law. Latin-English Edition* (Washington: Canon Law Society of America, 1999). The English translation of the *Codex Canonum Ecclesiarum Orientalium* is that of the *Code of Canons of the Eastern Churches. Latin-English Edition* (Washington: Canon Law Society of America, 2001). Translations of the four sets of canons of the Eastern Catholic Churches promulgated *motu proprio* by Pope Pius XII (1949-1957) are adapted from the translation of Victor J. Pospishil, *Code of Oriental Canon Law. Law on Persons* (Ford City, PA: St. Mary's Ukrainian Catholic Church, 1960) and *Code of Oriental Canon Law. The Law on Marriage* (Chicago: Universe Editions, 1962). All other translations are the responsibility of the English Editor unless indicated otherwise.

The work would not have been possible without the collaboration of Sean Doyle, J.C.L., who painstakingly reviewed the Latin translations and proofread the text for clarity and consistency.

John D. Faris
Utica, New York
Feast of the Holy Cross 2012

Introduction

On 18 October 1990, the *Code of Canons of the Eastern Churches* was promulgated. The supreme ecclesiastical legislator intentionally situated this significant legislative event in the wake of conciliar insights. The occasion permits us to engage in a broader discourse in order to deepen the points of cultural, ecclesiological and institutional encounters between the Eastern tradition and the Latin tradition, as well as the practical and challenging relationship between the two models of Catholic codifications.

It is particularly interesting that both Codes were promulgated in the same temporal context. The forty-year period between the 1917 Code and the four *Motu Proprios* of Pius XII for the Eastern Churches make it difficult to compare the two codifications. However, the two present codifications, the *Code of Canon Law* of 1983 and the *Code of Canons of the Eastern Churches* of 1990, are expressions of the same temporal context, and, therefore, of the same cultural and ecclesiological matrix, a matrix that has its roots in the magisterium of Vatican II.

For this reason, I wanted to begin this work with the Council as the point of departure, particularly *Lumen gentium*, the Dogmatic Constitution on the Church, and *Orientalium Ecclesiarum*, the Decree on the Eastern Catholic Churches, both promulgated on 21 November 1964, in order to justify the two-fold legislation for the one Catholic Church. This conciliar matrix provides for the juxtaposition of one with the other, an approach taken by John Paul II during the exhortation devoted to canonical science in a particularly qualified setting, the 18th General Congregation of the Synod of Bishops.

In this context, Pope John Paul II, presenting the new *Corpus Iuris Canonici* as constituted respectively by the Latin Code, the Apostolic Constitution *Pastor Bonus* regarding the reform of the Roman Curia and the *Code of Canons of the Eastern Churches*, stated: "appropriate comparative study of both codes should be promoted by the canon law faculties [...] which promote greater knowledge of all that constitutes the legitimate 'in unum conspirans varietas' of the ritual patrimony of the Catholic Church."[1]

My work operates in the wake of these teachings. Aware that it is a rather arduous task, I hope that it will offer useful points for future insights. Indeed, many themes are only touched upon or at most presented without further consideration. I decided to focus primarily on collaboration and on inter-ritual—or

---

1 John Paul II, *Discourse of Presentation of the Code of Canons of the Eastern Churches*, 25 October 1990: *Nuntia* 31 (1990) 18 and 20. Translation from G. Nedungatt, ed., *A Guide to the Eastern Code* (Rome: Pontificio Istituto Orientale, 2002) 27. Cf. E. Cappellini, "Con il Codex Canonum Ecclesiarum orientalium – Nuove prospettive didattiche per il Diritto Canonico," *L'Osservatore Romano*, 14 February 1991, 8.

rather, inter-ecclesial—issues in the two codes of the Catholic Church. I prefer to speak of inter-ecclesial relations between Churches, the Latin Church on one side and the Eastern Catholic Churches *sui iuris* on the other side, in the Catholic Church.

Human mobility today is facilitated not only by modern means of transport, but also by a series of historical-political events. For example, there is the collapse of communism in Eastern Europe and the opening of borders; the sad events in the Middle East which have uprooted hundreds of thousands of Christians, obliging them to be far from the lands of their forefathers; further, the notable economic inequality between the countries of the so-called third world and the industrialized countries causes many immigrants to seek better lives in the West. Consequently, millions of Christians belonging to every Eastern tradition are now found in Western Europe, Canada, the United States, Latin America, Australia, Africa and India.

This reality brings new problems of a pastoral and juridic nature regarding education and Christian formation, the religious life of the family, mixed marriages between Catholics of various Churches *sui iuris* and between Catholics and non-Catholics, pastoral care of isolated groups, etc. The migration of peoples undoubtedly promotes understanding and collaboration, witnesses and promotes the unity of the human family and creates a fraternal relationship among peoples "in which each party is at the same time a giver and a receiver" (AA 14). There is at the same time the urgency to consider the pastoral and juridic consequences of the increased presence of Catholic faithful belonging to different Eastern Churches *sui iuris* in the Latin dioceses as well as the preservation of their rites, that is, their spiritual, theological, liturgical and disciplinary patrimony. Therefore, it is necessary that everyone, Latin and Eastern faithful, consider the delicate implications of a situation that constitutes a true challenge both for the survival of the Christian East as well as a general rethinking of their own pastoral programs. Pastors of the Latin Church entrusted with Eastern faithful are invited especially to deepen their awareness of the existence and the patrimony (theological, spiritual, liturgical and disciplinary) of the Eastern Catholic Churches. Secondly, they are called to be promoters and defenders of the right of the Eastern faithful to live and to pray according to the tradition received from the Fathers of their own Church (cf. CCEO c. 39).[2] In doing so, the Latin dioceses

> are enriched by the heritage of the Eastern faithful who establish themselves there, and the preservation of such heritage is to be sustained and encouraged not only by the Eastern pastors but also by

---

2   See John Paul II, *Udienza alla Plenaria della Congregazione per le Chiese Orientali*, 1 October 1998: *L'Osservatore Romano*, 2 October 1998, 5.

the Latin ones of the immigration territories, because it wonderfully expresses the multicolored richness of the Church of Christ.[3]

To neglect, or worse, to block this right of the Eastern faithful, would perpetuate the sad and disdained experience of Latinization that, beyond trampling on the right of the faithful, risked (and perhaps still risks) depriving the Catholic Church of the riches of the Christian East, regarded by Vatican II as the patrimony of the universal Church (OE 5) and by Pope John Paul II as necessary in order for the Church to breathe with the two lungs of East and West. Therefore, Catholics of every rite are called upon to pay great attention to the pastoral exhortations regarding the Eastern Churches, rather than to pay mere lip service. "It is the responsibility of all to ensure that they grow and flourish in accord with their theological, spiritual and disciplinary patrimony."[4]

Why such a regard for the Eastern Churches? Because "in them shines the apostolic tradition handed down by the Fathers"; because they are "of venerable antiquity"; and lastly because this tradition "constitutes a part of the revealed and undivided patrimony of the universal Church" (OE 1). To lose or to compromise this tradition would constitute an irreparable loss for the entire universal Church.[5]

Taking all this into consideration, the essential points to be examined in this work are:

1. The reason for a two-fold legislation in the one Catholic Church.

2. Ascription to a Church *sui iuris* or to the Latin Church and the possible transfer from one Church *sui iuris* to another.

3. Pastoral assistance of the Eastern faithful, lacking their own Hierarch and entrusted by the norm of law to the care of a Latin diocesan Bishop. Each member of the Christian faithful, either by domicile or quasi-domicile, is part of the local Church according to the norm of law; each has a proper pastor and Ordinary according to the norm of law.

4. Ministers of Eastern faithful and their participation in the presbyteral council of the diocese, the college of consultors, as well as the participation of priests, religious and Eastern laypersons in the pastoral council of the diocese. This

---

3   Instr. 10; cf. John Paul II, Enc Ap *Orientale Lumen*, 2 May 1995, n. 5: *AAS* 87 (1995) 748-749.
4   P. Stasiuk, "Intervento all'Assemblea Speciale per l'Oceania del Sinodo dei Vescovi," *L'Osservatore Romano*, 25 November 1998, 6.
5   See John Paul II, *Ai Vescovi della Chiesa Armena Cattolica*, 19 November 1992: *S.I.C.O.* Suppl. to nn. 485-556, 52.

also entails provision for the support of Eastern clerics, who are to provide pastoral care for the Eastern faithful, as is the case for Latin clerics.

5. The various institutions that permit inter-ecclesial collaboration.

6. The administration of the sacraments of Christian initiation and of the other sacraments to the Eastern faithful according to the norms of the CCEO and CIC.

7. The complex issues of inter-ecclesial marriage.

8. Religious life: admission, transfer and collaboration with the Hierarch.

More research on the traditions and legitimate customs of each Church *sui iuris* will be necessary to better distinguish between what is constitutive for the proper rite and proper identity and what is of the practical order. The CCEO affirms that the rites of the Eastern Church are "the patrimony of the whole Church of Christ in which shines forth the tradition coming down from the Apostles through the Fathers" (CCEO c. 39). This is to affirm that the rites of the Eastern Churches have importance not only for these same Churches, an importance that explains the insistence of the CCEO on the observance and safeguard of the rite, but also an importance for the entire Church; if the rites of the Eastern Churches disappear, it is a loss for the entire Church. To keep this tradition alive and to maintain this variety in unity, there is a need to preserve and promote the rites of the Eastern Churches. These rites concern not only the Eastern faithful, but have an importance for the Church itself.

There is a need to ask if what is constitutive for the rite comes only from the tradition; moreover, in what measure can and must tradition be normative? On the other hand, in a conception of an on-going history, which does not stop in any given epoch, cannot the persons of today also make their own contribution to tradition? Do they not construct the tradition by continuing it and living the patrimony of their Church in a dynamic confrontation with the present circumstances? How does this "construction" take place? Our present situation is a tension between the past and the future: in the past we find our ancestral tradition and are obliged to be faithful to it and live it, but the future challenges us to grow so as not to die and disappear.

It appears that CCEO c. 28 emphasizes, in its description of the term "rite," the aspect of difference and distinctness of each Church in relation to the others: "[…] differentiated by the culture and the circumstances of the history of peoples […]." How does one deal with common elements that are manifested only in their unique manner in the rite? What is the form? What are the contents? Is it necessary to turn to philosophy in order to understand the details and the nuances?

On the other hand, there is a question more of a psychological order, which comes from our use of the term "identity" to indicate the patrimony and the specificity of each Church: what is it that creates the identity of a person or of a group, of a Church *sui iuris?* Is the identity to be constructed of various constitutive elements? What creates the cohesion among them? These are the issues to be explored, I hope, in future studies and research.

Chapter I

The Two-Fold Legislation of the Catholic Church

I.1. Unity and Diversity in the Ecclesial Communion
I.2. Ecclesiological Notes of Vatican II regarding the Eastern Catholic Churches
I.3. Canon 1 of the Respective Codes of the Catholic Church
   a. Prior Legislation
   b. Current Legislation

The Catholic Church, formed of all the baptized joined to Christ in bonds of faith, sacraments, and ecclesiastical government and governed by the Successor of Peter and the Bishops in communion with him, has been governed by a two-fold legislation since 18 October 1990: the *Codex Iuris Canonici* for the Latin Church[1] and the *Codex Canonum Ecclesiarum Orientalium* for the Eastern Catholic Churches.[2] To this two-fold legislation is added the apostolic constitution *Pastor Bonus* on the Roman Curia (28 June 1988),[3] thereby forming the one *Corpus Iuris Canonici* of the Catholic Church.

The two codes, while having their respective areas of application and passive subjects, are not completely separate from one another; both contain norms that either by the nature of the matter or through explicit or implicit mention concern all the faithful of the Catholic Church, both Latin and Eastern.

In this first chapter we shall demonstrate the need for a two-fold legislation in the Catholic Church, relying primarily on two conciliar documents: the dogmatic constitution on the Church, *Lumen gentium*, and the decree on the Eastern Catholic Churches, *Orientalium Ecclesiarum*, both promulgated on 21 November 1964.[4] We shall then examine the texts of canon 1 of the respective codes in the light of prior legislation.

---

1   The Code was promulgated with publication in *AAS* 75/II (25 January 1983). Later an Appendix was published containing the *errata-corrige* (*AAS* 75/II [1983] 321-324); other errors in the authentic edition were corrected in *AAS* 75 (1983) 1140 and 80 (1988) 1367, 1819.
2   The authentic edition was published in *AAS* 82 (1990) 1045-1363. The order of the texts is: *Præfatio*; *Codex Canonum Ecclesiarum Orientalium*, subdivided into *Canones Præliminares* and 30 titles; *Index*. The apostolic constitution, *Sacri Canones* (18 October 1990), which promulgated the Code, was published initially as a separate fascicle. An English edition of the CCEO is available in Canon Law Society of America, *Code of Canons of the Eastern Churches* (Washington, 2001).
3   *AAS* 80 (1988) 841-930.
4   Flannery, 350-426 and 441-451.

I.1. Unity and Diversity in the Ecclesial Communion

In the Creed, we profess: *I believe in the One, Holy, Catholic and Apostolic Church*. There is no other Church founded by Jesus Christ and entrusted to the pastoral vigilance of Peter and the Apostles. Where is this Church? Is it a concept or an abstract and spiritual reality? *Lumen gentium* describes it as follows:

> This is the sole Church of Christ, which in the Creed we profess to be one, holy, catholic and apostolic, which our Savior, after his resurrection, entrusted to Peter's pastoral care (Jn. 21:17), commissioning him and the other apostles to extend and rule it (cf. Mt 28:18, etc.), and which He raised up for all ages as "the pillar and mainstay of the truth" (1 Tim 3:15). This Church, constituted and organized as a society in the present world, subsists in the Catholic Church, which is governed by the successor of Peter and by the bishops in communion with him. Nevertheless, many elements of sanctification and of truth are found outside its visible confines. Since these are gifts belonging to the Church of Christ, they are forces impelling toward Catholic unity. (LG 8)

The text does not affirm that the Church is the Catholic community, but that it *subsists* in the Catholic Church: this the key word of the passage. What does it mean?

To subsist means to exist in a specific manner, in virtue of which an entity exists through itself and not through another as an accident. For example, John (soul + body) exists independently (*per se*) and needs nothing else to exist; therefore, he is a substance that exists *per se*. This is not to be confused with an entity that exists *ab se*, that is, an entity that possesses in itself everything which explains its existence (God alone). The accident is that which cannot exist *per se*: it does not exist except in another that is the true subject. An example is freedom; it is essential for John to be free, yet freedom does not exist *per se* but exists only in a subject *per accidens*.

Lumen gentium 8a means that the one Church of Christ exists in this world in the Catholic Church and that it is in no way completed by the other ecclesial communities. The Doctrinal Commission of the Council clarified that it was necessary to understand the expression *subsistit in* in the sense of *adest in*, "is present."[5] The Congregation for the Doctrine of the Faith has indicated:

> The council chose the word *subsistit* ("subsists") precisely to make clear that one sole "subsistence" of the true Church exists, whereas outside her visible structure only *elementa ecclesiæ* ("elements of Church") exist; these—being elements of the same Church—tend

---

5 *Acta Syn.* III/I, 177.

and conduct toward the Catholic Church (LG 8). The decree on ecumenism expresses the same doctrine (UR 3-4); it was restated precisely in the declaration *Mysterium Ecclesiæ*, n. 1 (Sacred Congregation for the Doctrine of the Faith, 24 June 1973: *AAS* 65 [1973] 396-398).[6]

The Church in this world, then, in its visible form of existence is fully formed in the one Catholic Church. The Church of Christ in this world with the totality of the signs / means of salvation is to be identified with the Catholic Church governed by the Roman Pontiff and by the Bishops in communion with him.

This *Ecclesia universa* is present in time and space in the more restricted communities which are the particular Churches constituted in its image. To say that the *Ecclesia universa* is a communion of the particular Churches does not mean that the former is a federation of the latter, nor that the sum of the particular Churches constitutes the *Ecclesia universa*.[7] The universal Church is thus the Body of Churches, a Communion of Churches: "The particular churches are constituted after the model of the universal Church; it is in these and formed out of them that the one and unique Catholic Church exists" (LG 23a; CCEO c. 177 §1 and CIC c. 369). From an external, sociological point of view, the universal Church represents the whole, while the particular Church represents the part. However, interiorly at a deeper, mysterious level, they are not. The Church is universal not through a juxtaposition or a sum of particular Churches, but through an awareness of the existence of a communion of love in the same "deposit" of faith received from the Apostles. The bond with Tradition enables every Church to be in continuity with the Apostles and for all the Churches be in communion among themselves. This universality or catholicity should not be understood in a geographic or quantitative sense, but in the sense of integrity or fullness of the faith and doctrine, in fidelity to the sacred "deposit."

The particular Church is a "portion of the People of God" and, more precisely, "a portion of the universal Church," so that the Bishops, properly governing their own Churches as a portion of the universal Church, contribute efficaciously to the good of the entire Mystical Body, which is the Body of the Churches. The particular Churches are not limited to being a quantitative part of the *Ecclesia universa*, except that in them *existit, inest et operatur* the one Church of Jesus Christ. The unity of the Church is constituted as a hierarchically structured communion of Churches. The relation of communion among the particular Churches and the *Ecclesia universa* is constituted internally and materially as a relationship of

---

6 Congregation for the Doctrine of the Faith, Notification *Il 12 febbraio 1982* regarding the writings of Rev. Leonardo Boff: *Chiesa: carisma e potere*, 11 March 1985: EV 9:1426.

7 Cf. Congregation for the Doctrine of the Faith, *Litteræ ad Catholicæ Ecclesiæ episcopos de aliquibus aspectibus Ecclesiæ prout est communio*, 28 May 1992 n. 8: *AAS* 85 (1993) 838-850.

identity (*de quibus*), externally and formally as a relation of differentiation (*ex quibus*).[8]

The universal Church realizes its mission when the Word is preached and the sacraments are celebrated in the particular Church. A proclamation or preaching of the Word of the particular Church with its own content, distinct from that of the universal Church, or vice versa, does not exist. The same is true for the sacraments.

The function of the universal Church in relation to the particular Church is to guarantee formally the unity of the particular Churches in doctrine, ecclesial communion and governance. The dimensions of universality and particularity intrinsically involve the unity of the Church and the essence of its constitution and, even if the universal Church and particular Church are related in historical and ontological simultaneity, the latter is hierarchically subordinate to the former.

The unity of the *Ecclesia universa* does not sacrifice the plurality and diversity of the particular Churches, which, in turn, do not impede unity, but rather confer the character of communion.[9] This plurality applies both to different ministries, charisms, forms of life and of apostolate internal to each particular Church, as well as to the diversity of liturgical and cultural traditions among the various particular Churches (cf. LG 23d). In this regard one recalls that the obligation of the one who presides over the universal communion of charity (the Bishop of Rome) is to protect legitimate variety, thus excluding every leveling uniformity and making room for liturgical, theological, spiritual and disciplinary pluralism.[10]

As we have said, the manner of living this diversity was not always viewed as a positive element. At times, it even evoked feelings of mistrust among the particular Churches, to the point of becoming a true and proper obstacle for understanding, collaboration and ecumenism, paralyzing common pastoral activity and giving counter-testimony to the world. Similar difficulties are overcome through sincere respect and in inter-ecclesial collaboration. The codified norms in the *Corpus Iuris Canonici* of the Catholic Church are not concerned with accentuating the differences, but rather emphasizing the unity while respecting the diversity.[11]

---

8   Cf. Congregation for the Doctrine of the Faith, *Responsa ad quaestiones de aliquibus sententiis ad doctrinam de Ecclesia pertinentibus*, 29 June 2007: *AAS* 99 (2007) 604-608; L. Lorusso, "Alcuni aspetti circa la dottrina sulla Chiesa utili al dialogo ecumenico," *O Odigos* 26 (2007/3) 22-28.
9   Cf. Congregation for the Doctrine of the Faith, *Litteræ ad Catholicæ Ecclesiæ episcopos de aliquibus aspectibus Ecclesiæ prout est communio*, 28 May 1992, n.15.
10 Cf. G. Cereti, *Per un'ecclesiologia ecumenica* (Bologna, 1996) 141.
11 Cf. John Paul II, Ap Exh *Una speranza nuova per il Libano*, 10 May 1997, n. 9: Suppl. to *L'Osservatore Romano*, 12-13 May 1997. "It is fundamental for this dialogue to recognize that the richness of this unity in faith and spiritual life must be expressed in

I.2. Ecclesiological Notes of Vatican II regarding the Eastern Catholic Churches

The fundamental texts on which we shall focus are: the dogmatic constitution *Lumen gentium* and the decree *Orientalium Ecclesiarum*. Let us begin with *Lumen gentium*:[12]

> In virtue of this catholicity each part contributes its own gifts to the other parts and to the whole Church, so that the whole and each of the parts are strengthened by the common sharing of all things and by the common effort to attain to fullness in unity. […] Hence, it is that the People of God is not only made up of various peoples but in itself is made up of different ranks. This diversity among its members is either by reason of their duties –some exercise the sacred ministry for the good of their brethren—or it is due to their condition and manner of life—many enter the religious state and, intending toward sanctity by a narrower way, stimulate their brethren by their example. Holding a right place in the communion of the Church there are also particular Churches that retain their own traditions, without prejudice the Chair of Peter, which presides over the whole assembly of charity and protects their legitimate variety, while at the same time taking care that these differences do not hinder unity but rather contribute toward it. (LG 13c)

> It has come about through divine providence that, in the course of time, different Churches set up in various places by the apostles and their successors joined together in a multiplicity of organically united groups which, while safeguarding the unity of faith and the unique divine structure of the universal Church, have their own discipline, enjoy their own liturgical usage, and inherit a theological and spiritual patrimony. Some of these, notably the ancient patriarchal churches, as mothers in the faith, gave birth to other daughter-Churches, as it were, and down to our own days they are linked with these by bonds of a more intimate charity in what pertains to the sacramental life and in a mutual respect for rights and obligations. (LG 23d)[13]

---

the diversity of forms. Unity—whether on the universal level or local level—does not mean uniformity or absorption of one group by the other. It is rather at the service of all the groups to live better those gifts that it has received from the Spirit of God": John Paul II, *Alla delegazione copta*, 22 June 1979: *Irenikon* 52 (1979) 377.

12 For the evolution of LG, see G. Philips, *La Chiesa e il suo mistero* (Milan, 1989) 17-66.

13 The common origins of the various Churches have produced a particular relationship among them and, consequently, a close union of the Bishops in the form of patriarchates: cf. *Acta Syn.* III/I, 239. LG 23 "does not attribute their foundation to the express will of Christ, but to the disposition of Divine Providence. To maintain regional or inter-regional communion, in the East as in the West, the episcopal sees, according to

In the conciliar documents, one generally finds an identification of the particular Church with the diocesan Church, while the Eastern Churches are called *cœtus Ecclesiarum particularium* or *Ecclesiæ locales* (LG 23). At times, the Council refers to the patriarchate and major archiepiscopate as a "particular Church," a communion of that portion of the people of God, which, without prejudice to the primacy of the Roman Pontiff, enjoys its own discipline, its own liturgy, its own theological, spiritual and cultural patrimony, which manifest a way of living the same faith. The variety of all these Churches, in the unity that they realize, demonstrates the catholicity of the one and undivided Catholic Church. Further, it should be noted that the Council uses the expression "particular Church" in designating the Eastern Churches when it speaks of the portion of the people of God with reference not only to territory, but also to rite, that is, the theological, spiritual and cultural tradition and governance. It uses the expression "local Church"[14] when referring to the same reality in terms of its territory. There is almost an identification of "particular Church" and "Rite" which is not entirely precise: that which constitutes a Rite, in the very broad sense of particular Church, is neither territory, nation, liturgical rite, liturgical language, particular discipline nor spirituality, but is all this at the same time, with a formal indispensable element—the constitution of an autonomous hierarchy of this community in relation to other similar communities within the *Ecclesia universa*.[15] The term "rite" offers a certain usefulness in common usage, but surely does not provide for clarity in the conciliar texts. For example, if we analyze the conciliar decree *Orientalium Ecclesiarum*, we discover the multiple meanings of the term *Ritus*: in nn. 2, 3, and 10, it means "particular Church"; in n. 3, it means "the complex of liturgy, ecclesiastical discipline and spiritual patrimony"; in n. 6 it means only "liturgy," distinct from discipline.

The Pontifical Commission for the Revision of the Eastern Code of Canon Law had a lengthy discussion on the question of the notion and terms "particular Church" and "Rite," used in *Orientalium Ecclesiarum*, as did the *Cœtus mixtus de lege Ecclesiæ fundamentali*; the latter came up with the follow formulation:

> Variæ Ecclesiæ particulares in plures coniunguntur cœtus organice constitutos, quorum quidem præcipui sunt Ecclesiæ peculiares secundum ritum, disciplinam atque propriam, infra supremam Ecclesiæ auctoritatem, hierarchicam ordinationem præsertim inter se distinctæ, videlicet Ecclesia latina et variæ Ecclesiæ orientales aliæque quæ suprema Ecclesiæ auctoritate, constituuntur; quæ

---

tradition founded by the Apostles or one of their immediate collaborators, were relied upon. This kind of division into more or less vast regions did not detract from the unity of the faith nor from the fundamental undivided constitution of the universal Church": G. Philips, *La Chiesa...*, 275.
14   The expression "local Church" is never used in the CIC or the CCEO.
15   Cf. N. Edelby and I. Dick, *Les Eglises Orientales Catholiques. Décret "Orientalium Ecclesiarum,"* Unam Sanctam 76 (Paris, 1970) 136-143.

> omnes, salva quidem fidei unitate et unica divina constitutione Ecclesiæ universæ, propria gaudent disciplina, proprio liturgico usu atque proprio theologico spiritualique patrimonio.[16]

But for the Eastern members of the Commission it was difficult to accept the expression *Ecclesiæ peculiares*. The Draft *De Episcopis* of January 1979, c. 1 and the Draft *De constitutione hierarchica Ecclesiarum Orientalium* of 1984, c. 145 were formulated as follows:

> Eparchia est populi Dei portio, quæ Episcopo cum cooperatione presbyterii pascenda concreditur, ita ut, pastori suo adhærens ab eoque per Evangelium et Eucharistiam in Spiritu Sancto congregata, Ecclesiam *singularem* constituat, in qua vere inest et operatur Una Sancta Catholica et Apostolica Ecclesia.[17]

In the *denua recognitio* of 1985 *singularem* was replaced with *particularem* in order not to give the impression that there is an Eastern peculiarity; the latter expression would have the same juridic meaning in the entire Catholic Church and would designate only the dioceses / eparchies and other equivalent ecclesiastical circumscriptions.[18] The wording is as follows:

> Eparchia est populi Dei portio, quæ Episcopo cum cooperatione presbyterii pascenda concreditur ita, ut Pastori suo adhærens et ab eo per Evangelium et Eucharistiam in Spiritu Sancto congregata Ecclesiam particularem constituat, in qua vere inest et operatur una sancta catholica et apostolica Christi Ecclesia. (CCEO c. 177 §1)[19]

With respect to the definition of Church *sui iuris* we have: "A community of the Christian faithful, which is joined together by a hierarchy according to the norm of law and which is expressly or tacitly recognized as *sui iuris* by the supreme authority of the Church, is called in this Code a Church *sui iuris*" (CCEO c. 27); while for *rite* we have the following: "A rite is a liturgical, theological, spiritual and disciplinary heritage, differentiated by the culture and the circumstances of the history of peoples, which is expressed by each Church *sui iuris* in its own manner of living the faith" (CCEO c. 28 §1).[20]

---

16   *Comm.* 8 (1976) 80-81; cf. É. Sleman, "De 'ritus' à 'Ecclesia sui iuris' dans la Code des Canons des Églises Orientales," *L'Année Canonique* 41 (1999) 253-276, especially 257-259.
17   *Nuntia* 9 (1979) 5; 19 (1984) 52.
18   *Nuntia* 2 (1976) 75-87; 23 (1986) 4; 24-25 (1987) 32.
19   Sources: CD 11; LG 25, 26, 28; SC 41; PO 4.
20   *Nuntia* 19 (1984) 21; 22 (1986) 22-24; 24-25 (1987) 5; I. Žužek, *Understanding the Eastern Code*, Kanonika 8 (Rome, 1997) 84-109.

Taking into consideration all these elements, it is possible to outline a description of an "Eastern Catholic Church": it is a portion of the people of God, composed of Bishops, priests, deacons, religious and laity, a part of the universal Church, which lives the Catholic faith (theology, liturgy, spirituality and discipline) in a manner corresponding to one of the great Eastern traditions (Alexandrian, Antiochene, Armenian, Chaldean and Constantinopolitan) and contains or is at least capable of containing several eparchial communities hierarchically joined under the guidance of a common Hierarch (Patriarch, Major Archbishop, Metropolitan, Bishop or another Hierarch) lawfully elected or appointed and in communion with the Roman Pontiff, whose Hierarch with his synod or another similar institution constitutes the superior instance for all affairs of an administrative, legislative or judicial character of those same communities, always with due regard for the right of the Roman Pontiff to intervene in individual cases.[21] So, up to this time each Eastern Church

> preserves its liturgy, which is a witness of the piety of the ages; it preserves its own proper discipline. Then there is the government, for which it has its own pastors, who, according to the statement of Leo XIII, are not simply vicars of the Pope, but are in the true sense pastors and successors of the Apostles, one in communion with the Roman Pontiff, who is acknowledged by all as the Supreme Pastor. It retains its language, its own means of propagating [the faith], its organization and its particular political relationship with the civil state.[22]

Thus, a portion of the people of God is a particular Church when it is formed in the image of the *Ecclesia universa*, that it is to say, when there are present all the essential elements of being Church (baptism, differentiation of the faithful through various hierarchical and charismatic gifts, acceptance of the entire order of the visible Church and of all the means of salvation instituted in it, bonds of the profession of faith, of sacraments, of ecclesiastical governance and of communion, the governance of the Roman Pontiff and the Bishops) and further, a certain accidental specifying element such as rite, territory, particular organs of governance. In this way *in* the particular Churches and *from* the particular Churches

---

21 Cf. I. Žužek, "Che cosa è una Chiesa, un Rito orientale?" *Seminarium* 27 (1975) 276; M. Brogi, "Le Chiese *sui iuris* nel Codex Canonum Ecclesiarum Orientalium," *Revista Española de Derecho Canónico* 48 (1991) 520-521. "A specific Church, that is governed by its own laws and customs, not only with regard to the form of the liturgy, but also with regard to hierarchical constitution, governance and discipline. Hence, rite in the canonical sense includes both the entire liturgy of a certain Church (Eucharistic sacrifice, sacraments and other liturgical offices) and the particularities of hierarchical constitution, governance, and discipline, introduced by law or legitimate custom": I. Řezáč, *Institutiones Iuris Canonici Orientalis* (Rome, 1958) 118.

22 A. Petrani, *De relatione iuridica inter diversos ritus in Ecclesia catholica* (Turin-Rome, 1930) 6.

exists the one and only Catholic Church, which is the communion among all the Churches.

The legitimate differentiation of the local or particular Churches is too little known in the West and could bring harm to uniformity; thus, "it is indispensable that in the Catholic Church there be promoted an ever deepening understanding of the Churches of the East."[23] Hence, Providence has disposed in the course of times a convergence of various Churches[24] in communion among themselves:

> The universality of the Church, on the one hand, involves the most solid unity, and on the other hand, a plurality and diversification, which do not impede unity, but rather confer the character of "communion"; legitimate diversity is opposed in no way to the unity in the Church, but rather enhances its beauty and contributes in no small way to the fulfillment of its mission.[25]

Subsequent to Vatican II, one no longer speaks of the "Eastern Church," but of the particular or local Churches or Rites (Churches *sui iuris* in the CCEO), the patriarchal Churches holding the first rank (LG 23; UR 14). One is not dealing with a terminological detail, but an ecclesiological evolution. Since their origins, the Churches of the East have possessed a treasure from which the Church of the West has drawn many elements of liturgy, spiritual tradition and law (UR 14). The harmonious coexistence of the various traditions is a benefit of ecclesial communion and for the glory of God, who thus receives a multiform of praise. The Decree on Ecumenism affirms that

> with regard to the theological traditions of the Orientals, we must recognize that they are admirably rooted in Holy Scripture, are fostered and given expression in liturgical life, are nourished by the living tradition of the apostles and by the works of the Fathers and spiritual writers of the East; they are directed toward a right ordering of life, indeed, toward a full contemplation of Christian truth. (UR 17)

---

23 A. Silvestrini, "Assemblea Speciale per l'America del Sinodo dei Vescovi," XVI Congregazione Generale: *L'Osservatore Romano*, 29 November 1997, 4.
24 For the origins of the Eastern Churches, see G. De Vries, *Oriente Christano ieri e oggi* (Rome, 1949); Sacred Congregation for the Eastern Churches, *Oriente Cattolico. Cenni storici e statistiche*, 4th ed. (Vatican City, 1974).
25 John Paul II, *Discorso nell'Udienza generale*, 27 September 1989, n. 2: *Insegnamenti di Giovanni Paolo II*, XII, 2 (1989) 679; *Id.*, Litt Enc *Ut unum sint*, 25 May 1995, n. 50: *L'Osservatore Romano*, 31 May 1995; cf. PB art. 11.

The salient points of the Decree *Orientalium Ecclesiarum*,[26] the Vatican II document specifically for the Eastern Catholic Churches, are:

- The Eastern Churches are part of the Catholic Church, and their ecclesial and spiritual patrimony is considered the *patrimony of the universal Church of Christ* (nn. 1 and 5);[27] the synods of the Eastern Churches constitute the supreme legislative instance;

- *The variety in the Church not only does not harm its unity, but rather manifests it* (n. 2). The presentation of these particular Churches differ in various ways from that contained in *Lumen gentium*; this is obvious, given their particular history, tradition, discipline, theology, liturgy and spirituality;

- All the Churches, both East and West, are *equally entrusted to the pastoral governance of the Roman Pontiff* and enjoy equal dignity, enjoy the same rights are held to the same obligations, even with regard to preaching the Gospel throughout the world (n. 3);[28]

- The fostering and growth of all the particular Churches, which must collaborate among themselves (n. 4);

- The Eastern faithful must preserve with the greatest fidelity the patrimony of their ancestral traditions, gain an ever deeper understanding of them and return to them *whenever they have fallen short because of contingencies of times or persons* (n. 6);

- They are invited to proceed with the erection of parishes and, when opportune, of their own hierarchy for the Eastern faithful (n. 4);[29] religious institutes and associations of the Latin Rite that work in Eastern regions and among Eastern faithful should establish houses or even provinces of an Eastern rite (n. 6);[30]

---

26 Cf. N. Edelby and I. Dick, *Les Églises…*; S. Manna and G. Distante, *Orientalium Ecclesiarum - Decreto sulle Chiese Orientali cattoliche* (Casale Monferrato, 1986); E. Said, *Les Églises orientales et leurs droits, hier, aujourd'hui… demain* (Paris, 1989).

27 CCEO c. 39: "The rites of the Eastern Churches, as the patrimony of the whole Church of Christ in which shines forth the tradition coming down from the Apostles through the Fathers, and which, in its variety, affirms the divine unity of the Catholic faith, are to be observed and promoted conscientiously."

28 CCEO c. 585 §1: "It is for each Church *sui iuris* continually to take care that, through suitably prepared preachers sent by a competent authority in accord with the norms of the common law, the gospel is preached in the whole world under the guidance of the Roman Pontiff." For the missionary activity of the Eastern Churches, see N. Edelby and I. Dick, *Les Églises…*, 169.

29 Cf. *Nuntia* 6 (1978) 17.

30 CCEO c. 432: "A dependent monastery, a house or province of a religious institute of any Church *sui iuris*, also of the Latin Church, that with the consent of

- Each and every Catholic, as well as baptized persons of any non-Catholic Church or community, should retain everywhere in the world their own rite (n. 4);[31] from the separated Easterners who, moved by the grace of the Holy Spirit, enter into Catholic unity, nothing is demanded more than the simple profession of the Catholic faith;[32] a cleric who comes into Catholic unity *has the faculty of exercising his proper order* (n. 25);[33]

- The Eastern Churches in communion with the Roman Apostolic See have the special task of promoting the unity of all Christians, especially Eastern Christians, according to the principles of the decree *Unitatis Redintegratio* (n. 24);[34]

- The juridic prescriptions delineated in the conciliar decree *are established for the present conditions, until the Catholic Church and the separated Eastern Churches come into the fullness of communion* (n. 30). The expression "for the present conditions" intends to emphasize the transitory nature of the juridic prescriptions of the Decree: they are in force as long as they are not abrogated by the supreme Legislator; but, in the actual situation, they are projected towards the desire of full communion between the Catholic Church and the Orthodox Churches.[35]

---

the Apostolic See is ascribed to another Church *sui iuris*, must observe the law of this latter Church, except for the prescripts of the typicon or statutes that regard the internal governance of the same institute or for the privileges granted by the Apostolic See."

31   CCEO c. 35: "Baptized non-Catholics coming into full communion with the Catholic Church should retain and practice their own rite and should observe it everywhere in the world as much as humanly possible. Thus, they are to be ascribed to the Church *sui iuris* of the same rite with due regard for the right of approaching the Apostolic See in special cases of persons, communities or regions."

32   CCEO c. 896: "For those who have been baptized in non-Catholic Churches or ecclesial communities and who ask of their own accord to enter into full communion with the Catholic Church, whether as individuals or as groups, no burden is to be imposed beyond what is necessary."

33   CCEO c. 899: "A cleric of an Eastern non-Catholic Church entering into full communion with the Catholic Church can exercise his sacred order in accord with the norms established by the competent authority; a bishop, however, cannot validly exercise the power of governance except with the assent of the Roman Pontiff, head of the college of bishops."

34   CCEO c. 903: "The Eastern Catholic Churches have a special function of fostering unity among all Eastern Churches, first of all through prayers, by the example of life, by conscientious fidelity to the ancient traditions of the Eastern Churches, by better knowledge of each other, by working together, and by fraternal respect for the feelings of others and their history."

35   Cf. Apcon *Sacri Canones*, 18 October 1990: *AAS* 82 (1990) 1036. "This must be understood to be in particular the rights and privileges of the Patriarchs and Major Archbishops and of their synods, since these are the questions treated by OE which most formally touch the law (except *communicatio in sacris* whose norms would then be moot)": E. Lanne, "Les Catholiques orientaux: liberté religieuse et Oecuménisme,"

Lumen gentium emphasizes the ecclesiology of communion of particular Churches, meaning primarily the diocesan Churches; in *Orientalium Ecclesiarum* this inter-ecclesial communion is treated at the level of the *cœtus*, stressing the synodal structure of the individual *cœtus Ecclesiarum particularium* and making these *cœtus* the subjects of inter-ecclesial communion.[36]

Irenikon 63 (1990) 20-46, especially 31; cf. D. Salachas, "Il nuovo Codice dei Canoni delle Chiese Orientali. Prospettive ecumeniche e limiti," *Euntes Docete* 49 (1996) 229-265, especially 231-233. Father Lanne, commenting on OE 30, affirms: "Given that union with the Orthodox Churches was a major preoccupation of Vatican II and the ecumenical activity of the Catholic Church since this council, there needed to be an explicit declaration in the text of the CCEO that it was of a provisory nature; even more since this code is called the *Code of Canons of the Eastern Churches* without mentioning that it deals only with the Eastern Catholic Churches": E. Lanne, "L'Oriente cristiano nella prospettiva del Vaticano II," in *Orientalium Dignitas*, Atti del Simposio commemorativo della recorrenza centenaria della Lettera Apostolica di papa Leone XIII, 2-4 November 1994, ed. L. Orosz (Nyíregyháza, 1995) 131-145, especially 135. Perhaps Fr. Lanne is ignoring that in CCEO c. 1, the *mens legislatoris* is expressed.

From 30 June to 6 July 1996, a study meeting of all the Eastern Catholic Bishops of Europe under the patronage of the Congregation of the Eastern Churches was held in Nyíregyháza, Hungary. The fundamental theme of this meeting was a reflection on the different dimensions of the Eastern Christian identity of these Churches. Prof. Salachas, commenting on OE 30, states: "Certain individuals have interpreted this phrase in the sense of the provisory character of the existence of the Eastern Catholic Churches and, consequently, in the sense of their disappearance in the future after the reestablishment of union between the Catholic Church and the Orthodox Church. This interpretation is erroneous and ecclesiologically unacceptable." The editor of *Irenikon* 70 (1997) 288-289 affirms rather the contrary and criticizes article n. 1 of the Declaration of the Bishops assembled in Nyíregyháza ("The Eastern Catholic Churches are an ecclesial reality in communion with the Apostolic See of Rome, confirmed in the course of history. This communion is not a provisory or precarious state, but the fullness of ecclesiality"). He criticizes the fullness of ecclesiality of the Eastern Catholic Churches because the major part of the Churches of the East is outside this communion. We do not agree with this assertion inasmuch as OE 2 speaks of the "admirable communion." How can the Eastern Catholic Churches promote the unity of Christians, as OE 24 states, if they are not in union with the Roman Apostolic See? CCEO c. 8 describes the fullness of communion: "In full communion with the Catholic Church on this earth are those baptized persons who are joined with Christ in its visible structure by the bonds of the profession of faith, the sacraments and ecclesiastical governance."

36   Cf. M. Brogi, "Le Chiese *sui iuris* nel Codex Canonum Ecclesiarum Orientalium," in *Il Diritto Canonico Orientale nell'ordinamento ecclesiale*, Studi Giuridici 34, ed. K. Bharanikulangara, (Vatican City, 1995) 49-75; F. McManus, "The Possibility of New Rites in the Church," *The Jurist* 50 (1990) 435-458, esp. 436-444; G. Nedungatt, *The Spirit of the Eastern Code* (Rome and Bangalore, 1993) 60-61; *Id.*, *A Companion to the Eastern Code*, Kanonika 5 (Rome, 1994) 20-21.

I.3. Canon 1 of the Respective Codes of the Catholic Church

a. Prior Legislation

The Latin Code[37] of 1917 expressed it in this way: "Although in the Code of canon law the discipline of the Oriental Church is frequently referenced, nevertheless, this [Code] applies only to the Latin Church and does not bind the Oriental, unless it treats of things that, by their nature, apply to the Oriental" (c. 1). Thus, it obligated only the Christian faithful of the Latin Church, while often mentioning the discipline of the "Eastern Church." However, there were in the Code some canonical dispositions which were applicable *ex ipsa natura rei* to the "Eastern Church"; these dispositions were those contained in the laws which were universal by their nature[38] and those which expressly concerned the Eastern faithful, for example, canons 98, 257, 804, 816, 819.[39] Certainly, the Eastern faith-

---

37 The *Codex Iuris Canonici* was promulgated on 27 May 1917 by Benedict XV with the Apcon *Providentissima Mater Ecclesia*: AAS 9/II (1917) 5-8; 11-456.

38 Laws that refer to dogmatic decisions are by their nature universal, as well as ones that declare divine law: "All persons are bound to seek the truth in those things which regard God and his Church and by virtue of divine law are bound by the obligation and possess the right of embracing and observing the truth which they have come to know" (CIC c. 748 §1).

39 CIC-17 c. 98: "§1. Among the various Catholic rites, one belongs to that one according to whose ceremonies one was baptized, unless perhaps baptism by a minister of an alien rite was brought about fraudulently, or in case of grave necessity when it was not possible to have a priest of one's own rite present, or if it came about by apostolic dispensation whereby the faculty was given to baptize one in a certain rite while remaining ascribed to the other rite.

"§2. Clerics shall not presume in any manner to induce latin-rite faithful to transfer to an oriental [rite], or an oriental-rite faithful to transfer to the latin [rite].

"§3. It is not lawful for anyone, without coming to the Apostolic See, to transfer to another rite, or, after legitimate transfer, to return to the former.

"§4. It is the right of a woman of a rite different than the rite of the man, either entering the marriage or during it, to transfer [rites]; when the marriage is ended, she has the power of freely returning to her former rite, unless by particular law it is provided otherwise.

"§5. The practice, however long in duration, of receiving the sacred Synax in a foreign rite does not bring about a change of rite."

CIC-17 c. 257: "§1. The Congregation for the Eastern Church is presided over by the Roman Pontiff. To this Congregation is reserved all those sorts of things that refer to persons or to the discipline or to the rites of the oriental Churches, even if they are mixed, that is, if either by reason of matter or persons they also affect latins.

"§2. Therefore, this Congregation enjoys all the faculties for all the oriental rites of the Church that other congregations obtain for the latin rites of the Church, without harm, nevertheless, to the rights of the H. Office, according to the norm of Canon 247.

ful were not obliged in virtue of the canons, but obliged because of their content; this also applies vice versa for the Latin faithful.

Despite the clarity of CIC-17 c. 1, Eastern canon law "was normally classified in the pre-conciliar manuals of canon law as particular law (special or personal), that is, relative and derived and placed at a lower level with respect to the norms of the CIC, considered as common law."[40]

Canon 1 of the texts of 1945 and 1946 of the Codex Iuris Canonici Orientalis was more complex and perhaps more clear: "Codex iuris canonici orientalis obligat christifideles ritibus orientalibus adscriptos, ubique terrarum commorantes, etsi Hierarchæ latini ritus subiectos; latinos autem non tenet, nisi ipsi expresse nominentur."[41] Latins were bound by the Eastern Code in cases wherein they were expressly mentioned. Alongside this canon, we compare PA c. 302 §2: "Whenever it is prescribed or recommended in these canons that a Hierarch of any rite seek counsel or proceed in another similar fashion, Latin rite Hierarchs who have jurisdiction in the region are also included."[42] Latin Hierarchs were subjected to the Eastern Code without the need of expressly mentioning them. One also had to take into account CS c. 1, made explicit by c. 15: "Clerics and faithful of any rite, including Latins, are bound by the prescriptions of cc. 1 §2, 4, 5, 7, 10, 11 §2, 13." The canons in question bound not only clerics, but also the laity.

The revision of the preliminary canons of the entire Eastern Code, that is, canons 1-8, brought about another formulation of CICO 1945 canon 1: "Canonibus huius Codicis omnes et solæ Ecclesiæ Orientales Catholicæ tenentur, nisi aliud

---

"§3. This Congregation decides controversies in a disciplinary manner; whatever it determines should be decided in a judicial manner, it remits to whatever tribunal it designates."

CIC-17 c. 804 §1: "A priest from outside the church in which he wishes to celebrate, showing an authentic and currently valid letter of commendation from his own Ordinary if he is secular, or from his Superior if he is religious, or from the Sacred Congregation for the Oriental Church if he is of an oriental rite, is to be admitted to the celebration of Mass unless in the meantime it is shown that he committed some deed that would require him to be prevented from the celebration of Mass."

CIC-17 c. 816: "A priest in the celebration of the Mass, according to his own rite, must use unleavened or leavened bread whenever he says the Holy [Mass]."

CIC-17 c. 819: "The sacrifice of the Mass is to be celebrated in the liturgical language approved by the Church for that rite."

40   E. Corecco and L. Gerosa, *Il diritto della Chiesa*, Amateca 12 (Milan, 1995) 49.
41   *Nuntia* 2 (1976) 54.
42   PA = Pius XII, Mp *Postquam Apostolicis Litteris*, 9 February 1952: *AAS* 44 (1952) 65-152, entered into the force of law 21 November 1952.

ex natura rei constet."⁴³ A consultative body had requested the substitution of the clause "nisi aliud ex natura rei constat" with "nisi de relationibus interritualibus agitur, quæ latinos quoque respiciunt," "in order to make the necessary connection between the two codes, in the ever more frequent cases of inter-ritual relations." The canon was thus formulated, "Canones huius Codicis omnes et solas Ecclesias orientales Catholicas respiciunt, iis exceptis, in quibus relationes cum Ecclesia latina quod attinet, expresse aliud statuitur."⁴⁴

In the 1986 CICO Draft, canon 1 had the following formulation: "Canones huius Codicis omnes et solas Ecclesias orientales catholicas respiciunt, nisi, relationes cum Ecclesia latina quod attinet, expresse aliud statuitur."⁴⁵ The promulgated canon is that of the novissimum draft (1989): "Canones huius Codicis omnes et solas Ecclesias orientales catholicas respiciunt, nisi, relationes cum Ecclesia latina quod attinet, aliud expresse statuitur" ["The canons of this Code concern all and only the Eastern Catholic Churches, unless, with regard to relations with the Latin Church, it is expressly established otherwise"].

b. Current Legislation

CIC c. 1⁴⁶ formulates the scope, force and juridic effect of the Code: "The canons of this Code concern only the Latin Church." The new Latin Code⁴⁷ no longer mentions the Eastern Catholic Churches,⁴⁸ which, according to the declaration of Vatican II, *have the right and obligation to govern themselves according to their own particular disciplines* (OE 5; LG 23), that is, they have their own authority and internal autonomy, with due regard for the supreme authority of the Church.

The direct and simple formulation of canon 1 was desired in order to avoid misunderstandings and in order to be clear. The non-inclusion of the Eastern Churches was a precise and determined choice,⁴⁹ but despite the absoluteness of the formulation, the CIC is also concerned with the relations of the Latin Catholics with members of the Eastern Churches and recognizes that some dispositions can involve them to the extent that they are in relation with Latin Catholics. The

---

43   *Nuntia* 10 (1980) 87; 19 (1984) 20.
44   *Nuntia* 22 (1986) 13-14.
45   *Nuntia* 24-25 (1987) 1.
46   The *Codex Iuris Canonici* was promulgated by John Paul II with the apostolic constitution *Sacræ disciplinæ leges* on 25 January 1983 and entered into the force of law 27 November 1983: *AAS* 75/II (1983) VII-XV; 1-317.
47   There was a desire to add *obbligant fideles Latini ritus etiam apud Orientales* in order to emphasize the personal character of the law: *Comm.* 23 (1991) 109.
48   Cf. F. J. Urrutia, "Canones præliminares codicis (CIC). Comparatio cum canonibus præliminaribus Codicis Canonum Ecclesiarum Orientalium (CC)," *Periodica* 81 (1992) 153-158.
49   The clause *nisi de iis agatur* was removed; it was unnecessary to insert the clause *quæ ex ipsa rei natura obbligant*: *Comm.* 23 (1991) 109.

supreme Legislator had to take into consideration also relations with other non-Latin but fully Catholic ecclesial communities: communities fully subject to the Roman Pontiff and conscious of this subjection, through which the supreme Legislator was able to overcome, at least *de facto*, the principle of non-interference stated in CIC c. 1 and to dictate binding norms for both parties, both Latin Catholics and members of the Eastern Catholic Churches. The same is true for the CCEO. Having made this choice, the Roman Pontiff had to make another choice regarding the inter-ecclesial relationships involving a Latin party: to include parallel norms in both codes to regulate these relationships, or to promulgate a third code of an inter-ecclesial character. The Legislator chose to use parallel norms, but since the two redactions occurred in different times, there is a certain dissonance and overlapping. Two parallel norms, one for the Latins and another for the Easterns, have been inserted independently in both codes. To summarize, the passive subject of the CIC, *primo et principaliter* is the Latin Church, *per accidens* all the others when it is stated expressly or when one is dealing with material that, by its nature, also touches the Eastern Churches. [50] This same is true for the CCEO, as we shall soon see.

---

50   For example, dogmatic laws (cc. 330, 331, 375); laws that regard divine law (c. 113); decrees of condemnation of errors, disciplinary decrees that also mention the Eastern Churches (c. 1015 §2). One must also take into consideration CCEO c. 1492: "Laws issued by the supreme authority of the Church, which do not expressly indicate the passive subject, affect the Christian faithful of the Eastern Churches only insofar as they concern matters of faith or morals or declarations of divine law, explicitly decide questions regarding these Christian faithful, or concern favors which contain nothing contrary to the Eastern rites."

The Eastern Churches now have their common Code,[51] which can be considered its first in the two millennia history of the Catholic Church.[52] But might not a single code for all the Eastern Churches be in opposition to the ecclesiastical

---

[51] For history on the codification process, consult the following: H. J. Cicognani, "De Codificatione canonica orientali," *Apollinaris* 5 (1932) 86-95; A. Coussa, "De Codificatione canonica orientali," in *Acta Congressus Iuridici Internationalis VII sæculo a Decretalibus Gregorii IX et XIV a Codice Iustiniano promulgatis Romæ, 12-17 novembris 1934*, v. 9 (Rome, 1937); A. Giannini, "Sulla Codficazione del diritto canonico orienatale," *Il Diritto Ecclesiastico* 58 (1947) 193-204; A. Coussa and C. Korolevskij, "Codificazione canonica orientale," s.v. in *Novissimo Digesto Italiano*, v. 3 (1967) 411-415; A. Coussa, "Codificazione Canonica orientale," in *Oriente cattolico. Cenni storici e statistiche*, 4th ed. (Vatican City, 1974); D. Faltin, "Codex Iuris Canonici Orientalis," in *Dictionarium morale et canonicum*, ed. D. Palazzini (Rome, 1962) 1:719-722; *Id.*, "La Codificazione del diritto canonico orientale," in *La Sacra Congregazione per le Chiese Orientali nel cinquantesimo della fondazione (1917-1967)*, ed. Congregazione per le Chiese Orientali (Rome, 1967) 121-137; *Id.*, "L'Unità della Chiesa e la legislazione canonica delle Chiese orientale," *Unitas* (1972) 176ff; R. Metz, "La première tentative di codifier le droit des Églises orientales catholiques au XXe siècle (1927-1958)," in *Melanges offerts à Jean Dauvillier* (Toulouse, 1979) 531-546; *Id.*, "La seconde tentative de codifier le droit des Églises orientales catholiques au XXe siècle (1972 à...). Latinisation or identité orientale?" *L'Année Canonique* 23 (1979) 289-309; *Id.*, "Le nouveau code de droit canonique des Églises orientales catholiques," *Revue de Droit canonique* 42 (1992) 101-106; *Id.*, *Le nouveau droit des Églises orientales catholiques* (Paris, 1997); O. Bucci, "Il Codice di Diritto Canonico Orientale nella storia della Chiesa," in *Miscellanea in onore dei Professori Anastasio Gutierrez e Pietro Tocanel*, ed. Pontificium Institutum Utriusque Iuris Apollinaris (Rome, 1982) 122-200; I. Žužek, "Presentazione del 'Codex Canonum Ecclesiarum Orientalium,'" *Monitor Ecclesiasticus* 95 (1990) 591-598; E. Eid, "La révision du Code de droit canonique oriental: histoire et principes," *L'Année canonique* 33 (1990) 11-27; T. J. Green, "Reflections on the Eastern Code Revision Process," *The Jurist* 51 (1991) 18-37; L Rohban, "Codification du droit canonique oriental," *Apollinaris* 65 (1992) 241-251; D. Salachas, *Istituzioni di diritto canonico delle Chiese cattoliche orientali* (Rome-Bologna, 1993) 45-54; *Id.*, "Teologia e nomotecnica del 'Codex Canonum Ecclesiarum Orientalium,'" *Periodica* 82 (1993) 320-328; F. R. McManus, "The Code of Canons of the Eastern Catholic Churches," *The Jurist* 53 (1993) 22-61; J. Faris, "La Storia della codificazione orientale," in *Il Diritto...*, ed. K. Bharanikulangara, 255-268.

[52] Certain authors are not in full agreement with this point. Msgr. E. Eid writes, "With the promulgation of the *Code of Canons of the Eastern Churches*, one has, for the first time in the history of the Church, a single body of law, complete and common to all the Eastern Catholic Churches" (*Apollinaris* 63 [1990] 475 and *Nuntia* 31 [1990] 24). Fr. I. Žužek holds a different opinion, affirming that "the opinions, frequently expressed this year, that the CCEO is the first code common to all the Eastern Churches in history, appear to be not entirely exact to me." According to Žužek, the CCEO is the first code to be promulgated by the Pope himself, but not the first as such for the Eastern Churches: "Common Canons and Ecclesial Experience in the Oriental Catholic Churches," in *Incontro*, 1:21-56. Indeed, John Paul II, on the day of the presentation of the Code, said that it is the first to be promulgated by the Vicar of Christ: *Discourse on the Presentation of the Code of Canons of the Eastern Churches*, 25 October 1990: *Nuntia* 31 (1990) 17.

patrimony of each of them? We believe not, since these Churches find a very clear expression and safeguard in the single Code.⁵³

CCEO c. 1 declares that "the canons of this Code concern all and only the Eastern Catholic Churches, unless, with regard to relations with the Latin Church, it is expressly established otherwise."⁵⁴ Again, this canon of the CCEO is required to determine the efficacy, scope and juridic force of the Code, as well as the faithful protection and diligent observance of all the Eastern rites. There are currently 21 Eastern Catholic Churches that are in perfect unity of faith and in full hierarchical communion with the Apostolic See of Rome;⁵⁵ these Churches use the five original traditions (cf. CCEO c. 28 §2): Alexandrian, Antiochene, Armenian, Chaldean and Constantinopolitan.⁵⁶ These different Eastern Catholic Churches are distinguished among themselves, even within the same liturgical tradition,⁵⁷

---

53   Cf. *Nuntia* 3 (1976) 4; R. Metz, "Quel est le droit pour les Églises orientales unies à Rome?" *L'Année Canonique* 30 (1987) 398-399.
   The editorial of *Irénikon* 63 (1990) 449-450, on the one hand affirms that "one can consider that (the Code) really represents the mind of the Eastern Catholic Churches and their heads and those responsible for them," while on the other hand says the very opposite: "Even if the content of this 'Code of Canons of the Eastern Churches' integrates a great number of elements of Eastern tradition, it remains that its conception is still quite Latin." We note that of the 35 members of the Revision Commission, 31 were Latin.
54   For the development of this canon, see M. Brogi, "Il nuovo Codice orientale e la Chiesa latina," *Antonianum* 66 (1991) 39-49; L. Lorusso, "L'ambito d'applicazione del Codice dei canoni delle Chiese Orientali. Commento sistematico al can. 1 del CCEO," *Angelicum* 82 (2005) 451-478.
   During the preparation of the CCEO, proposals that aimed to extend more broadly the force of the Eastern Code to Latin Catholics were rejected: *Nuntia* 22 (1986) 13-14; 28 (1989) 13.
55   M. Thériault, "Canonical questions brought about by the presence of Eastern Catholics in Latin Areas in the Light of the 'Codex Canonum Ecclesiarum Orientalium,'" *Ius Ecclesiæ* 3 (1991) 205-206, enumerates 22 entities addressed by the CCEO, including the Latin Patriarchate of Jerusalem among the Eastern Patriarchs.
56   PA c. 303 §1, 1° had another order: Alexandrian, Antiochene, Constantinopolitan, Chaldean and Armenian. In *Nuntia* 3 (1976) 45-46, there is a proposal to substitute "Constantinopolitan" with "Byzantine," but the proposal was rejected both because the Byzantine Empire extended beyond the boundaries of the rite of Constantinople and because the epithet "Byzantine" never qualified the rite of Constantinople before the ninth century. In *Nuntia* 22 (1986) 23, there is a proposal to enumerate the five traditions according to the order of precedence attributed to the patriarchal Churches: Constantinopolitan, Alexandrian, Antiochene, Chaldean and Armenian; but the proposal was not accepted inasmuch as all the traditions are of equal dignity and merit equal respect.
57   To have an idea of the variety of the Eastern Churches and their denominations, refer to the work of E. Saïd, *Les Églises*...: we have found 57 denominations; cf. N. Bux, *La liturgia degli orientali* (Bari, 1996) 57-80; F. Carcione, *Le Chiese d'Oriente. Identità, patrimonio e quadro storico generale 1997* (Cinisello Balsamo 1998); V. J. Pospishil, *Eastern Catholic Church Law*, 2ⁿᵈ ed. (New York, 1996) 15-41; H. L. Dalmais,

in part by their own discipline, and principally and fundamentally by their hierarchy. Each of them, in principle of law,[58] is a Church *sui iuris*, of its own law, in the sense that it is part of the universal Church with its own institutions and rules.[59] The Code is therefore for the Eastern Catholics, but also concerns the Latin Church when *expresse statuitur*.

The new Eastern Code mentions the Latin Church expressly in 9 canons:[60] 37, 41, 207, 322 §1, 432, 696 §§1-2; 830 §1, 916 §5, 1465. The CIC contains the following canons applicable to Eastern faithful: 111 §1: "ritual Church to which the father belongs"; 111 §2: "is to be baptized in another ritual Church *sui iuris*"; 112 §1, 1°: "are ascribed to another ritual Church *sui iuris*"; 112 §1, 2°: "to the ritual Church *sui iuris* of the other"; 112 §1, 3°: "lawfully to another ritual Church"; 112 §2: "rite of a certain ritual Church *sui iuris*"; 214: "according to the prescripts of their own rite"; 350 §1: "Eastern patriarchs who have been brought into the college of cardinals"; 350 §3: "Eastern patriarchs who have been made members of the college of cardinals"; 372 §2: "distinguished by the rite of the faithful or some other similar reason"; 383 §2: "If he has faithful of a different rite in his diocese"; 450 §1: "Ordinaries of another rite can also be invited"; 476: "over the faithful of a specific rite"; 479 §2: "or the faithful of a specific rite or group"; 518: "personal parishes are to be established determined by reason of the rite"; 535 §2: "and of change of rite"; 846 §2: "according to the minister's own rite"; 923: "can received in any Catholic rite"; 991: " to a legitimately approved confessor of his or her choice, even to one of another rite"; 1015 §2: "ordain licitly a subject of an Eastern rite"; 1021: "to a bishop of a rite different from the rite of the candidate"; 1109: "provided that one of them is of the Latin rite"; 1127 §1: "with a non-Catholic party of an Eastern rite"; 1248 §1: "celebrated anywhere in a Catholic rite."

The CCEO contains canons in which, even if the Latin Church is not expressly mentioned, it is included as a Church *sui iuris*[61] (29-41: ascription; 84 §1: pastoral

---

"Signification de la diversité des rites au regard de l'unité chrétienne," *Istina* 7 (1960) 311-318; D. Gelsi, "Orientali Liturgie," in *Nuovo Dizionario di Liturgia*, ed. D. Sartore and A. M. Triacca (Cinisello Balsamo, 1988) 983-1007.
58   Not all the Eastern Catholic Churches in existence today are *sui iuris* in the same way, from a juridic and formal perspective.
59   Cf. *Comm.* 12 (1980) 73.
60   Cf. I. Žužek, *Index analyticus Codicis Canonum Ecclesiarum Orientalium*, Kanonika 2 (Rome, 1992), especially 113, s.v. *Ecclesia latina* (c. 696 is missing); X. Ochoa, *Index verborum ac locutionum Codicis Iuris Canonici* (Rome, 1983), especially 144, s.v. *Ecclesia latina*.
61   I. Žužek, "Presentazione…," 604-606. We share the position of Žužek, who regards "the figure of the Latin Church entirely by itself and not comparable even by a distant analogy to the other Churches *sui iuris*. The Latin Church draws its juridic configuration from the fact that it has as its head the Vicar of Christ, successor of Saint Peter, who, in his primatial power over the universal Church by divine law, includes all power that exists in the Church of Christ, legislative, judicial, administrative": I. Žužek, "Un Codice per una *Varietas Ecclesiarum*," in *Studi sul Codex Canonum Ecclesiarum*

activity; 451, 517 §2: admission in religious institutes; 1013 §2: offerings; 1405 §3: penal laws). Alongside those canons are also others regarding the norms of marriage legislation. Be that as it may, it is necessary to note that the CCEO cannot be considered as a juridic complement to the CIC, since "it does not seem that the Eastern Code can oblige Latin Catholics directly if only by the nature of the things regulated in it (*ex natura rei*)";[62] thus, in the case of a contradiction with the Latin Code, the Eastern Code generally does not oblige that Latin faithful as a later norm of the same supreme Legislator,[63] since one is dealing with "two different legal systems."[64] In principle, the two codes cannot automatically constitute a suppletory source of law in the case of a *lacuna* of law. Nevertheless, we cannot speak of an airtight separation between the two legislations,[65] because the CCEO clearly states *nisi, relationes cum Ecclesia latina quod attinet, aliud expresse statuitur*.[66] A comparison of the codes will always give rise to new ideas to improve one or the other discipline, even if not always automatically, especially and principally through appropriate legislative acts. Moreover, in the interpretation of laws, beyond the proper meaning of words in the text and context,[67] if doubt or lack of

---

Orientalium, ed. S. Gherro (Padua, 1994) 4; cf. *Id.*, "Incidenza del 'Codex Canonum Ecclesiarum Orientalium' nella storia moderna della Chiesa universale," in *Ius in vita et in missione Ecclesiæ*, ed. Pontificium Consilium de Legum Textibus Interpretandis (Vatican City, 1994) 715-720; *Id., Understanding...*,104-105. Congar's study of the Pope as the Patriarch of the West is of interest: Y. Congar, *Eglise et papauté*, Congitatio Fidei 184 (Paris, 1994) 11-30. In any case, the fact remains that in CIC cc. 111 §2 and 112, the Latin Church is considered as a Church *sui iuris*, especially in the expressions *vel in alia Ecclesia rituali sui iuris, alii Ecclesiæ rituali sui iuris adscribuntur* and *ad aliam Ecclesiam ritualem legitime transierit*. The *Lex Ecclesiæ Fundamentalis* was more explicit; in enumerating the *Ecclesiæ rituales sui iuris*, it specified *videlicet Ecclesia latina et variæ Ecclesiæ Orientales...*: Cf. *Comm.* 12 (1980) 31, c. 2 §2. Thus, "the term *sui iuris*, although good and in use in the same Latin Code, has a specific meaning in reference to the Latin Church, which is not such that it can be applied to the Eastern Churches *cum grano salis*; likewise for the terms 'autonomous Church,' 'Church of its own status,' 'Church with a special status,' not to speak the term 'autocephalous,' used among the Orthodox. Such meanings do not have any sense when one speaks of the Latin Church. All that can be said of its *sui iuris* status is regulated on the basis of the *Codex Iuris Canonici*": I. Žužek, "Incidenza...," 720.

62   P. Erdö, "Questioni interrituali del diritto dei sacramenti (Battesimo e Cresima)," *Periodica* 84 (1995) 318; the updated version of the publication is found in *Folia Canonica* 1 (1998) 9-35.

63   P. Erdö, "Questioni interrituali...," 315-353, especially 315-322; F. J. Urrutia, "Canones...," 153-177, especially 158; M. Brogi, "Il nuovo Codice...," 46-49.

64   F. J. Urrutia, "Canones...," 158.

65   Cf. N. R. A. Rachford, "Two Lungs, two Ventricles: the Eastern Canons as Suppletory Law," *CLSA Proceedings* 56 (1994) 153-170.

66   G. Nedungatt, *The Spirit...*, 102: "But 'express' statement does not mean 'to mention by *name*,' which in law happens only rarely. In fact, 'express' can be either explicit or implicit."

67   The context is that legal body in which the norm is included. It is not simply the lexical or purely grammatical context, but the systematic position in which the norm

clarity remains, one must make recourse to parallel texts[68] for the purpose and circumstances of the law (ratio legis)[69] and to the mens legislatoris (cf. CIC c. 17; CCEO c. 1499). The *mens legislatoris* is not the will and the private intention of the legislator, but the particular motive which, in the exercise of his public functions, caused him to enact a specific law, with its precise meaning, content and expectation regarding the manner of understanding and applying the law itself. On the other hand, laws that determine the juridic conditions of persons within the ecclesiastical community, recognizing or denying them capacity to pose specific acts, are to be respected by any ecclesiastical superior, either Eastern or Latin.[70] Interpretation does not mean modification and, thus, does not always constitute a solution in cases of possible contradiction between the two codes. One should also take into consideration CIC c. 19 and CCEO c. 1501 that invoke the principle of suppletory law when one is faced with a *lacuna legis*;[71] laws enacted in similar cases (taking into account especially the canons of the Synods and the Fathers):[72]

---

is part of the legal body: cf. J. Otaduy, "Los medios interpretativos de la ley canónica y su relación con las distintas doctrinas de la interpretación," *Ius Canonicum* 35 (1995) 445-500, especially 489.

68   Parallel texts are those that treat the same or similar matters or persons, which are sometimes formulated more clearly or emphasize something that is not sufficiently emphasized in the text of the law. The parallel passage can also trace another canonical collection of universal or particular laws: cf. J. Otaduy, "Los medios...," 489; J. García Martín, *Le norme generali del Codex Iuris Canonici* (Rome, 1996) 115. CIC-17 c. 18 stated *ad locos Codicis parallelos*: "Ecclesiastical laws are to be understood according to the meaning of their own words, considered in their text and context; as for those things that remain unclear or in doubt, reference should be made to parallel provisions in the Code, if there are any, and to the purposes and circumstances of the law and to the mind of the legislator." However, one notes that the parallel places do not permit an extensive interpretation of penal laws and laws that restrict the exercise of rights or contain an exception to the law (CIC c. 18; CCEO c. 1500).

69   The *ratio legis* is in the order of *finis operantis*, not of *finis operis*. Cf. J. Otaduy, "Los medios...," 490-492; D. Salachas, "Principi di interpretazione del Codex Canonum Ecclesiarum Orientalium," in *Attuali problemi di interpretazione del Codice di Diritto Canonico*, Atti del Simposio Internazionale in occasione del I Centenario della Facoltà di Diritto Canonico della PUST (Roma, 24-26 ottobre 1996) (Rome, 1997) 245-268; J. Abbass, "Canonical Interpretation by Recourse to 'Parallel Passages': A Comparative Study of the Latin and Eastern Codes," *The Jurist* 51 (1991) 291-310.

70   Cf. M. Brogi, "Il nuovo Codice...," 55.

71   "For a norm to be suppletory, it is necessary that the material to be decided is not provided (considered) in law or custom": J. Otaduy, "Comentario al canon 19," in *Comentario exegético al Código de Derecho Canónico*, eds. A. Marzoa et al. (Pamplona, 1996) 1:384.

72   While CIC c. 19 speaks of *legibus latis in similibus*, CCEO c. 1501 speaks of *secundum canones Synodorum et sanctorum Patrum*. Therefore, when the CCEO contains laws that regulate matters treated in the CIC, Eastern norms can serve to fill the Latin *lacunæ*, but not vice versa. In any case, the interpretative principle of CIC c. 19 can be invoked only in individual cases because only the legislator has the authority to intervene or remedy such *lacunæ* in a definitive form.

analogia legis; general principles of canon law: *analogia iuris;* ecclesiastical jurisprudence; common and constant opinions of canonists. Hence, after all means internal to each code have been used and one still does not have a clear reading and interpretation of the juridic norm, it would be legitimate to make recourse to a parallel text of the other code, at least for direction or guidance to fill the *lacuna* or to make the norm understandable.[73] Moreover, bearing in mind that the Roman Pontiff in the apostolic constitution *Sacræ disciplinæ leges* says that the Code strives to transfer conciliar ecclesiology into canonistic language (and this applies also to the CCEO), when this translation is not fully achieved, the one who is called to interpret and apply the canon law must make recourse to the conciliar doctrine:[74]

> The instrument which the Code is fully corresponds to the nature of the Church, especially as it is proposed by the teaching of the Second Vatican Council in general, and in a particular way by its ecclesiological teaching. Indeed, in a certain sense, this new Code could be understood as a great effort to translate this same doctrine, that is, the conciliar ecclesiology, into canonical language. If, however, it is impossible to translate perfectly into canonical language the conciliar image of the Church, nevertheless, in this image there should always be found as far as possible its essential point of reference.[75]

Similarly in the apostolic constitution *Sacri Canones*: "We consider that this Code [...] must be considered to be assessed most of all according to the ancient law of the Eastern Churches. [...] The *Code of Canons of the Eastern Churches* should be considered as a new complement to the teaching proposed by the Second Vatican Council."[76] Each Code aims for the juridic translation of the Second Vatican Council. The fundamental hermeneutic principle is not that the Second

---

73   Cf. L. M. De Bernardis, "Possibilità e limiti dell'osmosi fra CIC e CCEO," in *Ius in vita et in missione Ecclesiæ*, ed. Pontificium Consilium de Legum Textibus Interpretandis (Vatican City, 1994) 785-790, especially 787; J. Abbass, *Two Codes in Comparison*, Kanonika 7 (Rome, 1997) 284-293. According to J. Otaduy, "Comentario al canon 19," 1:382: "The majority opinion is very clear: the four suppletory elements enumerated in the canon '*taxative* sunt intelligenda, ita ut ad adimplendas legislationis canonicæ lacunas *ad nullum aliud permittatur recursus*.' In particular this means there are no suppletory means either in the law of the state, or in the particular law outside its own jurisdictional sphere (including the law of the Eastern Churches), or in ancient canon law, or in Roman Law."
74   Such an interpretative value was already recognized by prior Eastern codification: C. Lefebre, "De orientalis codificationis auctoritate ad CIC interpretationem," *Apollinaris* 32 (1959) 87-104, especially 98-101.
75   *AAS* 75/II (1983) XI: Canon Law Society of America, *Code of Canon Law. Latin-English Edition* (Washington, 1999) xxx.
76   *AAS* 82 (1990) 1036, 1038: Canon Law Society of America, *Code of Canons of the Eastern Churches* (Washington, 2001) xxiii, xxv.

Vatican Council must be interpreted by the Code; rather the contrary. The conciliar ecclesiological doctrine has an external textual function that impedes the closure of the canonical text of the Code.

We can synthesize this argument by stating that in the Church there is one single juridic order, but subdivided into disciplinary systems that are equal in dignity. This distinction does not mean separation, but each, constituting an integral part, contributes to the formation of the general ordering of the Church. Interpretation, in order to carry out its function, rather than making note of the contrasts, wherever there exists only a necessary differentiation, must harmonize the multiplicity in the systematic unity of the juridic order, articulated in a multiplicity that is not disruptive but rather strengthens the cohesion.

Based on the principles set forth, the CCEO designates the Eastern Churches as *Ecclesiæ sui iuris*.[77] We prefer not to translate the phrase *sui iuris* because, in our opinion, it would run the risk of not fully expressing fully the relative autonomy of the various kinds of Eastern Catholic Churches. Indeed, "Church of its own law" in the broad sense is also an eparchy (diocese); further, in canonical doctrine, "of its own law" is also applicable to religious. Certainly to translate *sui iuris* with "of its own law" is better than "autonomous," but we prefer not to translate the term *sui iuris*, because it would be misleading and confusing; it has by now become a technical term in canonical literature.[78] The phrase "Churches *sui iuris*," as we have seen, is understood in the Eastern Code as "a community of the Christian faithful, which is joined together by a hierarchy according to the norm of law and which is expressly or tacitly recognized as *sui iuris*" (CCEO c. 27).

The *Ecclesia sui iuris* is differentiated from "rite," which is defined in CCEO c. 28 §1 in its essential elements:[79] "A rite is a liturgical, theological, spiritual and disciplinary heritage, differentiated by the culture and the circumstances of the history of peoples, which is expressed by each Church *sui iuris* in its own manner of living the faith."

Before Vatican II, there was a general tendency to establish a kind of identity between the universal Church and the Latin Church; the Eastern Catholic Churches appeared as some administrative divisions, a little anomalous in the midst of the Latin Church. But to want to reduce the Church of Christ to the Church of the Latin rite and to consider the Eastern rites as auxiliaries of the

---

77 Cf. D. Salachas, "Il concetto ecclesiologico e canonico di 'Chiese orientali' (*Ecclesia sui iuris*)," *Oriente Cristiano* nn. 1-2 (1990) 45-53; M. Brogi, "Le Chiese...," 517-544; I. Žužek, "Che cosa...," 263-277; J. E. Lynch, "The Eastern Churches: Historical Background," *The Jurist* 51 (1991) 1-17.
78 The French version of the CCEO translates the term *sui iuris* with the expression *de droit propre*; see the review in *Sapienza* 50 (1997) 361-366.
79 Cf. *Comm.* 12 (1980) 73; *Nuntia* 29 (1989) 36-61; for a historical note, see *Annuario Pontificio 2012* (Vatican City, 2012) 1817-1819.

Latin rite is to reduce the mandate Christ entrusted to his Church to go to all peoples and nations, both Western and Eastern.[80] The very expressions used by the CIC, "universal laws" and "universal customs," are "universal" only for the Latin Church, according to CIC c. 1.[81]

It has finally been rediscovered that the Catholic Church is, in effect, a communion of Churches of East and West, each having its own law, a specific rite and a distinct juridic person, which the Church calls a Church *sui iuris*, that is, a Church capable of self-governance, with due regard for the rights of the Roman Pontiff, the College of Bishops and an ecumenical council.

Even if the CCEO treats all and only the Eastern and Catholic Churches, that is, it is applicable to all of them, not all the Eastern Churches are *sui iuris* in the same manner.[82] According to CCEO cc. 27 and 174, the Eastern Catholic Churches are categorized into four kinds of Churches, that is, the patriarchal Churches[83] (LG 23; OE 7-9; CCEO cc. 55-150), with Patriarchs as heads who are

---

80   "To want to reduce the Church of Christ to the Church of the Latin Rite and to consider the Eastern rite as an auxiliary of the Latin Church is to reduce the mandate of Christ who entrusted his Church with the mandate to go out to every people and nation. The Church, faithful to the will of its Founder, strives to extend itself to every part without distinction of peoples of West or East": C. Pujol, "O recente Código das Igrejas de rito oriental," *Brotéria* 135 (1992) 178-200, especially 184. J. Beyer uses an expression that is not very appropriate, affirming that the CIC has a universal character while the CCEO is more restricted because of the territoriality of the Eastern Churches: J. Beyer, "Commento a un canone. Il primo canone del Codice," *Quaderni di diritto ecclesiale* 6 (1993) 298-306, especially 299.

81   N. R. A. Rachford, "Two Lungs…," *CLSA Proceedings* 56 (1994) 156-158.

82   Cf. G. Nedungatt, "Presentazione del CCEO," EV 12:889-894; J. Prader, *La legislazione matrimoniale latina e orientale* (Rome, 1993) 11-12; J. Chiramel, "Hierarchical Structuring in the Oriental Legislation," in *The Code of Canons of the Eastern Churches*, eds. J. Chiramel and K. Bharanikulangara (Alwaye, 1992) 91-107.

83   The patriarchal structure is the most ancient and the most traditional form of governance of the Eastern Churches (OE 11), as stated by Pope Pius XII in the preface of the Mp *Cleri Sanctitati*: "Indeed, the patriarchal institution seems to be worthy of mention before others, since it is truly known, as it were, as the preeminent institution of Eastern ecclesiastical organization": *AAS* 49 (1957) 435.

Currently, the patriarchal Churches are:

Armenian Church, whose head is the Patriarch *Ciliciæ Armenorum*, of the Armenian tradition, wherein Benedict XIV on 26 November 1742 confirmed the Patriarch Abraham Ardzivian (Abraham Peter I);

Chaldean Church, whose head is the Patriarch *Babylonensis Chaldæorum*, of the Chaldean tradition, wherein Julius III on 20 April 1553 confirmed Patriarch Sulaqa (Simon VIII);

Coptic Church, whose head is the Patriarch *Alexandrinus Coptorum*, of the Coptic tradition, erected by Leo XII on 15 August 1824 with the Aplet *Petrus Apostolorum princeps*, but later re-established by Leo XIII on 26 November 1895 with the Apletr *Christi Domini*;

Bishops of certain eparchies and have power over all members of the Church, governed by common and particular law enacted by the supreme authority of the Church and by their own legislative bodies; the major archiepiscopal Churches[84] (OE 10; CCEO cc. 151-154), in which the Major Archbishops are equated with the Patriarchs, except that they are Metropolitans with power over other ecclesiastical provinces beyond their own, while Patriarchs are eparchial Bishops with

---

Maronite Church, whose head is the Patriarch *Antiochenus Maronitarum*, of the Antiochene tradition, wherein Innocent III on 4 January 1216 with the bull *Quia divinæ sapientiæ* confirmed Patriarch Jeremiah II Al-Amshiti;

Melkite Church, whose head is the Patriarch *Antiochenus Græcorum Melkitarum*, of the Constantinopolitan tradition, wherein from Cyril VI (1724-1759) the series is of Patriarchs is uninterrupted;

Syrian Church, whose head is the Patriarch *Antiochenus Syrorum*, of the Antiochene tradition, wherein from 1783 the series of Patriarchs is uninterrupted.

Cf. D. Salachas, "Lo 'status *sui iuris*' delle Chiese patriacali nel diritto canonico orientale," *Periodica* 83 (1994) 569-609; *Id.*, "Il nuovo Codice...," 237-247. For the origins of the institution of Patriarchs both in the East and West, see F. Sollazzo, "I Patriarchi nel diritto canonico orientale e occidentale," in *Incontro*, 2:239-252; M. Miele, "I Patriarchi orientali nel collegio cardinalizio," in *Incontro*, 2:253-271; *Annuario Pontificio 2012* (Vatican City, 201) 1808-1809. See also G. De Vries, "La S. Sede ed i patriarcati cattolici d'Oriente," *Orientalia Christiana Periodica* 27 (1961) 313-361.

84   Currently the major archiepiscopal Churches are:

Ukrainian Church, whose head is the Major Archbishop *Leopolitanus Haliciensis et Camenecensis Ucrainorum*, of the Constantinopolitan tradition, elevated to major archiepiscopal status on 23 December 1963;

Malabar Church, whose head is the Major Archbishop *Ernakulamensis-Angamaliensis*, of the Chaldean tradition, elevated to major archiepiscopal status on 16 December 1992;

Syro-Malankara Church, whose head is the Major Archbishop *Travandrensis Syrorum Malankarensium*, of the Antiochene tradition, elevated to major archiepiscopal status on 10 February 2005;

Romanian Church, whose head is the Major Archbishop *Fagarasiensis et Albæ Iuliensis Romenorum*, of the Constantinopolitan tradition, elevated to major archiepiscopal status on 16 December 2005.

power over other Bishops, even Metropolitans;[85] the metropolitan Churches[86] (CCEO cc. 155-173), governed by Metropolitans appointed by the Roman Pontiff and assisted in the governance of the Churches by a Council of Hierarchs; and finally, other minor Churches *sui iuris*,[87] whose status is defined in Title VI, Chapter II (cc.174-176), with a Hierarch as head who is appointed by the Roman

---

85 The outstanding difference between the Patriarch and the Major Archbishop is their manner of election. After the election has been conducted by the Synod of Bishops of the patriarchal Church, the newly-elected can be immediately enthroned, although there is the obligation of informing the Roman Pontiff and requesting from him "ecclesiastical communion." The election of the Major Archbishop, conducted by the Synod, lacks finality because the confirmation of the Roman Pontiff is required before proceeding with the proclamation and enthronement. The qualification of "major" serves to distinguish him from other Archbishops who preside over an ecclesiastical province inside a Patriarchate.

86 Currently the Metropolitan Churches are:

Ethiopian Church, whose head is the Metropolitan of Addis Ababa *Neanthopolitanus*, of the Alexandrian tradition, elevated to metropolitan status on 20 February 1961;

Ruthenian Church of the United States, whose head is the Metropolitan *Pittsburgensis ritus byzantinti*, of the Constantinopolitan tradition, erected as a metropolia *sui iuris* on 21 February 1969;

Slovak Church, whose head is the Metropolitan *Prešoveniensis ritus byzantini*, of the Constantinopolitan tradition, erected as a metropolia *sui iuris* on 30 January 2008.

87 The status of these Churches are as follows:

Albanian Church, erected as the Apostolic Administration of Southern Albania (11 November 1939);

Belarusian Church, currently with an Apostolic Visitator;

Byzantine Eparchy of Križeci (17 June 1777), for the faithful of the Byzantine Rite;

Bulgarian Church, constituted as an Apostolic Exarchate for the Catholics of the Byzantine-Slav Rite residing in Bulgaria (31 July 1926);

Greek Church, constituted as an Apostolic Exarchate in Athens for the Greek Catholic of the Byzantine Rite (11 June 1932) and an Apostolic Exarchate at Istanbul (25 November 1996);

Italo-Albanian Church, constituted by the eparchies of Lungro (13 February 1919) and Piana degli Albanesi (26 October 1937) and the exarchic monastery of Grottaferrata (26 September 1937);

Macedonian Church, constituted as an Apostolic Exarchate for the Catholics of the Byzantine Rite residing in the former Yugoslav Republic of Macedonia (11 January 2001);

Russian Church, existing formally as an Apostolic Exarchate for Catholics of the Byzantine Rite (1917) and as an Apostolic Exarchate of Harbin for Russians of the Byzantine Rite and for all the Eastern Catholics in China (20 May 1928), but actually there is no hierarchy so this Church cannot be considered to be a Church *sui iuris*;

Slovak Church, constituted by the Eparchy of Prešov (22 September 1818), by the Apostolic Exarchate of Košice (27 January 1997) and by the Eparchy of Toronto (3 November 1956) for the faithful of the Byzantine rite;

Pontiff according the norms of common and particular law established by the Roman Pontiff. Obviously, this is a relative autonomy[88] of different degrees, not autocephaly,[89] delimited by the supreme authority of the Church,[90] which can always intervene *in casibus singulis* (OE 9). Indeed, these Churches exist through the will of the supreme authority of the Church, by which they can also be suppressed (CCEO cc. 27; 57 §1; 152; 155 §2).[91]

Hungarian Church, constituted by the Eparchy of Hajdùdorog (8 June 1912) and by the Apostolic Exarchate of Miskolc (4 June 1924).

88   It is understood to be bounded by the primacy of the Roman Pontiff; cf. *Nuntia* 26 (1989) 19; "To deal properly with the problem of autonomy within the Church, the canonist in particular, given the simultaneous roles of theologian and jurist, must distance himself from the conceptions of autonomy proper to the temporal sphere, in order to orient the research in an exclusive manner on the basis of a conception that considers the nature of the Church. Civil forms of organization such as those of the united, federated or confederated state and *a fortiori* those of communal autonomy, which imply a form of autonomous administration for the most part mixed with elements of delegation on the part of the State, cannot be translated to the ecclesial situation; one must consequently avoid working with analogies. The juridic term 'autonomy,' on the other hand, can be applied to the ecclesial situation because it does not prejudice any results. In the juridical sense, autonomy does not designate a situation of being totally unbound, but rather a sphere of liberty left to a community or rather between a specific community and the community as a whole, where they have the right to govern according to their own interests. Autonomy is consequently a relative concept because it designates the respective measure of self-determination and the measure of independence enjoyed within the context of the social entirety. In this sense, one can rightly pose the problem of autonomy also to the interior of the Church": K. Mörsdorf, "L'autonomia della Chiesa locale," in *Atti del congresso internazionale di Diritto Canonico: la Chiesa dopo il Concilio*, ed. Università di Roma (Rome, 1970) 1:168-169.

89   By "autocephaly" we mean full juridic independence, that is, the right of an ecclesiastical region to elect is own Bishops, its own Primate, Patriarch, Archbishops or Metropolitans.

90   Autocephaly is a characteristic of the Eastern non-Catholic Churches that have acquired a great autonomy of internal governance: the Church of Constantinople, of Alexandria, of Antioch and today the major part of the national Orthodox Churches of Eastern Europe (Greece, Russia, Bulgaria and Cyprus, etc.) or elsewhere (the Orthodox Church in America); cf. D. Salachas, "Le 'status' ecclésiologique et canonique des Églises catholiques orientales *'sui iuris'* et des Églises orthodoxes autcéphales," *L'Année Canonique* 33 (1990) 29-56; *Id.*, "Autocéphalie ou autonomie des Églises orthodoxes et status 'sui iuris' des Églises orientales catholiques," in *Incontro*, 1:372-380; *Id.*, "Le status d'autonomie des Églises catholiques orientales et leur communion avec le Siége Apostolique de Rome," *L'Année Canonique* 38 (1996) 75-90; E. Eid, "Authority and Autonomy (critical report in francese)," in *Incontro*, 1:428-447.

91   In our article that appeared in *O Odigos* 16 (1997/3) 3, it is affirmed: "However, although the CCEO had foreseen four models of Churches *sui iuris*, that is not to say that all Eastern Catholic Churches belong to one of these categories. One can have other Eastern Catholic Churches that are not *sui iuris*, but the CCEO also applies to them." These affirmations are not precise.

Bearing in mind what we have said, one sees that a Church *sui iuris* is identified neither with the universal Church nor with the particular Church (diocese / eparchy), but is a communion of particular Churches at the regional or interregional level.[92]

In the Latin Church there are also the Mozarabic or Visigoth rites in Spain and the Ambrosian rite in Milan;[93] neither of these, however, constitute a Church *sui iuris*. This expression, therefore, is not the same as a particular Church established on the basis of the rite of the faithful,[94] but signifies the liturgy or ceremony and the rules prescribed by the liturgy for the celebration of the divine office, the sacraments and religious functions in general.[95]

Hence, this diversity of rites in the Eastern Churches is defended and guaranteed because

> from the early days of the Church and from the Apostles themselves to a greater or lesser extent resound all the rites. Hence, their venerable antiquity, the apostolic name to which they are attached, the holiness of the Fathers and prelates who were their authors and the love and the veneration with which they are honored, the will of the Holy See, the intrinsic capacity to reject heresy, the decrees of the Councils that approved them, and finally the salvation of the Eastern nations, whose return to unity one could hardly hope if their rites were abolished, counsel their preservation, obliging the Holy See to cleanse them of those elements that have infiltrated them and obscured their genuineness.[96]

All this is made evident by the Vatican Council II:

---

92 Cf. D. Salachas, "Teologia...," 511-516.
93 Cf. A. M. Triacca, "Ambrosiana, Liturgia," in *Nuovo Dizionario di Liturgia*, eds. D. Sartore and A. M. Triacca (Cinisello Balsamo, 1988) 16-52.
94 Cf. CIC c. 372 §2. *Comm.* 12 (1980) 72-73: "One could say in place of 'Ritus' in our draft 'Ecclesia sui iuris" or 'ecclesia ritualis'; the first Consultor notes that 'ascription' of a baptized person in a Church *sui iuris* and the choice of a diocese are two different things."
95 Cf. F. McManus, "The Possibility of New Rites in the Church," *The Jurist* 50 (1990) 435-458, especially 444-458. The doctrine of the *præstantia ritus Latini*, used by the Roman Church, was formulated by Benedict XIV in *Etsi pastoralis*. For the origin of this expression, see H. L. Hoffman, *De Benedicti XIV latinizationibus*, 2nd ed. (Rome, 1958). According to Manna, this attitude was the result of a reaction to the accusations launched against it by those who were separated and out of a preoccupation to protect the Latin faithful from perversion. It was the practice that established the theory: cf. S Manna, *Chiesa latina e Chiese Orientali all'epoca del Patriarca Giuseppe Valerga (1813-72)*, Excerpta e dissertatione ad Lauream (Naples, 1972) 64-65; A. Petrani, "An adsit ritus præstantior," *Apollinaris* 6 (1933) 74-82.
96 S. Manna, *Chiesa...*, 61.

> This sacred Council thanks God that many Eastern children of the Catholic Church preserve this heritage and wish to express it more faithfully and completely in their lives, and are already living in full communion with their brethren who follow the tradition of the West. But it declares that this entire heritage of spirituality and liturgy, of discipline and theology, in the various traditions, belongs to the full catholic and apostolic character of the Church. (UR 17)

Elsewhere, the same Council declares:

> These individual Churches, whether of the East or the West, although they differ somewhat among themselves in "rite," that is, in liturgy, in ecclesiastical discipline, and spiritual tradition, are none the less all equally entrusted to the pastoral guidance of the Roman Pontiff, who by God's appointment is successor to Blessed Peter in primacy over the Universal Church. Therefore these churches are of equal rank, so that none of them is superior to the others because of its rite. They have the same rights and obligations. (OE 3)[97]

> Finally, in faithful obedience to tradition, the sacred Council declares that Holy Mother Church holds all lawfully recognized rites to be of equal right and dignity; that she wishes to preserve them in the future and to foster them in every way. The Council also desires that, where necessary, the rites be revised carefully in the light of sound tradition, and that they be given new vigor to meet present-day circumstances and needs. (SC 4)

The ecclesiological and juridic consequence of these principles is the solemn declaration of the Council:

> For that reason this Council solemnly declares that the churches of the East like those of the West have the right and duty to govern themselves according to their own special disciplines. For these are guaranteed by ancient tradition, and seem to be better suited to the customs of their faithful and to the good of their souls. (OE 5)

This equal dignity is made evident by the fact that the CCEO was promulgated, like the CIC, by the supreme Legislator of the Catholic Church in virtue of his primatial power and was solemnly presented to the entire Catholic Church; in the apostolic constitution *Sacri Canones*, it is declared:

---

[97] Cf. P Valdrini, "L'*æqualis dignitas* des Eglises d'Orient et d'Occident," in *Acta Symposii Internationalis circa Codicem Canonum Ecclesiarum Orientalium, USEK, 24-29 aprilis 1995*, eds. Al-Ahmar, A., A. Khalife and D. Le Tourneau (Kaslik, 1996) 51-68.

Thus it happens that the canons of the *Code of Canons of the Eastern Churches* must have the same firmness as the laws of the *Code of Canon Law* of the Latin Church, that is, that they remain in force until abrogated or changed by the supreme authority of the Church for just reasons.[98]

The two Codes are destined for the same purpose: the tranquility of order that provides for the development of love, grace and charisms.[99] The CCEO, on a basis equal to the CIC and PB, belongs to one *Corpus Iuris Canonici* of the Catholic Church,[100] and "nothing else is possibly more wonderful in illustrating the note of *catholicity* in the Church of God"[101] because

> in the Church of Jesus Christ, as it is neither Latin, nor Greek, nor Slavonic, but Catholic, no distinction comes between her children, and all of them, whether Latin, Greek, Slavonic or of other nations, have the same place before the Apostolic See.[102]

---

98   Apcon *Sacri Canones*, 18 October 1990: *AAS* 82 (1990) 1036: CCEC, xxiii; cf. *Nuntia* 29 (1989) 34.
99   Apcon *Sacri Canones*, 18 October 1990: *AAS* 82 (1990) 1042-1043: CCEC, xxvi-xxvii.
100   Apcon *Sacri Canones*, 18 October 1990: *AAS* 82 (1990) 1038: CCEC, xxv; *Nuntia* 31 (1990) 11 and 13.
101   Apcon *Sacri Canones*, 18 October 1990: *AAS* 82 (1990) 1036: CCEC, xxiii.
102   Benedict XV, Mp *Dei providentis*, De S. Congregatione pro Ecclesia Orientali, 1 May 1917: *AAS* 9 (1917) 529-531, especially 529.

Chapter II

Ascription and Transfer to a Church *Sui Iuris* in the Two Codes

II.1. Criteria of Membership in a Church
II.2. Membership in a Specific Church
II.3. Parents Ascribed in Different Churches
II.4. Membership of Only One Parent in the Catholic Church
II.5. Child Born to Unmarried Parents
II.6. Child Born to Unknown Parents
II.7. Child Under the Age of Fourteen of Non-Baptized Parents
II.8. Child Under the Age of Fourteen of Baptized Non-Catholics
II.9. Baptizing Persons at Least Fourteen Years Old
II.10. Transfer of a Spouse to the Church
II.11. Transfer of Parents or, in a Mixed Marriage, of the Catholic Spouse to Another Church *sui iuris*
II.12. Transfer to Another Church
II.13. Baptized Non-Catholics
II.14. Final Observations

Given the accelerated rate of emigration, the preservation of the rites, as articulated in CCEO c. 28 §1, is one of the most urgent problems the Church must face. Certain Eastern communities already have a large proportion of their population—perhaps nearly half—in Latin territory. Sometimes these families have abandoned their rite and completely adapted themselves to the Latin rite. Consequently, the next generation does not even take the matter into consideration and practically identifies itself as Latin. Therefore, we shall examine in a detailed manner how the norms of the Codes provide for the safeguard of the rites in the Church.

II.1. Criteria of Membership in a Church *sui iuris*

CCEO Title II, "The Church *sui iuris* and Rites," comprises two chapters: ascription to a Church *sui iuris* (cc. 29-38)[1] and the observance of rites (cc. 39-41). The CIC regulates ascription of the faithful to the Latin Church or to another "ritual Church" in only two canons of Book I, "General Norms," Title VI, "Physical and Juridic Persons," Chapter I, "The Canonical Condition of Physical Persons," canons 111-112.

"Rite" is understood in the meaning of CCEO c. 28 §1:

---

1 There was an extensive debate in the elaboration of these canons; see *Nuntia* 29 (1989) 36-51.

A rite is a liturgical, theological, spiritual and disciplinary heritage, differentiated by the culture and the circumstances of the history of peoples, which is expressed by each Church *sui iuris* in its own manner of living the faith.[2]

Each Church *sui iuris* by means of its rite is called to witness, profess, live and celebrate the one faith in Christ. In this sense, a member of the Christian faithful cannot be ascribed in a rite, but rather to a Church *sui iuris*, which has its own rite. Rite does not constitute a juridic element of the Church *sui iuris*. According to CCEO c. 921 §2, it is the Church *sui iuris* that constitutes a juridic person, represented by the one who presides over it according to the norm of law.[3] Rite "is obviously secondary, that is, with regard to the constitution of the Church *sui iuris*, it is not indispensable, however important it might be from other points of view."[4]

---

[2] The original concept of the term "rite" is quite broad: the habitual way of doing things; the totality of things done in the observance or practice in religious matters; a particular form of liturgical worship, that is, an individual liturgical act such as the mixing of water in the wine in the Divine Liturgy, or a complexity of acts such as the rite of baptism. Accordingly, it indicates the universality of liturgical laws and customs. From the liturgical meaning of rite, the spectrum extends from disciplinary laws treating liturgical usages to the entire discipline of the Churches that have a characteristic liturgical rite. The term "rite" can also be applied to the community itself or to the Church governed by such a totality of laws and customs. In the Eastern Churches, "rite" has at least five meanings: the global sense of a particular liturgy comprising not only the Eucharistic liturgy, but also all the functions of the Churches; the particular doctrine of a Church, distinct and possibly opposed to that of other Churches; the historical traditions of a particular group of Christians; the language and national culture that is reflected in the liturgy; finally, a nation that possesses and lives all this. "Rite" is a manner of living Christianity in a global sense on the part of a given group of Christians. See Y. Congar, *Diversités et communion*, Cogitatio Fidei, 112 (Paris, 1982) 114-125; É. Eid, "Rite – Église de droit proper – Juridiction," *L'Année Canonique* 40 (1988) 7-18, especially 7-10; É. Sleman, "De 'Ritus' à 'Ecclesia *sui iuris*' dans le Code des Canons des Églises Orientales," *L'Année Canonique* 41 (1999) 253-276.

[3] CCEO c. 921 §2: "Churches *sui iuris*, provinces, eparchies, exarchies, as well as other institutes expressly established as such in common law are by the law itself juridic persons."

[4] P. Szabò, "Opinioni sulla natura delle Chiese '*sui iuris*' nella canonistica odierna," *Folia Canonica* 7 (1996) 239.

Prior Latin and Eastern legislation[5] regulated ascription in CIC-17 c. 98 and CS[6] cc. 6-15. Both the CIC and CCEO establish an explicit principle for ecclesial and juridic ascription of Catholic faithful to the Latin Church or to an Eastern Church *sui iuris*, different than the former norms that generally established ascription by means of the liturgical rite[7] of the baptism itself. CIC-17 c. 98 §1 stated:

> Among the various Catholic rites, one belongs to that one according to whose ceremonies one was baptized, unless perhaps baptism by a minister of an alien rite was brought about fraudulently, or in the case of grave necessity when it was not possible to have a priest of one's own rite present, or if it came about by apostolic dispensation whereby the faculty was given to baptize one in a certain rite while remaining ascribed in the other rite.[8]

CS c. 6 states:

> §1. Among the various rites a person belongs to that one according to whose ceremonies he / she was legitimately baptized.
>
> §2. If the baptism was conferred by a minister of another rite in case of grave necessity, when a priest of the proper rite could not be present, or because of some other just reason with the permission of

---

5   See C. De Clercq, "De ritu et adscriptione ritui apud Orientales Catholicos," *Ephemerides Liturgicæ* 46 (1932) 473-480; D. Salachas, "L'appartenenza giuridica dei fedeli a una Chiesa orientale '*sui iuris*' o alla Chiesa latina," *Periodica* 83 (1994) 19-55, especially 19-23; N. Halligan, "Some Inter-Ritual Norms," *The Jurist* 42 (1982) 164-169, especially 165-166. For a summary presentation of Mp *Cleri Sanctitati*, see A. Wuyts, "Le droit des personnes dans l'Église orientale," *Nouvelle Revue Théologique* 80 (1958) 359-383.

6   CS = Pius XII, Mp *Cleri Sanctitati*, 2 June 1957: *AAS* 59 (1957) 433-603; acquired force of law on 25 March 1958.

7   This position is perhaps still held by L. Mistò, "Il libro IV: la funzione di santificare della Chiesa," *La Scuola Cattolica* 112 (1984) 297-307, especially 291: "It is good to remember the importance of rite, in the technical sense of the term (Western and Eastern) through which one is baptized, because precisely on the basis of the rite of baptism, one belongs to the Latin or Eastern Church." See also J. García Martín, *Le norme generali del Codex Iuris Canonici* (Rome, 1996) 19: "In the Latin Church are incorporated all those who validly receive baptism in the Latin Rite." One can also be incorporated validly in the Latin Church by receiving baptism in an Eastern rite. Further, Martín De Agar states, "Rite determines membership in a ritual Church [...]. Generally, a member of the faithful belongs to the rite in which he or she receives baptism, which, in turn, is received in the Church of the parents, but one to be baptized who is at least fourteen years old can choose his or her own rite": J. T. Martín de Agar, *Elementi di Diritto Canonico* (Rome, 1996) 37.

8   "The profession of the assumed rite, Latin or Greek, is to occur through baptism": Benedict XIV, Apcon *Etsi pastoralis*, 26 May 1742, §2, n. 11.

the proper hierarch, or because of fraud, the person thus baptized shall be regarded as belonging to that rite according to whose ceremonies he / she ought to have been baptized.

We note a difference between the two prior legislations: CS required the permission[9] of the proper Hierarch to administer baptism to the faithful of another rite. CIC-17 required a dispensation from the Apostolic See.[10] The new principle, based on Vatican II ecclesiology, is better formulated. In fact, OE 2 refers to the Eastern Catholic Churches as *Ecclesiæ particulares seu Ritus*, and situates them in the body of the one, holy, catholic and apostolic Church,[11] while LG 13 speaks of *Ecclesiæ particulares* that enjoy their own traditions in ecclesiastical communion. The concept of *Ecclesiæ rituales sui iuris* in the CIC and the concept of *Ecclesiæ sui iuris* in the CCEO emerge from these principles. The components a Church *sui iuris* are: a grouping of faithful, that is, the ecclesial community; its own hierarchy, legitimately constituted; express or tacit recognition on the part of the supreme authority of the Church. What is the criterion of membership in the various *Ecclesiæ sui iuris*?

By virtue of being born in Italy, in Greece or in Hungary, one is called an Italian, Greek or Hungarian. One is not born a Christian. Membership in the Church is neither hereditary nor acquired by place of birth. One enters the Church through a free act of the will and the reception of baptism. CIC c. 96 states: "By baptism one is incorporated into the Church of Christ and is constituted a person in it." [12] The Council of Florence proclaimed: "Through [baptism] we become members of Christ and of the body of the church."[13] This bond between baptism and law is the natural consequence of incorporation, effected by baptism, in the Church, which is the Body of Christ, and at the same time a constituted and ordered in this world.

---

9   Permission is an administrative act of the competent ecclesiastical authority which, while not affecting the juridic capacity of a subject, has the effect of making the subject able to complete some act. Therefore, permission constitutes, on a case-by-case basis, conditions for conformity to the law of individual acts in the exercise of a faculty which already belongs to a particular juridic subject; once he or she has received authorization, this subject can do that which was earlier prohibited.

10   This is understood to be the general dispensation given to Latin priests in the United States to baptize the children of Eastern faithful: see G. Michiels, *Principia generalia de personis* (Lublin, 1937) 275.

11   The CCEO shows that the characteristic element of the *Ecclesiæ particulares seu ritus* of OE is not rite, but rather the express or tacit recognition of their specific juridic status on the part of the supreme authority of the Church; see *Nuntia* 19 (1984) 5.

12   This is not found in the CCEO; see L. Örsy, "Interpretation in View of Action: A Quest for Clarity and Simplicity (Canon 96)," *The Jurist* (1992) 587-597; I. Žužek, "La 'Lex Ecclesiæ Fundamentalis' et les deux Codes," *L'Année Canonique* 40 (1998) 19-48, especially 22-24.

13   Council of Florence, Sess. VIII, Bull of Union with the Armenians, *Exsultate Deo*, 22 November 1439: DEC, 1:542.

We have a two-fold effect of baptism: incorporation into the Church, making the *human being* a *Christian* (religious aspect) and a *person* (juridic aspect). This double effect reflects the double character of the Church: community of faith and human society. One becomes a member of the *Ecclesia universa* by means of baptism[14] received in the particular or local Church to which one is ascribed, whatever the liturgical rite of the celebration:

> A direct juridic-organizational membership in the Catholic Church does not exist, but only an indirect membership by way of ascription to one of the Catholic Churches *sui iuris*, upon which all the consequences of membership depend in one of the two spheres of law in the Catholic Church.[15]

Through the sacrament of baptism, each member of the faithful is incorporated in the Body of Christ which is the Church; however, this incorporation is not indefinite, but realized in time and space.

> For it is not a group of certain persons who, of their own will, come together for some common undertaking, but rather a gift coming down from the Father of lights. It must also not be considered as merely an administrative division of the people of God, since it, in its own way, contains and manifests the nature of the Church universal, which flows forth from the side of Christ crucified, and immediately lives and increases by the Eucharist; it is joined to Christ and is the mother of the faithful.[16]

> [...] Non est enim cœtus hominum quorundam qui sponte sua conveniunt ad commune aliquod opus, sed donum desursum a Patre luminum descendens. Neque consideranda est ut mere administrativa populi Dei divisio, quia ipsa suo modo continet et manifestat naturam Ecclesiæ universalis, quæ e latere Christi

---

14   The Codes speak of baptism of water, not of desire nor the so-called baptism of blood, because juridic personality is obtained in the Church only by means of this sacrament.

15   C. G. Fürst, "Interdipendenza del diritto canonico latino ed orientale," in *Il Diritto Canonico Orientale nell'ordinamento ecclesiale*, Studi Giuridici 34, ed. K. Bharanikulangara (Vatican City, 1995) 18. Insertion in the *Ecclesia universa* by means of baptism does not happen in a mediate way, by way of membership in a particular Church, but in an immediate way, even if it is realized necessarily in a particular Church: see Congregation for the Doctrine of the Faith, *Litteræ ad Catholicæ Ecclesiæ episcopos de aliquibus aspectibus Ecclesiæ prout est communio*, 28 May 1992, n. 10: *AAS* 85 (1993) 844.

16   *Cæremoniale Episcoporum ex decreto Sancrosancti Œcumenici Concilii Vaticani II instauratum auctoritate Ioannis Pauli PP. II promulgatum*, editio typica (Vatican City, 1985) 13, n. 2.

crucifixi profluit, Eucharistia continuo vivit et crescit, Christo iugata, fidelium mater; [...].

The Church is a mystery of communion, a visible and spiritual reality that is incarnated in each particular Church: "The whole Church lives and acts in the various Christian communities, that is, in the particular Churches dispersed in the whole world."[17]

The Church that exists in a definite place, East and West, is manifested as such in its assembly presided over by the Bishop. This principle is codified in CCEO c. 7 §§1-2, drawn verbatim from the Council (see LG 14), while CIC c. 204 states:

> §1. The Christian faithful are those who, inasmuch as they have been incorporated in Christ through baptism, have been constituted as the people of God. For this reason, made sharers in their own way in Christ's priestly, prophetic, and royal function, they are called to exercise the mission which God has entrusted to the Church to fulfill in the world, in accord with the condition proper to each.
>
> §2. This Church, constituted and organized in this world as a society, subsists in the Catholic Church governed by the successor of Peter and the bishops in communion with him.

To summarize, ascription is made to a Church *sui iuris*, not to a rite, usually through the parents or in a general way as established in law (rescript, declaration…); the determining factor of Church membership of one who is baptized is not the liturgical ceremony, but the membership of the parents in a specific juridically-organized ecclesial community. Even if, for various reasons and circumstances, someone was baptized, even lawfully, according to the liturgical rite of a specific Church *sui iuris*, that person belongs to his or her Church established by the law, and not by the rite as such; indeed

> [...] the term "ritus" is found unsuitable to indicate fully the reality of a particular Catholic community gathered around its own hierarchy and with particular specific ethnic-religious elements, especially after the "status" of this community has been recognized as a Church "*sui iuris*," which does not imply, as such, any territorial connotation. The terminological ambiguity in use in the 16th century identified those communities as *ritus*, which focused on the liturgical particularities, to the detriment of the spiritual, cultural and disciplinary particularities; this ambiguity has been overcome, hopefully, in a definitive manner.[18]

---

17   Paul VI, Apcon *Vicariæ potestatis*, 6 January 1977: *AAS* 69 (1977) 6; cf. LG 15; PB art. 1 and Appendix II, n. 1.
18   *Nuntia* 28 (1989) 19.

This was also true in the preceding legislation (CIC-17 c. 98; CS c. 6), which contained three possibilities:

1. If the minister of another rite fraudulently administered the baptism;

2. If the minister of another rite administered the baptism in the case of grave necessity, the minister of one's own rite not being present;

3. If the baptism was received in virtue of an apostolic dispensation granted so that a person could be baptized in a rite without belonging to it.

In these three cases the person belonged to the "rite" in which he or she would normally be obliged to be baptized.

Let us now examine ascription to a determined Church *sui iuris* in the respective Codes.

II.2. Membership in a Specific Church *sui iuris*

The two legislations present particular differences:

CCEO	CIC
29 §1. A son or daughter who has not yet completed fourteen years of age is ascribed by virtue of baptism to the Church *sui iuris* to which his or her Catholic father is ascribed; or if only the mother is Catholic, or if both parents are of the same mind in requesting it, to the Church *sui iuris* of the mother, without prejudice to particular law enacted by the Apostolic See.	111 §1. Through the reception of baptism, the child of parents who belong to the Latin Church is enrolled in it, or, if one or the other does not belong to it, both parents have chosen by mutual agreement to have the offspring baptized in the Latin Church. If there is no mutual agreement, however, the child is enrolled in the ritual Church to which the father belongs.
§2. If, however, a person who has not yet completed fourteen years of age:	
1° is born of an unwed mother, he or she is ascribed in the Church *sui iuris* to which the mother belongs;	
2° is born of unknown parents, he or she is ascribed in the Church *sui iuris* to which belong those to whose care he or she has	

CCEO (continued)

been legitimately entrusted; if, however, it is a case of an adoptive father and mother, §1 should be applied;

3° is born of non-baptized parents, he or she is ascribed in the Church *sui iuris* to which belongs the one who has undertaken his or her education in the Catholic faith.

Through baptism, a person is incorporated in the Church of Christ and, through an indelible sign (see CIC c. 845 §1 and CCEO c. 672 §1) which, according to the doctrine of the faith, is imprinted on the soul by baptism, the baptized person is enabled to worship.[19] However, in the Church there are different ritual Churches *sui iuris* (CIC) or Churches *sui iuris* (CCEO).[20] The first criterion of belonging to a certain Church *sui iuris* is baptism and the general norm provides that a person, if an adult, should be baptized in his or her own parish; otherwise, he or she should be baptized in the parish of the parents (CIC c. 857; CCEO c. 687).

CIC c. 111 §1 does not mention the age of the person to be baptized, but it can be deduced from §2 which states, "Anyone to be baptized who has completed the fourteenth year of age [...]." Therefore, before the age of fourteen the norms of §1 are applied. In addition, both Codes apply the principle established in CIC c.

---

19   "The sacrament of baptism [...] is an act through which a person becomes juridically a member of the Church. [...] Baptism, beyond the conferral of sanctifying grace (and consequently the cancellation of original sin) and of sacramental grace, produces a permanent and indelible juridic effect, which, in theological terminology, indicates that baptism is one of the sacraments that imprint character [...]. Character is a spiritual sign imprinted on the soul; that which is imprinted by baptism produces in the baptized person the capacity to receive all the other sacraments (with the exception of orders in the case of a woman) and the perpetual membership in the Church, i.e., the quality of Christian. One can therefore say that the most important juridic effect of baptism is precisely that of giving character. [...] Given the indelibility of the character imprinted by baptism, membership the Church that is a consequence of baptism is not extinguished (juridically) except through the death of the person": P. Ciprotti, *Lezioni di diritto canonico. Parte generale* (Padua, 1943) 173-177.

20   *Comm.* 12 (1980) 72: "Relator: Regarding the expression '*Ecclesiæ ritualis sui iuris*' our text was made as a compromise in order to be in accord with the Eastern Commission, which later rejected what had been accepted."

98 §2 and in CCEO c. 910 §2, according to which minors are subject to the power of parents or guardians.[21]

The manner of designating guardians is ordinarily done according to the prescriptions of civil law,[22] but there are exceptions: if it is so determined by common law or particular law of the proper Church *sui iuris* (only in the CCEO) or so prescribed by a judge (see CIC c. 1479 and CCEO c. 1137); if it is determined by the eparchial Bishop, excluding vicars general and episcopal vicars (CIC c. 134 §3 and CCEO c. 987) for a particular case and for a just cause. In the last case, the power of the guardian is established by the eparchial Bishop; in the two preceding cases, it is determined by civil law or canon law respectively.

A child who has not completed the fourteenth year of age belongs, through baptism, to the Church of the parents: if both are Latin Catholic, to the Latin Church; if both are Eastern Catholic, to the proper Eastern Church *sui iuris*. This also means that if the child, in certain cases, is baptized according to a rite different than that of the parents or by a minister of another Church *sui iuris*, the administration of the baptism is valid, but the child nonetheless is a member of the Church *sui iuris* of the parents.[23] For example, if a minor child (under the age of fourteen years) of parents belonging to the Italo-Albanian Church was baptized by a pastor of the Latin Church, with or without the permission of the pastor of the parents, whether or not in the case of necessity, the baptized child is not ascribed in the Latin Church, but to the Italo-Albanian Church of the parents. It is logical that, for lawfulness, there must be a just cause for the administration of this baptism (cf. CIC c. 857 §2 and CCEO c. 687 §1); otherwise it would be unlawful out of a lack of competence (cf. CIC c. 862). With due regard for CIC

---

[21] "A minor, in the exercise of his or her rights, is subject to the power of parents or guardians except in those matters in which minors are exempted from their authority by divine law or canon law. Regarding the appointment of guardians, the prescripts of civil law are to be observed unless canon law or the particular law of his or her Church *sui iuris* provides otherwise and with due regard for the right of the eparchial bishop, if necessary, personally to appoint guardians" (CCEO c. 910 §2); "A minor, in the exercise of his or her rights, remains subject to the authority of parents or guardians except in those matters in which minors are exempted from their authority by divine law or canon law. In what pertains to the appointment of guardians and their authority, the prescripts of civil law are to be observed unless canon law provides otherwise or unless in certain cases the diocesan bishop, for a just cause, has decided to provide for the matter through the appointment of another guardian" (CIC c. 98 §2).

[22] In Italian law, it is necessary to refer to Law 184 of 4 May 1983. In the case of adoption, the new parents substitute for the natural parents in all matters. In the case of granting custody, one must take into account the various cases and interacting subjects (the Tribunal for minors, probate judges, social services, housing community, educational institutions, foster families and natural parents) who contribute to the determination of the type of education for the baby, for which it is not possible to give general directions. Rather, the individual situation is to be evaluated in the individual cases.

[23] Cf. *AAS* 11 (1919) 478.

c. 846 §2 (CCEO c. 674 §2), there may be reasons that justify the baptism of a child of Latin parents to be celebrated in another rite (for example, because they cannot approach a Latin priest, or because kinship or friendship with an Eastern minister, or because of their affinity for a Church *sui iuris* other than the Latin Church). The same is true for Eastern parents.

In the case of fraud on the part of the minister, the minor child under fourteen years old always belongs to the Church of the parents; for example, if Maronite parents, deceived by a Ukrainian pastor, allow for their child to be baptized in the Ukrainian parish, the child belongs to the Maronite Church. The same principle also applies when, according to CCEO c. 916 §4, the pastoral care of faithful belonging to one Church *sui iuris* is entrusted to a pastor of another Church *sui iuris*; for example, if Ethiopian Catholics are entrusted to the pastoral care of a Latin pastor, the minor children of these faithful are lawfully baptized by the Latin pastor, but will be ascribed to the Ethiopian Church.

With regard to communicating that baptism has been administered, the Codes do not call for communicating this information to the other Church *sui iuris*, but only recommends registering it in the baptismal register (CCEO cc. 37, 296 §2 and 689 §1; CIC cc. 535 §2 and 877 §1); it would be appropriate, however, to notify the relevant Church *sui iuris* that it has a new member.[24]

In territory in which a Church *sui iuris* does not have its own hierarchy, the faithful of such a Church, with baptism, are ascribed automatically to this Church *sui iuris* and to a particular Church (diocese / eparchy) of another ritual Church or Church *sui iuris*.

II.3. Parents Ascribed in Different Churches *sui iuris*

According to CCEO c. 29 §1, when parents belong to different Churches *sui iuris*, membership in the Church of the father prevails, conforming to Eastern traditions and to the laws of the Personal Statutes in force in the East. By *father*, we must understand "he whom a lawful marriage indicates unless clear evidence proves the contrary" (CIC c. 1138 §1). The children can be ascribed in the Church of the mother if both parents consent. In CIC-17 c. 756 §2, in the case of a difference of rite, *the children are baptized according to the rite of the father*, but admitted the possibility of a different arrangement: *unless provided otherwise by*

---

24   A. Celeghin, "L'iniziazione cristiana nel CIC 1983. Seconda parte: alcune questioni particolari," *Periodica* 84 (1995) 292. The opinion of Abbass seems to be restrictive: "Although CIC canon 535 §2 does not require the baptized person's ascription to a certain Church to be noted in the baptismal register, CCEO c. 37 obliges the Latin pastor to make such a notation": J. Abbass, "The Interrelationship of the Latin and Eastern Codes," *The Jurist* 58 (1998) 1-40, especially 5.

*special law.*²⁵ If, for example, one of the parents belongs to the Latin Church and the other to an Eastern Church, the child, according to CCEO c. 29 §1, belongs to the Church of the father, either Eastern or Latin, unless there was an agreement between the parents to ascribe the child to either the Eastern or Latin Church of the mother.

According to CIC c. 111 §1, in the case of parents, one of whom (either the father or mother) is Latin and the other Eastern, the child belongs to the Latin Church if both parents through a common accord have opted for the baptism of their child in the Latin Church; but what if the parents through common accord have opted for the baptism of their child in the Eastern Church? The canon

> does not consider the possibility for the son of a Latin Father to be ascribed to the Eastern rite. The reason of this apparent anomaly is the fact that the Latin Code of 1983 wanted to address itself only to ascription to the Latin Church, leaving the Eastern Code to regulate the institute through Eastern law.²⁶

Certainly, if we take into account only the text of CIC c. 111 §1, it does not grant the parents the faculty of being able to ascribe their infant to an Eastern Catholic Church if the mother is Eastern and the father Latin. This could bring about the dissolution of the Eastern Catholic Churches established outside the Eastern regions, which is neither the *mens legislatoris* nor the *mens* of the Council.²⁷ Therefore, when the parents agree on the Eastern Church of the

---

25   The final clause was applied to the Italo-Albanians: with the agreement of the parents, an infant born of an inter-ecclesial marriage was able to be baptized in the Latin Church of the mother (Benedict XIV, Apcon *Etsi pastoralis*, 26 May 1742, §2, n. 10). Among the Ruthenians of Galicia male children were obliged to be baptized in the Church of the father and female children in the Church of the mother; however, if the father was a cleric, all the children had to be baptized in his Church and thereby to be ascribed to it (Decr of 6 October 1863: CollPF, I:684-688, n. 1243, D.)

26   A. Gauthier, *Principi generali dell'attività giuridica nella Chiesa (Commentario dei canoni 96-203 del Libro I del Codice di Diritto Canonico)* (Rome, 1993) 24. "Ascription to a specific rite of children of parents who do not belong to the Church of the Latin rite is irrelevant to the CIC, in that it regulates questions relative only to the Church of the Latin Rite": M. Benz, "Nota al c. 111," in *Código de Derecho Canónico. Edición bilingüe, fuentes y comentarios de todos los cánones*, ed. A. Benlloch Pouedà (Valencia, 1993) 73.

27   John Paul II, *Discourse of Presentation of Code of Canons of the Eastern Churches*, 25 October 1990: *Nuntia* 31 (1990) 21-22: "May this code be received, therefore, in its entirety and in each of its canons by the whole Church [...]. This is an appeal that concerns particularly those norms of the Code which have been repeatedly at the centre of my attention [...]. Among these norms are to be included those [...] concerning the common will of spouses regarding the choice of the ritual heritage of their children."

other spouse, the child *must* belong to the Eastern Church,[28] taking into account the principle of reciprocity with the CCEO and the Council's statement desiring the flourishing of the Eastern Churches (OE 1). If there is no common agreement, the child is ascribed in the Church of the father, either Latin or Eastern. In practice, there is no opposition between the two norms regarding the last point, because in both the CCEO and the CIC, in the absence agreement between the parents, the child is always ascribed to the Church of the father. Thus, if the father is Eastern and the mother Latin, the child belongs to the Eastern Church of the father; if the parents are in agreement, the child can be ascribed in the Latin Church of the mother; if the father is Latin and the mother Eastern, the child is ascribed in the Latin Church of the father, at least if they do not agree to ascribe the children to the Eastern Church of the mother. But in the last case, "the agreement has no practical effect because even in its absence, the offspring would still be ascribed in the Latin Church, the Church of the father."[29] There should be no differences between the two Codes, even if the CIC is apparently more restrictive. The possible cases are:

- Parents of the same Church: the child to the Church *sui iuris* of the parents;
- Latin father, Eastern mother: Latin child;
- Latin father, Eastern mother: Eastern child by common agreement;
- Eastern father, Latin mother: Eastern child;
- Eastern father, Latin mother: Latin child by common agreement;
- Lacking common agreement, the child is always ascribed to the Church of the father.

CCEO c. 29 §1 offers parents the option to ascribe a minor child under fourteen years old to the Church *sui iuris* of the mother; a clause in the canon refers to the *ius particulare a Sede Apostolica statutum*. This means that particular law

---

[28] "If both parents belong to the Latin Church, the child receiving baptism also is ascribed to it. If, however, one of them does not belong to the Latin rite, they decide by common agreement in which to have the child baptized": G. Mazzoni, "Le norme generali," in *La normativa del nuovo Codice*, 2nd ed., ed. E. Cappellini (Brescia, 1985) 51. "In CIC c. 111, there is the same possibility": *Nuntia* 28 (1989) 20.

[29] M. Brogi, "I Cattolici orientali nel Codex Iuris Canonici," *Antonianum* 58 (1983) 224. See L. Sabbarese, "Cultura, lingua e rito: aspetti canonici," *Euntes Docete* 56 (2003) 91-116: "Ascription to the Latin Church of both parents to the Latin Church comes with baptism; if both parents do not belong to the Latin Church there must be an agreement for the child to be ascribed to the Latin Church through baptism, which must be manifested at the time of the baptism" (p. 101). If both parents are not ascribed to the Latin Church, the child under fourteen years of age cannot be ascribed to the Latin Church.

enacted by the Apostolic See for a Church *sui iuris* can maintain the principle of ascribing the children to the Church to which the father is ascribed, whenever particular circumstances demand it and for the good order of the Church, which leads to the salvation of souls.[30] Pope John Paul II, on the day of the presentation of the Eastern Code in the Synodal Hall, commented on the clause and affirmed it.

> A similar phrase is to be found also in the canon concerning the common will of spouses regarding the choice of the ritual heritage of their children, to show the way and apply the right remedy so long as this proves to be really necessary for the protection and growth of the Eastern Churches in places where they are a minority.[31]

This phrase, though not appearing in CIC c. 111 §1, also involves the Latin Church, because it is the disposition of the supreme authority.[32] It would be appropriate to regulate the formalities of this option at the local level, for example, by indicating it in the baptismal register of the parish,[33] so as not to leave a place for uncertainty regarding membership in a Church *sui iuris*.

The CCEO and the CIC leave open the possibility for parents to make different decisions regarding the ritual membership of the individual children because the Codes do not speak of the offspring, but of the child (in the singular). This formula "might create many difficulties in the observance of their own traditions, since certain children should follow those of one Church, and others that of another."[34] On the other hand the children would share the interecclesial reality of the parents and thus it could be considered as a richness in the family. However, it appears that the CCEO aims for the unity of the family: "In families in which the spouses are ascribed in different Churches *sui iuris*, it is permitted to observe the norms of one or the other Church *sui iuris* in the matter of feast days and days of penance" (CCEO c. 883 §2).

---

30   Cf. *Nuntia* 22 (1986) 29; Sacred Congregation for the Eastern Church, Decr *Græci-rutheni ritus*, 24 May 1930, art. 47: *AAS* 22 (1930) 353: "Those born in Canada of parents of different rites are to be baptized in the rite of the father."
31   John Paul II, *Discourse of Presentation of Code of Canons of the Eastern Churches*, 25 October 1990: *Nuntia* 31 (1990) 22; *Guide*, 29.
32   See the long debate on the redaction of CCEO c. 28 in *Nuntia* 29 (1989) 36-41 and 44-46.
33   P. Erdö, "Questioni interrituali del diritto dei sacramenti (Battesimo e Cresima)," *Periodica* 84 (1995) 333-334.
34   M. Brogi, "I Cattolici...," 225. For a different opinion, see F. J. Urrutia, *Les normes générales* (Paris, 1994) 183: "It seems that the parents are not free to baptize, for example, the sons in the Church of the father and the daughters in the Church of the mother, for this would be contrary to the spiritual unity of the family, the 'domestic Church' (LG 11). The letter itself of §1 opposes it."

II.4. Membership of Only One Parent in the Catholic Church

If only the mother is Catholic, obviously the child belongs to the Church of the mother, according to CCEO c. 29 §1.[35] This is not found in the CIC, but

> it seems that c. 111 §1 refers—in the meaning of CIC c. 11—only to Catholics (cf. CIC-17 c. 756 §3; CIC c. 6 §2). The analogy foreseen in CIC c. 19 is applicable in this case to fill the lacunae of the law. Even if the Eastern Code does not oblige Latin Catholics, CCEO c. 29 constitutes "a law given for a similar case."[36]

It is also necessary to take into account the canons on mixed marriage that require the Catholic party to do as much as it is in his or her power for the children be baptized and raised in the Catholic Church (CIC c. 1125, 1°; CCEO c. 814), as well as the penal disposition of canon 1366: "Parents or those who take the place of parents who hand over their children to be baptized or educated in a non-Catholic religion are to be punished with a censure or other just penalty" (cf. CCEO c. 1439). So, if only the father is Catholic, the child is ascribed in the Church of the father, as stated in the CCEO c. 29 §1.[37] The possible cases are:

- Latin father and non-Catholic mother: Latin child;
- Latin mother and non-Catholic father: Latin child;
- Eastern father and non-Catholic mother: Eastern child;
- Eastern mother and non-Catholic father: Eastern child.

When the mother is Catholic and the father is Orthodox, there can be some problems, especially in the Middle East; children born of a mixed marriage belong to the Church of the father. According to Salachas and Nitkiewicz, the practice adopted until now by the Congregation for the Eastern Churches is clear: children born of a mixed marriage belong to the Catholic Church, notwithstanding the fact of their baptism in the Orthodox Church.[38]

---

35   In the Middle East, children born of a mixed marriage belong to the Church of the father, according to the Accord of 14 October 1996 of Catholic and Orthodox Patriarchs: *Le Lien* (October-December, 1996) 30-34; cf. D. Salachas, "I matrimoni misti nel Codice latino e in quello delle Chiese Orientali Cattoliche," in *I Matrimoni misti*, Studi Giuridici 47, ed. C. Gullo (Vatican City, 1998) 57-91.
36   P. Erdö, "Questioni...," 332.
37   If only one [parent] is Catholic, the children are to be baptized in that rite (CIC-17 c. 756 §3).
38   D. Salachas and K. Nitkiewicz, *Rapporti interecclesiali tra cattolici orientali e latini* (Rome, 2007) 99.

Another case could be presented: to what Church *sui iuris* would a baby baptized heterodox, but through the express desire of the parents raised as a Catholic, belong? The *dubium* was presented to the then Holy Office, which on 5 November 1953 responded that he belonged to the Church in which he had received his Catholic upbringing.[39] Therefore, taking into account the 1953 response, a child born of Orthodox parents or (in a mixed marriage) of an Orthodox father and a Catholic mother (or vice versa), who was baptized in the Orthodox Church, but through the express desire of the parents is brought up as a Catholic, is to be considered as a Catholic. Having completed the fourteenth year of age, this person can return to the Orthodox Church; if this person wants to remain Catholic, obviously the profession of faith is not required. Conversely, a child of Catholic parents or, in a mixed marriage, of an Orthodox father and Catholic mother or vice versa, who was baptized in the Catholic Church but through the express desire of the parents is raised in the Orthodox Church, is to be considered as an Orthodox. Having completed the fourteenth year of age, the person can return to the Catholic Church after having made a Catholic profession of faith. We believe that in these cases, it is better to formalize the intention of the party concerned, beginning at the age of fourteen or at the age of majority.

There is yet another case. If a non-Catholic parent enters a Catholic Church *sui iuris* different than that of the other parent, can he / she ascribe to his / her own Church *sui iuris* a child less than fourteen years old? It is our opinion that the general rule of CCEO c. 29 §1 should be applied.

II.5. Child Born to Unmarried Parents

The child of an unwed mother is ascribed to the Church of the mother, according to CCEO c. 29 §2, 1°;[40] this norm *ex natura rei* also involves the Latin

---

39   This information was obtained from the Greek-Catholic Exarchate of Athens. The *dubium* was formulated in these terms: (1) If a child is baptized heterodox, but through the desire of the parents or guardians is raised as a Catholic until puberty or legal majority, by this act alone is he or she to be considered as a Catholic? (2) Must this child, having reached the age of puberty or legal majority, make a profession of faith expressly or in writing? (3) If such a profession is necessary, but through forgetfulness or neglect, is not made at the prescribed time, is the subject, who continues to observe the Catholic religion, to be considered a Catholic in all juridic effects, especially marriage? Response: To the first, affirmative. To the second, negative (unless a non-Catholic upbringing, drawn out even after the acquisition of the use of reason, preceded the Catholic one; then a profession of faith or abjuration must be demanded before admission to the Sacraments). To the third, affirmative (even if a non-Catholic upbringing preceded the Catholic one).

40   In the 1984 Draft *De constitutione hierarchica Ecclesiarum Orientalium*, it was affirmed that "a child born after the death of the father and a natural (illegitimate) child pertain to the Church of the mother, unless in the latter case he or she is publicly acknowledged by the father" (c. 10 §2): *Nuntia* 19 (1984) 22.

Church,[41] at least by way of guidance. Consequently, the child of parents not joined in an ecclesiastical marriage must be ascribed to the Church of the mother. For example, the minor child (under the age of fourteen), born of an Hungarian Eastern Catholic unmarried mother and of a Ukrainian man who has acknowledged his paternity, who was baptized in the Church of the father, belongs to the Eastern Church of the mother because she is unmarried. If the parents should subsequently celebrate a valid ecclesiastical marriage, can the father claim the right of ascription into his Church *sui iuris* of a minor child under the age of fourteen years? We believe that in this case, the general rule regarding adoption should be applied. Further, in the case of the declaration of nullity of marriage, must a minor child of less than fourteen years ascribed to the Church *sui iuris* of the father transfer to the Church of the mother? We believe that in this case CCEO c. 29 §2, 1° should be applied.

II.6. Child Born to Unknown Parents

According to CCEO c. 29 §2, 1°, the child of unknown parents is ascribed in the Church of the one in whose care the child has been lawfully entrusted; in the case of adoption[42] the norms of c. 29 §1 are applied. CIC c. 110 treats only true and proper adoption, not legal guardianship. In CIC c. 98 §2, there is a reference to civil legislation but

> if in a country there exists a clear separation between State and Church, connected with the "religious neutrality of the State," minors under the age of fourteen years, entrusted to the care of the State, will need another guardian appointed for this purpose by the Bishop, according to the Latin Code (cf. CIC c. 98 §2).[43]

---

41   J. Prader, *La legislazione matrimoniale latina e orientale* (Rome, 1993) 16. Cf. P. Szabò, "Diritto particolare e coordinazione interordimentale. Osservazioni alla luce di un caso concreto," *Folia Canonica* 10 (2007) 167-178.

42   Neither code regulates the institution of adoption. The former discipline canonized the civil prohibitive and diriment marriage impediment. The current discipline, both Latin and Eastern, no longer makes any reference to the civil impediment, but uses civil law only to infer from it the fact of a legal kinship arising from adoption, regardless of whether adoption constitutes a civil impediment or not. Thus, there is a need to take into account within what limits civil adoption constitutes a relationship of legal kinship and if adoption also constitutes a marriage impediment. A possible definition of adoption: a direct juridic act to create an artificial bond of filiation, that is, independent of the natural fact of procreation; it creates between the adopter and the adoptee the same juridic bond that exists between parents and children. This is what is commonly called "full adoption." On the other hand, "partial adoption," provided in some civil legislations, creates a civil bond, a legal kinship, normally only between the adopter and the adoptee, while the rights and obligations towards the family of origin of the adopted continue to exist.

43   P. Erdö, "Questioni...," 336. Cf. *Communicationes* 6 (1974) 95.

Logically, the Bishop will give this task to the godparents who, according to CIC, are not able to choose freely a ritual Church for the child; CCEO c. 29 §2, 2° provides for this.

In the case of true and proper adoption, if the adopted child has already received baptism, because adoption determines the same juridic relationship that exists between parents and children, the baptized adopted child of less than fourteen years transfers to the same Church *sui iuris* of the adopted parents because adoption establishes the same juridic relationship that exists between parents and children. If the parents belong to different Churches *sui iuris*, the principles of CCEO c. 29 §1 and CIC c. 111 §1 are to be applied. For example, when a child of less than fourteen years of age, who was baptized in the Hungarian Greek-Catholic Church, is adopted by a Latin couple, CCEO canon 29 §1 is applied; the child is ascribed in the Latin Church without requesting the consent of the Apostolic See. The same is true for analogous Eastern cases. Reaching the age of fourteen years, the person can return to the original Church of the natural parents, applying, by analogy, CCEO c. 34 and CIC c. 112 §1, 3°. An adopted Orthodox minor can be ascribed in the Church *sui iuris* of the same rite as the natural Orthodox parents.[44]

If the parents are dead or are impeded in the exercise their rights, or were considered dead but later appear, the general rule is applied (CIC c. 111 §1 and CCEO c. 29 §1).

II.7. Child Under the Age of Fourteen of Non-Baptized Parents

According to CCEO c. §29, 3°, the child of non-baptized parents who request baptism for the child in the Catholic Church is ascribed by baptism in the Church *sui iuris* of the one responsible for the child's Catholic upbringing. The consent of at least one of the parents is required (cf. CCEO c. 681 §1, 2°), except if the child is in danger of death (CCEO c. 681 §4). For example, Buddhist parents request the Latin pastor to baptize their child of less than fourteen years, choosing a Syro-Malabar godparent; the child will be ascribed in the Syro-Malabar Church. The CIC does not contain anything about this matter, except for the consent of at least one parent or of the one in whose care the child was lawfully entrusted, except in danger of death (c. 868 §1, 1° and §2).[45] In the case of adoption, the principles of CCEO c. 29 §2, 2° are applied. But if the parents should subsequently be baptized, can they claim the right to ascribe their child in their own Church *sui iuris*? We believe that in this case the general rule must be applied.

---

44   Cf. *Roman Replies and CLSA Advisory Opinions 2003*, 23.
45   In prior norms issued by the Holy See, the assignment required a practicing Catholic for the religious upbringing of a child born of parents who are not ready to make the profession of faith or personally to assume the responsibility of the Catholic upbringing of the child. See Congregation for the Doctrine of the Faith, Instructio *Pastoralis actio*, De baptismo parvulorum, 20 October 1980: *AAS* 72 (1980) 1153.

II.8. Child Under the Age of Fourteen of Baptized Non-Catholics

The child of baptized non-Catholics who request baptism for their child in the Catholic Church will be baptized only if one of them or the one who lawfully takes their place requests it and if it is physically or morally impossible to approach their own minister (CCEO c. 681 §5; cf. CIC c. 868 §1, 1°).[46] Whenever baptized non-Catholic parents ask for their child to be received into the Catholic Church, the child will be received only if grave harm to the Church or the child is not foreseen and there exists the founded hope that the child will be brought up in the Catholic faith. Otherwise, it is appropriate to postpone reception of baptism to the fourteenth year of age, at least if there is no imminent danger of death (CCEO cc. 681 §1, 1° and 900). The child will be ascribed *mutatis mutandis* (CCEO c. 29 §2, 3°) in the Church *sui iuris* of the one who has assumed responsibility for the upbringing of the child. It is appropriate that the latter belong to the Church *sui iuris* corresponding to that of the baptized non-Catholic parents, thus retaining the principle of CCEO c. 35; hence, the parents and child will be in the same liturgical-cultural tradition. If the parents should enter into full communion with the Catholic Church, can they claim the right to ascribe their child to their own Church *sui iuris*? We believe that in this case the general rule is to be applied. Another possibility is ascription of the child to the Catholic Church *sui iuris* corresponding to that of the non-Catholic parents.

II.9. Baptizing Persons at Least Fourteen Years Old

CCEO	CIC
30. Anyone to be baptized who has completed the fourteenth year of age can freely select any Church *sui iuris* in which he or she then is ascribed by virtue of baptism received in that same Church, with due regard for particular law established by the Apostolic See.	111 §2. Anyone to be baptized who has completed the fourteenth year of age can freely choose to be baptized in the Latin Church or in another ritual Church *sui iuris*; in that case, the person belongs to the Church which he or she has chosen.

A candidate for baptism who has completed fourteen years of age[47] is free to choose the Church *sui iuris* to which he / she wishes to belong; "care should be taken lest anything should be recommended that might prevent their ascription in the Church *sui iuris* more appropriate to their culture" (CCEO c. 588). The norm is to be applied regardless of whether the parents of the one to be baptized are Catholic, non-Catholic or non-baptized. The clause "with due regard for particular law established by the Apostolic See" (CCEO c. 30) does not affect the

---

46   Cf. J. H. Provost, "Baptism of an Orthodox by Catholic Priest, Opinion," *Roman Replies and CLSA Advisory Opinions 1997*, 102.

47   CIC-17 c. 745 §2 gave the person the freedom to choose a rite beginning at the age of seven.

fundamental liberty of persons, but serves to regulate the particular situations of persons or regions; in certain circumstances or in certain countries, particular law established by the Apostolic See can oblige the one to be baptized to follow the Church *sui iuris* of the parents or of the father, provided they are Catholic. The same particular law can require an age of majority for someone to be able to choose a Church *sui iuris*. This clause, not found in *Cleri Sanctitati*, will also affect the Latin Church, since it is a disposition of the Apostolic See.[48]

II.10. Transfer of a Spouse to the Church *sui iuris* of the Other Spouse

CCEO	CIC
33. A wife is at liberty to transfer to the Church of the husband at the celebration of or during the marriage; when the marriage has ended, she can freely return to the original Church *sui iuris*.	112 §1. After the reception of baptism, the following are enrolled in another ritual Church *sui iuris*: 1° a person who has obtained permission from the Apostolic See; 2° a spouse who, at the time of or during marriage, has declared that he or she is transferring to the ritual Church *sui iuris* of the other spouse; when the marriage has ended, however, the person can freely return to the Latin Church.

In the case of case of a marriage between two Catholics belonging to different Churches *sui iuris*,[49] CCEO c. 33 states that the Eastern wife has the full right to be ascribed to the Church *sui iuris* of the husband (cf. CS c. 9),[50] in accordance with the Eastern tradition of the prevalence of the husband, while the husband does not have this right.[51] In order for an Eastern man to transfer to the Church

48   Cf. *Nuntia* 29 (1989) 45 and 47; CS c. 12: "A non-baptized person may freely choose a rite when embracing the faith."

49   "[…] in marriages of mixed rite between Latins and Italo-Greeks, neither Clement VIII nor Benedict XIV permitted Latins to follow the Greek rite of their spouse, but conversely, the Greek wife or husband was always able to follow the Latin rite of the spouse; indeed, if the wife adopted the Latin rite, she was not able to return to the Greek rite after the death of her husband": A. Petrani, *De relatione iuridica inter diversos ritus in Ecclesia catholica* (Turin-Rome, 1930) 36-37.

50   Cf. *Nuntia* 3 (1976) 50; CS c. 9: "A wife who belongs to another rite is free to join the rite of her husband at the time of the marriage or during its duration. When the marriage has been dissolved she is free to resume her own rite." In the 1984 Draft *De Constitutione hierarchica Ecclesiarum Orientalium* (c. 12) and in the 1986 Draft (c. 31), no difference was made between the spouses.

51   See the debate in *Nuntia* 29 (1989) 37 and 43-48.

of his Latin wife or another Church *sui iuris* different than his, he must make recourse and obtain consent of the Apostolic See, with due regard for CCEO c. 32 §2.[52] On the other hand, CIC c. 112 §1, 2° does not admit any distinction between the spouses,[53] so that each of them could be ascribed, if they wanted, to the Church *sui iuris* of the other spouse. However, if the husband is Latin and desires to transfer to the Eastern Church of his wife, can the Hierarch or the Eastern pastor validly ascribe him without the consent of the Apostolic See? These officials can ascribe him, because one is dealing with the personal right of the Latin faithful, which must always be respected by any Hierarch. Hence, the Eastern husband needs the consent of the Apostolic See to transfer to the Church *sui iuris* of his wife, with due regard for CCEO c. 32 §2, while a Latin husband does not need this consent. But what if the Latin wife desires to transfer to the Eastern Church of her husband? Can the Hierarch or Eastern pastor ascribe her without making recourse to the Apostolic See? Again, the same principle for the Latin husband is valid and recourse is not necessary.

When recourse to the Apostolic See is required for the Eastern husband, consent is normally granted with a rescript that is effective for six months after its concession.[54] The change must be noted in the baptismal register (CIC c. 535 §2; CCEO cc. 37 and 296 §2) both by the parish *a quo* and that *ad quem*, observing the form of CCEO c. 36.[55] Children under the age of fourteen years are ascribed *ipso iure* in the new Church *sui iuris* of the father or mother, if both consent, according to CCEO c. 34; their names, together with that of the father or, in a mixed marriage, of the mother, are to be noted in the baptismal register of the parish *ad quem*.

Even when recourse to the Apostolic See is not required, the spouse must make a declaration of will before the authority determined by law:

> Every transfer to another Church *sui iuris* takes effect at the moment a declaration is made before the local hierarch of the same Church or the proper pastor or a priest delegated by either of them and two witnesses, unless the rescript of the Apostolic See provides otherwise. (CCEO c. 36)

---

52   See the long debate on the question of CCEO c. 33 in *Nuntia* 29 (1989) 37 and 43-48.

53   In CIC-17 c. 98 §4, only the wife could transfer to the rite of her husband; cf. *Comm.* 6 (1974) 87-98; 21 (1989) 124.

54   See Appendix I and II. F. J. Urrutia holds a different opinion: "A Latin husband will not be accepted in the Eastern Church of his spouse even if our canon recognizes this right": *Les normes générales* (Paris, 1994) 184.

55   Formerly in CS c. 13; Prader states that CCEO cc. 36-37 fill a lacuna of the CIC, but this does not seem to be correct, since it fills only the lacuna regarding the manner, because CIC c. 535 §2 considers the notation of the change of rite in the baptismal register: cf. J. Prader, *La legislazione…*, 20.

There is no corresponding canon in the prior or current Latin Code, but we should consider, by analogy, CIC cc. 1125-1126 on mixed marriages. This transfer of the spouse is not obligatory, but depends on the free choice of the person;

> upon dissolution of the marriage by widowhood, by declaration of nullity, or by intervention of the Roman Pontiff in the case of marriage *ratum non consummatum*, the woman can return to her original rite, provided that it is not prohibited by particular law.[56]

In summary:

- The husband, in the celebration of the marriage: the Latin husband can transfer to the Eastern Church of his wife after a declaration to this effect; this is not the case for an Eastern husband, who needs to make recourse to the Apostolic See, with due regard for CCEO c. 32 §2;

- The wife, in the celebration of the marriage: the Latin wife can transfer to the Eastern Church of her husband after a declaration to this effect; the Eastern wife can transfer to the Latin Church of her husband after a declaration to this effect;

- The Latin husband, during the marriage, can transfer to the Eastern Church of his wife after a declaration to that effect; this not the case for an Eastern husband, who needs to make recourse to the Apostolic See, with due regard for CCEO c. 32 §2;

- The wife, during the marriage: the Latin wife can transfer to the Eastern Church of the husband after a declaration; the Eastern wife can transfer to the Latin Church of the husband after a declaration;

- The marriage having been terminated (death, dissolution, declaration of nullity): the Latin spouse can return to the Latin Church after a declaration (this declaration, implicit in CIC c. 112, is necessary, because it must be recorded in the baptismal register), the Eastern wife can return to the Church *sui iuris* after a declaration (CCEO c. 36); for the husband, CCEO c. 32 is applicable.

Building on these situations, one can examine particular cases. A Latin man marries an Eastern woman and transfers to the Church *sui iuris* of his wife: can he receive sacred orders? Ordinarily, yes, at least if there are no norms restricting this, as is the case for the Italo-Albanian Church,[57] and where the norms con-

---

56   M. Brogi, "I Cattolici...," 229.
57   Benedict XIV, Apcon *Etsi pastoralis*, 26 May 1742, §7, n. 25; Benedict XV, Apcon *Catholici fideles*, 13 February 1919: *AAS* 11 (1919) 222-226; Pius XI, Apcon *Apostolica Sedes*, 26 October 1937: *AAS* 30 (1938) 213-216.

tained in the Decree *Qua solerti* are not in force. An Eastern married priest married to a Latin woman, transfers, according to the norm of CCEO c. 32 §2, to the Latin Church; can he exercise his ministry? Probably in these cases one must take into account CCEO c. 758 §3.[58] To avoid any malicious intention on the part of the interested party, one should always include the clause *vetita tamen sacrorum Ordinum receptione* in the document which grants a transfer; this clause may, at a later time, be revoked according to the merits of the case at the request of the proper Hierarch.

II.11. Transfer of Parents or, in a Mixed Marriage, of the Catholic Spouse to Another Church *sui iuris*

CCEO	CIC
34. If the parents, or the Catholic spouse in the case of a mixed marriage, transfer to another Church *sui iuris*, children who have not completed fourteen years of age by the law itself are ascribed in the same Church; if, however, in a marriage between Catholics, only one parent transfers to another Church *sui iuris*, the children transfer only if both parents have given consent. Upon completion of the fourteenth year of age, the children can return to the original Church *sui iuris*.	112 §1. After the reception of baptism, the following are enrolled in another ritual Church *sui iuris*: 3° before the completion of the fourteenth year of age, the children of those mentioned in nn. 1 and 2 as well as, in a mixed marriage, the children of the Catholic party who has legitimately transferred to another ritual Church; on completion of their fourteenth year, however, they can return to the Latin Church.

CIC-17 did not take this matter into consideration,[59] while CS c. 10 filled the *lacuna*: "If the father or, in a mixed marriage, the Catholic mother lawfully transfers to another rite, the children who have not yet reached the age of puberty are by the law itself transferred to the same rite." Hence, all minor children [*filii impuberes*] *ipso iure* followed the father into his new rite, while, in a mixed marriage in which the mother was a Catholic, the children followed the mother into her new rite. The new codes established that the children of those who transfer to another Church *sui iuris*, if they are less than fourteen years old, follow the parents;[60] in a mixed marriage, the children under the age of fourteen years follow the Catholic party, if this one changes rite (cf. CIC c. 1125, 1° and CCEO c. 814, 1°). Brogi correctly notes that the new Latin legislation does not determine which of the two parents the children must follow, the father or mother, if only

---

58   "The particular law of each Church *sui iuris* or special norms established by the Apostolic See are to be followed in admitting married men to sacred orders."
59   Cf. *Comm.* 12 (1980) 75-76; 21 (1989) 125-126.
60   This is an application of the principle established in CIC c. 98 §2 and CCEO c. 910 §2.

one of them changes rite: "it also sets no time limit for the exercise of the right of returning to the Latin Church (or the Eastern Church), nor establishes any formality."[61] In any case, we are of the same opinion that in a marriage between two Catholics, if only one of the parents transfers to another Church *sui iuris*, the children transfer to this Church if both parents consent, as is the case in CCEO.

The transfer of the Catholic party together with the children, in a mixed marriage, can be justified, for example, in the case of when the husband belongs to the Greek Orthodox Church and the wife to the Latin Church. If the wife transfers to the Greek Catholic Church, with the consent of the Apostolic See, the children follow the mother and the family would be integrated into the same liturgical-cultural tradition.

The children, having completed fourteen years, can return freely to the Church of origin; but both Codes are silent as to whether they must make an express request and to whom such a request would be made. The change must be recorded in the baptismal register (CIC c. 535 §2; CCEO cc. 37 and 296 §2), observing the formalities of CCEO c. 36.

II.12. Transfer to Another Church *sui iuris*

CCEO	CIC
32 §1. No one can validly transfer to another Church *sui iuris* without the consent of the Apostolic See.	112 §1. After the reception of baptism, the following are enrolled in another ritual Church *sui iuris*:
§2. In the case of Christian faithful of an eparchy of a certain Church *sui iuris* who petition to transfer to another Church *sui iuris* which has its own eparchy in the same territory, this consent of the Apostolic See is presumed, provided that the eparchial bishops of both eparchies consent to the transfer in writing.	1° a person who has obtained permission from the Apostolic See.

Ascription to a Church *sui iuris*, other than through baptism, can occur through transfer in exceptional circumstances and should be properly documented. One who desires to change their ascription to a Church *sui iuris* for reasons other than those connected to marriage must request and obtain the permission or consent of the Apostolic See.[62] The CIC speaks only of the "permission

---

61 M. Brogi, "I Cattolici…," 231-232.
62 Cf. Benedict XIV, Enc *Demandatum*, §15; Leo XIII, Aplet *Orientalium dignitas*, 30 November 1894, art. 7: *ASS* 27 (1894-95) 261; Sacred Congregation for the

of the Apostolic See," without specifying anything else, while the CCEO requires consent *ad validitatem*. However, because transfer implies a change of discipline, liturgy and doctrine, it cannot be left to the whims of pastors or Ordinaries, lest there arise a distorted or misunderstood apostolic spirit, close to ritual proselytism and certainly contrary to the universality of the Church.[63] Taking into account what we have said, CIC c. 17 and CCEO c. 1499 on the interpretation of laws, as well as the tenor of the rescript of the Secretary of State of 26 November 1992 that we shall examine, it is our opinion that the permission of the Apostolic See is necessary for validity of such a transfer; this permission is normally granted with a rescript that remains in force for six months after its concession.[64] The change must be recorded in the baptismal register, both in the parish *a quo* and in that *ad quem*, following the form of CCEO c. 36, that is, there must be a declaration of intent in the presence of the authority determined by law. There is no corresponding canon in the former or current Latin Code, but we must take into account, by analogy, CIC cc. 1125-1126 on mixed marriages. The validity of marriages can depend on these canons.[65] If there are children under the age of fourteen years old, they are ascribed *ipso iure* to the new Church *sui iuris* of the father or the mother according to CCEO c. 34, noting in the baptismal register of the parish *ad quem* their names together with that of the father or, in a mixed marriage, of the mother.

Regarding the presumed permission of the Apostolic See provided in CCEO c. 32 §2, applicable when the transfer occurs in jurisdictions in the same territory,

---

Propagation of the Faith for Eastern Rite Matters, Decr *Fidelibus ruthenis*, 18 August 1913: *AAS* 5 (1913) 397; Pius X, Aplet *Ea semper*, 14 June 1907: *ASS* 41 (1907) 8; Sacred Congregation for the Eastern Church, Decr *Nemini licere*, de venia apostolica transitus ad alium ritum a Romani Pontificis Legatis concedenda, 6 December 1928: *AAS* 20 (1928) 416-417. Petrani states, "when it is a case of transfer from one Eastern rite to another Eastern rite and when both, i.e., the rite *a quo* and the rite *ad quem*, have the same Eucharistic matter, the consent of both Bishops suffices": *De relatione*..., 40. CS c. 8 §1: "No one can validly transfer to another rite, nor after a lawful transfer return to the former rite without permission of the Apostolic See." CIC-17 c. 98 §3: "It is not lawful for anyone, without coming to the Apostolic See, to transfer to another rite, or after legitimate transfer, to return to the former."

Until 6 December 1928, the faculty was granted by the Sacred Congregation for the Eastern Church; from that date, it was delegated to the Nuncios and Pontifical Legates for lay persons: *AAS* 20 (1928) 416. With the Decr *Quo firmior* of 23 November 1940 (*AAS* 33 [1941] 28), the grant of the faculty again pertained to the Eastern Congregation; in the United States the Congregation granted the faculty to the Apostolic Delegate provided that the Ordinary *a quo* and that *ad quem* consented; cf. *Nuntia* 3 (1976) 50.

63   Cf. T. I. Jiménez Urresti, "Nota al c. 32," in J. L. Acebal Luján et al., *Código de cánones de las Iglesias orientales. Edición bilingüe comentada*, B.A.C. 542 (Madrid, 1994) 37.
64   Cf. Appendix I and II; the rescript can prohibit access to sacred orders.
65   Cf. J. Prader, *La legislazione*..., 20.

the rescript *Ad normam can. 112* of Pope John Paul II of 26 November 1992[66] extends the meaning of CIC c. 112 §1, 1°, with the implication that the disposition of CCEO c. 32 (not cited in the rescript) was not able to oblige the Latin faithful and Bishops, not even *ex natura rei*, before the publication of the rescript. The permission for the transfer can be presumed whenever a member of the Christian faithful of the Latin Church has requested to transfer to another Church *sui iuris* that has an eparchy within the same territory provided that both Bishops have consented in writing.[67] It should be noted, however, that the rescript considers transfer from the Latin Church to an Eastern Church, but does not consider the inverse case (i.e., from an Eastern Church *sui iuris* to the Latin Church), which, according to Brogi, continues to require the explicit consent of the Holy See.[68] We do not share this restrictive interpretation of Brogi, because in CCEO c. 32 §2, we should understand "Church *sui iuris*" in the broad sense to include the Latin Church. Although the rescript employed the expression *Christifidelis*, we should understand only lay persons, because for religious and clerics there are specific procedures established by the Apostolic See.

The transfer of a man ascribed to an Eastern Church *sui iuris* to the Latin Church should only be granted rarely to avoid the dissolution of the Eastern Churches. The transfer of a Latin man to an Eastern Church should only be granted rarely to avoid fraudulent intent on the part of the interested party; the clause *vetita tamen sacrorum Ordinum receptione* should always be included in the indult. Obviously the Apostolic See at a later time could revoke the clause consequent to a request of the local Hierarch in whose eparchy the interested party is ascribed.

II.13. Baptized Non-Catholics

In the expectation of the restoration of full communion, the Catholic Church cannot refuse the free and spontaneous request of those Christians who, moved

---

66   *AAS* 85 (1993) 83: "According to the norm of CIC c. 112 §1, 1°, it is forbidden for anyone, after having received baptism, to transfer to another Church *sui iuris* if permission has not been given by the Apostolic See. In this matter, the Roman Pontiff, John Paul II, after having approved the judgment of the Pontifical Council for the Interpretation of Legislative Texts, established that such permission can be presumed whenever a member of the Christian faithful of the Latin Church should request to transfer to another ritual Church *sui iuris* that has its own eparchy within the same borders, provided that the diocesan Bishops of both the dioceses consent in writing." Cf. M. Brogi, "Licenza presunta della Santa Sede per il cambiamento di Chiesa '*sui iuris*,'" *Revista Española de Derecho Cánonico* 50 (1993) 661-668; J. Canosa, "La presunzione della licenza di cui al can. 112 §1, 1° del Codice di Diritto Canonico," *Ius Ecclesiæ* 5 (1993) 613-631.

67   Possible reasons can be the return to the faith of one's forefathers, the unity of the family or benefit to one's spiritual life. It is for the competent authority to judge if the possible motives are beneficial for the *salus animarum*.

68   Cf. M. Brogi, "Licenza…," 666.

by the grace of the Holy Spirit, enter into Catholic unity (OE 25; UR 4); however, every form of proselytism must be avoided.

Before 1957, an Eastern non-Catholic[69] who entered into communion with the Catholic Church was able to be ascribed to any Eastern rite he / she wanted, but could transfer to the Latin Church only if this was posed as a condition *sine qua non* for conversion to the Catholic Church.[70] CS c. 11 §1 gave to baptized non-Catholics the right to choose the rite they preferred, but also stated, "however, it is desired that they retain their own rite." This canon provoked protests on the part of the Melkite Church.[71] There was a change of perspective in OE 4, taken up in CCEO c. 35.

> Baptized non-Catholics coming into full communion with the Catholic Church should retain and practice their own rite and should observe it everywhere in the world as much as humanly possible. Thus, they are to be ascribed in the Church *sui iuris* of the same rite with due regard for the right of approaching the Apostolic See in special cases of persons, communities or regions.

For non-Catholics who enter into full communion with the Catholic Church, CCEO c. 35 conforms to the norm of Vatican II, OE 4, and, contrary to CS c. 11, states that they must maintain their own rite and be ascribed to the Church *sui iuris* of the same rite, with due regard for recourse to the Apostolic See in special cases of persons, communities or regions.[72] The text of OE 4 states that the Apostolic See will itself or through another provide for their needs and provide

---

69   Regarding the use of the term "non-Catholic" (*acatholicus*) in the CCEO see D. Ceccarelli-Morolli, *Il Codex Canonum Ecclesiarum Orientalium e l'Ecumenismo*, Quaderni di "Oriente Cristiano," Studi 9 (Palermo, 1998) 36-40.

70   "But as for what pertains to heretics and schismatics, who return to the bosom of the Church, this Sacred Congregation thinks that it is to be permitted that they embrace the Eastern rite which they prefer": CollPF, I:500, n. 878. "And so if one of the heretics or schismatics of an Eastern rite afterwards should follow western heresies, he or she is not to be considered legitimately joined to the Latin rite because of this, since no right can arise from the profession or heresy or schism; but he or she must be considered (to remain) in the Eastern rite which they followed earlier. And so he or she, returning to the Catholic Church, would be able to choose and follow the Eastern rite they prefer": CollPF, II:96, n. 1458. Cf. Leo XIII, Aplet *Orientalium dignitas*, arts. 1 and 11: *ASS* 27 (1894-95) 260 and 262.

71   N. Edelby and I. Dick, *Les Églises Orientales Catholiques. Décret Orientalium Ecclesiarum*, Unam Sanctam 76 (Paris, 1970) 216.

72   "Finally, each and every Catholic, and also the baptized members of every non-Catholic church or community who come to the fullness of the Catholic communion, must retain each his or her own rite wherever he or she is, and follow it to the best of his or her ability, without prejudice to the right of appealing to the Apostolic See in special cases of persons, communities or districts. The Apostolic See, which is the supreme judge of inter-Church relations, will provide for all such needs in an ecumenical spirit, acting

appropriate norms, decrees or rescripts. Thus, it is left to the interested Churches themselves to provide for the regulation of ascription, transfer or bi-ritualism. CCEO c. 35 is, however, more restrictive: only the Apostolic See can do this, to avoid, I believe, possible abuses and arbitrariness of lower authorities who often ignore its dispositions. On this point, a question immediately arises: is the consent of the Apostolic See in this regard required *ad validitatem* or only *ad liceitatem*? Both OE 4 and c. 35 appear to be exhortative. It was proposed to formulate the canon as an obligation, but "today no one argues that the Council wanted to provide a norm in this matter *ad validitatem*."[73] For Salachas-Nitkiewicz, the norm of c. 35 is binding.[74] If, for example, an Orthodox Christian desires to be ascribed in the Latin Church, permission from the Congregation for the Eastern Churches and the approval of the Latin Ordinary is required according to current practice.[75] But what if, for example, an Anglican wishes to be ascribed in the Maronite Church? We believe that this is possible in virtue of CCEO c. 35 which states: "with due regard to recourse to the Apostolic See in special cases of persons, communities or regions."[76] Thus, an Orthodox Christian who becomes Catholic ordinarily belongs to the Eastern Church of his rite, while a Protestant, coming traditionally from the Church of the West, belongs to the Latin Church.[77]

---

directly or through other authorities, giving suitable rules, decrees or rescripts" (OE 4). Cf. CS c. 11; *Nuntia* 3 (1976) 51.

73   *Nuntia* 22 (1986) 31.
74   D. Salachas and K. Nitkiewicz, *Rapporti...*, 14.
75   Cf. Appendices 3 and 4. Recently, an American woman belonging to the Armenian Apostolic Church, frequenting a Latin parish, transferred to the Catholic Church, being ascribed to the Armenian Catholic Church, while continuing to frequent the Latin parish. Later she requested transfer to the Latin Church, but the Congregation for the Eastern Churches refused the transfer, stating that there is a need to preserve the continuity with one's origins, above all when one is dealing with an ethnic Church; there is no need to give the impression to non-Catholics that becoming Catholic means the loss of one's own national and religious identity: cf. *Roman Replies and CLSA Advisory Opinions 1995*, 28-31.
76   Nevertheless, the contrast between CCEO c. 35 and c. 901 seems to continue to exist: "If non-Catholics, who do not belong to an Eastern Church, are received into the Catholic Church, the norms given above are to be observed with the necessary adaptations, provided they have been validly baptized."
77   V. J. Pospishil does not share this opinion. He describes the discussions that took place during the elaboration of the canon: "One can ask if those must be considered as of the Latin Rite if they have up to now deviated from their traditions and customs that define this Church. This problem cannot be left unresolved, because of the daily needs of the Eastern Churches in North America, where Protestants constitute the majority of the population and not rarely marry Eastern Catholics. Contracting such a marriage they not rarely decide to be united to the Catholic party also with regard to religion. They—and all the other Christians—should be permitted to choose the Church "*sui iuris*" of the Catholic party without any other legal or formal obstacle" (*Eastern Catholic Marriage Law* [New York, 1991] 65); "The presumption that all Protestants have a kind of affiliation with the Latin Church is highly questionable, because their ecclesial communities, different than the Orthodox, have little or no similarity with the Latin Church, from which they are

If, for example, a Romanian Orthodox Christian wishes to enter into full communion with the Catholic Church and in his country there is no Romanian Catholic hierarchy, but only a Latin hierarchy, the Latin Bishop will receive him into the Catholic Church; he will be subject to the Latin Bishop in accord with CCEO c. 916 §5, but will be ascribed to the Romanian Catholic Church. Any policy of Latinization is excluded by this policy, and "these principles should be implemented in dioceses, even at the risk of complicating pastoral duties. The greater good, the richness of the patrimony of the Church in its diversity, calls for it."[78]

Nothing more than a simple profession of Catholic faith is required of Eastern non-Catholics (cf. OE 25; UR 18; CCEO cc. 896-897);[79] while not treated in the CIC, this also involves Latins, since it is provided for in the *Ordo initiationis christianæ*.[80] What about non-Catholics of non-Eastern separated ecclesial communities? "If non-Catholics, who do not belong to an Eastern Church, are received into the Catholic Church, the norms given above are to be observed with the necessary adaptations, provided they have been validly baptized" (CCEO c. 901). When they are received into the full communion of the Catholic Church in the Latin Rite, the profession of Catholic faith is required (Nicene-Constantinopolitan Creed) with the addition of these words: "I believe and profess all the truths which the holy Catholic Church teaches and proclaims as revealed by God." Baptism is not called into the question, unless there is a prudent doubt that requires baptism under condition. The celebrant imposes his right hand on the head of the candidate saying, "N., the Lord receives you into the Catholic Church. His loving kindness has led you here, so that in the unity of the Holy Spirit you may have full communion with us in the faith that you have professed in the presence of his family."[81] It is for the

---

detached. Thus individual Protestants and their communities should be free to choose a Church *sui iuris* when they enter into full communion with the Catholic Church. It is important that the future Code resolve this question because in the United States, Protestants constitute the majority and mixed marriages are not rare. In the case of a Protestant who marries a Catholic and wishes to become Catholic himself, if it is logical to first be ascribed to the Latin Church, almost as a *fictio iuris* and only subsequently in the Eastern Church of the wife": *Nuntia* 28 (1989) 27.

78   M. Baudoux, cited by *La Civiltà Cattolica*, (1965) I, 596.
79   *Nuntia* 17 (1983) 58: *fundamentale in hac re*. "Eastern non-Catholics who come to the fullness of Catholic communion do not have need of absolution from excommunication, nor is there a need for any 'liturgical rite,' as is required for non-Catholics belonging to other Churches and ecclesial communities of the West. In fact, the new *Rite of Christian Initiation for Adults*, found in the Roman Ritual, includes the 'rite of admission to full Communion of the Catholic Church of those who are already validly baptized'": D. Salachas, *L'iniziazione cristiana nei Codici orientale e latino* (Rome-Bologna, 1991) 128-129.
80   SC 69b: "And a new rite is to be drawn up for converts who have already been validly baptized; it should indicate that they are now admitted to communion with the Church." Cf. UR 3.
81   Cf. Sacred Congregation for Divine Worship, Decr *Ordinis baptismi adultorum*, 6 January 1972: *AAS* 64 (1972) 252ff. The English text from National Conference of

Bishop to admit the candidate; however, the priest to whom he has entrusted the celebration has the faculty to confirm the candidate during the rite of admission itself, if the candidate has not already validly received confirmation.[82] This faculty also includes the case of re-admission of an apostate from the faith who is not yet confirmed.[83]

II.14. Final Observations

We have seen the cases and modes of ascription to a Church *sui iuris* through being incorporated in the Catholic Church, in which subsists the Church of Christ (cf. CCEO c. 7 §2; CIC c. 204 §2), but in addition to these canons one should never lose sight of the following, lest disagreements arise.

Eastern Catholics who live in the territory of Latin dioceses and are subjects of the Latin Church do not transfer to the Latin Church, according to CCEO c. 38: "Christian faithful of Eastern Churches, even if committed to the care of a Hierarch or pastor of another Church *sui iuris*, nevertheless remain ascribed in their own Church *sui iuris*."[84] The same is applicable for the reverse scenario: Latin faithful subject to an Eastern hierarchy. CIC c. 112 §2 adds: "The practice, however prolonged, of receiving the sacraments according to the rite of another ritual Church *sui iuris* does not entail enrollment in that Church."[85] Eastern Catholics

---

Bishops, *Rite of Christian Initiation of Adults* (Washington, 1988) 280. Cf. ED 101.

82   ED 101: "In the present state of our relations with the ecclesial Communities of the Reformation of the 16th century, we have not yet reached agreement about the significance, the sacramental nature, or even the administration of the sacrament of Confirmation. Therefore, under present circumstances, persons entering into full communion with the Catholic Church from one of these Communities are to receive the sacrament of Confirmation according to the doctrine and rite of the Catholic Church before being admitted to Eucharistic communion." According to Faris, they should also receive the sacrament of reconciliation: J. D. Faris, "The Reception of Baptized Non-Catholics into Full Communion," in *Acta Symposii Internationalis circa Codicem Canonum Ecclesiarum Orientalium, USEK, 24-29 Aprilis 1995*, eds. A. Ahmar, A Khalife and D. Le Tourneau (Kaslik, Lebanon, 1996) 159-177, especially 174.

83   *Responsum ad propositum dubium* della Pontificia Commisione per l'Interpretazione dei Decreti del Concilio Vaticano II, 25 April 1975: *AAS* 65 (1975) 348. An apostate is one who has totally rejected the Christian faith.

84   Leo XIII, Aplet *Orientalium dignitas*, art. IX, established the following principle: "Anyone of an Eastern rite that resides outside the patriarchal territory will be under the administration of the Latin clergy; they shall, however, remain reckoned as belonging to his / her own rite. Hence, neither length of time nor any other reason shall in any way alter a person being subject to his / her Patriarch once he / she returns to his territory." The same principle is substantially contained in CIC-17 98 §3; CS cc. 8 §1 and 14; and CA c. 86 §3, 3°. Cf. Pius X, *Ea semper*, 14 June 1907: *ASS* 41 (1908) 3-12.

85   Pius X, Apcon *Tradita ab antiquis*, 14 September 1912, n. 6: *AAS* 4 (1912) 616: "Each will remain in his own rite, even if for a long time he was communicating in another rite; nor will anyone be given the faculty to change rite, except for a just and

always remain ascribed in their own Church *sui iuris*, even if they regularly attend a Latin parish in which they receive the sacraments,[86] because such a habit or custom cannot obtain the force of law. Further, CCEO c. 31 states "No one is to presume to induce in any way the Christian faithful to transfer to another Church *sui iuris*."[87] This norm is more generic than that of CCEO c. 588, which treats missionaries in particular: "Catechumens are free to be ascribed in any Church *sui iuris*, in accord with the norm of canon 30; however, care should be taken lest anything should be recommended that might prevent their ascription in the Church *sui iuris* more appropriate to their culture."

The Decree *Orientalium Ecclesiarum* declares that:

> [These Churches of East and West] are of equal rank, so that none of them is superior to the others because of rite. They have the same rights and obligations, even with regard to the preaching of the Gospel in the whole world (cf. Mk 16:15), under the direction of the Roman Pontiff. (OE 3)

> Finally, each and every Catholic, and also the baptized of every non-Catholic church or community who comes to the fullness of Catholic communion, must retain each his own rite wherever he is, and follow it to the best of his ability. (OE 4)

These norms implicitly include the absolute prohibition against carrying out ritual proselytism among faithful belonging to different Churches *sui iuris*; thus, "the various rites cannot be considered as competitors within the one Catholic Church, but spiritual paths which, each in its own way, bring the richness of their

---

legitimate cause as determined by the Sacred Council of the Propagation of the Faith for Eastern Affairs. The custom of communicating in another rite will not be counted as such a cause."

86   It is a principle already found in CIC-17 c. 98 §5, though only with reference to the sacrament of the Eucharist: "The practice, however long in duration, of receiving the sacred Synax in a foreign rite does not bring about a change of rite." It is not found in CS, perhaps because it was considered superfluous, given that *no one can validly transfer to another Rite, nor after a lawful transfer return to the former rite, without permission of the Apostolic See* (c. 8 §1) and that *the faithful of an Eastern rite who are lawfully subject to a hierarch or pastor of another rite continue to remain members of their own rite* (c. 14).

87   There is a precedent in reference to clerics in CIC-17 c. 98 §2: "Clerics shall not presume in any way to induce Latin-rite faithful to transfer to an oriental [rite], or oriental-rite faithful to transfer to the latin [rite]"; it was formerly provided for in CS 7: "No one shall presume to induce in any manner anyone from among the faithful to join another rite." For the history of this institute, see I. Řezáč, *Institutiones Iuris Canonici Orientalis* (Rome, 1958) 135-138.

ancient traditions and are fruitful for all and in service of communion."[88] Further, there is the absolute obligation to respect the freedom of conscience of each member of the Christian faithful. This applies especially to those who by reason of their office or their apostolic ministry (canonists, Bishops, clerics, religious, catechists and laity) have frequent contact with the Eastern Churches and their faithful:

> The Christian faithful of any Church *sui iuris*, even the Latin Church, who by reason of their office, ministry, or function have frequent dealings with the Christian faithful of another Church *sui iuris*, are to have an accurate formation in the knowledge and practice of the rite of the same church in keeping with the importance of the office, ministry or function they hold. (CCEO c. 41)

There is also a penal canon in this regard, CCEO c. 1465:

> A person who, ascribed in any Church *sui iuris*, including the Latin Church, and exercising an office, a ministry or another function in the Church, has presumed to induce any member of the Christian faithful whatsoever to transfer to another Church *sui iuris* contrary to can. 31, is to be punished with an appropriate penalty.[89]

Although there is no equivalent in the CIC, this canon also involves the Latin Church, because it is necessary to take into account the dictate of the Council, contained in OE 6:

> Those who, by reason of their office or apostolic ministry, have frequent dealings with the Eastern Churches or their faithful should be instructed as their office demands in the theoretical and practical knowledge of the rites, discipline, doctrine, history and character of the members of the Eastern Churches.

---

88 John Paul II, *Discorso ai membri della Conferenza inter-rituale dei Vescovi della Romania*, 7 December 1996: *L'Osservatore Romano*, 8 December 1996, 5.
89 Cf. Leo XIII, Aplet *Orientalium dignitas*, art. 1: *ASS* 27 (1894-1895) 260; Benedict XIV, Ep Enc *Demandatam*, §5.

Chapter III

Ecclesiastical Hierarchy and the Pastoral Care of the *Christifideles*: Structures of Collaboration

III.1. Apostolic Exarchates and Ordinariates for Eastern Faithful
III.2. Syncelli and Episcopal Vicars
III.3. Extra-Territorial Executive Power
III.4. Erection of Parishes
III.5. The Formation of Clerics
III.6. Ascription or Incardination of Clerics
III.7. Episcopal Conferences
III.8. Eastern Synods
III.9. Patriarchal and Eparchial Assembly
III.10. Inter-ecclesial Assemblies
III.11. Eastern Hierarchs and the College of Cardinals
III.12. Inter-ecclesial Associations
III.13. Evangelization of Peoples
III.14. Preaching of the Word of God
III.15. Catechetical Activity
III.16. Catholic Education
III.17. Pre-matrimonial Investigations
III.18. Ecumenism
III.19. Taxes
III.20. Penal Laws
III.21. Procedural Law
III.22. Ecclesiastical Dignities

The Christian faithful, transferring their domicile or quasi-domicile[1] from their place of origin to another place, near or distant, often find themselves in a territory under the jurisdiction of a pastor or Bishop different than that of their

---

1   In both CCEO c. 912 and CIC c. 102, domicile is acquired with residence, either perpetual or protracted for five complete years, in the territory of a parish or diocese (eparchy). The intention of establishment in a place in a permanent manner can result from an express declaration or from other indications or facts (for example, the construction of a house or the acquisition of an apartment). Quasi-domicile is acquired with protracted residence in a place for at least three complete months. It is not, therefore, the place of work, but the place where one sleeps, where one relaxes. According to prior legislation (CIC-17 c. 92; CS c. 20), domicile was acquired with residence that was perpetual or protracted for ten complete years; quasi-domicile was acquired by residing in a place for the greater part of the year. For an interesting historical inquiry into the subject, see R. G. Mailleux, "Domicile légal et domicile des religieux dans l'histoire de la doctrine canonique," *Antonianum* 66 (1991) 62-139.

place of origin. The problem is juridical and pastoral, especially when the faithful do not belong to the same ritual tradition of the hierarchy (cf. CCEO c. 28 §1) to which they are subject: this situation is governed by both the CCEO and the CIC.[2]

In this third chapter we shall focus principally on the condition of Eastern faithful lawfully entrusted to the pastoral care of an Ordinary or a pastor of another Church *sui iuris*, the Latin Church in particular, and on the various Eastern and Latin institutions that provide inter-ecclesial collaboration *pro bono animarum*.[3]

III.1. Apostolic Exarchates and Ordinariates for Eastern Faithful

The decree on the pastoral office of Bishops states:

> Accordingly, where there are believers of different rites, the bishop of that diocese should make provision for their spiritual needs either by providing priests of those rites, or special parishes, or by appointing episcopal vicars, with the necessary faculties. If necessary, such a vicar may be ordained bishop. Alternatively, the bishop himself may perform the functions of an Ordinary for each of the different rites. And if the Apostolic See judges that, on account of some special circumstances, none of these alternatives are practicable, a special hierarchy should be established for each different rite. (CD 23, 3)

The Council of Nicea I (325) prohibited the presence of two Bishops in the same city. Lateran Council IV (1215) re-affirmed:

> Since in many places peoples of different languages live within the same city or diocese, having one faith but different rites and customs, we therefore strictly order bishops of such cities and dioceses to provide suitable men who will do the following in the various rites and languages: celebrate the divine services for them, administer the church's sacraments, and instruct them by word and example. We

---

[2] For the prior legislation, see C. Pujol, "Condicio fidelis orientalis ritus extra suum territorium," *Periodica* 73 (1984) 489-504; I. Řezáč, *Institutiones Iuris Canonici Orientalis* (Rome, 1958) 102-104.

[3] There are cases in which Latin faithful are subject to an Eastern jurisdiction, that is, the exclusive jurisdiction of an Eastern Bishop over a given territory, with the consequent extension of his power also over the faithful of other Churches *sui iuris*. This occurs in Italy, for the Byzantine Italo-Albanian Bishops of Lungro and Piana degli Albanesi; in Ethiopia, with the Ethiopian rite Archbishop of Addis Ababa and the Ethiopian rite Bishop of Adigrat; in Eritrea, whose territory is entirely subject to Bishops of the Ethiopian rite; and in India, in eight of the new eparchies of the Syro-Malabar Church located outside of Kerala (with the exception of Kalyan, whose territory is the same as that of the Latin diocese of Mumbai and some other surrounding Latin dioceses).

altogether forbid one and the same city or diocese to have more than one bishop, as if it were a body with several heads like a monster. But if for the aforesaid reason urgent necessity demands it, the bishop of the place may appoint, after careful deliberation, a catholic bishop who is appropriate for the nations in question and who will be his vicar in the aforesaid matters and will be obedient and subject to him in all things. (Const. 9)[4]

From a formal point of view, this principle remained in force in CIC-17, which did not provide for ritual dioceses, but admitted the presence of only one Ordinary of different "rites," even if, *de facto* from the beginning of the Crusades in an exceptional manner, and after the Council of Florence as a matter of course, the practice of creating ritual dioceses had spread with the consequent presence of several Bishops in the same territory.

In accordance with these principles, CIC c. 372 §1 establishes the rule that every diocese be circumscribed within a determined territory; therefore, territory is the principal and general criterion to determine, through the domicile or quasi-domicile, the proper pastor of the baptized person, and to render concrete the sphere of ministerial activity and of the jurisdiction of pastors.[5] The canon adds: "Nevertheless, where in the judgment of the supreme authority of the Church it seems advantageous after the conferences of Bishops concerned have been heard, particular churches distinguished by the rite of the faithful or some other similar reason can be erected in the same territory."

There are five types of ecclesiastical circumscriptions of a personal character in the Latin canonical arrangements: personal dioceses (CIC c. 372 §2),[6] personal prelatures[7] (CIC cc. 294-297), and three others not directly provided for in the CIC, that is, military ordinariates, Latin ordinariates for Eastern faithful and personal ordinariates.

---

4   DEC, 1:239. One notes the difference with CD 23, which considers the possibility of several jurisdictions in the same territory.
5   While it is the primary and general criterion, territory is not the essential element, but is a spatial determination of the activity of the one Catholic Church, for a more orderly execution of this activity. In CD 11, territory does not enter in the definition of a diocese: "A diocese is a section of the People of God entrusted to a bishop to be guided by him with the assistance of his clergy so that, loyal to its pastor and formed by him into one community in the Holy Spirit through the Gospel and the Eucharist, it constitutes one particular church in which the one, holy, catholic and apostolic Church of Christ is truly present and active."
6   According to the Accord of 3 January 1979 between the Holy See and Spain (*AAS* 72 [1980] 47-55), the military vicariate is a personal and not territorial diocese.
7   A personal prelature is not a particular Church, that is, it does not belong to the constitutional hierarchy of the Church. CIC c. 265 places it on the same level as the religious institutes of pontifical right.

These personal circumscriptions are true *cœtus fidelium*, circumscribed according to a personal criterion (for example, rite) and not principally in virtue of domicile or quasi domicile; they are erected by the Apostolic See; they have their own special law that determines their own specific elements; they require a form of collaboration and coordination with the local territorial Hierarchies; they have a certain territorial dimension that is juridically relevant, a church-see of the Ordinary, the curia, the seminary; they are bound to the *ad limina* visit, to the quinquennial report, etc.

Therefore, the law contemplates the possibility of distinct ecclesiastical circumscriptions in the same territory on the basis of the rite of the faithful.[8] This possibility must be understood as a true exception to the rule that more than one hierarchy must not exist in the same territory.[9] Personal circumscriptions can be created for Eastern Catholics, even within a given territory of particular Latin Churches.[10] These circumscriptions take the name of apostolic *exarchates* and *ordinariates* for the faithful of an Eastern Rite.

Ordinariates are erected by means of a decree of the Congregation for the Eastern Churches, having heard the interested Bishops' conferences[11] and having consulted the dicastery competent for the constitution of a particular Church in

---

8   According to the *Annuario Pontificio 2012* (Vatican City, 2012) 1029-1033, there are 17 apostolic exarchates. For example: John XXIII, Apcon *Cum ob immane bellum*, 17 April 1959: *AAS* 51 (1959) 789-791; *Id.*, Apcon *Æterni Pastoris*, 22 July 1960: *AAS* 53 (1961) 341-342; *Id.*, Apcon *Sacratissima*, 22 July 1960: *AAS* 53 (1961) 343-344; Paul VI, Apcon *Byzantini Melkitarum*, 10 January 1966: *AAS* 58 (1966) 563-564; *Id.*, Apcon *Cum supremi*, 10 January 1966: *AAS* 59 (1967) 529-530; John Paul II, Apcon *Qui benignissimo*: *AAS* 72 (1980) 1075-1076. For commentary: P. Tocanel, "Constitutio Apostolica. In natione germanica Exarchia constituitur pro fidelibus ruthenis byzantini ritus ibidem commorantibus. Adnotationes," *Apollinaris* 34 (1961) 15-16; D. Faltin, "Annotationes ad Constitutiones Apostolicas de Exarchatibus Orientalibus," *Apollinaris* 34 (1961) 278-279.
9   "The Draft admits personal dioceses in virtue of rite; if this can be held [as justified] as a lesser evil because of particular temporary circumstances, nevertheless this [proposal] cannot not be accepted as the ordinary rule because it would harm the local manifestation of the unity of the Church": P. L. Seitz, in *Acta Syn.* II/IV, 429; "Experience in Egypt has shown that personal dioceses are the cause of damage and difficulty. In the East, a unity of direction in governance and in external relations with the civil government is necessary. It is desirable that for the various rites only vicars general be appointed": S. Sidarouss, *ibid.*, 429 and 901; "[…] Thus, one can maintain the principle of the unicity of jurisdiction in the same territory and at same time provide properly for the needs of the faithful and the integrity of the rite by establishing that, in truly special cases, a proper hierarchy for different rites could be constituted": *Acta Syn.* III/VI, 162.
10   Cf. Synod of Bishops, Relatio "*Principia quæ*," 7 October 1967: *Comm.* 1 (1969) 77-85.
11   There is no explicit norm in this matter, because the ritual Ordinariates are institutions born out of practice.

the same territory; but their structure does not coincide with the circumscriptions typified by Eastern law, which always deal with faithful belonging to a specific Church *sui iuris*. As a matter of fact, a ritual ordinariate generally comprises all the Eastern Catholic faithful residing in a country,[12] regardless of the rite or the Church *sui iuris* to which they belong. It is entrusted to a Latin pastor in the manner of a proper Ordinary, who, given the experiences of recent years, is the diocesan Bishop of the capital of the nation in which the ordinariate is located.[13] The Ordinary enjoys jurisdiction over his faithful that must take into account simultaneous membership both in these personal communities and in the territorial community, as well as coordination among the respective episcopal offices. The decree of erection determines the nature of the power of the Ordinary and the kind of coordination and dependence with regard to the local Ordinary or the Eastern Catholic Hierarch.[14] In exercising his office, the Ordinary is invested with powers proper to a diocesan Bishop, such as building churches, erecting

---

12 The ordinariates began with Pius X, Aplet *Officium supremi*, 15 July 1912: *AAS* 4 (1912) 555-556. In this letter, among other things, the pope states: "I. The Ruthenian Bishop is to exercise full personal jurisdiction over all members of the faithful of the Ruthenian rite who reside in the said region, under the dependence only of our venerable brother the Apostolic Delegate." According to the *Annuario Pontificio 2012* (Vatican City, 2012) 1029-1033, there are eight ordinariates. For example, Sacred Congregation for the Eastern Church, Decr *Annis præteritis*, 19 February 1959: *AAS* 54 (1962) 49-50; Decr *Cum fidelium*, 14 November 1951: *AAS* 44 (1952) 382-383; Decr *Nobilis Galliæ*, 27 July 1954: *AAS* 47 (1955) 612-613. There are exceptions: in the Ordinariate of Austria for the faithful of the Byzantine Rite; of Eastern Europe for the Armenian Catholics; of Greece for the Catholics of the Armenian Rite; of Romania for Catholics of the Armenian Rite. For a commentary, see M. Rizzi, "Decretum. Ordinariatus pro omnibus christifidelibus ritus orientalis in Gallia degentibus instituitur. Adnotationes," *Apollinaris* 28 (1955) 211-216; A. Herman, "Decretum. Ordinariatus pro omnibus christifidelibus ritus orientalis in Gallia degentibus instituitur. Adnotationes," *Monitor Ecclesiasticus* 81 (1956) 27-30.
13 The situation of the country can recommend another arrangement; for example, the Ordinary of the Ordinariate for Eastern Europe is a religious, the Ordinary of Romania is an Apostolic Administrator, that of Greece is an Apostolic Visitator.
14 In France the jurisdiction of the Ordinary is cumulative with that of the local Ordinaries and the latter must act only in a subsidiary manner, even though their consent is needed for the validity of acts that affect them: Cf. Sacred Congregation for the Eastern Churches, Decr *Gallia: ordinariatus pro fidelibus orientalibus ritus* [*Déclaration interpretative du décret du 27 juillet 1954*], 30 April 1986: *AAS* 78 (1986) 784-786, nn. I and II (cf. Appendix V); J. Passicos, "L'Ordinariat des catholiques de rite oriental résidant en France," *L'Année Canonique* 40 (1998) 151-163, especially 157-161; D. Le Tourneau, "Le soin pastoral des catholiques orientaux en dehors de leur Église de rite propre. Le cas de l'Ordinariat français," *Ius Ecclesiæ* 13 (2001) 391-419. In Argentina, "the power of jurisdiction of the Ordinary over the above-mentioned Eastern faithful will be exclusive": Sacred Congregation for the Eastern Church, Decr *Annis præteritis*, 19 February 1959: *AAS* 54 (1962) 49-50. The same is true in Brazil: Decr *Cum fidelium*, 14 November 1951: *AAS* 44 (1952) 382-383; cf. C. De Clercq, "Decretum. Ordinariatus fidelibus ritus orientalis in Argentina erigitur. Adnotationes," *Apollinaris* 35 (1962) 24.

Eastern parishes, appointing priests who should provide pastoral care,[15] seeing to the formation of seminarians, providing for the necessary educational and social programs, etc.

The jurisdiction and the tasks of the Ordinary for Eastern faithful can be drawn, for example, from the *Declaratio* of 1986 of the Congregation for the Eastern Churches:[16] first of all, the jurisdiction of the Ordinary of the Eastern faithful is primary, while that of the local ordinaries is secondary, but the former will not make any decision without the agreement *ad validitatem* of the other interested ordinaries. It is for the Ordinary of the Eastern faithful:

1. To authorize the constitution of new communities attached to the Eastern Churches, having heard the opinion of the superior authority of the concerned Eastern Churches;

2. To recognize, after hearing the opinion of the superior authority of the Eastern Churches, groups and associations of Latin faithful who intend to live according to the traditions of an Eastern Church, celebrating the liturgy and living the spirituality;

3. To construct churches and places of worship; to authorize their construction or their adaptation for the Eastern faithful;

4. To erect Eastern parishes,[17] to appoint their pastors and priests entrusted with a ministry for the faithful or communities attached to an Eastern Church, after having consulted or subsequent to the proposal of the superior authority of this Church;

---

15   The decrees issued for the ordinariates in Brazil, France and Argentina indicate: "Since in certain places there is no priest assigned for the faithful of an Eastern rite, the local pastor is to provide for the spiritual good of these faithful, having obtained faculties from the Ordinary for the faithful of Eastern rites residing in Brazil" (Brazil);
"In a place where there is no parish for the faithful of a certain Eastern rite, the local pastor of the Latin rite is to provide for the spiritual good of these faithful, having obtained faculties from the Ordinary of the faithful of the Eastern rite or from the local Ordinary" (France);
"In a place where there is no parish for the faithful of a certain Eastern rite, the local pastor of the Latin rite is to provide for the spiritual good of these faithful, having obtained faculties from the Ordinary of the faithful of the Eastern rite" (Argentina).
16   Congregation for the Eastern Churches, Decr *Gallia: ordinariatus pro fidelibus orientalibus ritus* [*Déclaration interpretative du décret du 27 juillet 1954*], 30 April 1986: *AAS* 78 (1986) 784-786; cf. Appendix V.
17   Actually in Rome there is only one Eastern personal parish, that of Saints Sergius and Bacchus of the Ukrainians: *Le Chiese Orientali in Roma nel cammino del Sinodo Pastorale Diocesano*, ed. Vicariate of Rome (Rome, 1992) 34.

5. To approve *ad normam iuris* the statutes of monasteries and institutes of consecrated life and all other associations or groups attached to an Eastern Church.

The ordinariate for the Eastern faithful is an institution that responds to the pastoral needs of the faithful; however, where there is a significant presence of faithful belonging to a given Church *sui iuris*, it would be better to constitute their own hierarchy.

Apostolic exarchates are erected by means of an apostolic constitution of the Roman Pontiff,[18] and always concern faithful belonging to a specific Eastern Church. The exarchate is entrusted to an Exarch in the manner of a proper Hierarch. The Hierarch is responsible for the faithful of a jurisdiction that must take into account the simultaneous membership in both the personal and the territorial community. The apostolic constitution of erection determines the nature of the power of the Hierarch and the kind of coordination and dependence with regard to the local Ordinary or with respect to the Roman Pontiff.

The ordinariates and the exarchates depend on the Congregation for the Eastern Churches (PB arts. 59-60).

III.2. Syncelli or Episcopal Vicars

Bearing in mind CD 23, 3, the same conciliar decree in n. 27 adds:

> In the diocesan curia, the office of the vicar general is preeminent. When, however, the good government of the diocese requires it, the bishop may appoint one or more episcopal vicars who by the very fact of their appointment will enjoy in specified parts of the diocese, or in specific types of affairs, or in regard to the faithful of particular rites, that authority which is conferred by the general law on the vicar general.

CIC c. 383 §2 (cf. CCEO c. 193 §2) states that the Bishop, "if he has faithful of a different rite in his diocese, is to provide for their spiritual needs either through priests or parishes of the same rite or through an episcopal vicar."[19] The Latin legislation, like CD 23, does not clearly state that the episcopal vicar can be of the

---

18   On the contrary, within the boundaries of the territory of a patriarchal Church, the erection of an exarchate is the competence of the Patriarch with the consent of the permanent synod (CCEO c. 311 §2).

19   Regarding the vicar general, CIC-17 c. 366 §3 stated: "Only one [vicar general] shall be consituted, unless diversity of rites or the size of the diocese requires otherwise;" For the appointment of priests from another Church *sui iuris*, see Sacred Congregation for the Propagation of the Faith for Eastern Rite Matters, *Fidelibus ruthenis*, 18 August 1913: *AAS* 5 (1913) 397.

same rite or of the same Church *sui iuris* of the faithful, while the Eastern legislation clearly affirms that the Syncellus (=Episcopal Vicar) is not necessarily of the same rite or of the same Church *sui iuris* of the faithful; indeed, CCEO c. 247 §4 allows for the possibility that the eparchial Bishop could appoint a syncellus even from another eparchy or another Church *sui iuris*, with the consent of his own eparchial Bishop, although CS was not very clear: "It is not prohibited for a bishop to appoint a syncellus from another eparchy" (CS c. 433 §3).

The episcopal vicar is a figure constituted by Vatican II (CD 27);[20] he is a priest (or Bishop) who assists and represents the diocesan Bishop concerning, in our case, the faithful of a specific rite or a specific Church *sui iuris*. In this case, he enjoys the same power that the law attaches to the office of vicar general. The difference between the vicar general and the episcopal vicar is not in the nature of the power they possess, but in the area to which it extends. They enjoy power that is ordinary (attached to their office) and vicarious (they exercise it in the name of the diocesan Bishop); but the vicar general possesses it in the entire diocese, over all persons and all matters not explicitly reserved to the Bishop or which the Bishop has reserved to himself; the episcopal vicar possess power only for a certain zone, sector, or for certain persons (in this case, the Eastern faithful).[21] Both are freely appointed by the diocesan Bishop, except if they are Bishops (CIC c. 406; CCEO c. 215 §§1-2); they must not be blood relatives of the diocesan Bishop up to the fourth degree (CIC c. 478 §2; CCEO c. 247 §3); they must belong to the secular / regular clergy (CIC c. 478 §1; CCEO c. 247 §2); they must have minimum age of thirty years, be doctors or licentiates in canon law or in theology, or at least have a true understanding of these disciplines, according to CIC c. 478 §1, while CCEO c. 247 §2 speaks of doctorates, licentiates or at least experts in some sacred science. The episcopal vicar, unlike the vicar general, is appointed only when the diocesan Bishop considers it opportune for the purpose of the good governance of the diocese, except if he is an auxiliary Bishop.

It is appropriate that the diocesan Bishop, before designating a priest as assistant, or pastor, or even as episcopal vicar for the Eastern faithful, be in contact both with the Congregation for the Eastern Churches and the proper hierarchy of these faithful, or even to ask this Hierarch to present a candidate to him.[22] The Bishop is free to take other paths, e.g., entrusting the task to a Bishop of his own diocese or even one lawfully residing in it, even of another ritual tradition or ecclesial membership as provided for in CCEO c. 247 §4. In this case an indult of biritualism issued by the Apostolic See (Congregation for the Eastern Churches)

---

20   Cf. Paul VI, Mp *Ecclesiæ Sanctæ*, 6 August 1966, I, 14 §1: *AAS* 58 (1966) 757-787.
21   Cf. A. Abate, *I ministeri nella missione e nel governo della Chiesa* (Rome, 1976) 92-95.
22   Cf. M. Brogi, "I Cattolici orientali nel Codex Iurix Canonici," *Antonianum* 58 (1983) 237; CCEO cc. 193 §3 and 916 §4.

is needed.²³ When the faithful belong to a patriarchal or major archiepiscopal Church, as we shall see later, it seems the freedom of the Bishop is limited. The instruction *Erga migrantes*²⁴ applies by analogy the Eastern norm also to Latin Bishops. Thus, as Gefaell states, although it is reasonable that one makes recourse to the Patriarch in these cases, technically speaking, the obligation of an Eastern canon should not be applicable to Latin Bishops by analogy, because it would then be a limitation on the rights of the diocesan Bishops and, thus, the norm would not be susceptible to application by analogy.²⁵ The Eastern Catholic priest designated by his own Hierarch will receive the *missio canonica* from the diocesan Bishop that will establish an agreement regarding economic matters, social security (CIC cc. 281 §§1-2 and 1274 §1-2; CCEO cc. 390 §§1-2 and 1021 §§1-2) and residence (CIC c. 533 §1 and CCEO c. 292 §1). Under n. 49 of the above-cited instruction, while for Latin migrants the pastoral object is their "full and rapid insertion in the local territorial parishes," for Eastern faithful their pastoral care should be organized "in view of the erection of parishes or a proper hierarchy of the faithful of specific Churches *sui iuris*." Hence, for a Latin Bishop, the ultimate goal should be that of helping Eastern faithful to organize themselves in their own parishes and eventually an exarchy or eparchy of the respective Church *sui iuris* with its own Hierarch.

According to CIC c. 214 and CCEO c. 17, the pastoral care of the faithful is a duty that arises out of the right of the faithful to worship God according to the lawful prescriptions of their own rite;²⁶ this right obliges the authority to constitute pastoral structures of various rites wherever there are a sufficient number of persons of this rite (GE 2; LG 37; OE 2, 3, 5; PO 9; SC 4, 19; UR 4). The faithful are also called upon to deepen their understanding of their own liturgical, spiritual, disciplinary, and theological patrimony (CCEO c. 405) and live according to their own spirituality;²⁷ this is a personal right, which should certainly be guaran-

---

23   The indult authorizes the priest (or deacon) of a Church *sui iuris* who had made the request to observe the liturgical prescriptions of the patrimony of another Church *sui iuris*. Cf. Appendices VIII, IX and X.

24   Pontifical Council for the Pastoral Care of Migrants and Itinerant People, Instructio *Erga migrantes caritas Christi*, 3 May 2004: *AAS* 96 (2004) 762-822.

25   Cf. P. Gefaell, "Rapporti tra i due 'Codici' dell'unico 'Corpus iuris Canonici,'" in *Metodo, Fonti e Soggetti del Diritto canonico*, Atti del Convegno Internazionale di Studi, "La Scienza Canonistica nella seconda metà del '900. Fondamenti, metodi, prospettive in D'Avack, Lombardia, Gismondi e Corecco," Roma 13-16 novembre 1996, Pontificia Università della Santa Croce, Università di Roma Tor Vergata, eds. J. I Arrieta and G. P. Mialno (Vatican City, 1999) 664.

26   This is understood in the context of CCEO c. 28 §1. The right to follow one's own method of spiritual life is also manifested in the rite.

27   Cf. E. Corecco, "Il Catalogo dei doveri-diritti nel CIC," in *I diritti fondamentali della Persona Umana e la libertà religiosa*, Atti del V Colloquio Giuridico (8-10 marzo 1984), ed. F. Biffi (Rome, 1985) 111-114; L. Okulik, *La condición jurídica del fiel cristiano. Contribución al studio comparado del Codex Iuris Canonici y del Codex Canonum Ecclesiarum Orientalium* (Buenos Aires, 1995); I. Žužek, "La 'Lex Ecclesiæ

teed both to the faithful who are in their homeland and to those in the diaspora. Thus, all those who are responsible for pastoral care

> have the obligation to be prepared adequately, to foster a respect of the people they intend to serve, resisting the temptation to "colonize" them, even by "advancing" them by means of their conversion to the culture of the missionaries (presumed by them to be higher). This is an approach of which we must continually become more cognizant.[28]

In fact, the goal of pastoral care for the Eastern Catholics "is not to assimilate them into the faithful of the Latin Church, but to preserve their understanding and practice of their own rite."[29] Recognizing this right means recognition and defense of the action of the Holy Spirit, which enriches the Church always with new gifts for the benefit of all. This right pertains to all the faithful who, in order to exercise it, have other rights:

CCEO	CIC
15 §2. The Christian faithful are free to make known their needs, especially their spiritual needs, and their desires to the pastors of the Church.	212 §2. The Christian faithful are free to make known to the pastors of the Church their needs, especially spiritual ones, and their desires.
16. The Christian faithful have the right to receive from the pastors of the Church assistance out of the spiritual goods of the Church, especially from the word of God and from the sacraments.	213. The Christian faithful have the right to receive assistance from the sacred pastors out of the spiritual goods of the Church, especially the word of God and the sacraments.

Fundamentalis' et le deux Codes," *L'Année Canonique* 40 (1998) 19-48, especially 25-34.

28   M. Brogi, "Il diritto all'osservanza del proprio rito (CIC c. 214)," *Antonianum* 68 (1993) 114.

29   Card. A. Silvestrini, "Assemblea Speciale per l'America del Sinodo dei Vescovi," XVI Congregazione Generale: *L'Osservatore Romano*, 29 November 1997, 4. Pius IX had this to say: "It is absolutely necessary that the liturgical discipline of the proper Church be observed by all Bishops and priests, and that it never be left to the decision of the individual prelates, but is to be determined by the authority of this Apostolic See. It was never permitted, nor is it permitted, for anyone lightly to change, alter, innovate or diminish the liturgy in any way, especially as it was established and taught in the apostolic letters of Benedict XIV (*Demandatam*, 21 December 1743) and Gregory XVI (*Inter gravissimas*, 3 February 1832); these letters and the regulations in their prescriptions we also confirm by our supreme authority and order them to be observed most carefully by all the Eastern Churches": *Allocutio consistorialis* die 12 iulii 1867, cited in A. Petrani, *De relatione iuridica inter diversos ritus in Ecclesia catholica* (Turin-Rome, 1930) 10-11.

These canons refer to the right of individual or collective requests and the obligations on the part of pastors to organize the administration of the sacraments, the preaching of the Word and the means which lead to holiness that appropriately respond to the needs of the faithful. In this way, all can use these spiritual aids according to their vocation (cf. CIC-17 c. 682; LG 37).[30] There is also an obligation of justice when, in a given situation, the right of the faithful can be satisfied only by a specific well-prepared sacred minister. Practices that unduly allow for the reception of sacraments and those which force someone to receive sacraments in a manner not prescribed by the law (i.e., pastoral practices that transform into obligations practices not compelled by the law or contrary to the law) are considered an abuse against this right.

Assistance to Eastern Catholic faithful is also the object of other canons treating episcopal vicars and pastors ; CIC c. 476 (cf. CCEO c. 246) prescribes:

---

30 The following is a summarized list of the rights and obligations of the Christian faithful in the CIC and the CCEO:

Obligation to maintain communion with the Church and to observe the laws of the universal Church and of one's own particular Church (CCEO c. 12 and CIC c. 209);

Obligation to seek personal sanctity as a means of growth of the Church and the promotion of its continual sanctification (CCEO c. 13 and CIC. c. 210);

Right and obligation to collaborate in the message of salvation (CCEO c. 14 and CIC c. 211);

Obligation of obedience towards the pastors, representatives of Christ, as teachers of the faith and guides of the Church (CCEO c. 15 §1 and CIC c. 212 §1);

Right to petition and to make known their own needs, especially spiritual, and their desires to their pastors (CCEO c. 15 §2 and CIC c. 212 §2);

Right and, at times, obligation, to make known their own opinions regarding the common good of the Church, and the right to participate in the formation of public opinion of the Church (CCEO c. 15 §3 and CIC c. 212 §3);

Right to receive from the pastors spiritual goods, and especially the Word of God and the sacraments (CCEO c. 16 and CIC 213);

Right to worship God according to one's own rite and the right to one's own spirituality (CCEO c. 17 and CIC c. 214);

Right of association and meeting for the purposes of charity, piety or to foster the Christian vocation (CCEO c. 18 and CIC c. 215);

Right of apostolic initiative (CCEO c. 19 and CIC c. 216);

Right to Catholic education (CCEO c. 20 and CIC c. 217);

Right to just freedom of inquiry in the sacred sciences (CCEO c. 21 and CIC c. 218);

Right to freedom from coercion in the choice of a state of life (CCEO c. c. 22 and CIC c. 219);

Right to a good reputation and privacy (CCEO c. 23 and CIC c. 220);

Right to juridic protection (CCEO c. 24 and CIC c. 221);

Obligation to provide for the needs of the Church (CCEO c. 25 §1 and CIC c. 222 §1);

Obligation to promote social justice and see to the needs of the poor (CCEO c. 25 §2 and CIC c. 222 §2).

> Whenever the correct governance of a diocese requires it, the diocesan bishop can also appoint one or more episcopal vicars, namely, those who in a specific part of the diocese or in a certain type of affairs or over the faithful of a specific rite or over certain groups of persons possess the same ordinary power which a vicar general has by universal law, according to the norm of the following canons.

This provision was not found in CIC-17, while CS stated:

> One syncellus only shall be appointed, unless the size of the eparchy or another reasonable cause should require several. However, for an absent or impeded syncellus the Bishop can appoint another or substitute for him. (c. 432 §3)

> If in a diocese of the Latin rite there are communities of faithful of the Eastern rite, a syncellus shall be appointed to take care of them. If possible, he should be of an Eastern rite; otherwise, a Latin rite priest may be appointed, who is qualified and well-versed in Eastern matters. (c. 432 §4, 1°)

Regarding this matter, CCEO c. 916 §5 states:

> In places where not even an exarchy has been erected for the Christian faithful of a certain Church *sui iuris*, the local Hierarch of another Church *sui iuris*, even the Latin Church, is to be considered as the proper Hierarch of these faithful, with due regard for can. 101. If, however, there are several local Hierarchs, that one whom the Apostolic See has designated is to be considered as their proper Hierarch or, if it concerns the Christian faithful of a certain patriarchal Church, the one whom the patriarch has designated with the assent of the Apostolic See.[31]

One is obviously dealing with Eastern faithful who are outside the territory of the patriarchal / major archiepiscopal Church; inside the proper territory, the Patriarch / Major Archbishop is considered the eparchial Bishop of the faithful where there is not even an exarchate:[32] "In his own eparchy, in stauropegial monasteries and other places where neither an eparchy nor an exarchy has been erected, the patriarch has the same rights and obligations as an eparchial bishop"

---

31   CS c. 22 §3: "Outside the territory of their own rite, in the absence of a Hierarch of that rite, the local Hierarch shall be regarded as their proper Hierarch. When there are several, the one designated by the Apostolic See is to be regarded as the proper Hierarch, with due regard for c. 260 §1, n. 2, d."
32   CCEO c. 311 §1: "An exarchy is a portion of the people God which, because of special circumstances, is not erected as an eparchy, and which being delimited territorially or on some other criterion, is entrusted to an exarch to be shepherd."

(CCEO c. 101).[33] Within the territory of the patriarchal Church, "the patriarch, with the consent of the permanent synod, can erect, change or suppress exarchies" (CCEO c. 85 §3);[34] for the other exarchies, such a right belongs to the Apostolic See.

In the case of Eastern faithful living in a territory where they lack their own Hierarch, if there is only one Bishop with jurisdiction, the case is resolved without difficulty: they will have the local Ordinary as their own Hierarch. If there is more than one Bishop with jurisdiction in the same territory, none of whom is ascribed to the same Church *sui iuris* as the faithful, the proper Hierarch is the one designated as such by the Apostolic See.[35] If they are faithful of a patriarchal or major archiepiscopal Church (Armenian, Chaldean, Coptic, Melkite, Syrian, Maronite, Romanian, Syro-Malabar, Syro-Malankara and Ukrainian), the Patriarch or Major Archbishop can proceed with a designation of a Hierarch with the assent of the Apostolic See;[36] the Metropolitan, head of another Church *sui iuris*, cannot designate such a Hierarch because it is the exclusive competence of the Apostolic See. Therefore, entrustment of the faithful of a given Church *sui iuris* to a Bishop of another Church *sui iuris* is not done in virtue of the authority of the Church *sui iuris* to which these faithful are ascribed, but by the authority of the one competent to modify and provide for the entire diocese, entrusting it to the care of the Bishop. The faculty given to Patriarchs and Major Archbishops is not in the sense of a power over the diocese of another Church *sui iuris*[37] but an exercise of their *ius vigilantiæ* that extends beyond the boundaries of their Church.[38]

CCEO c. 312: "The exarch governs the exarchy either in the name of the one who appointed him or in his own name. This must be established in the erection or modification of the exarchy."

33   CS c. 282 did not include the stauropegial monastery. A *stauropegial* monastery is a monastery in the territory of the patriarchal Church and directly dependent on the Patriarch, that is, of patriarchal right.

34   Formerly in CS c. 248 §2.

35   Cf. R. Metz, "La désignation des évêques dans le droit actuel: étude comparative entre le Code latin de 1983 et le Code oriental de 1990," *Studia Canonica* 27 (1993) 321-334.

36   Cf. Sacred Congregation for the Eastern Churches, Declaratio *Apostolica Sedes*, 25 March 1970: *AAS* 62 (1970) 179; CLD 7:9-10.

37   John Paul II recalled that the ecumenical councils had foreseen patriarchal jurisdiction only in the territory of the patriarchate and that Vatican II did not accept the request to extend such jurisdiction outside such boundaries; in any case, the pope left open the possibility of making special and *ad tempus* law for particular situations.: cf. *Nuntia* 29 (1989) 27.

38   John Paul II, *Udienza ai Patriarchi delle Chiese Orientali Cattoliche*, 29 September 1998: *L'Osservatore Romano*, 30 September 1998, 5: "You, who are the heads, have received from the Holy Spirit the mission to preserve and promote a specific patrimony, so that the Gospel may be given with ever greater abundance to the Church and to the World. The Successor of Peter has the obligation to assist you and help you in this mission"; Id., *Udienza alla Plenaria della Congregazione per le Chiese Orientali*,

A realization of CCEO c. 916 §5 in an entirely singular manner is found in the Diocese of Rome, which has the Roman Pontiff as its proper Ordinary; thus, all the Eastern faithful who have a domicile and quasi-domicile in Rome have the pope as their Hierarch.

By the term *Ordinary* in the CIC or *Hierarch* in the CCEO is understood, beyond the diocesan (eparchial) Bishop, also those who enjoy general ordinary executive power, that is to say, vicar generals or protosyncelli, episcopal vicars or syncelli (CIC c. 134 §1; CCEO c. 984 §2). Accordingly, at Rome the proper Hierarch of the Eastern faithful is, beyond the Roman Pontiff, also the Vicar of Rome and the episcopal vicar for the Eastern faithful.

When the Eastern faithful entrusted according to the norm of law to the care of a Latin Ordinary belong to a patriarchal or major archiepiscopal Church, both the Patriarch or Major Archbishop and the Latin Ordinary must keep in mind CCEO c. 148:

> §1. It is the right and the obligation of the patriarch to seek appropriate information concerning the Christian faithful who reside outside the territorial boundaries of the Church over which he presides, even through a visitor sent by himself with the assent of the Apostolic See.
>
> §2. The visitor, before he begins his function, is to go to the eparchial bishop of those faithful and present his letter of appointment.
>
> §3. When the visitation is completed, the visitor is to send a report to the patriarch, who, after discussing the matter in the synod of bishops of the patriarchal Church, can propose suitable measures to the Apostolic See, in view of providing everywhere in the world for the protection and enhancement of the spiritual good of the Christian faithful of the Church over which he presides, even through the erection of parishes and exarchies or eparchies of their own.

Comparing CCEO c. 148 with CS c. 262 §1,[39] we find certain important points. The CCEO speaks of a visitator in a generic manner and of the report to be sent

---

1 October 1998, n. 6: *L'Osservatore Romano*, 2 October 1998, 5: "The Pastors of the Eastern Churches, on the other hand, will not cease to be responsible for their faithful who have left the homelands, committing to discern the forms in which to manifest their own tradition, in a way that responds to the modern expectations of these faithful, in the particular conditions of the society in which they live."

39   "The patriarch is entitled to send, with the consent of the Apostolic See, as often as he considers it appropriate, a suitable secular or religious priest to communities of faithful residing outside the patriarchal territory, if he has power over these faithful according to the norm of c. 216 §2, 2°; this priest shall paternally visit them and report everything to the Sacred Congregation for the Eastern Church as well as to the patriarch" (CS c. 262 §1, 1°).

to the Patriarch who, together with the Synod of Bishops, can propose appropriate remedies to the Apostolic See; CS spoke of an *idoneum sacerdotem secularem vel religiosum* ("suitable secular or religious priest"), who was to submit a report of the visit not only to the Patriarch but also to the Sacred Congregation for the Eastern Church.

Further, CCEO c. 193 §3, not found in CS, states:

> Eparchial bishops who appoint this kind of presbyters, pastors or syncelli for the care of the Christian faithful of patriarchal churches are to draw up a plan in consultation with the respective patriarchs. If these agree, they are to act on their own authority and inform the Apostolic See as soon as possible; should the patriarchs disagree for whatever reason, the matter is to be referred to the Apostolic See.

It seems that the faithful ascribed to a patriarchal or major archiepiscopal Church are not true subjects of the diocesan Bishop; hence, he is not free in the choice of priests to be appointed as pastors or syncelli, but must discuss it with the Patriarch or Major Archbishop and needs their consent. One might ask if this consent refers to the fact of the appointment or to the specific persons who are to be appointed. The text says *huiusmodi* ["of this kind"]; therefore, it seems to refer to the appointment and not to the specific person. In any case, the Patriarch is not completely autonomous because in the case of disagreement, the matter is referred to the Apostolic See. The Pontifical Commission for the Revision of the *Codex Iuris Canonici Orientalis* wanted to extend this norm to the Latin Church, but the promulgated text does not mention it; according to CCEO c. 1, it juridically binds only the Eastern faithful.[40] The Latin Bishops must keep in mind that for the Eastern mentality, ascription to a ritual community has great social-political importance and can prevail even over the factor of citizenship. Moreover, according to CIC c. 214, Latin Bishops are bound to see that the faithful entrusted to their care worship God according to the prescriptions of their own rite; thus, Latin Bishops must share in the concern of the Apostolic See that Eastern faithful are able to practice their rite everywhere.

From the nature of the matter, the priest to whose care the faithful are entrusted can be of the same or another Church *sui iuris* as the faithful. With regard to the visitor, PB art. 59 should also be kept in mind: "The Congregation [for the Eastern Churches] pays careful attention to communities of Oriental Christian faithful living within the territories of the Latin Church, and attends to their spiritual needs by providing visitors […]."[41] The reference to the Latin Church is explicit and leaves no doubt regarding interpretation.

---

40   1986 Draft, c. 191: *Nuntia* 24-25 (1987).
41   If he is a Bishop, the visitator can confer sacred orders on the faithful of the respective rite who have been called by the proper Latin diocesan Bishop; he can help

Regarding the *ad limina* visit, CCEO c. 207 states: "An eparchial bishop of any Church *sui iuris*, even of the Latin Church, is to inform the Apostolic See on the occasion of the quinquennial report, about the state and needs of the Christian faithful who, even if they are ascribed in another *sui iuris*, are committed to his care."[42]

CIC c. 399 §1 is more generic: "Every five years a diocesan bishop is bound to make a report to the Supreme Pontiff on the state of the diocese entrusted to him, according to the form and time determined by the Apostolic See." [43] Thus, the Latin Bishops, in anticipation of the *ad limina* visit, send six months prior (PB art. 32) their quinquennial report to the competent dicastery, which is, as appropriate, the Congregation for Bishops, the Congregation for Evangelization of Peoples or even Congregation for the Eastern Churches, or to the second section of the Secretariat of State, and report also on the state of the Eastern faithful entrusted to their pastoral care. It is then the responsibility of the dicastery that received the report to transmit this information to the Congregation for the Eastern Churches.[44] In the form for the quinquennial report, in the section regarding the episcopal ministry there is a reference to possible structures or specific positions for the pastoral care of Catholics of other rites subject to the jurisdiction of the diocesan Bishop; there is also a reference to the collaboration with Bishops of other rites who have jurisdiction over their own faithful in the diocese. Further, the report asks for a report on other rites possibly present in the diocese.[45]

III.3. Extra-Territorial Executive Power

The power of governance in divided into legislative, executive and judicial (CIC c. 135 §1; CCEO c. 985 §1). This executive power can be exercised also while outside the territory:

---

the Latin Ordinary in providing pastoral care for the respective Eastern faithful with information, counsel, teaching and liturgical aids, etc.

42   CS c. 406: "Bishops, even of the Latin rite, shall inform the Sacred Congregation for the Eastern Church on the occasion of their quinquennial report of the situation and needs of groups of faithful of another Eastern rite who reside in their territory and lack a Hierarch of their rite."

43   Formerly in CIC-17 c. 340 §1.

44   Cf. V. Che Chen-Tao, "Aspetti giuridici della visita 'ad limina,'" in *Ius et vita et in misisone Ecclesiæ*, ed. Pontificium Consilium de Legum Textibus Interpretandis (Vatican City, 1994) 325-336. For a comparison between the prior and current discipline, see J. A. F. Arruty, "La visita ad limina de los obispos de rito latino y de rito oriental," in *Incontro*, 2:229-237.

45   Cf. Congregation for Bishops, *Formulary for the Quinquennial Report* (Vatican City, 1997).

CCEO	CIC
986. Unless common law provides otherwise or it is evident from the nature of the matter, a person can exercise executive power over his subjects even when he is outside his own territorial boundaries or they are absent; he can also exercise this power over travelers actually living in the territory if it concerns granting favors or executing either common law or particular law by which they are bound according to the norm of can. 1491, §3.	136. Unless the nature of the matter or a prescript of law establishes otherwise, a person is able to exercise executive power over his subjects, even when he or they are outside his territory; he is also able to exercise this power over travelers actually present in the territory if it concerns granting favors or executing universal laws or particular laws which bind them according to the norm of can. 13, §2, n. 2.

The exercise of executive power has both a personal and territorial dimension, specified in these canons in which its active and passive subjects are indicated. The holder of this power can exercise it while outside his territory, at least if it is not established otherwise *ex natura rei* or by a disposition of the law, on behalf of his subjects and also on behalf of travelers in certain specific cases.[46] In determining the scope of executive power, the personal element has an important role. The condition of the faithful belonging to a given particular Church follows the person, even when he or she is outside the territory of his or her own diocese: indeed, the juridic relationship between the authority and the passive subject of the power is personal. Territory is only one of the factors in the determination or delimitation of such a relationship. We can, therefore, assert that the relationship between the authority and the faithful does not come through territory, but is a personal relationship, even if determined initially by a territorial factor, domicile or quasi-domicile.[47] Because the relationship between the authority and the faithful, even if determined or specified by territory, is of a personal nature, this power remains and can be exercised also in cases in which the faithful are found outside their own territory, and even when the authority itself is outside the territory.

Another element in the determination of the relationship between the authority and the faithful is incardination. According to CIC c. 266 §1 and CCEO c. 358, one becomes a cleric with diaconal ordination and is incardinated in the particular Church in whose service he was admitted. Thus, the personal nature

---

[46] E. Labandeira, *Trattato di Diritto Amministrativo Canonico* (Milan, 1994) 138: "With reference to persons, executive power—like every power of governance—can be territorial or personal: in both cases it can be exercised on behalf of subjects wherever they are. When the power is territorial, it can also be exercised on behalf of foreigners present in the territory and when it is a question of granting favors or applying particular or universal laws to which these are bound by c. 13 §2, 2°."

[47] Cf. J. Hervada, "Significado actual del principio de territorialidad," *Fidelium Iura* 2 (1992) 235.

of the relationship with one's own particular Church is even clearer in the case of priests, since for them, the criterion which determines membership in a particular Church is in itself a personal criterion, incardination, which establishes his own Ordinary. Clerics of a particular Church, in any place they are found, are members of the faithful of this Church and are part of its presbyterate.

On this point we can ask: could not the eparchial Bishop, according to CCEO cc. 986 and 246 (CIC cc. 136 and 476), appoint a personal syncellus (=episcopal vicar) outside his own territory for a given *cœtus* of faithful of his eparchy that reside in a determined city?[48] For example, could the eparchial Bishop of Hajdùdorog (Hungary) appoint a syncellus for his priests and seminarians who reside in Rome, with a prior *nihil obstat* of the vicar general of the pope for the Diocese of Rome? The syncellus, beyond the competency that the canonical legislation in force already provides for him, could promote spiritual values, priestly friendship, common life, could take into account appropriate consideration for the situation of these clerics, their obligations, needs and diverse requirements, could collaborate with the rectors of the ecclesiastical institutes of education and formation, etc. We hold, however, that the Bishop of Hajdùdorog could not appoint a syncellus for the other Christian faithful who by reason of domicile or quasi-domicile reside in a given diocese, because CCEO c. 986 states: "unless common law provides otherwise." CCEO c. 916 §5 states:

> In places where not even an exarchy has been erected for the Christian faithful of a certain Church *sui iuris*, the local Hierarch of another Church *sui iuris*, even the Latin Church, is to be considered as the proper Hierarch of these faithful, with due regard for can. 101. If, however, there are several local Hierarchs, that one whom the Apostolic See has designated is to be considered as their proper Hierarch or, if it concerns the Christian faithful of a certain patriarchal Church, the one whom the patriarch has designated with the assent of the Apostolic See.

The proper Hierarch of these faithful is the local Hierarch and, consequently, these faithful are subject to him; thus, it is solely for him to appoint a syncellus for these faithful, and not the Hierarch of the Church *sui iuris* to which they are ascribed.

III.4. Erection of Parishes

Every particular Church is divided into parishes, that is, into communities of faithful constituted stably and entrusted to pastors, under the authority of the eparchial Bishop (cf. CCEO c. 279; CIC c. 515 §1). According to CIC c. 107 §1, ev-

---

48   Cf. Archidiocesis de Valencia, "Decreto por el que se nombra Vicario Episcopal personal para los sacerdotes diocesanos residentes en Roma y se determinan las competencias de su oficio, 22 enero 1995," *Ius Ecclesiæ* 8 (1996) 383-384.

ery member of the Christian faithful obtains a proper pastor through domicile or quasi-domicile; according to CCEO c. 916 §1, one obtains a pastor of the Church *sui iuris* to which one is ascribed always through a domicile or quasi-domicile. If, in a given eparchy, there is a region without parishes, the eparchial Bishop designates a pastor of another Church *sui iuris*, including the Latin Church, with the consent of the pastor to be designated (CCEO c. 916 §4). In those places where there is not even an exarchy, CCEO c. 916 §5 is applied.

The eparchial Bishop must be zealous and solicitous in his ministry, both towards the faithful in general, towards the non-Catholic brethren, the non-baptized and the non-believers, and towards the priests who for various reasons reside in the territory of his diocese, because he is responsible for all before God and the Church. On the basis of this norm established in both codes, wherever there is in a Latin diocese the stable presence of a sufficient number of faithful belonging to different Churches *sui iuris*, one might eventually consider the possibility of constituting in the diocese some personal parishes according to the various Churches *sui iuris*, with the consequent appointment of Eastern (or Latin) pastors, the necessary pastoral and organizational structures,[49] and the use of their own parish registers,[50] because these communities have

> the right to have a priest as its own pastor, who *vi officii ipsi ab Episcopo commissi in hac tali communitate* must exercise his pastoral *munus* with jurisdiction *in foro interno vi ipsius officii*, with the administration of the sacraments, with the preaching of the Word of God.[51]

---

49   The parochial council for economic affairs and the pastoral parochial council. The constitution of the pastoral parochial council is left to the discretion of the diocesan Bishop if, given the circumstances, he sees its opportuneness; to be able to make a judgment of this kind, hearing the counsel of the presbyteral council is required. Cf. P.G. Marcuzzi, "Il Consiglio pastorale parrocchiale," in *Ius in vita et in missione Ecclesiæ*, ed. Pontificium Consilium de Legum Textibus Interpretandis (Vatican City, 1994) 437-464.

50   The *ratio* for the constitution of a personal parish is the *utilitas curæ pastoralis*; cf. *Comm.* 4 (1972) 42.

51   Sacred Congregation for the Propagation of the Faith, *In Litteris Encyclicis diei 8 Nov. 1882 ad Delegatos Apostolicos pro Orient. quoad obligationem vi Constit. In suprema 10 Iun. 1882*, cited in F. Cappello, *De administrativa amotione parochorum* (Rome, 1911) 28.

It is expressed in the codes as follows:

CCEO	CIC
192 §1. In the exercise of his pastoral function, the eparchial bishop is to show that he is concerned for all the Christian faithful who are committed to his care, regardless of age, condition, nation or Church *sui iuris*, both those who live within the territory of his eparchy and those who are staying in it temporarily; he is to extend his apostolic spirit also to those who cannot sufficiently avail themselves of ordinary pastoral care due to their condition in life as well as to those who are far from the practice of their religion.	383 §1. In exercising the function of a pastor, a diocesan bishop is to show himself concerned for all the Christian faithful entrusted to his care, of whatever age, condition, or nationality they are, whether living in the territory or staying there temporarily; he is also to extend an apostolic spirit to those who are not able to make sufficient use of ordinary pastoral care because of the condition of their life and to those who no longer practice their religion.
193 §1. The eparchial bishop to whose care the Christian faithful of another *sui iuris* have been committed is bound by the serious obligation of providing everything so that these Christian faithful retain the rite of their respective Church, cherish and observe it as far as possible. He is also to ensure that they foster relations with the superior authority of their churches.	771 §1. Pastors of souls, especially bishops and pastors, are to be concerned that the word of God is also proclaimed to those of the faithful who because of the condition of their life do not have sufficient common and ordinary pastoral care or lack it completely.
246. As often as the good governance of the eparchy requires it, one or several syncelli can be appointed, who have by virtue of the law itself the same authority as that which is attributed by common law to the protosyncellus but limited to a given section of the eparchy, or to certain kinds of affairs or for the Christian faithful ascribed to another *sui iuris* or for a certain group of persons.	476. Whenever the correct governance of a diocese requires it, the diocesan bishop can also appoint one or more episcopal vicars, namely, those who in a specific part of the diocese or in a certain type of affairs or over the faithful of a specific rite or over certain groups of persons possess the same ordinary power which a vicar general has by universal law, according to the norm of the following canons.
280 §1. As a rule, a parish is to be territorial, that is, it is to embrace all the Christian faithful of a certain territory. If, however, in the judgment of the eparchial bishop it is advisable, after consulting the presbyteral council, personal parishes are to be erected, by reason of nationality, of language, of ascription of the Christian faithful to another Church *sui iuris* or indeed of some other clearly distinguishing factor.	518. As a general rule a parish is to be territorial, that is, one which includes all the Christian faithful of a certain territory. When it is expedient, however, personal parishes are to be established determined by reason of the rite, language, or nationality of the Christian faithful of some territory, or even for some other reason.

It would be beneficial for the pastoral service of the Eastern faithful residing in Latin dioceses to have some Eastern eparchial clergy or religious, rather than using Latin priests (or Eastern clerics belonging to another ritual tradition) who are able to celebrate according to an Eastern rite through an indult of biritualism.[52] One should make recourse to biritualism, granted by the Congregation for the Eastern Churches for a determined time, only in the case of the absolute lack of priests belonging to the same Church *sui iuris* of the concerned faithful, avoiding every unlawful liturgical syncretism and granting the indult of bi-ritualism only *devotionis causa*.

CIC c. 518 (CCEO c. 280 §1), after enunciating the general principle of the territoriality of the parish, states that, where it is appropriate, personal parishes are to be constituted on the basis of rite, language or nationality of the faithful belonging to a territory, or even other reasons. Hence, territory is not an essential element, either for the parish or for the diocese, but is only an instrument for the determination of a certain community.[53] The general rule does not prevent the diocesan Bishop from erecting personal parishes (CD 23; OE 4) when he is presented with the objective need *bono animarum id exposcente* ["the good of souls demanding it"], and with the real unity of such persons *non in præfinitio territorio exstante sed ex unitate quadam sociali membrorum suorum* ["not existing in a defined territory, but from a certain social unity of its members"].[54] For the institution of personal parishes according to the prior legislation, a special apostolic indult was needed (CIC-17 c. 216 §4),[55] but the 1951 Apcon *Exul Familia* granted to local Ordinaries the faculty of erecting personal parishes for immigrants without the need of requesting an apostolic indult.[56] In the legislation in force, this act is the competency of the diocesan Bishop, after having consulted the presbyteral council (CIC c. 515 §2; CCEO c. 280 §2).[57]

---

52   Cf. Appendix VIII.
53   Cf. *Principia quæ Codicis Iuris Canonici recognitionem dirigant* (n. 8), in *Comm.* 2 (1969) 84: "When, however, we set about to determine and define this portion of the People of God which constitutes a particular Church, the territory in which the faithful live might often serve as a criteria. Territory retains its importance, not indeed as a constitutive element, but as an element determining a specific portion of the People of God, by which this Church is defined and identified." John Paul II, *All. al convegno internazionale del movimento parrocchiale*, 4 May 1986, in *La Traccia* 7 (1986/5) 427-429: "The parish is not principally a structure, a territory or a building. The parish is in the first place a community of faithful that is born of the word, has as its center the celebration of the Eucharist and is animated by love.
54   Sacred Congregation for Bishops, Directorium *Ecclesiæ imago*, 22 February 1973, n. 174.
55   Cf. Appendix VI.
56   Cf. Pius XII, Apcon *Exul Familia*, 1 August 1952, n. 32: *AAS* 44 (1952) 649-704.
57   Cf. *Comm.* 18 (1986) 71: "The Most Reverend Secretary responded that the erection of parishes is the competency of the diocesan Bishop, whatever may be

While the pastor enjoys stability in his office, nevertheless he can be appointed for a determined time:

CCEO	CIC
284 §3. The pastor is permanent in his office, therefore he is not to be appointed for a determined period of time unless: 1° it concerns a member of a religious institute or society of common life in the manner of religious; 2° a candidate agrees to this in writing; 3° it concerns a special case, in which case the consent of the college of eparchial consultors is required; 4° the particular law of his Church *sui iuris* permits it.	522. A pastor must possess stability and therefore is to be appointed for an indefinite period of time. The diocesan bishop can appoint him only for a specific period if the conference of bishops has permitted this by a decree.

Both codes emphasize the stability that a pastor enjoys in his office, but this stability is something different than the immovability spoken of in CIC -17 and CS. Indeed, while immovability was viewed as a privilege, stability is considered as a requirement for the efficacy of the ministry: "Pastors should enjoy in their respective parishes that stability of office which the good of souls demands" (CD 31). Ordinarily, the appointment should be made without a predetermined time limit, that is, without a fixed expiration of the term of the appointment, the duration depending on the circumstances and the assessment of the Bishop. The innovation in the legislation consists in the introduction of the appointment for a determined time, which does not contradict the principle of stability, which "can coexist with the concept of a definite time,"[58] meaning that in such a case, for the entire pre-determined time, the pastor cannot be removed from office. By this solution, one can appeal to the determined conditions considered in the above-mentioned canons.

The Italian Bishops' Conference [CEI – Conferenza Episcopale Italiana], under the norm of CIC c. 522, established that Bishops have the faculty to appoint pastors *ad certum tempus*; these appointments have a period of nine years.[59]

---

the criteria—that is, personal, territorial or mixed—according to which the faithful are circumscribed."

58   *Comm.* 13 (1981) 272.

59   ECEI 3:1593, 1977. It should be noted that the Italian Bishops Conference cannot establish this as an obligation, but only as a possibility.

For the erection of a parish in the church of an Eastern monastery situated in a Latin diocese and for the appointment of a monk as pastor, the diocesan Bishop must keep in mind that the consent of the Apostolic See is necessary, differing with the Latin legislation that requires only the consent of the competent superior (CCEO c. 480; CIC c. 520). This rigidity in the Eastern legislation was required because of the fact that it is not for monks to have the pastoral care of the faithful, but only in truly exceptional and particular cases, even if often the faithful go to the monastery for confessions, for preaching, for the direction of souls and for brief retreats. On the other hand, if the pastor is a member of a religious institute or a society of the common life in the manner of religious, according to CCEO c. 284 §, 1° he is appointed for a determined time.

We find that among the functions entrusted to the pastor in a special way (CIC c. 530 and CCEO c. 290), there is also the administration of the sacrament of confirmation. While the Latin pastor administers the sacrament of confirmation ordinarily only for those who are in danger of death, the Eastern pastor ordinarily administers the sacrament for all his faithful.

The Eastern parochial vicar ordinarily does not have the faculty of blessing a marriage (CCEO c. 290 §2), but the pastor grants it to him (CCEO c. 302 §2); the Latin parochial vicar does not have this faculty *ipso iure*, but must be delegated by the pastor or the local Ordinary. It could be granted to him either by the diocesan statutes or by the letter of appointment of the diocesan Bishop (CIC c. 548).

III.5. The Formation of Clerics

Because it is for the Church to form its ministers (CIC c. 232; CCEO c. 328), it does so by means of the erection of seminaries:

CCEO	CIC
332 §2. A major seminary must be erected that serves either one very large eparchy or, if not a whole Church *sui iuris*, at least, by agreement, several eparchies of the same Church *sui iuris*, or even of different Churches *sui iuris* that have an eparchy in the same region or nation so that, whether by the appropriate number of students or the number of properly qualified moderators and teachers, as well as by sufficient material resources, and the best combined efforts, formation is provided for which nothing is left wanting.	237 §1. Where it is possible and expedient, there is to be a major seminary in every diocese; otherwise, the students who are preparing for the sacred ministries are to be entrusted to another seminary, or an inter-diocesan seminary is to be erected. §2. An inter-diocesan seminary is not to be erected unless the conference of bishops, if the seminary is for its entire territory, or the bishops involved have obtained the prior approval of the Apostolic See for both the erection of the seminary and its statutes.

CCEO (continued)

333. Even if it is preferable that a seminary, especially minor seminaries, be reserved to students of one Church *sui iuris*; on account of special circumstances, students of another Church *sui iuris* can be admitted into the same seminary.

334 §1. A seminary is erected by the eparchial bishop for his own eparchy; a seminary common to different eparchies is erected by the eparchial bishops of the same eparchies or by a higher authority, however, with the consent of the council of Hierarchs if it is the case of a metropolitan of a metropolitan Church *sui iuris* or with the consent of the synod of bishops of the patriarchal Church if it is the case of a patriarch.

The CCEO provides for the possibility of an eparchial major seminary or an inter-eparchial major seminary, but of the same Church *sui iuris*, or even a major seminary that serves different Churches *sui iuris* that have an eparchy in the same region or nation. The CIC provides the possibility of sending seminarians to a seminary of another diocese or even to an inter-diocesan seminary (regional, central or national) that serves several Latin dioceses,[60] without reference to other Churches *sui iuris*. Certainly the constitution of a major seminary in each diocese (eparchy) is preferable, since it better expresses the meaning of the particular Church. But it is necessary take cognizance of reality: the small number of candidates for the priesthood, the difficulty in finding suitable and prepared persons, the lack of financial resources, etc.

---

60 "Juridically, the inter-diocesan seminary is that which is erected through the initiative of several Bishops involved or the Bishops' conference, with the approval of the Apostolic See. If, therefore, several Bishops send their own students to a major seminary of a particular diocese, such a seminary remains 'diocesan,' subject to the proper authority of the local Bishop. In an inter-diocesan seminary, the management and operation are instead in the competence of all the Bishops involved, or of the entire Bishops' conference in the case of a national seminary": L. Chiappetta, *Il Codice di Diritto Canonico. Commento giuridico-pastorale*, 2nd ed. (Rome, 1996) 1:346, n. 1480.

CCEO c. 343 prescribes: "Students, even if admitted into a seminary of another Church *sui iuris* or into a common seminary for several Churches *sui iuris*, are to be formed in their own rite; any contrary custom being reprobated,"[61] so that

> [...] in the diversified ecclesial experiences, and by means of studies that present the historical, theological, juridical and spiritual patrimony of their own Churches of membership, the young Eastern faithful can appropriately find an educational environment suitable to develop the universal meaning of their dedication to Christ and the Church.[62]

A similar norm does not exist in the CIC, but this arrangement must also involve the Latin Church, because there are members of the Eastern faithful who study in Latin faculties, seminaries or theological institutes. This formation applies to all dimensions of the proper patrimony of the Eastern Churches: to the theological, spiritual and disciplinary dimension, but in an eminent way to the liturgical dimension because liturgy is the molder of Christian life and the most complete synthesis of its various aspects.[63] The plan of priestly formation should organize the basic courses about the Eastern Churches, their theological principles and their liturgical and spiritual traditions. This will help the students to understand the diversity that exists in the one Church of Christ and to create bonds of friendship that will also serve in future pastoral collaboration. Further, not only universal laws must be considered, but also appropriate adaption to the

---

61   CCEO c. 6: "With the entry into force of the Code:

"1° all common or particular laws contrary to the canons of the Code or which concern matters which are integrally reordered in this Code are abrogated;

"2° all customs reprobated by the canons of this Code or which are contrary to them, unless they are centennial or immemorial, are revoked."

62   Pontifical Work for Ecclesiastical Vocations. *Nuove vocazioni per una nuova Europa*, Documento finale del Congresso sulle Vocazioni al Sacerdozio e alla Vita Consecrata in Europa (Rome, 5-10 May 1997): Suppl.to *L'Osservatore Romano*, 28 January 1998, n. 21.

63   Cf. John Paul II, *Discorso ai partecipanti alla riunione sui problemi pastorali della Chiesa cattolica di rito bizantino in Romania*, 22 January 1994: *L'Osservatore Romano*, 22 January 1994, 5; *Id., Discorso ai Vescovi della Turchia*, 5 September 1994: *AAS* 87 (1995) 351; *Id.*, Ep Ap *Orientale Lumen*, 2 May 1995, n. 24: *AAS* 87 (1995) 771; Sacred Congregation for Seminaries and Universities, Litt *Quod catholicis hominibus*, de studiis Orientalium rerum et de catechesi in seminariis impensius excolendis, 28 August 1929: *AAS* 22 (1930) 146-148; Congregation for Catholic Education, *Circular Letter Concerning Studies of the Oriental Churches*, 6 January 1987: CLD 12:130-134; Instr. 71; OT 16; ED 76-78, 88.

CCEO c. 346 §2: "Those aspiring to the sacred ministry are to be formed in such a way that they learn to cultivate in the Holy Spirit an intimate familiarity with Christ and to seek God in all things so that, impelled by the love of Christ the Pastor, they become solicitous to gain all people for the kingdom of God by the gift of their very lives." Cf. CCEO cc. 369 §1 and 377.

particular circumstances of time and place, "so that the priestly training will always be in tune with the pastoral needs of those regions in which the ministry is to be exercised" (OT 1). The same conciliar decree recommends, among other things, the need for the study of the liturgical language proper to each rite (OT 13). John Paul II said:

> Also as regards priestly formation in general are to be recommended initiatives such as, for example, courses of information or study days, which promote greater knowledge of all that constitutes the legitimate "in unum conspirans varietas" of the ritual patrimony of the Catholic Church.[64]

Keeping in mind all that has been said, it would be beneficial to have in every Latin seminary a professor of Eastern discipline; further, the rectors of Latin seminaries must permit their Eastern seminarians to participate, at least on Sundays and feast days, in the liturgies of their own Churches, whenever they are in the locale. It would also be desirable to provide Eastern seminarians with facilities in the seminary for liturgical celebrations.

The plan of formation of clerics can be common to different Churches *sui iuris*, with the caveat that the character of the rites not be harmed (CCEO c. 330 §2), faithfully observing common law and keeping in mind the tradition of the proper Church *sui iuris* (CCEO cc. 40 §2 and 330 §3).[65]

In formation there is a need to form in the candidates concern and interest not only for the needs of their own particular Church, but also for those of the universal Church (PO 10);[66] they should be ready to dedicate themselves to the Churches that are particularly needy, ardently collaborating in evangelization (CCEO c. 593§1) and in the pastoral care of given groups of faithful:

---

64   John Paul II, *Discourse of Presentation of the Code of Canons of the Eastern Churches*, 25 October 1995: *Nunita* 31 (1990) 20: *Guide*, 27; cf. E. Cappellini, "Con il Codex Canonum Ecclesiarum Orientalium—Nuove prospettive didattiche per il Diritto Canonico," *L'Osservatore Romano*, 14 February 1991, 8.

65   On 2 May 1995, the Congregation for the Eastern Churches issued a decree concerning executive norms for an integrated program of formation for students of the Eastern Churches who frequent educational institutions not belonging to the Eastern Churches: *S.I.C.O.* 50-51 (1995-1996) 91-94.

66   "The text was revised, attentive especially to two comments submitted by Fathers in the Observations, namely: a) there should be a distribution of secular clergy not only for the different nations and regions of the world, but also for different social groups in the entire world, who for a particular reason require pastoral assistance, namely for certain special works of the apostolate to be exercised in any region of the world": *Acta Syn.* III/IV, 878.

CCEO	CIC
352 §3. Even though students are preparing themselves for the ministry in their own Church *sui iuris*, they are to be formed in a truly universal spirit by which they are internally prepared to respond in the service of souls everywhere in the world. Therefore, they are to be instructed about the needs of the entire Church and especially about the apostolate of ecumenism and evangelization.	257 §1. The instruction of students is to provide that they have solicitude not only for the particular church in whose service they are to be incardinated but also for the universal Church, and that they show themselves prepared to devote themselves to particular churches which are in grave need.

The work of promotion of vocations and the formation of clerics are the obligation of the entire Christian community, especially parents, educators, priests and pastors; but it is the principal obligation of the eparchial Bishop to animate his flock, joining forces with other Hierarchs for the promotion of vocations and the coordination of initiatives (CCEO c. 329 §1, 3°).

A norm of a pastoral character especially valid in those seminaries that receive students from other Churches *sui iuris* is the following:

> The rector is to send a report regarding the progress of the formation of the students each year to their respective eparchial bishop or, as the case may be, to their major superior; with regard to the status of the seminary, to those who erected it. (CCEO c. 356 §1)

III.6. Ascription or Incardination of Clerics[67]

Ascription or *incardination* is understood in the CIC to be the membership of a cleric in a particular Church or personal prelature,[68] or in an institute of consecrated life or a society of apostolic life that has the faculty to incardinate, in such a way that there are no clerics who are *acephali seu vagi* (c. 265). The CCEO does not have personal prelatures, but, beyond the eparchy, exarchy, religious institute and society of common life in the manner of religious, there is also the possibility of ascription in an institute or association that has obtained from

---

67 This section is to be read in conjunction with IV.8.
68 Secular jurisdictional structures of a personal character are designated as "personal prelatures," that is, not circumscribed according to the criterion of territoriality, and constitute an absolute innovation in the new CIC. They are quite distinct from "territorial prelatures" that constitute true and proper particular Churches, comparable to dioceses.

the Apostolic See the faculty to ascribe clerics (c. 357 §1);[69] the Patriarch and the Major Archbishop also have this faculty inside their territory with the consent of the permanent synod.[70]

Incardination is a determining element in the life and ministry of the priest, "which is not restricted to a purely juridical bond, but also involves a series of attitudes and spiritual and pastoral choices, which contribute to confer a specific physiognomy on the vocational image of the priest."[71] It is, therefore, not a simple bond of submission to the Bishop, but the incorporation into a particular Church to serve it and, through it, the *Ecclesia universa*.[72]

---

69   The CIC contemplated this during the codification process, but finally excluded it.

70   For the Armenian Church, there is the Patriarchal Institute of Bzommar. The first statutes date back to 18 April 1788. An examination of these statutes (cf. M. Terzian, *L'Institut Patriarcal de Bzommar*, Collection Bzommarienne, n. 1 [Bzommar, 1983]) reveals that the Patriarch himself and the Bishops are members of the convent, that is, religious who govern the religious priests bound to the patriarchal see that is identified with the monastery. The see and the monastery form one institute, which regulates the common life, stable and regular, under a well-determined authority, with the exercise of evangelical poverty, chastity and obedience. Thus, the Patriarch was the superior and the first member of the institute. In virtue of their vow of obedience to the Patriarch and his lawful successors, the members of the Institute of Bzommar were at the disposition of the Patriarch both in the monastery and in the dioceses and missions of the patriarchate. At the time of Gregory-Peter VIII (1843-1866) the series of local superiors of the monastery began, despite the permanent presence of the Patriarch at the convent. These local superiors ensured the observance of the internal rule redacted by Patriarch Gregory-Peter VIII, who constituted also a Chapter, improperly called a Chapter of Canons, as an auxiliary body of the permanent Synod of Bishops with a consultative voice. In 1888, Patriarch Stephan-Peter X constituted a council of the monastery with only a consultative voice to assist the local superior. This lasted until 1913, when the Institute of Bzommar obtained from the Holy See a new rule, which provided for a monastery council with a deliberative voice. This was retained in the rule of 1934 and subsequent rules. With the rule of 1976, the system of "patriarchal vicar for the Institute of Bzommar" was re-established, whereby the institute was endowed with broader jurisdiction within the limits of internal autonomy. By the decrees *Apostolica Sedes* (30 March 1908) and *Sacra Congregatio* (15 August 1934), the Institute of Bzommar is an institute of pontifical right for service of the Armenian patriarchate in all the dioceses and missions of the patriarchate itself (cf. M Terzian, *L'Institut Patriarcal de Bzommar,* 151-153.)

71   John Paul II, Ap Exh *Pastores dabo vobis*, March 25, 1992, n. 30: *AAS* 84 (1992) 657-804.

72   Congregation for Clergy, *Dives Ecclesiæ*, Directory on the Ministry and Life of Priests, 31 March 1994: "Therefore, the membership to a particular Church, through incardination, must not enclose the priest in a restricted and particularistic mentality, but rather should open him to the service of other Churches, because each Church is the particular realization of the only Church of Jesus Christ, such that the universal Church lives and fulfills her mission in and from the particular Churches in effective communion

Excardination means the cessation of membership of a cleric in a particular Church or institute of consecrated life, etc., not in an absolute manner, but to be incardinated in another particular Church or institute of consecrated life, etc.

There is a need to distinguish between the ascription of a candidate to orders to a Church *sui iuris* and the ascription (or incardination) to an eparchy (diocese). The first takes place by means of CCEO cc. 29-38 (CIC cc. 111-112), and the second takes place as follows.

Ascription or incardination as a cleric can be two-fold: original or derived. Original ascription is that which is acquired initially with the reception of diaconate or, according to the norm of particular law, another minor order (CCEO c. 358);[73] one who professes perpetual vows is ascribed definitively in the religious institute, but ascription as a cleric occurs with diaconal ordination; in clerical societies of the apostolic life in the manner of religious, it occurs with diaconal ordination, with due regard that the constitutions do not provide otherwise; in a secular institute, with diaconal ordination one is ascribed to the particular Church in whose service one was admitted, unless the Apostolic See or the Patriarch had not granted the right of ascription to the institute itself (CCEO c. 565; CIC 266 §3).

Derived ascription or incardination is that which is acquired afterwards; it can be two-fold:

1. *Formal*: that which takes place by means of two distinct acts: dismissal and ascription (a letter which releases in an absolute and complete form on the part of the Bishop *a quo*, and the letter of admission on the part of the Bishop *ad quem*);

2. *Ipso iure*: that which takes place by means of the disposition of the law:

    a. After five years, when a cleric who lawfully moves to another eparchy requests in writing from the Bishop *a quo* and the Bishop *ad quem* to be ascribed in the new eparchy and neither of the Bishops expresses a contrary intention within four months;

    b. When a secular cleric who has been admitted in a religious institute or society of apostolic life or in a society in the manner of religious makes perpetual vows;

---

with her. Thus, all the priests must have a missionary heart and mind and be open to the needs of the Church and of the world" (n. 14).

73   The canonical discipline of the Eastern Churches was not modified by the Mp *Ministeria quædam* of 15 August 1972 of Paul VI (*AAS* 64 [1972] 529-534), which exclusively treats the Latin Church, in which the minor orders were suppressed. Those who receive ministries instituted by the above-mentioned *motu proprio* are no longer considered clerics.

c. When a religious cleric, having obtained an indult to leave the religious institute, society of the apostolic life or society in the manner of religious, is accepted on a probationary basis in an eparchy, if he is not dismissed by the Bishop after a five-year period. The Eastern religious cleric will exercise his orders when he has found a Bishop who will ascribe him in his eparchy or at least receive him on a probationary basis. The Latin religious cleric will receive an indult of separation from the institute when he has found a Bishop who incardinates him or at least receives him on a probationary basis (CIC c. 693).

The proper diocese of the secular cleric is the one in which he is incardinated; his proper Bishop is that of the proper diocese; the Bishop he had in virtue of baptism is irrelevant. A cleric in a Church *sui iuris* can be ascribed in an eparchy (diocese) of another Church *sui iuris*, including the Latin Church (cf. CCEO c. 366 §1, 2°; CIC 269) without a change of rite in order to meet the needs of the entire Church (cf. OT 20).[74] For the change of rite, CCEO c. 32 is obviously applied,[75] that is, the consent of the Apostolic See, express or presumed, is required. Also, CCEO c. 36 is applied, that is, the declaration to assume the new rite is made before the Hierarch or pastor of the new Church or a priest delegated by one or the other in the presence of two witnesses; the pastor or the Hierarch will record the transfer in the baptismal register of the new parish and notify the pastor of the place of baptism that a change of rite occurred so that it will be recorded in the baptismal register. It is necessary to observe the procedure of CCEO c. 359 (dimissorial letter from his Bishop and a letter of ascription from the Bishop who receives him).[76] Thus, a Latin Bishop can ascribe in his diocese an Eastern cleric for service of the faithful who belong to the same Church *sui iuris* of the cleric and have a domicile in his diocese. In the same way, an Eastern Bishop can do so with regard to Latin faithful.

A cleric ascribed in a Church *sui iuris* different than that of his eparchial (diocesan) Bishop always remains ascribed in his own Church *sui iuris*, and there are certain consequences for the local Bishop.[77] But before being able to ascribe a cleric lawfully and definitively, the Bishop must consider the needs of or the usefulness for the diocese (eparchy), the aptitude and needs of the cleric, and inform the Bishop of origin:

---

74 The ascription of clerics to a particular Church is no longer as it was in the past, that is, *perpetua et absoluta*, even if there was explicit or implicit excardination or through religious profession; transfer from one diocese to another was discouraged: cf. CIC-17 cc. 112-117.
75 Cf. Appendix VII.
76 If particular law of a Church *sui iuris* so prescribes, for the licit transfer to the eparchy of another Church *sui iuris*, the eparchial Bishop who is releasing the cleric can be required obtain the consent of the authority determined by particular law (CCEO c. 365 §2). For example, in a patriarchal Church, it can be the Patriarch.
77 Cf. *Nuntia* 15 (1982) 45.

CCEO	CIC
366 §1. The eparchial bishop is not to ascribe an extern cleric to his eparchy unless:	269. A diocesan bishop is not to allow the incardination of a cleric unless:
1º the needs or advantage of the eparchy require it;	1° the necessity or advantage of his own particular church demands it, and without prejudice to the prescripts of the law concerning the decent support of clerics;
2º he is convinced that the cleric has the aptitude to carry out the ministry, especially if the cleric came from another Church *sui iuris*;	2° he is certain from a legitimate document that excardination has been granted and, in addition, has appropriate testimonials from the excardinating diocesan bishop, under secrecy if necessary, concerning the life, behavior, and studies of the cleric;
3º he is convinced by a legitimate document that the cleric has obtained legitimate dismissal from his eparchy; and he has obtained from the dismissing eparchial bishop, secretly if appropriate, suitable testimonials concerning the background and morals of the cleric;	3° the cleric has declared in writing to the same diocesan bishop that he wishes to be dedicated to the service of the new particular church according to the norm of law.
4º the cleric has declared in writing that he is devoting himself to service of the new eparchy in accord with the norm of law.	

With incardination, the cleric assumes the same rights and obligations of the other clerics of the diocese, as well as the possibility of participating in the various diocesan bodies, such as the episcopal council, which assists the Bishop in carrying out his fundamental pastoral obligations, the presbyteral council,[78] which assists the Bishop in the governance of the diocese, and the college of consultors, called to intervene in cases as indicated by the law. Further, he also has the right to receive some office, ministry or function (CCEO c. 371; CIC c. 274). If in the future an Eastern hierarchy is constituted in the Latin territory, what will be the canonical situation of the Eastern clerics incardinated in Latin dioceses? Salachas

---

78   Priests who are not incardinated in the diocese can also participate, provided that they have a domicile or quasi-domicile (CIC c. 498 and CCEO 267), but not those who have lost the clerical state or who have abandoned the exercise of sacred ministry; cf. G. Di Mattia, "I Consigli presbiterali: qualificazione e collocazione ecclesiologico-giuridica," *Ius in vita et in missione Ecclesiæ*, ed. Pontificium Concilium de Legum Textibus Interpretandis (Vatican City, 1994) 407-426; G. Sarzi Sartori, "Presbiterio e Consiglio presbiterale nelle fonti conciliari della disciplina canonica," *Quaderni di diritto ecclesiale* 8 (1995) 6-47; M. Rivella, "Le funzioni del Consiglio presbiterale," *ibid.*, 48-60; M. Marchesi, "Il Consiglio presbiterale: gruppo di sacerdoti, rappresentante di un presbiterio," *ibid.*, 61-71; P. Bianchi, "Gli statuti del Consiglio presbiterale," *ibid.*, 72-93.

states the following: "Obviously, [...], the Eastern clerics ascribed in a Latin diocese pass *ipso iure* to the respective Eastern hierarchy; therefore, in that territory, the Eastern faithful for whom the proper hierarchy was established cease to be subjects of the local Ordinary."[79] Instead, we hold that even in this case, it is necessary to follow the procedure provided by the codes: the letter of excardination of the Bishop *a quo* and a letter of incardination of the Bishop *ad quem*. "If the cleric comes from another Church *sui iuris*, the norm of CCEO c. 32, regulating ascription to a Church *sui iuris*, must also be observed."[80] This is not always the case because one can be incardinated in an eparchy of another Church *sui iuris* without transferring to another Church *sui iuris*. Another criterion for incardination might be this: the cleric will be incardinated in the new eparchy if the office he exercises is found in it; for other clerics, the new incardination is determined by the lawful domicile in the territory of the new eparchy. The problem does not arise if the canonical situation of the Eastern clerics is indicated explicitly in the document of the erection of the new eparchy.

The permission to move is not excardination and new incardination, but it is the permission to offer to serve in a diocese other than one's own; in this case, "the cleric represents his own Church as a witness and in a service of inter-ecclesial communion, and reaffirms the will and purpose to serve his own Church in the sister Church."[81] The cleric remains incardinated in his own diocese, and his obligations and rights ought to be established in a written agreement between his own Bishop and that of the diocese (eparchy) in which he is transferred (CIC c. 271; CCEO cc. 360 §1, 361 and 362). The agreement should contain, among other things, the length of service, the specific tasks of the priest and the place of ministry and residence, assistance he will receive and the one who is to give it

---

79   D. Salachas, "Lo stato giuridico delle minoranze di fedeli cattolici orientali nei territori della Chiesa latina," Seminario di storia delle istituzioni religiose e relazioni tra Stato e Chiesa, Università degli Studi di Firenze, Facoltà di Scienze Politiche "C. Alfieri," *Reprint Series No. 23* (Florence, 1997) 24. This is also affirmed in D. Salachas and L. Sabbarese, *Chierici e ministero sacro nel Codice latino e orientale. Prospettive interecclesiali* (Vatican City, 2004) 339 and 341. This is also supported by L. Sabbarese, *Girovaghi, migrani, forestieri e naviganti nella legislazione ecclesiastica* (Vatican City, 2006) 87-88.
80   D. Salachas and L. Sabbarese, *Chierici e ministero sacro nel Codice latino e oriental. Prospettive interecclesiali* (Vatican City, 2004) 106.
81   D. Mogavero, "I ministri sacri o chierici," in *Il diritto nel mistero della Chiesa*, 2nd ed., ed. Gruppo Italiano Docenti di Diritto Canonico (Rome, 1990) 2:112.

CCEO c. 393: "Clerics, whatever their condition, are to have in their heart a solicitude for all the Churches, and therefore manifest a disposition to be of service wherever there is an urgent need and especially to exercise, with the permission or encouragement of their own eparchial bishop or superior, their ministry in the missions or in regions suffering from a shortage of clerics."

to him, insurance for health, disability and old age, etc.[82] This permission can be given only for a determined period of time, even if it is renewable several times. In this case, while it is not incardination, the priests who exercise some office for the good of the diocese fully belong to the presbyterate of that diocese where "they have an active and passive voice in constituting the presbyteral council" (CIC c. 498 §1, 2°; CCEO c. 267 §1, 2°).[83] It would be opportune in the lands of emigration to facilitate the relocation of a number of Latin priests of Eastern origin in order for them to offer their services in the proper rite, at least partially, to their mother Churches which are so much in need.

Can the Latin Bishop ascribe in his diocese an Eastern married priest, or can he ordain one of his Eastern married subjects destined for an Eastern parish? We hold yes, with due regard for the special norms of the Apostolic See established for specific regions (cf. CCEO c. 758 §3).[84] In fact, if the ordination of married

---

[82] Sacred Congregation for Clergy, Notæ directivæ *Postquam Apostoli*, 25 March 1980: *AAS* 72 (1980) 343-364: CLD 9:760-787. See also Conferenza Episcopale Italiana, *Convenzione per il servizio pastorale in missione dei presbiteri diocesani*, in *Notiziario CEI* 2/1998, 66-72.

[83] See Congregation for Clerics, Directorium *Dives Ecclesiæ*, 31 March 1994, n. 26.

[84] The restrictive norms of the Apostolic See have existed since 1880, when thousands of Greek-Ruthenians emigrated to the United States together with their married clergy. The Latin Bishops protested against the exercise of ministry by married clergy among those faithful because of *gravissimum scandalum* for own Latin their faithful. For this reason, the Congregation for the Propagation of the Faith, with a decree of 1 October 1890, prohibited married Greek-Ruthenian priests from living in the United States. In 1913, the same Congregation decreed that in Canada, among the Eastern faithful, only celibates could be ordained priests.

The Sacred Congregation for the Eastern Churches established celibacy for the clergy of the diaspora with the Decr *Cum data fuerit* of 1 March 1929 (*AAS* 21 [1929] 152-159) for the Ruthenians and Ukrainians in the United States and the Decr *Græci-rutheni ritus* of 23 December 1930 (*AAS* 22 [1930] 346-354) for the Ukrainians-Ruthenians in Canada. With the Decr *Qua sollerti alacritate* of 24 May 1930, art. 6, it established that in America and in Australia, "secular priests who have wives shall not be admitted to exercise the sacred ministry in these countries, but only celibate priests or widowers. Widowers may, however, for just cause be excluded by this Sacred Congregation from those dioceses and places in which they may have children living or in any way present; and the same is true of the adjoining localities": *AAS* 22 (1930) 99-105, especially 102-103: CLD 1:20-21.

For the genesis of CCEO c. 758 §3, see R. Cholij, "An Eastern Catholic Married Clergy in North America: Recent Changes in Legal Status and Ecclesiological Perspective," *Studia Canonica* 31 (1997) 311-339, especially 319-323. The Synod of Bishops of the Melkite Greek-Catholic Church, assembled in Rabweh, Lebanon, from 21-26 July 1997, discussed the problem of married priests in the diaspora: "The Fathers consider that 'what is good for our faithful in the East cannot be bad for those in the West,' especially since one is dealing with a very ancient tradition [...]. They cannot give it up. They ardently

men is truly a part of the disciplinary patrimony of a specific Church *sui iuris* and if the entire Church must preserve and promote the rites of the Eastern Churches, how is it possible to prohibit the ordination of married men and the exercise of their functions in the diaspora?[85] Is the principle that *ex ministerio enim talis cleri uxorati inter latinos timetur scandalum et cum eo non minus detrimentum religionis et disciplinæ ecclesiaticæ* ("from the ministry of married clergy among the Latins there is the fear of scandal, and with it also harm to religion and ecclesiastical discipline") still valid?[86] We don't believe so, because converted Anglican priests with families were accepted into the Latin Church. To avoid misunderstanding, there should be an explicit intervention on the part of Apostolic See to abrogate the prohibition against sending married priests to the diaspora or ordaining married candidates. Certainly it will be necessary to insist on the proper preparation of married candidates to receive or exercise orders in the diaspora, a preparation that will also involve their wives; at the same time, in the Eastern territories, there should be an insistence on promoting vocations to the celibate priesthood, to avoid the reduction of eparchial priest candidates for the episcopate.[87]

---

propose a search for a common position on this question with all the other Eastern Catholic rites and even with the Latin Church in the diaspora. They note that blocking this issue does not serve our relations with the Orthodox, nor the good of our Church and nor even that of the universal Church" (*Le Lien* 62 [1997] fasc. 4, 31). The Australian Bishops Conference, in the session held 19-28 May 1998, abrogated motion n. 8 of 9 November 1949, in which the Australian episcopate had ordered that "only celibate clergy will be admitted to the exercise of ministry in Australia" (*Irénikon* 71 [1998] 380). On 1 September 1998, the Council of Hierarchs of the Catholic Church of Ruthenian rite in the United States decided that married Greek-Catholic priests can exercise the ministry in the Ukrainian-Ruthenian dioceses of North America (*Il Regno-attualità* [16 /1998] 526). On 4 March 1998, Cardinal Sodano, Secretary of State, sent a letter to the Apostolic Nuncio in Poland (published in *Chrétiens en marche*, n. 60, October-December 1998, 4); it deals with return to Ukraine of Ukrainian Catholic priests because they were married, who exercise their ministry in the region of Przemysl in southeastern Poland. After protests by the Ukrainian Church, Cardinal Sodano withdrew his decision, promising to examine the matter further.

85 Cf. R. Cholij, "Celibacy, Married Clergy, and the Oriental Code," in *Acta Symposii Internationalis circa Codicem Canonum Ecclesiarum Orientalium, USEK, 24-29 aprilis 1995*, eds. Al-Ahmar, A. Khalife and D. Le Tourneau (Lebanon, 1996) 179-202.

86 A. Petrani, *De relatione…*, 48.

87 The *quæstio disputata* today is if, after Vatican II and the promulgation of the CCEO, these three prohibitive decrees are still in force or if they have been abolished. Some authors respond *affirmative*, that is, they consider that they were abolished, while others are doubtful on the permanence of the prohibition. The doubt was proposed to the Congregation for the Eastern Churches, which responded that the prohibition is still in force. Cf. R. Cholij, "An Eastern Catholic Married Clergy in North America: Recent Changes in Legal Status and Ecclesiological Perspective," *Studia Canonica* 31 (1997) 331-339; N. R. A. Rachford, "Norms of Particular Law for the Byzantine Metropolitan Church *sui iuris* of Pittsburgh, USA," *CLSA Proceedings* 62 (2000) 233-243; G. Nedungatt, "Clerics (cc. 323-398)," in *Guide*, 303. G. Nedungatt, in referring to this response of the Congregation, states:

Let us pose another case. A Latin married permanent deacon asks to transfer to an Eastern Church *sui iuris*, to be ascribed in an eparchy and to be eventually ordained a priest. Along with the letters of excardination and incardination, the consent of the Apostolic See will be needed to give permission for the transfer and biritualism, but quite probably with the clause *excepta sacrorum Ordinum receptione*, a clause which at a later time, on the request of the proper Hierarch, will be able to be eliminated.

The Bishop must consider the following canons for the ordination of a candidate to sacred orders who does not belong to the same Church *sui iuris*:

CCEO	**CIC**
747. A candidate to the diaconate or presbyterate should be ordained by his own eparchial bishop or by another bishop with legitimate dimissorial letters.	1015 §1. Each person is to be ordained to the presbyterate or the diaconate by his proper bishop or with legitimate dimissorial letters from him.
748 §2. An eparchial bishop cannot ordain a candidate subject to him who is ascribed to another Church *sui iuris* without the permission of the Apostolic See; if, however, it is a case of a candidate who is ascribed to a patriarchal Church and has a domicile or quasi-domicile within the territorial boundaries of the same Church, the patriarch can also grant this permission.	§2. If not impeded by a just cause, the proper bishop is to ordain his own subjects personally; without an apostolic indult, however, he cannot ordain licitly a subject of an Eastern rite.

The permission of the Apostolic See or, in certain cases, of the Patriarch / Major Archbishop, to ordain a cleric ascribed to another Church *sui iuris* affects only the liceity of the celebration of the ordination and "more appropriately refers to the case in which the celebration takes place in a liturgical rite different from that of the one to which the candidate belongs, or when the ordaining eparchial Bishop asks permission to celebrate the ordination in the rite of the candidate."[88]

To challenge the validity of sacred ordination pertains, beyond to the cleric himself, also to the Hierarch to whom the cleric is subject or in whose eparchy he was ordained (CCEO c. 1385; CIC c. 1708).

"But this reply is widely ignored in practice, and a new custom is developing which does not regard that the Eastern discipline of married clergy is applicable only within territorial limits" (*Guide*, 303).
88   Instr. 77.

III.7. Episcopal Conferences

The episcopal conference[89] is a permanent Latin institute that gathers the Bishops of a given nation or a given territory, who collegially exercise some pastoral functions for the benefit of the faithful of that territory (CIC c. 447). Once erected, it enjoys its own juridic personality (CIC c. 449 §2), that is, it is the subject of rights and obligations.[90] These rights and obligations are of a pastoral character, *quædam pastoralia munera* (cf. CIC c. 447); the episcopal conference has limits with respect to the Holy See and the individual diocesan Bishop. With respect to the Holy See, the episcopal conference must act in its specific field *ad normam iuris*, that is, only within the limits of its competence, observing the general norms of the Holy See and availing itself of the particular indults granted by the Holy See (cf. CIC c. 455 §1). With respect to the diocesan Bishop, it must respect fully the rights of the Bishop, except if all the Bishops of the episcopal conference granted the episcopal conference the faculty to intervene in individual cases.[91] It is a body that embraces a territory or a nation, but does not have a proper territory, that is, erected as such; it is a territorial unity distinct from dioceses or as one conceives a province or ecclesiastical region. "It is of no concern that the conference of Bishops be an expression of a particular territory; the sphere of activity of each individual conference is given by the corresponding circumscriptions of the particular dioceses that comprise the same conference."[92]

The actions of the Episcopal Conference in Italy (CEI) generally take the form of decrees; for example, decrees concerning Italian typical editions of the new li-

---

89   There are currently more than 100 episcopal conferences in addition to 10 international assemblies of episcopal conferences and, always at the continental level, the Conseil des Patriarches Catholiques d'Orient (C.P.C.O), the Consilium Conferentiarum Episcoporum Europæ (C.C.E.E.), the Consejo Episcopal Latinoamericano (C.E.L.A.M.), the Secretariado episcopal de América central y Panamá (S.E.D.A.C.), the Commissio Episcopatum Communitatis Europensis (COM.E.C.E.): *Annuario Pontificio 2012* (Vatican City, 2012) 1076-1093 and 1096-1099.

For an updated bibliography, see F. Guillemette, *Théologie des conferences épiscopales. Une herméneutique de Vatican II*, Collection Brèches théologiques 21 (Montreal - Paris, 1994). For the history and activity of the CEI, see ECEI 1:17-34; 2:19-36; 3:xiii-xxviii; 4:xvii-xxvii; A Ricciardi, "La CEI nel postconcilio," *Communio* 149 (1996) 15-29; S. Gaeta, "Cronologia della CEI (1952-1996)," *Communio* 149 (1996) 85-94.
90   Cf. G. Ghirlanda, "Conferenza dei Vescovi," in *Nuovo Dizionario di Diritto Canonico*, eds. C.C. Salvador, V. De Paolis and G. Ghirlanda (Cinisello Balsamo, 1993) 252-257; L. Bianco, "Conferenza Episcopale Italiana," *ibid.*, 257-261 with an extensive bibliography; L. Chiappetta, *Prontuario di diritto Canonico e Concordatario* (Rome, 1994) 295-300.
91   Cf. John Paul II, Mp *Apostolos Suos*, on the theological and juridical nature of episcopal conferences, 21 May 1998: Suppl. to *L'Osservatore Romano*, 24 July 1998.
92   *Comm.* 12 (1980) 248.

turgical books (some enriched with new *prefaces*[93]) and concerning the decisions in liturgical matters in the implementation of the new CIC. Among the latter we recall those that refer to the obligation of the Liturgy of the Hours for permanent deacons, the age for confirmation and marriage, the age and qualities of lay candidates for ministries, the place for confessions, the *mensa* for a fixed altar.[94] Other actions of the CEI were issued under the form of an instruction, document and pastoral note, decision, disposition, clarification, communication or norm.

CD 38, with the aim of promoting the organic collaboration of the Bishops of a predominant rite in a given territory with the hierarchy of the ritual minorities present, provided that all the local ordinaries of each rite participate with equal rights.[95] During the revision process of the CIC, consideration was given to the fact that the conferences of Bishops concern only the Latin Church, especially since they enjoy legislative powers in matters such as liturgy, regulated by specific norms in the individual rites.[96]

The CIC limits to Latin Bishops (or their equivalents) the full participation in the episcopal conferences (CIC cc. 450 §1 and 454), leaving to the statutes of the conference itself to determine the participation of the ordinaries of another rite.[97] The CIC does this for three reasons: circumstances are very different in the various regions; the presence of an Ordinary of another rite in a conference of Bishops does not create difficulty in the formulation of norms that affect only the Latin Church, as this occurs also in ecumenical councils; finally, in order to observe the norms of Vatican II. The exclusion of Eastern Bishops from the episcopal conferences could have negative consequences in a given country. Often there are common problems with should be dealt with by all the Bishops of the country through a frank discussion and possible collaboration.

---

93   Cf. *I Prænotanda dei nuovi testi liturgici*, ed. A. Donghi (Milan, 1989).
94   ECEI 3:914-915, 1316, 1318-1320.
95   "Members of the episcopal conference are all local Ordinaries of every rite – excluding vicar generals – and coadjutors, auxiliaries and other titular bishops who perform a special work entrusted to them by the Apostolic See or the episcopal conferences": CD 38.
96   *Comm.*12 (1980) 265: "Some consultors do not accept that a deliberative vote be conceded to Ordinaries of other rites for the following reasons:

    a) The episcopal conference is a hierarchical instance with a legislative function; it is not logical that Ordinaries of another rite have a deliberative vote;

    b) For common pastoral problems, special meetings or assemblies are provided in which the concerned Ordinaries of the various rites in the same territory can participate."
97   Making the participation of the Ordinaries of another rite optional is intended to safeguard the autonomy of their Churches. For the institutional and juridical foundations of this disposition, see P. Erdö, "La participation des Évêques orientaux à la Conférence épiscopale," *Apollinaris* 64 (1991) 295-301.

The statutes of the conference of Bishops can provide for certain possible solutions:

1. Say nothing regarding the participation of the Eastern Bishops and thus, conforming to CIC c. 450 §1, the Eastern Hierarchs will be invited to the sessions without having a deliberative vote;

2. They can contain an invitation expressly directed to the Eastern Hierarchs with a general character, without according them a deliberative vote;

3. They can contain a permanent invitation that implies the concession of the deliberative vote;

4. They can contain the possibility of a simple invitation, reserving to the invited persons the right of a deliberative vote;

5. They can authorize (when the Apostolic See confirms it) the plenary assembly to concede, when necessary, a deliberative vote. [98]

Let us examine the statutes of the CEI to see what they say regarding the Eastern Hierarchs.

The first statute of the CEI dating from 1 August 1954 states, "The Italian Episcopal Conference (CEI) is the assembly of Archbishops and Bishops of Italy, presidents of regional conferences, representing the Ordinaries of their respective regions (I, 1).[99] The statue of 16 December 1965, art. 2 states: "The following are members by right of the CEI with a deliberative vote: Archbishops and residential Bishops […]."[100] The statute of the CEI of 8 May 1971, confirmed by art. 1 of the Bylaws of 15 December 1974, states: "The following are members by right of the CEI with a deliberative vote according to the norm of common law or by the present statute: Archbishops and diocesan Bishops *of any rite* and those having personal jurisdiction […]."[101] The statue of 19 November 1977, art. 4 states: "The following are members by right of the CEI with a deliberative vote: a) according to the norm of common law: the Cardinal Vicar of His Holiness for the City of Rome, the diocesan Archbishops and Bishops *of any rite*."[102] Art. 1 of the Bylaws of 30 June 1978 confirms the statute.[103] After the 1983 CIC acquired the force of law, art. 7 of the new statute of 18 April 1985 states: "The following are members by right of the CEI with a deliberative

---

98 Cf. P. Erdö, "La participation…," 304-305.
99 ECEI 1:77.
100 ECEI 1:509.
101 ECEI 1:3715, 2:1700.
102 ECEI 2:2908.
103 ECEI 2:3066.

vote [...]: a) diocesan Bishops of the territory."[104] This was taken up again by the Bylaws of 28 May 1985, art. 1.[105] Are the Eastern Bishops also included? In a later Statute of the CEI, definitively approved by the Congregation for Bishops with the decree of 25 March 1985, Prot. N. 1029/53 and no longer *ad experimentum*,[106] there is a derogation of CIC c. 450 §1, by which there is granted "also to the local ordinaries *of another rite* membership with full right" to the CEI. In the Statute promulgated on 19 October 1998,[107] participation with full right was provided to the ordinaries of another rite. Lastly, in the Statute promulgated 1 September 2000, art. 6 counts "the Ordinaries of another rite" as included among the members of the CEI, as is also stated in the Bylaws, art. 5.[108] One is dealing with the two ordinaries of the eparchies of the Italo-Albanians, Lungo (Cosenza, erected with the Apcon *Catholici fideles* of 13 February 1919)[109] and Piana degli Albanesi (Palermo, erected with the Apcon *Sedes Apostolica* of 26 October 1937),[110] as well as the Exarchial Abbey of Grottaferrata (Rome, erected with the Apcon *Pervetustum Crytæferatæ Cœnobium* of 26 September 1937).[111]

Where there is a significant presence of Eastern faithful in a Latin territory, it would be appropriate to create, as a part of every episcopal conference, a Committee for Eastern Churches with the mandate to study pastoral, liturgical, canonical or other problems. This fraternal cooperation will offer valuable assistance to the Eastern Churches and at the same time will permit the Latin particular Churches to be enriched with the spiritual patrimony of the Eastern Christian tradition.

The juridic structure of the Eastern Churches does not include episcopal conferences, "which appear to close the individual Churches *sui iuris* in on

---

104   CEEI 3:2311.
105   ECEI 3:2517.
106   *Notiziario CEI* 3/1985, 65: "[...] Furthermore, the same Supreme Pontiff, derogating from the norm of CIC c. 450 §1, grants that local Ordinaries of another rite also pertain to the said conference of Bishops."
107   Cf. *Notiziario CEI* 9/1998, arts. 6 and 7 §2. See J. Faris, *Eastern Catholic Churches, Constitution and Governance, According to the Code of Canons of the Eastern Churches* (New York, 1992) 642: "In the United States, the Eastern Catholic bishops participate in the National Conference of Catholic Bishops / United States Catholic Conference and enjoy a deliberative vote in all matters excluding those that affect only the Latin Church (cfr. 83 CIC c. 450, §1)."
108   ECEI 6:3072, 3150.
109   "To the Diocese of Lungro, we attribute and assign perpetually the following parishes with all the faithful of both the Greek rite and the Latin rite (if there are any) who inhabit them; and we divide and separate them from the Latin dioceses to which they belong": Benedict XV, Apcon *Catholici fideles,* 13 February 1919: *AAS* 11 (1919) 222-226, especially 224.
110   *AAS* 30 (1938) 213-216.
111   *AAS* 30 (1938) 183-186.

themselves."[112] Some canonists have attempted to compare the episcopal conferences to the synods of Bishops of the patriarchal Churches,[113] but this seems to be hazardous since the two institutions are similar only inasmuch as they are composed exclusively of Bishops. In fact, as opposed to the episcopal conferences, the synods of Bishops of the patriarchal Churches can, for their respective patriarchal Churches, enact laws that have the force of law in virtue of CCEO c. 150 §§2 and 3 (c. 110 §1); further, the same synod is a tribunal according to CCEO c. 1062 §2, and elects the Patriarch, Bishops and candidates for office mentioned in CCEO c. 149 §3. As such, administrative acts are not within the competency of the Synod of Bishops of the patriarchal Church, with due regard for those specific acts for which the Patriarch has determined otherwise or the common law established otherwise (CCEO c. 110 §4). The same Mp *Apostolos suos*, on the theological and juridic nature of the conferences of Bishops, emphasizes that one cannot make an analogy between them and the Synod of Bishops of the patriarchal or major archiepiscopal Church.[114] We can say only that the synods of the patriarchal Churches are in a certain sense the *analogatum princeps* (cf. LG 23d) of the episcopal conferences.[115]

III.8. Eastern Synods

The Synod of Bishops gathers all the Bishops of a specific patriarchal or major archiepiscopal Church, including those constituted outside the territorial boundaries. It has legislative and judicial power; it is convoked to elect the Patriarch / Major Archbishop and Bishops constituted inside the patriarchal territory, and any other time there is the need. In the metropolitan Churches *sui iuris*, the assembly that gathers all the Bishops of the same Church constituted anywhere is called the Council of Hierarchs.

Speaking of the Synod of Bishops of the patriarchal Church, CCEO c. 102 §3 states:

> To expedite certain matters, according to the norm of particular law or with the consent of the permanent synod, others can be invited by the patriarch, especially Hierarchs who are not bishops and experts to give their opinions to the bishops gathered in the synod with due regard for can. 66, §2.

---

112 M. Brogi, "Commento agli Statuti dell'Assemblea degli Ordinari cattolici di Terra Santa," *Ius Ecclesiæ* 6 (1994) 842.
113 Cf. U. Betti, *La dottrina sull'episcopato nel capitolo II della costituzione dommatica Lumen Gentium* (Rome, 1968) 390.
114 John Paul II, Mp *Apostolos suos*, 21 May 1998, note 1: Suppl. to *L'Osservatore Romano*, 24 July 1998.
115 Cf. G. P. Montini, "Le Conferenze episcopali e i Sinodi delle Chiese orientali," *Quaderni di diritto ecclesiale* 9 (1996) 433-448.

The canon, without making any distinction, recognizes the possibility of also inviting Latin ordinaries to the Synod of Bishops of the patriarchal Church, in order to hear their opinions. This can be determined either by particular law or by the Patriarch with the consent of the permanent synod. This provision differs from preceding legislation found in CS c. 340 §3, which required the permission of the Roman Pontiff for Hierarchs *plurium rituum*: "Bishops and other Hierarchs of several rites can convene in a synod after they have obtained the permission of the Roman Pontiff, who designates the place where the synod shall meet, and appoints his legate who is to call together and preside over the synod." It is almost a customary practice in some patriarchal Churches to invite the superiors general of religious orders and sometimes representatives of the clergy.[116] CCEO c. 102 §3 has origins in the Council:

> Prelates of the various individual Churches who have jurisdiction in the same territory should meet at regular intervals for consultation, and thus foster unity of action and strive together to meet their common tasks, so as better to further the good of religion and to safeguard more effectively the discipline of the clergy. (OE 4)

> It is earnestly recommended to prelates of the Eastern Churches that when engaged in the improvement of morals in their own Church and the promotion of activities beneficial to religion, they should take into consideration the common good of the whole of a region in which there happen to be Churches of different rites. (CD 38)

Other canons of the CCEO take the same approach:

> All and only the ordained bishops of the metropolitan Churches *sui iuris*, wherever they are constituted, must be called to the council of Hierarchs, except those mentioned in can. 953, §1 or those who have been punished with the canonical penalties mentioned in cann. 1433 and 1434. Bishops of another Church *sui iuris* can be invited as guests only if the majority of the members of the council of Hierarchs agrees. (c. 164 §1)

> The eparchial bishops of several Churches *sui iuris* exercising power in the same territory are to ensure that through the exchange of views in periodic meetings, they foster unity of action and, by combined resources, help advance common works more readily to promote of the good of religion and more effectively safeguard ecclesiastical discipline. (c. 202)

---

116   Cf. D. Salachas, *Istituzioni di diritto canonico delle Chiese cattoliche orientali* (Rome-Bologna, 1993) 174.

While not found explicitly in the CIC, given its importance and since it is by invitation only, this provision involves the Latin Bishops. The Council of Hierarchs is similar to the episcopal conference of the Latin law, even if the competency of the Council of Hierarchs, as a legislative body of the metropolitan Church *sui iuris*, is greater.[117]

II.9. Patriarchal and Eparchial Assembly

The patriarchal assembly is a consultative assembly of the entire Church presided over by the Patriarch and offers its own collaboration to the Patriarch and to the synod of the patriarchal Church. The same applies for the major archiepiscopal and metropolitan Churches *sui iuris* (CCEO cc. 152 and 172). There is also in every eparchy the eparchial assembly, which helps the Bishop in those matters that concern the special needs or advantage of the eparchy (CCEO c. 235).[118]

These assemblies serve to promote a unity of action for the benefit of religion, to protect more effectively ecclesiastical discipline and to foster the unity of all Christians (CCEO c. 84 §1). To these assemblies must also be convoked some superiors of institutes of consecrated life (CCEO cc. 143 §1, 3° and 238 §1, 9°), rectors of Catholic universities and of ecclesiastical universities and deans of the faculties of theology and of canon law found in the territories of the Church in which the assembly is held (CCEO c. 143 §1, 4°); among such persons can be faithful of the Latin Church who carry out these tasks.[119] Persons from other Churches *sui iuris*, including the Latin Church, can be invited and granted the right to vote:[120]

> Persons of another Church *sui iuris* can be invited to the patriarchal assembly and can take part in it according to the norm of the statutes. (CCEO c. 143 §3)

---

117   Cf. *Nuntia* 19 (1984) 14.
118   An exhaustive presentation on the eparchial assembly is given by D. Salachas, "L'istituzione ecclesiale dell''assemblea eparchiale' nel diritto delle Chiese orientali," *Apollinaris* 61 (1988) 861-877.
119   According to J. Faris, the right of these persons to participate in the assembly is based on the presumption that they are members of the Church that is involved; otherwise, they can be invited as members of another Church *sui iuris* and their participation will be determined by the statutes of the assembly: J. Faris, *Eastern...*, 346.
120   Certain reservations were raised regarding the participation of other persons belonging to other Churches *sui iuris*, but they were not accepted because it is a case of consultative votes and the concession of such a right is entrusted to the discretion of the eparchial Bishop: *Nuntia* 23 (1986) 53. In the decree of the convocation of the first Eparchial Assembly of Lungro (22 June 1994) it is stated: "According to the sacred canons, other participants considered qualified and beneficial for the work of the assembly from other Churches *sui iuris*, including the Latin Church, will be invited": Eparchia di Lungro degli Italo-Albanesi dell'Italia Meridionale, *Dichiarazioni e decisioni della I^a Assemblea Eparchiale 1995-1996* (Lungro, 1997) 202.

The eparchial bishop, if he judges it opportune, can invite to the eparchial assembly others also, not excluding persons of other Churches *sui iuris*, to all of whom he can even grant the right to vote. (CCEO c. 238 §2)

The CIC, while not making explicit reference to the Eastern Churches, deals with them in relation to the diocesan synod: "The diocesan Bishop can also call others to a diocesan synod as members of the synod; they can be clerics, members of institutes of consecrated life, or lay members of the Christian faithful" (CIC c. 463 §2). Among the members by law are the episcopal vicars, members of the presbyteral council, priests representing each vicariate, religious superiors, lay persons and representatives of the associations of the faithful.[121]

The diocesan synod is the assembly that gathers and involves equally all the components of the particular Church with their specific ministers: the Bishop, who convokes and presides at the synod; clerics, religious and laity, as they are called to offer their work by reason of their competence with opinions and counsels. The areas in which the synod can intervene are very vast and varied, which go from the accommodation of universal laws, to the elaboration of pastoral methodologies, to the solution of problems concerning the apostolate and governance of the diocese, to the proposal of activities that involve the diocesan community and the examination and correction of any errors in matters of faith and morals. In the diocesan synod, the diocesan Bishop becomes the promoter of normative renewal and the center of unity of the involvement of all the faithful who, in a manner proportionate to the knowledge, competence and prestige that they enjoy, have the right or at times even the obligation of manifesting their opinions to their pastors (CIC c. 212 §3 and CCEO c. 15 §3).

The norms regarding the diocesan (eparchial) pastoral council, which has the task of studying and examining pastoral activity and proposing practical conclusions in order to promote conformity of life and of action of the People of God with the Gospel (CIC c. 511; CCEO c. 272),[122] emphasize inter-ecclesial collaboration; indeed, "it is strongly recommended that, where possible, the pastoral council should be inter-ritual, that is, consisting of clerics, religious and laity of the different rites."[123] This recommendation became the norm of CCEO c. 273

---

121 For the preparation, execution and post-synodal legislation, see J. Beyer, "De synodo diœcesana," *Periodica* 81 (1992) 381-423.

122 The pastoral council has as its object the same care of the diocese that is entrusted to the presbyteral council, but primarily touches that part of the concern for the good of the diocese that consists in the study of the pastoral problems, while the presbyteral council examines them from the perspective of the decisions taken by the Bishop.

123 Paul VI, Mp *Ecclesiæ Sanctæ*, 6 August 1966: *AAS* 58 (1966) 57-787; Id., *Normæ ad exsequenda decreta SS. Concilii Vaticani II 'Christus Dominus' et 'Prebyterorum Ordinis'*, art. 16 §5: Flannery, 601.

§3: "Along with these Christian faithful, if it is opportune, the eparchial Bishop can also invite others to the pastoral council, even if they are of another Church *sui iuris*."

III.10. Inter-ecclesial Assemblies

The inter-ecclesial assembly (other names are also used, even "episcopal conferences," creating a certain confusion)[124] is a periodic meeting in which the Patriarchs, Metropolitans of the metropolitan Churches *sui iuris*, eparchial Bishops and, if the statutes so provide, all the local Hierarchs of the various Churches *sui iuris*, even the Latin Church, that exercise their power in the same nation or region, as well as priests and lay persons participate:[125]

> Where it seems advisable in the judgment of the Apostolic See, periodic assemblies are to be held of patriarchs, metropolitans of metropolitan Churches *sui iuris*, eparchial bishops, and, if the statutes so state, other local Hierarchs of various Churches *sui iuris*, even of the Latin Church, exercising their authority in the same nation or region. These assemblies are to be convoked at regular intervals by the patriarch or another authority designated by the Apostolic See. The purpose of these meetings is that, by sharing the insights of wisdom born of experience and by the exchange of views, the pooling of their resources is achieved for the common good of the churches, so that unity of action is fostered, common works are facilitated, the good of religion is more readily promoted and ecclesiastical discipline is preserved more effectively. (CCEO c. 322 §1)[126]

These assemblies are similar to episcopal conferences, at least at an institutional level: although these assemblies do not properly possess the legislative power of episcopal conferences, nevertheless they possess the animating and coordinating

---

124 According to the *Annuario Pontificio 2012* (Vatican City, 2012) 1094-1095, they are: Assemblea della Gerarchia Cattolica d'Egitto; Assemblea dei Patriarchi e dei Vescovi Cattolici nel Libano; Assemblea della Gerarchia Cattolica in Siria; Assemblea degli Ordinari Cattolici di Terra Santa; Riunione Interrituale dei Vescovi dell'Iraq; Conferenza Episcopale Iraniana.
125 Cf. *Comm.* 13 (1981) 77; CS c. 4.
126 The canon (like others, e.g., cc. 84, 99 §2 and 202) completes the exhortations and prescriptions of the CCEO to Patriarchs and eparchial Bishops in the meetings with Hierarchs of other Churches *sui iuris* who exercise power in the same territory. The prior legislation stated: "Local Hierarchs who exercise jurisdiction in the same territory shall in mutual agreement promote unity of action among the clergy of various Rites, and they shall by concerted efforts work toward common goals, in order to advance more expeditiously the good of religion and to insure with better efficiency the discipline of the clergy" (CS c. 4).

functions of the episcopal conferences.[127] The decisions of these assemblies can have obligatory force whenever they do not prejudice the rite of each Church *sui iuris* or the power of the Hierarchs and their *cœtus*, are accepted by two-thirds of the members and are approved by the Apostolic See (CCEO c. 322 §2).

The purpose of these assemblies, whose institution is reserved to the Apostolic See, is to coordinate the Gospel witness and service to the community, to study together the problems of the region, to foster the exchange of information and common experiences, to establish common pastoral activity for the benefit of the entire Church, to promote initiatives and collective actions so that the welfare, promotion and defense of religion and its rights be better achieved and so that the proper observance of ecclesiastical discipline might be more easily promoted.[128] The sectors of competence are not specified, but they can easily be deduced: relations with the State or with non-Catholic Christians (cf. CCEO c. 904); inter-religious dialogue; problems regarding universities or centers of study; the press and social media; catechetical programs; the erection and approval of associations of the faithful in a national or inter-ecclesial context; strengthening the bond between the faithful of the diaspora and their Churches; promoting justice, peace, development, respect for human rights, especially those of women and families, etc.[129] This structure of ecclesial collaboration

> does not constitute a holy synod (proper to the patriarchal Churches) nor an episcopal conference (proper to the Churches of the Latin tradition) but a practical and flexible arrangement that enables the Churches that participate in it to respond together to common problems at a national level.[130]

These inter-ecclesial assemblies, once constituted, preserve and promote the same meaning of the faith in the various Churches in such a way that they do not bring harm to the integrity and unity of the faith, but put in a better light the catholicity of the Church through legitimate diversity (cf. CCEO c. 604).

---

127   Cf. *Nuntia* 23 (1986) 103; the Mp *Apostolos Suos*, on the theological and juridical nature of the conferences of Bishops, 21 May 1996: Suppl. to *L'Osservatore Romano*, 24 July 2998, in note 1 states that the document treats the assemblies constituted in regions where there are several Churches *sui iuris* and governed by CCEO c. 322 and the respective Statutes approved by the Apostolic See, to the degree that they approximate episcopal conferences.
128   Cf. Assemblea degli Ordinari Cattolici di Terra Santa, *Statuti*, 9 December 1991, in *Ius Ecclesiæ* 6 (1994) 832-836; M. Brogi, "Sinodi Patriarcali, Assemblee e Conferenze Episcopali di rito orientale," *Antonianum* 51 (1976) 256-265; John Paul II ,Ep Ap *Orientale Lumen*, 2 May 1995, n. 26: *AAS* 87 (1995) 772-773.
129   Cf. "Règlement intérieur du Conseil des Patriarches catholiques d' Oriente," *Le Lien* 61 (1996/2) 44-48.
130   *Lettera pastorale del Consiglio dei Patriarchi cattolici d'Oriente (CPCO)*, Christmas 1996, n. 46: *Il Regno-documenti* 11/1997, 371.

III.11. Eastern Hierarchs and the College of Cardinals

The College of Cardinals is an institution of ecclesiastical law not directly found in the CCEO. CIC Book II, Part II, Section I, Chapter III, cc. 349-359 is specifically dedicated to this institution. It has its origins in the group of deacons, priests and Bishops who, during the first millennium, assisted the Bishop of Rome in the pastoral governance of the Church: "[...] the title of *clericus cardinalis* or simply *cardinalis* [...] cannot, at least for now, be substantiated by normative texts prior to the end of the thirteenth century."[131]

The primary role of the College of Cardinals is the election of the Roman Pontiff. The cardinals also assist the Roman Pontiff in the governance of the universal Church, either collegially or individually. This College comprises three orders: the episcopal order, the presbyteral order and the diaconal order. The participation of Eastern Hierarchs in the College of Cardinals is of a relatively recent time.[132] Eastern Patriarchs who are included in the College of Cardinals are part of the episcopal order, differing however in that while the other cardinal Bishops have the title of a suburbicarian Church, the Patriarchs have as a title their own patriarchal see (CIC c. 350 3); this was the intention of Paul VI with the Mp *Ad purpuratorum patrum* of 11 February 1965, establishing also that they are preceded only by the suburbicarian cardinal Bishops.[133] All other Eastern Hierarchs receive the title of a titular Roman Church.

In the consistory of 21 February 2001, the Major Archbishops of the Ukrainian Church and the Syro-Malabar Church were created cardinals; they received the title of Santa Sofia a Via Boccea and S. Bernardo alle Terme. CCEO c. 152 equates Major Archbishops to Patriarchs "unless the common law expressly provides otherwise or it is evident from the nature of the matter." Could not the provision for cardinal Patriarchs also be applied to the cardinal Major Archbishops?

It would be appropriate on the part of the Apostolic See to modify the norms of precedence of the cardinals: the Eastern Patriarchs, different than the other cardinals, are fathers and heads of their respective Churches, exercising a true ordinary, proper and personal power according to the norm of law over faithful, clergy, religious, Bishops and Metropolitans of their respective Churches. The same can be said about Major Archbishops. Likewise, Metropolitans, placed as heads of a metropolitan Church *sui iuris*, enjoy ordinary, proper and personal su-

---

131   M. Miele, "I Patriarchi orientali nel Collegio Cardinalizio," in *Studi sul Codex Canonum Ecclesiarum Orientalium*, ed. S. Gherro (Padua, 1994) 119-138, especially 120-121.
132   The exceptions are Bassaron of Nicæa and Isidore of Kiev, created after the Council of Florence; there would not be others until the second half of the nineteenth century.
133   *AAS* 57 (1965) 295-296. The suburbicarian Churches are: Ostia, Albano, Frascati, Palestrina, Porto-Santa Rufina, Sabina-Poggio Mirteto and Velletri-Segni.

per-episcopal power, different than the Metropolitans who are heads of an Eastern or Latin ecclesiastical province. It should be established that the Patriarchs of the Eastern Churches have precedence in the entire world over cardinals and Bishops of any degree. They should be followed by the Major Archbishops and, immediately after, the Metropolitans who preside over a metropolitan Church *sui iuris*.

Regarding the correctness of including Eastern Hierarchs in the College of Cardinals, Paul VI stated the following on 5 March 1973:

> Patriarchs of the Eastern Churches are not included in the list of Cardinals which We are going to read. This is so because We have resolved to satisfy a desire expressed by some of them. Nevertheless, in the days ahead We shall find more ways to avail Ourself of their advice, which We value highly, and of their fraternal cooperation. We wonder whether it might not be good to consider the advisability of making use of their services when electing a Pope.[134]

Hierarchs included in the College of Cardinals are bound to the obligations and have the rights of this college, but, I believe, we must take into account CS c. 180, "Eastern rite clerics promoted to the dignity of cardinal retain their own rite. They shall, however, abstain from the use of those privileges which are not in concord with their rite," and, indirectly, CCEO c. 1492:

> Laws issued by the supreme authority of the Church, which do not expressly indicate the passive subject, affect the Christian faithful of the Eastern Churches only insofar as they concern matters of faith or morals or declarations of divine law, explicitly decide questions regarding these Christian faithful, or concern favors which contain nothing contrary to the Eastern rites.

Once promoted to the cardinalatial dignity, they are bound by the obligation to make personally the profession of faith (CIC c. 833, 2°); they enjoy the faculty everywhere to hear the confessions of the faithful (CIC c. 967 §1); they can be buried in their own churches (CIC c. 1242); in ecclesiastical causes they are judged exclusively by the Roman Pontiff (CIC c. 1405 §1, 2°); as witnesses they can be heard in the place of their choice (CIC c. 1558 §2).[135]

---

134   Paul VI, *All. Concistoriale del 5 marzo 1973*: *AAS* 65 (1973) 163: *The Pope Speaks* 18 (1973) 58-59.

135   CS c. 283 gave a long list of faculties and privileges enjoyed by the Patriarchs outside the territory of their Church: "Besides other privileges of common law, granted or recognized by the Roman Pontiff, all patriarchs enjoy after the enthronement has been performed according to c. 235, the following faculties and privileges: 1° to hear everywhere the confessions of the faithful of Eastern Rites, also of the religious of both sexes, and to absolve from all sins and censures, including reserved ones, with the

I believe that for the election of the Roman Pontiff it would be good to have also representatives of the Eastern Catholic Churches or to grant to Patriarchs the right to vote on certain questions, independent of membership in the College of Cardinals.

III.12. Inter-ecclesial Associations

By the term "associations of the faithful" are understood those associations, distinct from institutes of consecrated life and societies of the apostolic life, in which faithful, either clerics or laity, or clerics and laity together, join for a common action, with a precise purpose, for a more perfect life or for other apostolic works (initiatives of evangelization, works of piety or of charity, animation of the temporal order through the Christian spirit), constituting an autonomous subject, distinct from the individual members, with its own entities and rules. In a time of socialization such as ours, in which persons organize themselves to promote projects for the improvement of people and society, such associations of Christians—who want to be present in an active way and aware of the collective reality of our society—are of particular value. Christian movements are not only a support for the faith, but also a collective sign of the Gospel. The Church favors and supports Christian action, consistent with the faith, at all national and inter-

---

exclusion of those excepted in c. 185 §1, 1°; 2° to preach the word of God everywhere; 3° to bless everywhere merely with the sign of the cross, with all the indulgences which the Apostolic See usually grants, crosses, rosaries and other prayer beads, medals, statutes, scapulars approved by the Apostolic See and impose them without the obligation of inscribing the names of the persons invested; 4° to grant an indulgence of three hundred days, even *toties quoties*, in all places of his patriarchate, also exempt ones, in churches of his Rite outside the boundaries of the patriarchate, and everywhere to the faithful of his Rite; 5° to declare one of the altars in any church of his Rite, even outside the patriarchate, forever a daily privileged altar; 6° to make use, in accordance with liturgical laws, of the pastoral staff and pallium in the entire patriarchate, not excluding places that are exempt from his jurisdiction; of the pastoral staff alone, also outside the patriarchate, but only in the churches of his Rite; to celebrate in the manner of a bishop in churches of his Rite even outside an Eastern region or territory, with the use also of the pastoral staff, but having informed the local Hierarch if it is the case of a cathedral; 8° to make use in documents given by him, if this is the lawful custom, of a specific formula of blessing, even calling it apostolic, excluding formulas exclusively used by the Roman Curia; 9° to make use of the insignia and decorations of his dignity also outside an Eastern region or territory; 10° the title of Beatitude; 11° to take precedence, also outside an Oriental region or territory, over all primates, archbishops and other metropolitans, bishops of whatsoever Oriental Rite, although they are each in his own territory; 12° to be an assistant at the throne of the Roman Pontiff in public divine services and other papal ceremonies, with observance of the order of precedence; 13° to appoint procurators or delegates who are to represent his person or act in his name in business transactions of the patriarchate, without prejudice to c. 260 §1, 2°."

national levels. Because life and the future of people are determined within the collective reality, Christians must be present, and their Gospel witness assumes a new value if it is collective: for people it is a revelatory sign of Christ the Savior. Especially for laity, the participation in the mission of the Church is expressed in combined forms. Free association is a right that flows from baptism and must be realized with respect to the criteria of ecclesiality (CL 29-30).

The codes recognize the right of association in the Catholic Church, because it is connatural to the concept of Church (cf. AA 18, 19 and 24; PO 8; GS 68)[136] and "by his innermost nature man is a social being, and if he does not enter into relations with others, he can neither live nor develop his gifts" (GS 12). Further, among the tasks of the eparchial Bishop[137] is that of promoting associations of the Christian faithful that pursue directly or indirectly a spiritual end, erecting, approving, praising or commending them, if so necessary, according to the norm of law (CCEO c. 203 §3).

CCEO	CIC
18. The Christian faithful are free to found and to direct associations which serve charitable and pious purposes or which promote the Christian vocation in the world and, therefore, to hold meetings to pursue together these purposes.	215. The Christian faithful are at liberty freely to found and direct associations for purposes of charity or piety or for the promotion of the Christian vocation in the world and to hold meetings for the common pursuit of these purposes.

The participation of faithful belonging to different Churches *sui iuris* is implied, but without losing view of OE 6: "Religious and associations of the Latin Rite working in Eastern countries or among Eastern faithful are earnestly counseled to found houses or even provinces of the Eastern rite, as far as this can be done."

For example, the Ordinariate of France for Eastern faithful offers the possibility of creating in their own area associations of Latin faithful who desire to live according to the traditions of an Eastern Church, celebrating the respective liturgy and participating in its spirituality.[138]

---

136   Cf. Pius XI, Litt Enc *Quadragesimo Anno*, 15 May 1931: *AAS* 23 (1931) 177-178; John XXIII, Litt Enc *Pacem in terris*, 11 April 1963: *AAS* 55 (1963) 263.
137   Cf. C. Redaelli, "Il vescovo di fronte alle associazioni," *Quaderni di Diritto Ecclesiale* 8 (1995) 349-371.
138   Sacred Congregation for the Eastern Churches, Decr *Gallia: ordinariatus pro fidelibus orientalibus ritus* [*Déclaration interpretative du décret du 27 juillet 1954*], 30 April 1986: *AAS* 78 (1986) 784-786: "III. In consideration of the above, it pertains to the Ordinary of the Eastern Catholics to take the following actions: [...] 2. To recognize, after having notified the superior authority of the ritual Church, groups and associations of Latin faithful who intend to live according to the traditions of an Eastern Church, in

Among the associations of Christian faithful are also the so-called Third Orders, whose members, belonging to any Church *sui iuris*, living in the world in the spirit of a religious institute, lead the apostolic life and aim for Christian perfection. Such associations carry out their activity under the direction of the major superior of the corresponding religious institute.[139]

The following is a norm of an exhortative character:

> Those who preside over associations of the laity, even those which have been erected by virtue of apostolic privilege, are to take care that their associations cooperate with other associations of the Christian faithful where it is expedient and willingly assist various Christian works, especially those in the same territory. (CIC c. 328)

This is an implicit reference to inter-ecclesial collaboration also at the level of associations of the faithful, especially for that work which is done in the same territory. Pope John Paul II invited, whenever possible, the constitution of inter-parochial associations of different Churches *sui iuris* to foster dialogue, consultation, collaboration and reciprocal material, spiritual and pastoral assistance.[140]

Regarding ascription as clerics to associations of the faithful, CCEO c. 597 requires the special concession of the Apostolic See or, if it is a case of associations erected or approved by the Patriarch which have their principal center in the territory of the patriarchal Church, the concession given by the Patriarch with the consent of the permanent synod. There is no counterpart in the CIC.

III.13. Evangelization of Peoples

CCEO c. 585 §1 translates into a canonical norm the statement of OE 3: "It is for each Church *sui iuris* continually to take care that, through suitably prepared preachers sent by a competent authority in accord with the norms of the common

---

celebrating the Liturgy and in living the spirituality." Leo XIII, with the brief *Romanorum Pontificum*, 18 April 1896, instituted at Notre Dame de France in Jerusalem the pious association "for rightly offering prayers for the souls of deceased faithful from both the East and the West who are detained in the fires of purgatory."

139 The supreme moderator of the Order of Preachers (Dominicans), in virtue of the faculty granted to him by the Holy See, can erect everywhere confraternities proper to the Order, even in the rite of the Eastern Churches, having obtained always the consent of the respective Bishop; Eastern priests can use the formula used by the Latin priests for blessing of rosaries, beads and other similar things, and in the ceremony for the erection of such confraternities or in the reception of members, always translated into their own language. All this was conceded by the Sacred Congregation of Indulgences, 21 June 1893 (CollPF, II:293, n. 1837), which, in conformity with CIC c. 4, remains in force.

140 Cf. John Paul II, Ap Exh *Una speranza nuova per il Libano*, 10 May 1997, n. 67: Suppl. to *L'Osservatore Romano*, 12-13 May 1997.

law, the gospel is preached in the whole world under the guidance of the Roman Pontiff."

Notwithstanding this norm, not all the Eastern Catholic Churches can devote themselves freely to the mission *ad gentes*, because this activity is often monopolized by the Latin Church, mission territories being the exclusive competence of the Latin Bishops. In some mission territories, Eastern religious are obliged to carry out evangelization in the Latin Rite.

CCEO c. 594 states: "Mission territories are those recognized as such by the Apostolic See." PB art. 85 states: "It pertains to the Congregation for the Evangelization of Peoples to direct and coordinate throughout the world the actual work of spreading the Gospel as well as missionary cooperation, without prejudice to the competence of the Congregation for the Eastern Churches." Regarding the competence of the Congregation for the Eastern Churches, PB art. 60 states: "In regions where Eastern rites have been preponderant from ancient times, apostolic and missionary activity depends solely on this Congregation, even if it is carried out by missionaries of the Latin Church."

Can the Eastern Churches perform missionary activity *ad gentes* also outside the regions in which, from ancient times, the Eastern rites were prevalent? For example, in India, why restrict the missionary activity of the Syro-Malabar Church or Syro-Malankara Church to a very reduced territory? Such Churches are capable of providing for the pastoral needs of their faithful throughout India and even outside India in an effective way, as well as performing missionary activity throughout India with the same efficacy of the Latin Church.

It is necessary to review the question of the "mission territories," regarding their boundaries and the mandate given by the supreme authority of the Church to the various Churches, Eastern or Latin, to carry out evangelization. It would be expedient to ensure a unity of purpose and the coordination of evangelization; to "restrict" Eastern religious to a "Latin" evangelization impoverishes missionary work and injures the right of evangelization according to one's own ritual character.[141]

Pope John Paul II, in his apostolic exhortation *Ecclesia in Asia* affirmed:

> The situation of *the Catholic Eastern Churches*, principally of the Middle East and India, merits special attention. From Apostolic times they have been the custodians of a precious spiritual, liturgical

---

141   "According to the millennial tradition of the Church, members of institutes of the entire Church should dedicate themselves to the mission *ad gentes*, always with respect for the equal rights and obligations of the Churches of every rite": Ninth Synod of Bishops, Propositions *Placet ut* (28 October 1994), especially proposition 37: "La missione *ad gentes*," EV 14:1645

and theological heritage. Their traditions and rites, born of a deep enculturation of the faith in the soil of many Asian countries, deserve the greatest respect. With the Synod Fathers, I call upon everyone to recognize the legitimate customs and the legitimate freedom of these Churches in disciplinary and liturgical matters, as stipulated by the Code of Canons of the Eastern Churches. Following the teaching of the Second Vatican Council, there is an urgent need to overcome the fears and misunderstandings which appear at times between the Catholic Eastern Churches and the Latin Church, and among those Churches themselves, especially with regard to the pastoral care of their people, also outside their own territories. As children of the one Church, reborn into the newness of life in Christ, believers are called to undertake all things in a spirit of common purpose, trust and unfailing charity. Conflicts must not be allowed to create division, but must instead be handled in a spirit of truth and respect, since no good can come except from love. (n. 27)[142]

III.14. Preaching of the Word of God

It is the particular responsibility of the Roman Pontiff and the College of Bishops to preach the word of God to the entire world and in every place, because Christ Himself entrusted this mandate and made it a common duty (LG 23; CIC c. 756 and CCEO c. 596). Therefore, every Bishop in communion with the Roman Pontiff and with the College of Bishops can preach everywhere, except if the local Bishop in a particular case has explicitly prohibited it (cf. CIC c. 763 and CCEO c. 610 §1).

Priests and deacons do not have the right to preach everywhere, but have the faculty to preach, which the Ordinary can limit or withdraw. While Latin priests and deacons enjoy the faculty to preach anywhere with at least the presumed consent of the rector of the church in which they preach, at least if the same faculty had not be restricted or withdrawn entirely on the part of the competent Ordinary or if particular law requires express permission (CIC c. 764),[143] Eastern priests can exercise this faculty wherever they are lawfully sent or invited (CCEO c. 610 §2),[144] as can deacons "unless particular law establishes otherwise" (§3). It would seem that there is a difference between Latin clerics and Eastern clerics

---

142   *Origins* 29:23 (November 18, 1999) 373.
143   A Bishop can withdraw the faculty to preach for a just reason, either from a sacred minister of his diocese or from a minister of another diocese who would attempt to preach in the diocese he governs: cf. Sacred Consistorial Congregation, Normæ *Ut quæ Beatissimus,* 28 June 1917, arts. 29-33: *AAS* 9 (1917) 333.
144   PO 4 is cited as a source for CCEO c. 610 §2 (cf. Pontificium Consilium de Legum Textibus Interpretandis, *Codex Canonum Ecclesiarum Orientalium auctoritate Ioannis Pauli pp. II promulgatus. Fontium annotatione auctus* [Vatican City, 1995] 222), but we do not see the connection.

regarding the faculty to preach, but this is not so since for both there is a presumed invitation. The CCEO contains the norm: "Against a decree of a Hierarch forbidding someone to preach there is recourse *in devolutivo* only, which must be resolved without delay" (CCEO c. 613).

Lay persons can also receive the mandate to preach, except for the homily,[145] but the CIC refers the matter to the provisions of the episcopal conference (CIC c. 766);[146] the CCEO refers it to the decision of the eparchial Bishop (CCEO c. 610 §4). The same expression *admitti possunt* emphasizes that it is not a right, such as that proper to Bishops, or a faculty, like that of priests or deacons.[147]

The homily is reserved to the priest and, by common law, also to the Latin deacon (CIC c. 767§1); the Eastern deacon should observe the particular law of his own Church *sui iuris* (CCEO c. 614 §4).[148] The homily cannot be entrusted in any case to priests or deacons who have lost the clerical state or who have likewise abandoned the exercise of sacred ministry.[149]

One might consider a specific case: can a Latin deacon who is invited to an Eastern Catholic Church preach there, even if the particular law of that Church prohibits deacons from preaching? Since it is a personal right of the deacon, he should not be impeded from preaching anywhere at the invitation of the parish or the local Hierarch.[150]

---

145   The diocesan Bishop cannot dispense: *Authentic Response* of 26 May 1987: *AAS* 79 (1987) 1249.
146   According to AA 17, there is a great need, for example, where the freedom of the Church is gravely impeded; according to AG 17, there is a true benefit where the communitarian prayer is normally presided over by catechists because of a lack of priests. The CEI has established that, if necessity requires it in specific circumstances or usefulness recommends it in particular cases, lay persons, who possess an orthodox faith, theological-spiritual preparation, an exemplary life at a personal and communitarian level, the capacity to communicate and have received the mandate for the local Ordinary, can be permitted to preach (but not to deliver the homily) in churches and in oratories when the necessary requirements are present: *Delibera n. 22*, 18 April 1985: *Notiziario CEI* 11 (1985) 44.
147   Cf. Congregation for the Clergy et al., *Istruzione su alcune questioni circa la collaborazione dei laici al ministero dei sacerdoti*, 15 August 1997, art. 2 §3: Suppl. to *L'Osservatore Romano*, 14 November 1997.
148   According to the particular law of the Maronite Church, prepared in May 1993, "Homilies on Sundays or feast days are reserved to the pastor. He can authorize the deacon to deliver the homily in his parish": *Particular Law of the Eastern Catholic Churches*, ed. K. Bharanikulangara (New York, 1996) 203, art. 62.
149   *Ibid.*, art. 3 §5. For the redactional *iter* of the canons on preaching, see T. J. Green, "The Teaching Function of the Church: A Comparison of Selected Canons in the Latin and Eastern Codes," *The Jurist* 55 (1995) 93-140.
150   D. Salachas holds the contrary position: *Il magistero e l'evangelizzazione dei popoli nei codici latino e orientale* (Bologna, 2001) 70.

III.15. Catechetical Activity

The teaching of Christian doctrine in an organic and systematic way, to lead the faithful progressively to the fullness of Christian life according to their capacity and needs, belongs in a particular way to each Church *sui iuris* and to its Hierarch; but if in the same territory or social-cultural region several Churches *sui iuris* are present, a catechetical commission or center can be constituted for several Churches *sui iuris* in order for catechesis or theological formation to be presented with a complete awareness of the living tradition of the Christian East and West. "In each Church *sui iuris* there is to be a catechetical commission, which can be established together with the other Churches *sui iuris* for the same territory or socio-cultural region" (CCEO c. 622 §1).[151] According to the CIC, it is for the episcopal conference, if it seems opportune, to publish catechisms with the prior approval of the Apostolic See (CIC c. 775 §2),[152] otherwise, the local Ordinary (CIC cc. 775 §1 and 827 §1);[153] for the CCEO, the Synod of Bishops of the patriarchal Church or the Council of Hierarchs can do so, without the permission of the Apostolic See (CCEO c. 621 §3), otherwise, the eparchial Bishop (CCEO c. 623 §1).[154]

III.16. Catholic Education

The issue of education is one of the most important issues in civil and religious society. The Vatican II document *Gravissimum educationis* of 28 October 1965 states that every person has a right to a civil and moral education integrated by a religious education, for which the family and the Church have a grave responsibility; the State has a subsidiary function with regard to educational programs.

The two codes indicate the subjects and the purpose of Catholic education as well as the erection, approval and suppression of Catholic schools, but of immediate concern to us is the collaboration among the pastors of the Churches and the other components of the Christian community.

The diocesan Bishop has the right to visit all the Catholic schools in his diocese, but the CCEO speaks explicitly of the canonical visit, stating that schools that are exclusively open to students of an institute of consecrated life of pon-

---

151   For the redactional *iter* of the canons on catechesis, see T. J. Green, "The Teaching Function of the Church: A Comparison of Selected Canons in the Latin and Eastern Codes," *The Jurist* 55 (1995) 93-140.
152   "Given the substantial differences between the Latin episcopal conferences and the Eastern synods, it is not appropriate to apply in this case CIC c. 775 §2": *Nuntia* 28 (1989) 78.
153   For a diocesan catechism, the approval of the Apostolic See is not necessary: *Comm.* 15 (1987) 93.
154   For the collaboration among Hierarchs, one must take into account CCEO cc. 604, 662 and 663, and CIC c. 824.

tifical or patriarchal status are exempt (CCEO c. 638 §1); CIC c. 806 §1 speaks generically of a visit and includes those schools founded or directed by religious institutes, while CIC c. 683 §1, in treating the pastoral visit, excludes schools restricted to students of the institute. Thus, leaving aside the difference between a pastoral and canonical visit, the Eastern Bishop in his territory can also visit schools reserved to students of an institute of consecrated life, but only of eparchial right, while the Latin Bishop does not have this faculty.

Whenever there are several eparchial Bishops in the same territory, the canonical visit to a Catholic school is the competence of the one who founded or established the school or the one designated by the statutes of the foundation or agreement among the Bishops themselves (CCEO c. 638 §2).

It is for the eparchial Bishop to provide for the pastoral care of university students (CIC c. 813), but in territories with several Hierarchs, a mutual agreement is preferable in order to organize the pastoral programs for the university (GE 10; CCEO c. 645).

In order to preserve the Eastern Christian patrimony, it would be appropriate to create centers of higher studies *pro Oriente* (theology, liturgy, spirituality, etc.) within universities or Catholic schools.[155]

III.17. Pre-matrimonial Investigations

CCEO	CIC
784. In the particular law of each Church *sui iuris*, after consultation with the eparchial bishops of other Churches *sui iuris* exercising their power in the same territory, norms are to be established concerning the examination of the couple and other means for inquiries that are to be carried out before the marriage, especially those that concern baptism and the freedom to marry, which are to be diligently observed so that the celebration of the marriage can proceed.	1067. The conference of bishops is to establish norms about the examination of spouses and about the marriage banns or other opportune means to accomplish the investigations necessary before marriage. After these norms have been diligently observed, the pastor can proceed to assist at the marriage.

The CCEO rightly provides for inter-ecclesial collaboration in the jurisdictions in the same territory for the examination of engaged couples and pre-matrimonial investigations. The CIC entrusts the entire matter to the episcopal

---

155 For the redactional *iter* of the canons on Catholic education, see T.J. Green, "The Teaching Function of the Church: A Comparison of Selected Canons in the Latin and Eastern Codes," *The Jurist* 55 (1995) 93-140.

conferences,[156] but one must take into account that Eastern Bishops could be part of the episcopal conference. The prior Latin and Eastern legislation entrusted the matter to the local Bishop (CIC-17 c. 1020 §3; CA c. 10 §3).[157]

Other canons that manifest inter-ecclesial collaboration are:

CCEO	CIC
787. The pastor who has made the investigation is immediately to notify the pastor who is to bless the marriage of the results of this investigation by means of an authentic document.	1070. If someone other than the pastor who is to assist at marriage has conducted the investigations, the person is to notify the pastor about the results as soon as possible through an authentic document.
841 §2. Furthermore, the local pastor is to record in the baptismal register that the spouse celebrated marriage in his parish on a certain day. If the spouse was baptized elsewhere, the local pastor is to send an attestation of marriage himself or through the eparchial curia to the pastor of the place where the spouse's baptism was recorded. He is not to be satisfied until he receives notification that the information has been entered in the baptismal register.	1122 §2. If a spouse did not contract marriage in the parish in which the person was baptized, the pastor of the place of the celebration is to send notice of the marriage which has been entered into as soon as possible to the pastor of the place of the conferral of baptism.

Additionally, we have:

CCEO	CIC
792. Diriment impediments are not to be established by the particular law of a Church *sui iuris* except for a most grave cause, after having consulted with eparchial bishops of other Churches *sui iuris* who have an interest, and after consultation with the Apostolic See; however, no lower authority can establish new diriment impediments.	1075 §2. Only the supreme authority has the right to establish other impediments for the baptized.

---

156   Cf. Conferenza Episcopale Italiana, *Decreto generale sul matrimonio canonico*, Roma, dalla Sede della CEI, 5 November 1990: *Notiziario CEI* 16 (1990) 258-279.
157   CA = Pius XII, Mp *Crebræ allatæ*, 23 February 1949: *AAS* 41 (1949) 89-117, acquired the force of law on 2 May 1949.

Impediments of ecclesiastical law for the valid or licit celebration of marriage can be established in conjunction with other Churches *sui iuris* that are concerned, that is, with those who are working in the same territory; this differs from prior legislation that limited this right exclusively to the Apostolic See (CIC-17 c. 1038; CA c. 28).

III.18. Ecumenism

With regard to the promotion of ecumenism, that is, the movement for unity in which participate all those who invoke the Trinity and profess faith in Jesus Christ, Lord and Savior, the CCEO has a canon on inter-ecclesial collaboration that does not have a corresponding canon in the CIC, but involves, given its importance, the Latin Church:

> For this purpose, there should be in each Church *sui iuris* a commission of experts on ecumenism, that is to be set up, if circumstances so suggest, in consultation with the patriarchs and eparchial bishops of other Churches *sui iuris* who exercise their power in the same territory. (CCEO c. 904 §2)

ED 42 recommends the constitution of an ecumenism commission or secretariat that involves several dioceses wherever the circumstances require it:

> In addition to the diocesan officer for ecumenical questions, the diocesan Bishop should set up a council, commission or secretariat charged with putting into practice any directives or orientations he may give and, in general, with promoting ecumenical activity in the diocese. Where circumstances call for it, several dioceses grouped together may form such a commission or secretariat.

Eastern Catholics in Latin dioceses have a particular task in the ecumenical field. CIC cc. 755 §2 and 383 §3 recommend that Bishops promote ecumenism as it is understood by the Church, both individually for their own dioceses and collegially for the entire Church. The CCEO directly devotes an entire title to ecumenism.[158] In this regard, one can refer to the Vatican II decree *Orientalium Ecclesiarum*: "The Eastern Churches in communion with the Apostolic See of Rome have a special duty of promoting the unity of all Christians, especially Eastern Christians, in accordance with the principles of the decree on Ecumenism" (n. 24).[159] CCEO c. 903 recommends conscientious fidelity to the ancient traditions of

---

[158] Cf. D. Salachas, "The Ecumenical Significance of the New Code," in *The Code of Canons of the Eastern Churches*, eds. J. Chiramel and K. Bharanikulangara (Alwaye, 1992) 258-275; D. Ceccarelli Morolli, *Il Codex Canonum Ecclesiarum Orientalium e l'Ecumenismo*, Quaderni di "Oriente Cristiano," Studi 9 (Palermo, 1998).

[159] John Paul II, *Omelia alla Divina Liturgia in Rito Armeno*, Rome, 21 November 1987: *S.I.C.O.* Suppl. to nn. 485-556, 6: "The Church desires that the Armenian Catholic

the Eastern Churches, especially the liturgical traditions, as an effective means for Eastern faithful to promote unity among the Eastern Churches, thereby witnessing that communion with Rome is not detrimental to their own tradition. In this sense, the presence of Eastern faithful in the ecumenical commissions and in the various other ecumenical initiatives of the dioceses must be active and appreciated, especially in this particularly delicate period in the relations between Catholics and Orthodox. Thus, full integration in the life of the local Church will be a witness to all the Churches of the unity and plurality of the Catholic Church. Through the variety of rites and for the richness of their patrimony of spirituality and liturgical life, these venerable communities constitute a gift for the local Church and a permanent memory of the ancient Eastern Christian Churches, of their fidelity and their current needs. The consideration, respect and affectionate reception that the Latin dioceses concretely demonstrate towards the Eastern Catholic Churches will verify their ecumenical spirit and render them more credible also to the Churches not in full communion, taking into consideration that the divisions in the history of the Church were born often not for theological or spiritual reasons, but because of a diversity of culture and traditions.

One can add to these norms CCEO c. 192 §2, which invites the eparchial Bishop to attend to the promotion of Christian unity; CCEO cc. 350 §4 and 352 §3, on the formation of candidates to sacred orders in the principles of ecumenism (CIC c. 256 §2); and CCEO c. 634 §2, on the adaptation of Catholic school principles to particular circumstances if the majority of its pupils are non-Catholics, under the direction of the competent ecclesiastical authority.

Further, according to ED 41, it is for the Bishop to appoint a diocesan delegate for ecumenical matters. In Latin dioceses with Eastern communities, this person could be an Eastern Christian member of the faithful who would represent the Catholic community in its relations with other Churches and ecclesial communities and their leaders, which would facilitate relations with the local Bishop, the clergy and laity at various levels. This applies also to the various institutes of consecrated life and societies of apostolic life, as well as organizations of Catholic faithful of a particular territory, or of a national or international character (cf. ED 51-52).[160]

---

community and all the Eastern communities in full communion with this See of Peter strive to become always greater models of authenticity, with respect and full appreciation of their own identity, rediscovering it, as the absolutely primary task, wherever it becomes weakened or blurred. This will be a most efficacious means to prepare the way that leads to the unity of all Christians in a single profession of faithful and in the communion of the same chalice" (n. 3); *Id., Udienza ai Patriarchi delle Chiese Orientali Cattholiche*, 29 September 1998: *L'Osservatore Romano*, 30 September 1998, 5: "Your Churches represent in the midst of the Catholic Church that Christian East, towards which we never cease to extend our arms for a fraternal encounter in full communion."

[160] For the redactional *iter* of the canons on ecumenism, see T. J. Green, "The Teaching Function of the Church: a Comparison of Selected Canons in the Latin and

III.19. Taxes

The Church, while having supernatural ends, cannot work towards these ends without the goods of this world, since it reaches such goals with its worldly actions. Temporal goods, by participating in the spiritual work of the Church, are spiritualized and elevated to a certain sacrality. The proper ends of the goods of the Church are: divine worship, the works of the apostolate, the works of charity and the decent support of ministers. In this section, we shall examine temporal goods of the Church in the two codes; we shall direct our attention to those norms that require collaboration among the various Churches *sui iuris*, including the Latin Church.

There is a need to make a distinction between taxes and offerings: in the first case, one is dealing with an amount that is received for a specific action of an administrative character; in the second case, one is dealing rather with free donations for the administration of sacraments or sacramentals.

With regard to taxes and offerings, the codes provide:

CCEO	CIC
1013 §2. Patriarchs and eparchial bishops of various Churches *sui iuris* exercising their power in the same territory are to take care that, after mutual consultation, the same norm is established regarding fees and offerings.	952 §1. It is for the provincial council or a meeting of the bishops of the province to define by decree for the entire province the offering to be given for the celebration and application of Mass, and a priest is not permitted to seek a larger sum. Nevertheless, he is permitted to accept for the application of a Mass a voluntary offering which is larger or even smaller than the one defined.

Again, the CCEO requires an understanding between the various Hierarchs who work in the same territory, including the Latin ordinaries. CIC-17 left this matter to the disposition of the local Ordinary: "It is for the local Ordinary to determine by decree the stipend for the manual Masses in his diocese, [and this decree] as far as possible [is to be] laid down in a diocesan synod; nor is it permitted for a priest to demand one higher" (c. 831 §1); it was provided for by PA c. 245 §2: "Hierarchs of different rites having jurisdiction in the same territory will see to it that, having consulted one another, the same customary and regular fees be established for all."

The CIC establishes that the provincial council or assembly of Bishops of the province is to establish the amount to be offered for Mass intentions. If there is no decree, one follows the custom in force in the diocese (CIC c. 952 §2).

Regarding the collection of the alms, the two codes have different norms establishing that the Hierarchs and those subject to them, both Latin and Eastern faithful, must strive to avoid possible abuses or deception and to protect the rights of all:

CCEO	CIC
1015. Physical and juridic persons are not permitted to collect alms without the permission of the authority to which they are subject and without the written consent of the local hierarch where the alms are collected.	1265 §1. Without prejudice to the right of religious mendicants, any private person, whether physical or juridic, is forbidden to beg for alms for any pious or ecclesiastical institute or purpose without the written permission of that person's own ordinary and of the local ordinary.
	§2. The conference of bishops can establish norms for begging for alms which all must observe, including those who by their foundation are called and are mendicants.

The CIC expressly states that private persons, physical or juridic, need the permission of the local Ordinary where they intend to collect alms; hence, public juridic persons do not need this permission in the sphere of their competence. It remains that, with due regard for the rights of religious mendicants, law can be established also by the episcopal conference, but one must take into the consideration the Mp *Ecclesiæ Sanctæ* I, 27, according to which religious should not collect funds through public subscription without the consent of the local ordinaries where these alms are collected.[161]

The CCEO does not distinguish between public or private persons and eliminates the privilege of the mendicant orders that had been expected to remain in the law;[162] thus, a double permission is necessary: from the authority to which one is subject, and the written permission of the local Hierarch where the alms are collected.[163]

---

161   On 19-23 September 1983, the 22nd Extraordinary Assembly of the CEI decided that the issue regarding alms would be entrusted to a group of study for further examination.
162   *Nuntia* 18 (1984) 52.
163   The Sacred Congregation of the Propagation of the Faith for Affairs of the Eastern Rite, in a circular letter of 1 January 1912 sent to Latin local Ordinaries, prohibited

A norm found in both codes that manifests inter-ecclesial collaboration and the *sollicitudo omnium Ecclesiarum* is the following:

CCEO	CIC
1021 §3. Insofar as necessary, each eparchy is to establish, in a manner determined by the particular law of its own Church *sui iuris*, a common fund through which eparchial bishops can satisfy obligations towards other persons who serve the Church and meet the various needs of the eparchy and through which the richer eparchies can also assist the poorer ones.	1274 §3. Insofar as necessary, each diocese is to establish a common fund through which bishops are able to satisfy obligations towards other persons who serve the Church and meet the various needs of the diocese and through which the richer dioceses can also assist the poorer ones.

These organizations are, in principle, of eparchial (diocesan) character, but, according to various local circumstances, it is always possible to create a federation of eparchial organizations, a cooperative or even an association of various eparchies so that the more wealthy eparchies can provide help to the poorer eparchies and to missionary activities (PO 21). These organizations or institutes are public juridic persons with approved statutes, and, if possible, should be recognized by civil law. The administration of inter-eparchial funds must be agreed upon by the various Bishops who are involved.

III.20. Penal Laws[164]

Penal law of the Eastern Churches is one of the parts of the CCEO that significantly differs from the CIC.[165] The principal specific principles that guided the reaction of Eastern penal law, and that most distinguishes it from Latin penal law, are the following:[166] the medicinal character of penalties;[167] elimination of the *latæ sententiæ* penalties;[168] the restriction of penal law to the external forum;

Eastern faithful from collecting alms without the permission of the same Congregation: *AAS* 4 (1912) 532-533.

164   This section goes with IV.6 and VI.2.

165   Cf. L. Lorusso, "Le pene nei singoli delitti," *O Odigos* 19 (2000/unico) 23-28.

166   Synod of Bishops, Relatio *"Principia quæ,"* 7 October 1967: *Comm.* 1 (1969) 77-85; *Nuntia* 3 (1976) 3-10; 4 (1977) 74; 13 (1981) 59-66; 20 (1985) 4-11. For the redactional *iter* of the penal canons of the CCEO: T. Green, "Penal Law in the *Code of Canon Law* and in the *Code of Canons of the Eastern Churches*: Some Comparative Reflections," *Studia Canonica* 28 (1994) 407-451, especially 411-424.

167   Cf. R. Coppola, "Carattere della pena nel 'Codex Iuris Canonici' e nel 'Codex Canonum Ecclesiarum Orientalium,'" in *Ius in vita et in missione Ecclesiæ*, ed. Pontificium Consilium de Legum Textibus Interpretandis (Vatican City, 1994) 773-783.

168   "The specific penalty is attached to the law in such a way that one incurs it *ipso facto* at the moment of the commission of the crime, without the need for an intervention on the part of a superior to inflict it. The sentence and executive decree are written in the

the fundamental importance of the canonical warning prior to the imposition of the penalty;[169] the notion of a penalty consisting not only in the *privatio alicuius boni*, but also in the *impositio actus positivi*;[170] prior process for the imposition of any penalty. All this is well synthesized in the first canon of the penal section of the CCEO:

> Since God employs every means to bring back the erring sheep, those who have received from Him the power to loose and to bind are to apply suitable medicine to the sickness of those who have committed delicts, reproving, imploring and rebuking them with the greatest patience and teaching. Indeed, they are even to impose penalties in order to heal the wounds caused by the delict, so that those who commit delicts are not driven to the depth of despair nor are restraints relaxed unto a dissoluteness of life and contempt of the law. (c. 1401)[171]

As Di Mattia emphasizes, the norm is theological and pastoral, but is established as the source and foundation of the juridic norms, as the lintel of the Eastern penal structure, as the original expression of the *Sacri Canones* and patristic thought.[172]

---

same law for one who commits a specific crime": A. Urru, *Sanzioni penali nella Chiesa*, 2nd ed. (Rome, 1996) 31-32.
169   Cf. H. Alwan, "Les sanctions penales," in *Acta Symposii Internationalis circa Codicem Canonum Ecclesiarum Orientalium, USEK, 24-29 aprilis 1995*, eds. Al-Ahmar, A. Khalife and D. Le Tourneau (Lebanon, 1996) 369-414, especially 382-384.
170   *Nuntia* 3 (1976) 17.
171   CIC-17 c. 2214 §2: "She shall always have before her eyes the advice of the Coun. of Tr., sess.13, *on ref.*, chap. 1: 'Let Bishops and Ordinaries bear in mind that they are pastors and not prosecutors and that they ought so to preside over those subject to them so as not to lord it over them, but to love them as children and brethren and to strive by exhortation and admonition to deter them from what is unlawful, that they may not be obliged, should [their subjects] transgress, to coerce them by due punishments. In regard to those, however, who should happen to sin through frailty, that command of the Apostle is to be observed, [namely] that they reprove, entreat, rebuke them in all kindness and patience, since benevolence toward those to be corrected often effects more than severity, exhortation more than threat, and charity more than force. But if on account of the gravity of the offense there is need of the rod, then severity is to be tempered with gentleness, judgment with mercy, and severity with clemency, that discipline, so salutary and necessary for people, may be preserved without harshness and they who are chastised may be corrected, or, if they are unwilling to repent, that others may by the wholesome example of their punishment be deterred from vices.'"
172   Cf. G. Di Mattia, "La normativa di diritto penale nel Codex Iuris Canonici e nel Codex Canonum Ecclesiarum Orientalium," in *Incontro*, 2:511-534, especially 522.

Considering the principle of collaboration, we have the following canons, which also correspond to, among other things, the desires of Vatican II as expressed in OE 4:

CCEO	CIC
1405 §3. Insofar as it is possible, patriarchs and eparchial bishops are to take care that penal laws of particular law are uniform in the same territory.	1316. Insofar as possible, diocesan bishops are to take care that if penal laws must be issued, they are uniform in the same city or region.

The uniformity of penal laws is a demand of a pastoral nature. Bishops retain their own autonomy in the exercise of coercive power, and thus in the establishment of penal laws. Nevertheless, it is appropriate to reach an understanding, even if the norms will be issued by the individual eparchial (diocesan) Bishops; otherwise, there is a risk of great confusion among the faithful in the same territory.

The prohibitions imposed by excommunication vary in the two codes. With minor excommunication (*interdict* in CIC c. 1332), there is a prohibition against reception of the Divine Eucharist and possibly even exclusion from participation in the Divine Liturgy or from entering a church, if public worship is celebrated in it (CCEO c. 1431 §1). With an interdict (*minor excommunication* in the CCEO), there is a prohibition against participating in any way as a minister in the celebration of any act of public worship, celebrating the sacraments or sacraments and receiving the sacraments (CIC c. 1332). Regarding sacraments, applicable only to clerics, the CCEO also provides for a reduction to a lower order: "A cleric demoted to a lower grade is prohibited from exercising those acts of the power of orders or governance that are not consonant with this grade" (CCEO c. 1433 §1).[173]

Other penalties not provided explicitly by the CIC are: "If the gravity of the case demands and especially if it concerns recidivists, a Hierarch can, in addition to the penalties imposed by sentence in accord with the norm of law, place the offender under supervision in the manner determined by an administrative decree" (CCEO c. 1428). We, as does Di Mattia, have a certain reservation with this norm that has medieval resonances and the flavor of authoritarian and dictatorial orders.[174] Additionally, "a person who deliberately omits the commemoration of the Hierarch in the Divine Liturgy and in the divine praises as prescribed by law, and does not reconsider, though legitimately warned, is to be punished with an appropriate penalty, not excluding major excommunication" (CCEO c. 1438). This canon is very important in the East, because not commemorating one's Hier-

---

[173]   *Nuntia* 4 (1977) 89.
[174]   G. Di Mattia, "La normativa di diritto penale nel *Codex Iuris Canonici* e nel *Codex Canonum Ecclesiarum Orientalium,*" *Apollinaris* 65 (1992) 149-172, especially 163.

arch is considered as the denial of due dependence, and perhaps an initial public declaration of schism. In certain Churches *sui iuris*, it is prescribed to commemorate several Hierarchs, but not more than four: the Bishop, the Metropolitan, the Patriarch and the Roman Pontiff.[175] Therefore, the Eastern presbyter who is lawfully incardinated in a Latin diocese must commemorate the local Bishop *in signum subiectionis*. Further:

> A person who has approached the civil authority directly or indirectly to obtain by its intervention sacred ordination, an office, a ministry or another function in the Church, is to be punished with an appropriate penalty not excluding major excommunication and, in the case of a cleric, even deposition. (CCEO c. 1460)

Physical violence against the hierarchy is regulated differently:

CCEO	CIC
1445 §1. A person who has used physical force against a bishop or has caused him some other serious injury is to be punished with an appropriate penalty, not excluding deposition, if he is a cleric. However, if the same delict has been committed against a metropolitan, patriarch, or indeed the Roman Pontiff, the offender is to be punished with a major excommunication, whose remission, in the last case, is reserved to the Roman Pontiff himself.	1370 §1. A person who uses physical force against the Roman Pontiff incurs a *latæ sententiæ* excommunication reserved to the Apostolic See; if he is a cleric, another penalty, not excluding dismissal from the clerical state, can be added according to the gravity of the delict.
§2. A person who did the same to another cleric, religious, member of a society of common life in the manner of religious, or a lay person who is actually exercising an ecclesiastical function, is to be punished with an appropriate penalty.	§2. A person who does this against a bishop incurs a *latæ sententiæ* interdict and, if he is a cleric, also a *latæ sententiæ* suspension.
	§3. A person who uses physical force against a cleric or religious out of contempt for the faith, the Church, ecclesiastical power, or the ministry is to be punished with a just penalty.

One who uses physical violence against a Metropolitan or Patriarch incurs major excommunication; one who uses physical violence against the Roman Pontiff incurs major excommunication reserved to the Roman Pontiff according to the CCEO, a *latæ sententiæ* excommunication reserved to the Apostolic See according to the CIC; if he is a cleric, he can be deposed according to the codes. If the same crime was committed against a Bishop, according to the CCEO the offender must be punished with an appropriate penalty, not excluding deposition

---

175   *Nuntia* 4 (1977) 91. In some Eastern Churches, religious also commemorate their major superior.

for a cleric, while according to the CIC one incurs a *latæ sententiæ* interdict and, if a cleric, also a *latæ sententiæ* suspension. If the same crime was committed against a cleric or a religious, the crime must be punished with an appropriate and just penalty, but the CCEO also provides for an appropriate penalty for a crime that uses physical violence against a lay person who exercises an ecclesiastical function.

In the CCEO, but not in the CIC, there is the possibility of public rebuke, which is "to occur before a notary or two witnesses or by letter, but in such a way that the reception and tenor of the letter are established by some document" (CCEO c. 1427). In the penal process, the discussion of the case must take place orally in the presence of the accused, the promoter of justice and the advocate (CCEO cc. 1476-1477); in the CIC, the oral discussion is optional (c. 1725).[176]

There are also the canons on the cessation of penalties in the respective legislations, and also on the age of the persons on whom penalties can be inflicted:

CCEO	CIC
1420 §1. The following can remit a penalty imposed by virtue of the common law:	1355 §1. Provided that the penalty has not been reserved to the Apostolic See, the following can remit an imposed or declared penalty established by law:
1° the Hierarch who initiated the penal trial or imposed the penalty by decree;	1° the ordinary who initiated the trial to impose or declare a penalty or who personally or through another imposed or declared it by decree;
2° the local Hierarch where the offender actually resides, but after having consulted the Hierarch mentioned in n. 1.	
§2. These norms also apply regarding penalties imposed in virtue of particular law or a penal precept, unless the particular law of a Church *sui iuris* provides otherwise.	2° the ordinary of the place where the offender is present, after the ordinary mentioned under n. 1 has been consulted unless this is impossible because of extraordinary circumstances.
§3. However, only the Apostolic See can remit a penalty imposed by the Apostolic See, unless the remission of the penalty is delegated to the patriarch or others.	§2. If the penalty has not been reserved to the Apostolic See, an ordinary can remit a *latæ sententiæ* penalty established by law but not yet declared for his subjects and those who are present in his territory or who committed the offense there; any bishop can also do this in the act of sacramental confession.

---

176   For a comparative table, see L. Lorusso, "Le pene nei singoli delitti," *O Odigos* 19 (2000/unico) 23-28.

CCEO (continued)	CIC (continued)
1413 §1. A person who has not completed the fourteenth year of age is not subject to a penalty. §2. However, a person who has committed a delict between the fourteenth and eighteenth year of age can be punished only with penalties that do not include the loss of some good, unless the eparchial bishop or the judge, in special cases, thinks that the reform of that person can be better accomplished in another way.	1356 §1. The following can remit a *ferendæ sententiæ* or *latæ sententiæ* penalty established by a precept not issued by the Apostolic See: 1° the ordinary of the place where the offender is present; 2° if the penalty has been imposed or declared, the ordinary who initiated the trial to impose or declare the penalty or who personally or through another imposed or declared it by decree. §2. The author of the precept must be consulted before remission is made unless this is impossible because of extraordinary circumstances. 1323. The following are not subject to a penalty when they have violated a law or precept: 1° a person who has not yet completed the sixteenth year of age 1324 §1. The perpetrator of a violation is not exempt from a penalty, but the penalty established by law or precept must be tempered or a penance employed in its place if the delict was committed: 4° by a minor who has completed the age of sixteen years.

It should be noted that CCEO c. 1420 §1, 2° is more restrictive while CIC c. 1355 §1, 2° is more magnanimous: "[...] unless this is impossible because of extraordinary circumstances."[177] Is this consultation *ad validitatem*? Considering CIC c. 127 §2 and CCEO c. 934 §2, we must respond that the consultation is *ad validitatem* in order to avoid possible abuses,[178] because the persons to be consulted are designated by the law itself.[179] Thus, the obligation of consultation juridically binds the authority, but is not required if approval is obtained from the person consulted.[180] CIC cc. 87 and 91 (CCEO cc. 1538-1539), on the faculty of dispensing, cannot be invoked in this case because according to CIC c. 86 (CCEO c. 1537), one is dealing with a constitutive element of the capacity of the authority to posit a juridic act. But we can invoke CIC c. 10 and CCEO c. 1495, according to which laws are to be considered as nullifying or invalidating only if it is expressly stated that an act is null or that a person is incapable. In this case, at least according to CIC c. 1355 §1, 2°, there is a clause of exception that does not make the act obligatory in extraordinary circumstances. The *ratio legis* should be respect for the authority that had pronounced the judgment or inflicted or declared the penalty, but also the need to know the reasons for the imposition or declaration of the penalty in order to appraise better the advisability and appropriateness of its remission.[181]

A member of the Eastern Christian faithful of less than 14 years of age is not subject to a penalty, while a member of the Latin Christian faithful is not subject to a penalty until sixteen years. Regarding the mitigation of the penalty, according to the CCEO, if the crime was committed by someone between fourteen and eighteen years of age, the offender can be punished only with penalties that do not include the privation of a good, *nisi Episcopus eparchialis vel iudex in casibus specialibus aliter melius consuli posse censet eiusdem emendationi* (c. 1413 §2); for

---

177　It was proposed to make stricter the obligation to consult the Ordinary who had pronounced the judgment or inflicted the penalty by suppressing the clause *nisi propter extraordinarias circumstantias impossibile sit*, but it was decided to leave the text unchanged: *Comm.* 9 (1977) 169; 16 (1984) 45.

178　"When Maronite Bishops began to absolve Greek- Melkites from censures imposed on them by their own pastors, Benedict XIV with great severity and force censured the Patriarch and Maronite Bishops and declared all such actions to be absolutely void of value": A Petrani, *De relatione...*, 43; *Nuntia* 4 (1977) 85; *Comm.* 9 (1977) 169.

179　The same superior does not have the right to vote with the others, nor to settle a tie vote: Authentic response of 14 May 1985: *AAS* 77 (1985) 771. But this does not involve the CCEO: I. Žužek, *Understanding the Eastern Code*, Kanonika 8 (Rome, 1997) 390-391.

180　*Comm.* 16 (1984) 45.

181　A. Borras, *Les sanctions dans l'Église* (Paris, 1990) 133; D. Cito, "La remissione della pena canonica," in *Le sanzioni nella Chiesa*, XXIII Incontro Studio Abbazia di Maguzzano - Lonato (Brescia 1 iuglio-5 iuglio 1996), ed. Gruppo Italiano Docenti di Diritto Canonico (Milan, 1997) 113-132, especially 124; A. Calabrese, *Diritto penale canonico*, 2nd ed. (Vatican City, 1996) 238-239.

the CIC, the penalty is mitigated or substituted with a penance if the offender is a minor who has completed sixteen years of age (c. 1324 §1, 4°).

The Latin Ordinary who has been lawfully entrusted with the pastoral care of Eastern faithful must keep in mind in the imposition of a penalty that

> [u]nless another penalty is determined by law, according to the ancient traditions of the Eastern Churches, penalties can be imposed that require some serious work of religion or piety or charity to be performed, such as certain prayers, a pious pilgrimage, a special fast, alms, spiritual retreats.
>
> §2. Other penalties are to be imposed on that person who is not disposed to accept these penalties. (CCEO c. 1426)

With due regard for the right of the Roman Pontiff (CCEO c. 1423 §1) and of the Apostolic See (CIC c. 1354 §3) of reserving to himself / itself or to others the remission of any penalty, the CCEO also provides that the Synod of Bishops of the patriarchal / major archiepiscopal Church can reserve, by a law passed for grave circumstances, the remission of penalties to the Patriarch or Major Archbishop for subjects having a domicile or quasi-domicile in the territory of the Church over which he presides (CCEO c. 1423 §1). Thus, for the CIC only the Apostolic See can reserve to itself or to others the remission of a penalty, excluding this possibility for inferior legislators; instead, for the CCEO the Synod of Bishops of the patriarchal or major archiepiscopal Church can do so, but also other inferior legislators with the consent of the Apostolic See (CCEO c. 1423 §1).

III.21. Procedural Law

This section examines the inter-ecclesial collaboration provided for in the legislation of the Church, leaving aside the convergences or differences present in the procedural law of the two codes.[182]

The CCEO provides for the possibility of erecting a common tribunal for the various Churches *sui iuris* (including the Latin) found in the same territory to judge both contentious and penal cases; this tribunal is constituted by the eparchial Bishops concerned, who designate one from themselves who will exercise power over this tribunal. Appeal is made to the tribunal stably designated by the Apostolic See (CCEO c. 1068). In the prior Eastern legislation there was reference only to a tribunal within the patriarchate, with appeal to a tribunal designat-

---

[182] For example, J. Abbass, "Trials in General: A Comparative Study of the Eastern and Latin Codes," *The Jurist* 55 (1995) 838-874; M. Ventura, "Spunti di comparazione in diritto penale canonico dopo la promulgazione del Codice delle Chiese Orientali," *Il Diritto Ecclesiastico* 107 (1996) 637-666.

ed *a Patriarchis partium diversi ritus in causa* (SN cc. 39 §1 and 72 §1, 6°).[183] For the Latin Code, in order to constitute a tribunal that serves several dioceses, the approval of the Apostolic See is also needed (CIC c. 1423 §1). The reasons for the creation of such tribunals can be the paucity of clergy, the lack of qualified personnel or the few number of cases. CCEO c. 1068 does not speak of the approval of the Apostolic See, but we believe that this is necessary because CCEO c. 1067 §1, in treating the tribunal of the first instance for different eparchies of the same Church *sui iuris* situated outside the territory of the patriarchal Church, states the need for pontifical approval. Further, PB art. 124, 4°, while using language that is purely Latin, states that it is for the Supreme Tribunal of the Apostolic Signatura "to promote and approve the erection of inter-diocesan tribunals."[184]

Whenever a controversy arises between physical or juridic persons of different religious institutes, or between a religious person and a secular cleric or a lay person or a secular juridical person, the first instance of judgment is the diocesan tribunal (CIC c. 1427 §3; CCEO c. 1069 §2).

Even if there is no tribunal constituted to serve various Churches *sui iuris*, every tribunal has the right to ask for the assistance of another tribunal of any Church, except, however, if those acts involve the decisions of the judges (CCEO c. 1071; CIC c. 1418); to the right of one corresponds the juridic obligation in the other.[185] The collaboration among tribunals is indispensable to guarantee the same justice for all, across the diversity of judicial powers, and to prevent the possible manipulation of tribunals by approaching various jurisdictions.

The codes provide for the possible appointment of lay Christian faithful of any Church *sui iuris* as judges of ecclesiastical tribunals, but never as a single judge.[186] Their appointment is within the competence of the eparchial Bishop, but the permission to do so belongs to the Patriarch / Major Archbishop, having consulted the permanent synod, or to the Metropolitan who presides over a metropolitan Church *sui iuris*, having consulted the two eparchial Bishops senior by episcopal ordination; in other cases, the Apostolic See is to be approached regarding this matter (CCEO c. 1087 §2). For the Latin legislation, the permission is left to the episcopal conferences (CIC c. 1421 §2); the CEI granted permission to bring a lay person into an ecclesiastical tribunal as a judge as part of the college, provided that the person be qualified according to the canonical norms.[187] Further, according to CCEO c. 1102 §1, judges and other officers of the tribunal can be drawn

---

183 SN = Pius XII, Mp *Sollicitudinem nostram*, 6 January 1950: *AAS* 42 (1950) 5-120.
184 Cf. P. V. Pinto, *I Processi nel Codice di Diritto Canonico. Commento sistematico al Lib. VII* (Vatican City, 1993) 103.
185 *Comm.* 10 (1978) 228. This is the juridic institute of the *rogatoria*.
186 *Comm.* 10 (1978) 231.
187 *Delibera n. 12*, Rome, 23 December 1983: *Notizario CEI* 9 (1983) 210.

from any Church *sui iuris*, but with the written consent of their own eparchial Bishop or major superior.[188]

The eparchial Bishop who exercises power outside the territory of the patriarchal Church and does not belong to any province has the right to choose a Metropolitan, having consulted the Patriarch and with the approval of the Apostolic See (CCEO c. 139);[189] to this Metropolitan, who could even be a Latin, belongs the rights and obligations contained in CCEO c. 133 §1: to erect a Metropolitan tribunal; to be vigilant that the faith and ecclesiastical discipline are observed; to make a canonical visit if the eparchial Bishop neglected to do so; to appoint and confirm someone who was lawfully proposed or elected to an ecclesiastical office if the eparchial Bishop omitted to do so; to appoint an eparchial finance officer if the eparchial Bishop omitted to do so.

For all the other Churches *sui iuris* that depend directly on the Apostolic See, the Hierarch delegated by the Apostolic See erects the metropolitan tribunal (CCEO c. 175). The metropolitan tribunal is the tribunal of appeal of sentences of the eparchial tribunals (CCEO c. 1064 §1); for cases judged in the first instance before the Metropolitan or another eparchial Bishop who has no superior authority other than the Roman Pontiff, one must appeal to the tribunal stably designated by him with the approval of the Apostolic See (CCEO c. 1064 §2).

A tribunal of the Latin Church, in cases dealing with Eastern faithful in the diaspora who reside in territories of the Latin Church and lack their own hierarchy or are entrusted to the local Ordinary of the Latin Church, is competent to deal with cases of the nullity of marriages of Catholics of another Church *sui iuris*. This possibility is expressly provided in the instruction *Dignitas connubii*, which, although it concerns only tribunals of the Latin Church, states that they can judge marriage cases of Eastern faithful.[190] Art. 16 §1 mentions such a competency, which can be exercised in two ways: *ipso iure* or through an extension of competence. A case can be examined *ipso iure* when it occurs "in a territory where, besides the local Ordinary of the Latin Church, there is no other local Hierarch of any other Church *sui iuris*, or where the pastoral care of the faithful of the Church *sui iuris* in question has been entrusted to the local Ordinary of the Latin Church by designation of the Apostolic See or at least with its assent." The examination of a case of marriage nullity through extension of competence can be granted in a stable manner or *ad casum*; this competence is granted by the Apostolic Signa-

---

188   SN c. 71 does not mention written permission.
189   CS c. 323: "Bishops who are not subject to a patriarch, archbishop or metropolitan, exarchs with a territory of their own, and apostolic exarches, shall designate, with the previous approval of the Apostolic See, a neighboring metropolitan, to whom permanently are assigned all rights and obligations to which a metropolitan so designated is entitled according to common law."
190   Cf. Pontifical Council for Legislative Texts, Instruction *Dignitas Connubii*, 25 January 2005 (Vatican City, 2005).

tura. The formulation of art. 16 §2 is important: the Latin tribunal must observe its own procedural law, but the assessment of nullity must observe the substantive law of the Church *sui iuris* to which the parties are ascribed.

III.22. Ecclesiastical Dignities

It is the customary practice of the Roman Pontiff to grant honorific titles of Chaplain to His Holiness, Prelate of Honor and Apostolic Protonotary to clerics pertaining to the Latin Church and Eastern Catholic Churches. The Patriarch and the Major Archbishop inside the territory of their own Churches can confer ecclesiastical dignities recognized in their Church *sui iuris* to any cleric, even one of another Church *sui iuris* including the Latin Church, provided he has the written consent of the eparchial (diocesan) Bishop to which the cleric is subject or, if it is a case of a member of a religious institute or a society of common life in the manner of religious, the written consent of his major superior (CCEO c. 89 §3). To confer a dignity on a cleric outside the territory of the patriarchal or major archiepiscopal Church, one needs the written consent of the Ordinary or major superior and the *nulla osta* of the Congregation for the Eastern Churches. The Metropolitan of a metropolitan Church *sui iuris* can confer dignities only on clerics of his own Church, while an eparchial Bishop can do so only on his own subjects (CCEO c. 194). To confer a dignity on a cleric of another Church, he needs the written consent of his Ordinary or major superior and the *nulla osta* of the Congregation for the Eastern Churches. Clerics who have received a dignity according to the above-mentioned norms can wear the appropriate insignia only in the territory of the one who granted it. Clerics who have received a dignity from the Roman Pontiff can wear the appropriate insignia anywhere.

Chapter IV

Administration of the Sacraments

IV.1. Guiding Principles
IV.2. Christian Initiation
IV.3. Baptism
    IV.3.1. Minister
    IV.3.2. Sponsors
IV.4. Chrismation with Holy Myron or Confirmation
    IV.4.1. Minister
    IV.4.2. Sponsor
IV.5. Eucharist
    IV.5.1. Obligations of the Faithful
    IV.5.2. Participation
    IV.5.3. Minister of Distribution
    IV.5.4. Concelebration
    IV.5.5. Offerings for the Divine Liturgy
IV.6. Penance and Indulgences
IV.7. Anointing of the Sick
IV.8. Sacred Ordination
IV.9. Sacramentals

IV.1. Guiding Principles

This chapter will indicate not only the differences between the two codes regarding the administration of sacraments, which manifest the richness of the traditions of the one Church of Christ, but also possible inter-ecclesial collaboration, especially when Eastern faithful are lawfully entrusted to a Latin Ordinary or priest. The administration of the sacrament of marriage will be treated separately in the following chapter.[1]

---

[1] For a commentary on the individual canons of Title XVI, with the exception of the sacrament of marriage, see L. Lorusso, *Il Culto divino nel Codex Canonum Ecclesiarum Orientalium*, Analecta Nicolaiana 5 (Bari, 2008).

CCEO	CIC
667. Through the sacraments, which the Church is bound to dispense in order to communicate the mysteries of Christ under visible signs, our Lord Jesus Christ sanctifies people by the power of the Holy Spirit, so that they may become in a unique way true worshipers of God the Father and be inserted into Christ and the Church, His Body; therefore, all the Christian faithful, but especially the sacred ministers, are to observe diligently the prescripts of the Church in the conscientious celebration and reception of the sacraments.	840. The sacraments of the New Testament were instituted by Christ the Lord and entrusted to the Church. As actions of Christ and the Church, they are signs and means which express and strengthen the faith, render worship to God, and effect the sanctification of humanity and thus contribute in the greatest way to establish, strengthen, and manifest ecclesiastical communion. Accordingly, in the celebration of the sacraments the sacred ministers and the other members of the Christian faithful must use the greatest veneration and necessary diligence.

In the Church, the sacraments signify and create the one community of the Body of Christ because they assimilate those who believe in Jesus into his death and resurrection. The pneumatic dimension, that is, the work of the Holy Spirit in the liturgical life of the Church, is particularly emphasized in the CCEO: through the power of the Holy Spirit, the Church celebrates and administers the sacraments, sanctifying humans, and, through the power of that same Spirit "who dwells in man, deification already begins on earth; the creature is transfigured and God's kingdom inaugurated."[2] On the other hand, the CIC greatly emphasizes the Christological dimension, i.e., the sacraments are actions of Christ and the Church.[3]

CCEO	CIC
669. Since the sacraments are the same for the entire Church and belong to the divine deposit, it is for the supreme authority of the Church alone to approve or define those things required for their validity.	841. Since the sacraments are the same for the whole Church and belong to the divine deposit, it is only for the supreme authority of the Church to approve or define the requirements for their validity; it is for the same or another competent authority according to the norm of can. 838, §§3 and 4 to decide what pertains to their licit celebration, administration, and reception and to the order to be observed in their celebration.

---

2 John Paul II, Ep Ap *Orientale Lumen*, 2 May 1995, n. 6: *AAS* 87 (1995) 749-751.
3 Cf. A. M. Triacca, "Tradiciones sacramentarias Occidental y Oriental: originalidad y reciprocidad," *Phase* (1994) 265ff.

Both canons state that it is only for the Supreme Authority of the Church to approve or define the requirements for the validity of the sacraments (cf. SC 22), since they belong to the divine deposit. This principle is a part of the perennial theological-juridical-liturgical patrimony of the Church. Since the liturgy is a specific expression of the Church (*lex orandi, lex credendi*), it necessarily follows that only the ecclesiastical authority is competent to establish norms in this matter. At the universal level, both the Roman Pontiff and the College of Bishops are competent. The power of the Roman Pontiff is exercised either personally or by means of dicasteries of the Roman Curia: the Congregation for Divine Worship and the Discipline of the Sacraments for the Latin Church (PB arts. 62-70), the Congregation for the Eastern Churches for the various Churches *sui iuris* (PB arts. 56-61), with due regard for the competence of the Congregation for the Doctrine of the Faith. At the level of the particular Church, it is for the Bishop, as moderator of the entire liturgical life of his Church, the episcopal conferences and the *cœtus* of the various Eastern Churches *sui iuris*.

In the patriarchal Churches, liturgical laws are enacted by the Synod of Bishops of the patriarchal Church (in collaboration with the liturgical commission of the patriarchal Church [cf. CCEO cc. 114 §1 and 124]),[4] are promulgated by the Patriarch and have the force of law everywhere for the faithful ascribed to the same patriarchal Church.[5] The same is true for the major archiepiscopal Churches (cf. CCEO c. 152). Therefore, the faithful who reside outside the territory of their own patriarchal or major archiepiscopal Church are bound to the observance of their own liturgical laws, because the liturgy is an important part of the rite of every Church *sui iuris*. The liturgy expresses the theology, spirituality and discipline of the Church *sui iuris*. The laws and obligations of the Patriarch with regard to the liturgical books in the prior legislation were found in CS c. 279 §2. The Apostolic See had the right of *approbatio*, while the Patriarch had the right of *recognitio* of the text of the liturgical books and, on the basis of the approved text, could grant permission for a translation (*in vulgus emendi licentiam*).

The Council of Hierarchs of the metropolitan Churches *sui iuris* can also enact, according to the norm of law, liturgical laws and norms that the Metropolitan promulgates, in cases in which common law relegates the matter to the particular law of a Church *sui iuris* (cf. CCEO c. 167 §§1-3). In all the other Churches *sui*

---

[4] CS c. 302: "A council or so-called commission on liturgical matters is to be established by the Patriarch for the editing and printing of liturgical books, according to the norm of c. 279 §2, and for dealing with all matters that concern the liturgy."

[5] CCEO c. 150 §2: "Laws enacted by the synod of Bishops of the patriarchal Church and promulgated by the Patriarch, have the force of law everywhere in the world if they are liturgical laws. However, if they are disciplinary laws or in the case of other decisions of the synod, they have the force of law within the territorial boundaries of the patriarchal Church."

iuris, the competent authority is the Apostolic See[6] and, within limits established by the same, Bishops and their lawfully constituted *cœtus* (CCEO cc. 176 and 657 §1), with due regard for the right of the eparchial Bishop: "As the moderator, promoter and guardian of the entire liturgical life in the eparchy entrusted to him, the eparchial Bishop must be vigilant that it be fostered to the greatest extent possible and be ordered according to the prescriptions and legitimate customs of his own Church *sui iuris*" (CCEO c. 199; cf. CIC c. 835 §1).

The approval of liturgical texts, with the prior *recognitio* of the Apostolic See, pertains to the same authorities who issue the liturgical laws; this applies also to the publication of the same books intended for liturgical use,[7] after having made a report to the Apostolic See.[8] To re-publish liturgical books, translations of them, or part of them intended for liturgical use, it is required and sufficient that agreement with the approved edition be established through an attestation of the local Hierarch of the place of the author or of the local Hierarch where the texts are published, or by the superior authority who exercises executive power of governance over those persons or places.[9] Books of prayers or devotions intended for public or private use of the Christian faithful require ecclesiastical permission.

All this is evident in principle, but one encounters certain difficulties in practice. Some Eastern Catholic Churches lack a proper edition of all or at least some of the liturgical books and out of necessity use editions in use in the corresponding Orthodox Churches, which are objectively sometimes well-edited. Such a practice occurs traditionally with the tacit approval of the Apostolic See or the local authority. This necessity, having examined everything with prudence, can develop into a valuable custom, as a manifestation of the partial but profound and broad communion that exists today between the Catholic Churches and the Orthodox Churches that originate from a common strain, and can be a dynamic seed for the recovery of full communion. On the other hand, many editions of

---

6   For the role of the Apostolic See, see Instr. 24 and J. Abbass, "The Historical Basis for the Unqualified Use of *Apostolic See* in the Oriental Legislation," in *The Code of Canons of the Eastern Churches*, eds. J. Chiramel and K. Bharanikulangara (Alwaye, 1992) 230-257.

7   A *liturgical book* is a publication containing texts of ceremonies of public worship, the rubrics that regulate their execution and the order of the feasts. It is published by the competent ecclesiastical authority, or such an authority guarantees its authenticity. It should be kept in mind that, according to the practice of the Congregation for the Eastern Churches, in the case of an *editio typica* a decree *ad hoc* is not required: cf. P. Szabó, "I libri liturgici orientali e la Sede Apostolica. Sviluppo della prassi e dello stato attuale," *Folia Canonica* 7 (2004) 261-278, especially 275.

8   In the *Schema Canonum de Cultu Divino et præsertim de Sacramentis* of 1980, c. 3 §1 states: "Liturgiam ordinare atque libros liturgicos adprobare, in Ecclesiis Patriarchalibus Patriarchæ et Synodi Episcoporum est ad normam iuris […]."

9   Cf. C. Vasil', "Norme riguardanti l'edizione dei libri liturgici," in *Ius Ecclesiarum vehiculum caritatis*, ed. Congregazione per le Chiese Orientali (Vatican City, 2004) 363-391.

liturgical books published in Rome are appreciated and used by Orthodox brethren. One should avoid every unnecessary difference between the liturgical books of the Eastern Catholic Churches and the Orthodox Churches. It is desirable, insofar as it is possible, that there be common editions (cf. CCEO c. 656 and Instr. 29). Only those editions of Sacred Scripture that have ecclesiastical approval should be employed for liturgical and catechetical use; all the other editions should have at least ecclesiastical permission (cf. CCEO c 655 §3).[10]

Benedict XIV on 21 December 1743 wrote:

> Regarding the rites and practices of the Greek Church, we especially decreed that it be established that no one was or is permitted by virtue of any title, state, authority or dignity, even if he shine with patriarchal or episcopal dignity, to change something or to introduce anything that diminishes from the complete and precise observance of the same rites and practices.[11]

Pius XII added:

> In liturgical matters, as in many other in many other fields, with regard to the past it is necessary to avoid two extreme attitudes: a blind attack and contempt. [...] The current liturgy requires a concern for progress, but also for preservation and defense. [...] One is also preoccupied with numerous specific problems concerning, for example: the relation of the liturgy with the religious ideas of the present world, contemporary culture, social issues, in-depth psychology.[12]

Every Hierarch must with the greatest diligence see that the celebrations conform to the prescriptions of the liturgical books (CCEO c. 674 §1 and CIC c. 846 §1) and with lawful customs (CCEO cc. 1506-1507 and CIC cc. 23-26). The Hierarch, as the promoter of the liturgical life, will see also to the faithful preservation and accurate observance of his own rite, and not admit into it changes except by reason of organic development (cf. OE 6; CCEO c. 40 §1).[13] This means that it is

---

10   *Ecclesiastical permission* indicates that the edition is free from any errors regarding Catholic faith and morals. *Ecclesiastical approval* indicates that the work is accepted by the Church or conforms to the authentic doctrine of the Church.
11   Benedict XIV, Ep Enc *Demandatam*, 24 December 1743, §3.
12   Pius XII, *Discorso a conclusione del congresso internazionale di liturgia pastorale*, Assisi – Rome (18-22 September 1956): *AAS* 48 (1956) 723-724.
13   "In modifying ancient liturgical practice, it must be determined if the element to be introduced is coherent with the contextual meaning in which it is placed. Such a context should be understood beginning with possible references to Sacred Scripture, interpretations of the Holy Fathers, liturgical reforms previously made and mystagogical catechesis. Here it must be verified that the new change is homogeneous with the symbolic language, images and style specific to the liturgy of the particular Church. The

necessary that each possible adaptation of the liturgy be based on a careful study of the sources, on an objective understanding of the particularities of one own culture, on the preservation of the tradition common to the entire Church *sui iuris* of membership;[14] moreover, this

> implies taking into account first of all the roots from which the heritage of these Churches was initially developed, mainly in Jerusalem, Alexandria, Antioch, Constantinople, Armenia and in the ancient empire of Persia; and secondly, the manner in which such traditions were transmitted, adapting to the various circumstances and places but maintained in a coherent, organic continuity.[15]

It is necessary to abandon gradually, with firmness and delicacy, by means of appropriate catechesis, uses and practices that are extraneous to the tradition of the proper Church *sui iuris* and cannot be integrated in a coherent way with the proper spirituality and culture. Pope John Paul II said:

> I recommend to the Pastors to be vigilant in the liturgical reforms undertaken to preserve the beauty and dignity of the celebrations that form a common patrimony for the Eastern Churches; it is indispensable that such reforms not deprive the theological meaning of the Holy mysteries, so that, according to the norms of the Catholic Church and with respect to their own ecclesial traditions, the various particular Churches understand that they are in communion and in harmony with the entire Church.[16]

Next to the eparchial Bishop, there is another figure who has the task of overseeing the liturgy (CD 30):[17] the protopresbyter (= vicar forane). The Codes express this as follows:

---

new element will have its place if, required for serious pastoral reasons, it blends within the celebration without contrast but with coherence, almost as if it had naturally evolved from it. In addition, it should be ensured that it is not already present, perhaps in another form, in a different moment of the celebration or in another part of the liturgical *corpus* of that Church": Instr. 20; cf. John Paul II, Aplet *É una grande gioia*, al Sinodo dei Vescovi della Chiesa siro-malabarese, 14 March 1998: *Il Regno-Documenti* 9/1998, 269-270; Congregation for the Eastern Churches, *Orientamenti fondamentali concernenti la liturgia siro-malabarese*, 16 March 1998: *ibid.*, 270-271.

14   Cf. John Paul II, *Omelia alla Preghiera dell'Incenso in Rito Alessandrino-Copto*, Rome, 14 August 1988: *S.I.C.O.* Suppl. to nn. 485-556, 24.

15   Instr. 12; *Nuntia* 1 (1975) 6; CS c. 1 §§1-2.

16   John Paul II, Ap Exh *Una speranza nuova per il Libano*, 10 May 1997, n. 42: Suppl. to *L'Osservatore Romano*, 12-13 May 1997; cf. *Id.*, *Ai partecipanti al Sinodo del Patriarcato Cattolico Armeno*, 26 August 1989: *S.I.C.O.* Suppl. to nn. 485-556, 42.

17   *Nuntia* 9 (1969) 85.

CCEO	CIC
278 §1. Besides the powers and faculties conferred on him by particular law, the protopresbyter has the right and obligation: 3° to see that the Divine Liturgy and the divine praises are celebrated according to the prescriptions of the liturgical books; that the decor and neatness of the churches and sacred furnishings are carefully maintained especially in the celebration of the Divine Liturgy and the custody of the Divine Eucharist; that the parish registers are correctly entered and safely kept; that ecclesiastical goods are carefully administered; finally, that the rectory is looked after with due care.	555 §1. In addition to the faculties legitimately given to him by particular law, the vicar forane has the duty and right: 3° of seeing to it that religious functions are celebrated according to the prescripts of the sacred liturgy, that the beauty and elegance of churches and sacred furnishings are maintained carefully, especially in the eucharistic celebration and custody of the Most Blessed Sacrament, that the parochial registers are inscribed correctly and protected appropriately, that ecclesiastical goods are administered carefully, and finally that the rectory is cared for with proper diligence.

The sources of canonical norms in liturgical matters of the various Churches *sui iuris* are found in various conciliar documents, for example, LG 23, UR 14-17, and *Orientalium Ecclesiarum*, but also in the particular law contained in the liturgical books, in the laws (CCEO c. 150 §2), prescriptions (CCEO c. 199), rules (CCEO c. 668), liturgical norms and statutes, as well as lawful customs and the CCEO itself. The latter defines *public* worship as that carried out in the name of the Church by persons legitimately appointed for this and through acts approved by the ecclesiastical authority; otherwise, it is called private.[18]

CIC-17 c. 2 affirmed that the Code generally (*plerumque*) does not establish anything regarding rites and ceremonies prescribed in the liturgical books of the Latin Church for the celebration of sacred functions. Further, all liturgical laws in force at the time of the promulgation of the Code retained their force, except those that were expressly corrected by the Code itself.[19]

CIC c. 2 states: "For the most part the Code does not define the rites which must be observed in celebrating liturgical actions. Therefore, liturgical laws in

---

[18] CCEO c. 668 §1: "Divine worship, if carried out in the name of the Church by persons legitimately appointed for this and through acts approved by the ecclesiastical authority, is called public; otherwise, it is called private."

[19] CIC-17 c. 2: "The Code, for the most part, determines nothing concerning the rites and ceremonies that the liturgical books approved by the Latin Church determine are to be observed in the celebration of the most holy sacrifice of the Mass, in the administration of the Sacraments, and in conducting other holy Sacramentals. Therefore, all of these liturgical laws retain their force, unless something about them is expressly corrected in this Code."

force until now retain their force unless one of them is contrary to the canons of the Code."[20]

CCEO c. 3 states: "The Code, although it often refers to the prescripts of liturgical books, does not for the most part determine liturgical matters; therefore, these prescripts are to be diligently observed, unless they are contrary to the canons of the Code."

CIC c. 2 speaks of rite and liturgical laws; CCEO c. 3 speaks of prescriptions of the liturgical books. The reason for this subtle terminological distinction lies in the fact that the CIC is particular law of one Church, that is, the Latin Church, while the CCEO deals with the Eastern Catholic Churches, all of which can have their own liturgical laws.

The canons of the CCEO often refer to the prescriptions of the liturgical books, while the CIC states that most of the time it does not make reference to the liturgical laws in its canons. Hence, the CCEO generally does not determine liturgical matters (*de re liturgica plerumque non decernit*). The CIC, even if it does not make the general statement, makes the more precise assertion that it does not define the rites which must be observed in celebrating liturgical actions (*non definit ritus, qui in actionibus liturgicis celebrandis sunt servandi*). Synthesizing, we can affirm that while the CIC speaks of the manner of celebrating liturgical actions, the CCEO speaks, above all, of the other aspects of the *res liturgica* in addition to the manner of celebration. All the liturgical norms in force at the moment of the promulgation of the Codes that are not contrary to their norms retain their force in the part where they are not contrary; the parts that are contrary are abrogated.[21]

It is also necessary to take into account the *liturgical custom*. Regarding this point, it is beneficial to examine how custom is regulated in the two codes:

CCEO	CIC
1506 §1. A custom of the Christian community, insofar as it corresponds to the action of the Holy Spirit in the ecclesial body, can obtain the force of law.	23. Only that custom introduced by a community of the faithful and approved by the legislator according to the norm of the following canons has the force of law.

---

20   Cf. *Variationes in novas editiones, Librorum liturgicorum ad normam Codicis iuris canonici nuper promulgati introducendae*, in *Notitiae* 19 (1983) 541ff. For the relationship between the current and prior law, see M. Rivella, "Commento a un canone. Il rapporto fra Codice di diritto canonico e diritto liturgico (can. 2)," *Quaderni di Diritto Ecclesiale* 8 (1995) 193-200.
21   D. Salachas, "Le prescrizioni liturgiche del '*Codice dei Canoni delle Chiese Orientali*' alla luce dell'Istruzione della Congregazione per le Chiese Orientali (6 gennaio 1996)," *Ecclesia Orans* 15 (1998) 239-273, especially 240-243.

We note immediately that according to the CCEO, custom obtains the force of law (*vim iuris*) when it responds to the activity of the Holy Spirit (LG 12);[22] according to the CIC, custom obtains *vim legis* when it is approved by the legislator. According to CCEO c. 1507 §3, custom contrary to the law or outside canon law obtains *vim iuris* if it has been observed for thirty continuous and complete years, while only a centenary or immemorial custom can prevail over a canon law containing a clause that prohibits future customs; even before the expiration of this time, the competent legislator can approve a custom as legitimate at least through tacit consent (§4). The same thing applies for CIC c. 26, but there is the clause *nisi a competenti legislatore specialiter fuerit probata*. Further, with the entry into force of law of the codes, all those customs that are reprobated by the canons of the Codes, as well as all those contrary to it but not centenary or immemorial, are revoked (CCEO c. 6, 2° and CIC c. 5 §1). The CIC adds that those customs that, in the judgment of the Ordinary, cannot be removed for reasons of places or persons can be tolerated; those customs outside the law until now in force, either universal or particular, are retained (c. 5 §2).

Therefore, post-code liturgical legislation is governed according to CIC c. 20 / CCEO c. 1502, when one is dealing with laws; if one is dealing with liturgical norms established through administrative norms, one is dealing with the norms of administrative laws.

For inter-ecclesial questions, there is a need not to lose the view of what the Roman Pontiff said:

> Liturgical diversity can be a source of enrichment, but it can also provoke tensions, mutual misunderstandings and even divisions. In this field it is clear that diversity must not damage unity. It can only gain expression in fidelity to the common Faith, to the sacramental signs that the Church has received from Christ and to hierarchical communion.[23]

IV.2. Christian Initiation

Christian initiation renders the faithful into images of Christ through the ministerial priesthood, which serves the people of God and pronounces the epiclesis, "that the Spirit may place them in the presence of the divine majesty, to render

---

[22] *Nuntia* 10 (1980) 103: "It seems appropriate also to emphasize that the text does not speak of *consuetudines vim legis*, but rather *vim iuris*, because the Group believed it preferable to maintain for a specific term for all cases, appropriate for both *consuetudines constitutivæ* and *consuetudines abrogativæ*."

[23] John Paul II, Aplet *Vicesimus quintus annus*, 4 December 1988, n. 16: *AAS* 81 (1989) 912-913; cf. SC 21.

him glory and praise, and to express thanksgiving."[24] Christian initiation is nothing other than the initial participation in the death and resurrection of Christ.

CCEO	**CIC**
697. The sacramental initiation in the mystery of salvation is completed with the reception of the Divine Eucharist; therefore after baptism and chrismation with holy Myron, the Divine Eucharist is to be administered as soon as possible in accord with the norms of the particular law of each Church *sui iuris*.	842 §2. The sacraments of baptism, confirmation, and the Most Holy Eucharist are interrelated in such a way that they are required for full Christian initiation.
695 §1. Chrismation with holy Myron must be administered in conjunction with baptism, except in a case of true necessity, in which case, however, care is to be taken to have it administered as soon as possible.	891. The sacrament of confirmation is to be conferred on the faithful at about the age of discretion unless the conference of bishops has determined another age, or there is danger of death, or in the judgment of the minister a grave cause suggests otherwise.
§2. If the celebration of chrismation with holy Myron is not done together with baptism, the minister is obliged to notify the local pastor where the baptism was administered.	
710. Regarding the participation of infants in the Divine Eucharist after baptism and chrismation with holy Myron, suitable precautions are to be taken and the prescripts of the liturgical books of the respective Church *sui iuris* are to be observed.	913 §1. The administration of the Most Holy Eucharist to children requires that they have sufficient knowledge and careful preparation so that they understand the mystery of Christ according to their capacity and are able to receive the body of Christ with faith and devotion.
	§2. The Most Holy Eucharist, however, can be administered to children in danger of death if they can distinguish the body of Christ from ordinary food and receive communion reverently.
	866. Unless there is a grave reason to the contrary, an adult who is baptized is to be confirmed immediately after baptism and is to participate in the eucharistic celebration also by receiving communion.

---

24 Instr. 1.

The canonical discipline translates into practice the decision of the Second Vatican Council to re-establish the ancient discipline of the sacraments in force among the Eastern Churches as well as the practices regarding their celebration and administration (cf. OE 12).

Despite the theological principle of the unity of the three sacraments of initiation, confirmed by both codes, there is a difference between the disciplines in liturgical celebration. Generally in the East, the temporal unity of the liturgical celebration of the three sacraments, or at least of baptism and chrismation, was preserved; in the Latin Church,[25] this is the practice for adults, while in the case of children it is preferred to postpone confirmation in order to maintain contact between the baptized and the Bishop, thereby admitting a baptized who has not yet been confirmed to first Eucharist.[26] Undoubtedly, the natural order of the sacraments is baptism, chrismation, Eucharist, but

> for particular historical reasons, the Latin Church, already in antiquity, in some cases had placed chrismation after the Eucharist to allow for the presence of the Bishop. In time the Latin Church separated these sacraments in order to permit a preparation through catechesis, so that they would be sacraments of faith and not an almost magic rite. Thus, Eucharist and chrismation were distanced from baptism for reasons of catechesis.[27]

---

25   For the doctrine, the terminology and the Latin practice, see A. Celeghin, "L'iniziazione cristiana nel CIC 1983. Prima parte: alcuni aspetti generali," *Periodica* 84 (1995) 31-75, especially 31-41.

26   See the Western-Eastern theological debate in D. Salachas, *L'iniziazione Cristiana nei Codici orientale e latino* (Rome-Bologna, 1991) 52-64; cf. CCC 1233.

27   M. Magrassi, *La Gazzetta del Mezzogiorno*, 3 June 1986, cited by D. Salachas, *Il dialogo teologico ufficiale tra la chiesa cattolica-romana e la chiesa ortodossa* (Bari, 1994) 105. Theologically and Thomistically (cf. S. Th. III, q. 65) we shall be able to explain the Latin practice as follows. The life of the spirit has a certain analogy with the life of the body. In the physical life, the individual must achieve two perfections: personal and social. The sacraments correspond to this in the spiritual life in the following manner. Human personal perfection is two-fold: direct and indirect. The direct perfection comprises three steps of life (the sacramental trilogy of Christian initiation): generation or the beginning of life, corresponding to baptism or spiritual rebirth; growth to perfection (fullness) of stature and strength, corresponding to confirmation; nourishment to maintain life and strength, corresponding to the Eucharist, which is the culmination, the summit, the maturity of Christian initiation. Nourishment is a principle external to man: as a cause, it precedes human growth / fullness, while as a preservative, it follows growth. The Eucharist is Christ himself, superior to the Christian, so insofar as it is a cause of Christian perfection, it precedes chrismation; insofar as it conserves perfected life, it follows chrismation. Confirmation, although subordinate to the Eucharist (in the order of mystery), can be administered after the Eucharist (in the functional, pastoral order).

When a baptized person receives the Eucharist before confirmation, it is for that person a food, nourishment that sustains the Christian as the adopted child of God. When the person has already received confirmation, participation in the Eucharist is made positive and active; the person offers with Christ the sacrifice of the covenant for the salvation of the world.

The CCEO does not prohibit the sacraments of baptism and chrismation from being conferred at different times, but only in the case of necessity (c. 695 §1); hence, there must be a reason serious enough so as not to derogate absolutely the general principle. The Eucharist is administered *quam primum*, conjointly or separately from baptism or chrismation. Particular law, for example, could establish that the Eucharist is administered the Sunday following the reception of the sacraments of baptism and chrismation with holy Myron. Christian initiation, in both East and the West, is viewed as *one* sacrament that comprises three sacramental steps, and catechesis about one must always refer to the other two, which are strictly connected to it.

IV.3. Baptism

By means of the washing with natural water and with the invocation of the name of God the Father and the Son and the Holy Spirit, baptism is celebrated,[28] which incorporates us in Christ and constitutes the people of God, rendering us sharers in the priestly, prophetic and royal office of Christ. By virtue of baptism, the faithful are "consecrated to form a spiritual temple and a holy priesthood" (LG 10).

CCEO c. 675 §1 includes the entire Trinitarian invocation used in the celebration, while CCEO c. 683 refers to the liturgical prescriptions of the Church of ascription without any precise indication as to how the washing takes place.[29] Canon 10 §2 of the 1980 Draft and canon 672 §1 of the 1986 Draft of the Eastern Code spoke of immersion or washing. The CIC is more explicit on this point and affirms that baptism can be conferred through immersion or pouring, observing the dispositions of the episcopal conference (c. 854). The CIC modified prior legislation, excluding sprinkling; indeed, CIC-17 c. 758 stated: "Although baptism

---

28 The introductory canon of CIC-17 included a second paragraph, with the distinction between solemn baptism and private baptism (c. 737 §2).

29 Some consultors insisted on the triple immersion and pouring, but after a lively discussion, it was decided to refer to the tradition of each particular Church, making the observance of all the rites and ceremonies prescribed in the approved liturgical books obligatory: cf. *Nuntia* 4 (1977) 19-20. The CEI permits the rite through immersion only with the authorization of the Bishop: cf. *Resolution* n. 29, 18 April 1985: ECEI 3:2284; for a comment on this Resolution: M. Calvi, "Commenti alle Delibere della CEI: Forma del Battesimo ed età della Cresima," *Quaderni di diritto ecclesiale* 4 (1991) 390-399. For the decisions taken by other Bishops conferences, see J. Martin de Agar, *Legislazione delle Conferenze Episcopali complementare al CIC* (Milan, 1990) 21.

can be validly conferred by infusion, or by immersion, or by aspersion..." In the Latin Church, the triple pouring is accompanied by the words of the minster: "N., I baptize you in the name of the Father, and of the Son, and of the Holy Spirit." In the Eastern liturgies, while the catechumen is turned towards the East, the priest says: "The servant of God, N., is baptized in the name of the Father, and of the Son, and of the Holy Spirit." At the invocation of each person of the Most Holy Trinity, the priest immerses the candidate in the water and raises him up again.[30]

Eastern Catholics who practice total immersion are: Russians, Maronites for infants; Greek-Melkites, who recommend total immersion for infants although they approved pouring in the synod of 1924; Chaldeans generally. Eastern Catholics who practice pouring are: Ukrainians, Maronites for adults, Malabars; practically all the others when it is a case of baptizing adults. There is also total immersion with pouring practiced by the Syrians, the Copts and Chaldeans, almost exclusively in the baptism of infants, while for adults they use only pouring, as do the Armenians. The Ethiopians, even though their ritual speaks of total immersion, have the almost general custom of partial immersion together with pouring, not only on the head, but also on all parts of the body not immersed.[31]

All the Christian rituals, Eastern and Western, prescribe that there be appropriate preparation prior to the administration of baptism.[32] With regard to a case of danger of death, the CCEO is more sensitive than the CIC:

CCEO	CIC
681 §4. Infants whether of Catholic or even of non-Catholic parents who are in such a critical situation that it can be prudently foreseen that they will die before they reach the use of reason, are licitly baptized.	868 §2. An infant of Catholic parents or even of non-Catholic parents is baptized licitly in danger of death even against the will of the parents.

Regarding the time of baptism, both codes (CCEO c. 686 §1 and CIC c. 867) are not very precise: *intra priores hebdomadas baptizentur* ("in the first few weeks") for the CIC and *quam primum* ("as soon as possible") for the CCEO (cf. CIC-17 c. 770), leaving everything to the various traditions or customs.[33] For the proof of

---

30 CCC 1240.
31 See C. Pujol, *I santi sacramenti nel Codice dei Canoni delle Chiese Orientali*, dispense ad uso dei studenti (Rome, no date).
32 Cf. Instr. 44.
33 "In certain Churches, the baptism of boys is permitted after the fortieth day after their birth; the baptism of girls only after the eightieth day. In other Churches, one cannot baptize before the purification of the mother, that is, the fortieth day after having given birth": *Nuntia* 4 (1977) 27.

baptism, the CCEO speaks of a *declaratio* on the part of the baptized (c. 691) while the CIC speaks of a *iusiurandum* (oath) (c. 876).[34]

IV.3.1. Minister

CCEO	CIC
677 §1. Baptism is administered ordinarily by a priest; but, without prejudice to particular law, the proper pastor of the person to be baptized, or another priest with the permission of the same pastor or the local Hierarch, is competent for its administration. This permission is legitimately presumed for a serious cause. §2. In case of necessity, however, baptism can be administered by a deacon or, in his absence or if he is impeded, by another cleric, a member of an institute of consecrated life, or by any other member of the Christian faithful; even by the mother or father if another person is not available who knows how to baptize.	861 §1. The ordinary minister of baptism is a bishop, a presbyter, or a deacon, without prejudice to the prescript of can. 530, n. 1. §2. When an ordinary minister is absent or impeded, a catechist or another person designated for this function by the local ordinary, or in a case of necessity any person with the right intention, confers baptism licitly. Pastors of souls, especially the pastor of a parish, are to be concerned that the Christian faithful are taught the correct way to baptize.

Canonical legislation provides for an ordinary, lawful, delegated, and "extraordinary" minister. For the CIC, the deacon is also the ordinary minister of baptism,[35] but the "exercise of this faculty requires either the permission of the parish priest, who enjoys the particular right of baptizing those entrusted to his pastoral care, or in case of necessity";[36] for the CCEO it is the deacon only in a case of real need.[37] When there is no deacon or he is impeded, there is a scale of preference in the determination of a minister: another cleric (cf. CCEO c. 327), a religious or any other Christian faithful.[38] For the CIC, the order is the catechist, the person entrusted by the local Ordinary or any person with the right intention; this last differentiation "emphasizes that baptism saves the individual by introducing him or her into an ecclesiastical community. Therefore, only a

---

34   Avoidance of an oath conforms to Eastern tradition: cf. *Nuntia* 4 (1977) 52.
35   For the CIC-17, the deacon was an extraordinary minister. Such a disposition had its foundation in an ancient tradition, according to which, to use the words of Saint Thomas Aquinas, "it is not for the deacon to give the sacrament of baptism, but it is for him, in the conferral of this sacrament and others, to assist and serve high ministers" (S. Th. III, q. 67, art. 1c.). LG 29 changed this disposition.
36   Congregation for the Clergy, *Directory for the Life and Ministry of Permanent Deacons*, 22 February 1998, n. 31: Suppl. to *L'Osservatore Romano*, 13 March 1998.
37   See the historical-theological commentary of D. Salachas, *L'iniziazione*..., 92-97.
38   The 1980 Draft spoke of *laicus* (c. 12 §2).

member of the community can baptize."³⁹ The CCEO does not, as such, exclude the non-baptized, since it is the doctrine of the Church that "in the case of necessity not only can a priest or deacon baptize, but also a layman or woman, indeed, even a pagan or heretic, as long as the form is observed and the person intends to do what the Church does."⁴⁰ St. Thomas explains the fundamental theological rationale:

> It is due to the mercy of Him "Who will have all men to be saved" (1 Timothy 2:4) that in those things which are necessary for salvation, man can easily find the remedy. [...] And thus [. . .] it has been established that the minister of baptism should be anyone, even not in orders, lest from lack of being baptized, man should suffer loss of his salvation.⁴¹

However, one must be attentive to interpretations that are too broad and avoid granting the faculty habitually:

> Thus, for example, the absence or the impediment of a sacred minister, which renders licit the deputation of the lay faithful to act as an extraordinary minister of baptism, cannot be defined in terms of the ordinary minister's excessive workload, or his non-residence in the territory of the parish, or his non-availability on the day on which the parents wish the baptism to take place. Such reasons are insufficient for the delegation of the non-ordained faithful to act as extraordinary ministers of baptism.⁴²

But if each can confer baptism, it is for the priest to complete the "work" with the eucharistic sacrifice (cf. LG 17) and with the administration of Holy Myron as soon as possible.

Except in the case of danger of death or necessity, a problem arises if some Eastern faithful are subject to a local Latin Ordinary: in the case, can the Latin deacon lawfully baptize the child of Eastern parents? Which rule of law is to be applied? *Locus regit actum* ("The place governs the act") or *Ius personarum*

---

39 Instr. 46; cf. *Nuntia* 4 (1977) 20.
40 Council of Florence, Sess. VIII, Bull of Union with the Armenians, *Exsultate Deo*, 22 November 1439: DEC, 1:543; Council of Florence, Sess. XI, Bull of Union with the Copts, *Cantate Domino*, 4 February 1442: DEC, 1:576; CCC 1256; cf. A. Urru, "Ministro straordinario del battesimo: fondamento de tale potestà," in *Questioni canoniche*, Studia Universitatis S. Thomæ in Urbe 22, ed. Pontificia Università S. Tommaso d'Aquino (Milan, 1984) 200-213.
41 S. Th. III, q. 67, art. 3.
42 Congregation for the Clergy et al., *Istruzione su alcune questioni circa la collaborazione dei laici al ministero dei sacerdoti*, 15 August 1997, art. 11: Suppl. to *L'Osservatore Romano*, 14 November 1997. Cf. P. J. Vere, "Non-Baptized Person as Minister of Baptism," *Roman Replies and CLSA Advisory Opinions 2000*, 163-164.

adhœret ossibus ("The law of persons sticks to the bones")? Canonists differ on this; we favor the position that one must respect the personal law, of which every Bishop, Eastern or Latin, is the guarantor; thus, the deacon does not lawfully administer baptism to a child of Eastern Christian faithful. Further, when a member of the Eastern Christian faithful receives baptism, he or she ordinarily also receives the other sacraments of Christian initiation that the deacon absolutely cannot validly administer.

If the person to be baptized is the child of Latin parents, can an Eastern deacon administer baptism to him or her? In this case, he would act unlawfully since he is prohibited by common law. In each case, the Bishop must observe CCEO c. 678 §2 and CIC c. 383 §2, which provide for the faithful residing in a place lacking a priest of their own Church *sui iuris*: the local Ordinary has the obligation to appoint a pastor of the same Church of the faithful to administer baptism (cf. CCEO c. 193 §2). If this is not possible, it is enough to appoint a bi-ritual priest; otherwise, the competence will pass to the local pastor where these faithful reside. In dealing with the Eastern Christian faithful, the Bishop cannot designate a deacon (CCEO c. 677). It is also necessary to grant the designated Latin priest the faculty to administer conjointly the sacrament of chrismation (CCEO c. 695).

Given what has already been said regarding ascription to a Church *sui iuris*, one might pose particular cases in which it is necessary to determine the competence of the minister. For example, one could encounter a case when an infant to be baptized must be ascribed to a Church *sui iuris* different than that of his / her own pastor. If the parents belong to a Church *sui iuris* different than that of their pastor, he has the right to administer the baptism and will perform it according to the prescriptions of his own Church *sui iuris*. This will not impede, as we have seen, the baptized infant from being ascribed in the Church *sui iuris* of the parents. If there is a priest of the Church *sui iuris* to which the person to be baptized is to be ascribed, the proper pastor cannot refuse the required permission (CCEO c. 678 §1). One who receives baptism from a minister of a Church *sui iuris* different than the Church of ascription does not have the right to demand the celebration according the liturgy or rite of the Church of ascription. It is the baptized person who must observe it everywhere according to CCEO c. 40 (cf. OE 4). This is not to say that the faithful lack all rights in this matter; the diocesan Bishop has the grave obligation to offer the means necessary so that the Eastern Christian faithful can live according to their own rite (CIC c. 383; CCEO cc. 193 and 678 §2).

An infant born of unknown parents is ascribed in the Church *sui iuris* of the one to whom the infant is lawfully entrusted; the competent pastor, in this case, is the pastor of the latter.

An infant born of an unmarried mother is to be ascribed in the Church *sui iuris* of the mother; in this case, the proper pastor is that of the mother.

An adopted infant belongs to the Church *sui iuris* of the adoptive parents, with priority to that of the father (if he is Catholic) or the mother (if only she is Catholic), or, if both Catholic parents are in agreement, the Church *sui iuris* of the mother; in this case, the competent pastor is that of the adoptive parents.

When there is a difference of Church *sui iuris* between the competent pastor and the person to be baptized, the law recommends that the baptism be conferred by a minister of the Church *sui iuris* to which the baptized is to be ascribed, with the required permission of the pastor (CCEO c. 678 §1).[43] This does not remove the competence of the pastor, which is ordinarily determined by territory; hence, within the territory he is the only one who is competent, and no one else, without his permission, can administer the baptism. If his subjects give birth outside the parish territory, the pastor does not lose his right, but he cannot exercise it unless the infant cannot be brought into the parish territory without danger or inconvenience; if moving the infant is not possible, the local pastor where the infant was born is competent, but the proper pastor can baptize the infant with the permission of the local pastor. According to the current practice of the Apostolic See, for the celebration of baptism according to a rite different than that of the Church *sui iuris* to which the baptized must be ascribed, permission from the Apostolic See is required.

A norm found only in the CCEO is as follows: "Infants of non-Catholic Christians are licitly baptized if their parents or at least one of them or the person who legitimately takes their place request it and if it is physically or morally impossible for them to approach their own minister" (CCEO c. 681 §5). This disposition fills the *lacuna* of the CIC; hence, if these parents present themselves to a Latin priest, the pastor will baptize the infant, who will belong to the Church of the parents; the pastor will also administer chrismation if he has the required faculty (CCEO c. 696 §2).

If the non-Catholic parents request not only baptism, but that their child be Catholic and receive a Catholic education, it should be done in writing. The baptism should be recorded in the baptismal register of the Catholic parish, noting the membership in the Church *sui iuris* (CCEO cc. 296 §2 and 37). Christian non-Catholic parents could present the certificate of their baptism to determine membership in the corresponding Church *sui iuris*, or the child can be ascribed in the Church *sui iuris* of the sponsor. This norm is not found in the two codes. If possible, the minister should be an Eastern Catholic priest who will administer baptism conjointly with chrismation and Eucharist. Further, one should keep CCEO c. 900 in mind:

---

[43] According to CIC-17 c. 98 §1, the Eastern minister could baptize a Latin infant only with a special apostolic dispensation or in grave necessity.

§1. A person who has not yet completed his or her fourteenth year is not to be received, if the parents are opposed to it.

§2. If grave inconveniences are foreseen either to the Church or to the person from receiving such a person, the reception is to be deferred, unless there is imminent danger of death.

It may rarely happen that non-baptized parents request baptism in the Catholic Church for their minor child (who is not fourteen years old). The child will be baptized on the condition that an appropriate Christian education is provided. CCEO c. 29 §2, 3° states: "If, however, a person who has not yet completed fourteen years of age is born of non-baptized parents, he or she is ascribed to the Church *sui iuris* to which belongs the one who has undertaken his or her education in the Catholic faith."

IV.3.2. Sponsors

CCEO	CIC
685 §1. For a person to fulfill validly the role of a sponsor it is necessary that he or she:	874 §1. To be permitted to take on the function of sponsor a person must:
1° be initiated with the three sacraments of baptism, chrismation with holy Myron and the Eucharist;	1° be designated by the one to be baptized, by the parents or the person who takes their place, or in their absence by the pastor or minister and have the aptitude and intention of fulfilling this function;
2° belong to the Catholic Church, with due regard for §3;	
3° have the intention of carrying out the responsibility of sponsor;	2° have completed the sixteenth year of age, unless the diocesan Bishop has established another age, or the pastor or minister has granted an exception for a just cause;
4° be designated by the person to be baptized or the parents or guardians, or, if there are not any, by the minister;	
5° not be a father, mother or spouse of the person to be baptized;	3° be a Catholic who has been confirmed and has already received the most holy sacrament of the Eucharist and who leads a life of faith in keeping with the function to be taken on;
6° not be bound by excommunication, even a minor one, suspension, deposition or deprived of the right of acting in the function of a sponsor.	4° not be bound by any canonical penalty legitimately imposed or declared;
	5° not be the father or mother of the one to be baptized.

CCEO (continued)	CIC (continued)
§2. To assume licitly the role of sponsor, it is further required that the sponsor should be of the age required by particular law and lead a life in harmony with the faith and the function to be undertaken. §3. For a just cause, it is permitted to admit the Christian faithful of another Eastern non-Catholic Church to the function of a sponsor, but always at the same time with a Catholic sponsor.	§2. A baptized person who belongs to a non-Catholic ecclesial community is not to participate except together with a Catholic sponsor and then only as a witness of the baptism.

The conditions required to function as a sponsor[44] vary slightly in the two codes. The CIC permits a godfather or a godmother alone, or a godfather and a godmother (c. 873); the CCEO is less demanding as it states that the person to be baptized have at least one sponsor (c. 684 §1). Regarding the age of the sponsor, the CIC requires sixteen years old (however, a different age is possible either in virtue of a decree by the diocesan Bishop or by way of exception). It was different in the CIC-17: "In order that one be legitimately admitted as a sponsor, he ought to have attained the age of fourteen, unless it seems otherwise to the minister for a just cause" (c. 766, 1°). For the CCEO, the age required of a sponsor is determined by particular law.[45] In both codes there is a prohibition against parents functioning as sponsors, but in the CCEO there is also one against the spouse being a sponsor. This was also the case in CIC-17 c. 765, 3°; physical and spiritual parentage are not to be combined and it would not be proper that a spouse would have spiritual parentage over the other spouse. In the case of ritual diversity between the sponsor and the person to be baptized, each will be bound to the observance of his or her own law. A member of the Latin Christian faithful who has not received confirmation cannot function validly as a sponsor for an Eastern person to be baptized.

In the prior Latin legislation regarding the conditions of suitability to carry out the task of the sponsor at baptism, it was not required for the person to have received the sacrament of confirmation or of the Eucharist (cf. CIC-17 cc. 762-769), while the sponsor for confirmation was required to have been confirmed (cf. c. 785 §1); further it was prohibited for religious[46] and sacred ministers to serve as a sponsor:

---

44 *Vetustissimus Ecclesiæ mos*: CIC-17 c. 762 §1.
45 According to the particular law of the Maronite Church, prepared in May 1993, the required age is 18: *Particular Law of the Eastern Catholic Churches*, ed. K. Bharanikulangara, (New York, 1996) 203, art. 67.
46 For religious, permission of the superior is necessary only if constitutions require it: *Comm.* 10 (1978) 84.

In order that one be legitimately admitted as a sponsor, it is proper that one:

> 4° Not be a novice or professed as a religious, unless necessity urges and then with the express approval of the Superior at least of the place;
>
> 5° Not be constituted in sacred orders, unless he has received the express permission of his own Ordinary. (CIC-17 c. 766)

The admission of non-Catholics to the function of sponsor (for reasons of family or friendship) was prohibited by prior legislation[47] and is treated differently by both codes. The CCEO allows for Eastern non-Catholics, i.e., Orthodox, to act as sponsor, but does not permit an Orthodox Christian to be the only sponsor in the baptism of a Catholic. The CIC makes no distinction between Protestants and Orthodox and states that a non-Catholic cannot be admitted as a sponsor, but only as a witness along with a Catholic sponsor. However, from the *Acta Commissionis* one can deduce that non-Catholic Orthodox Christians are not included in this prohibition.[48] The *Rite of Christian Initiation of Adults*, n. 10, affirms that one can admit as a Christian witness of a baptism a baptized person not in Catholic communion; with regard to the Eastern non-Catholics, the special discipline for the Eastern Churches must be observed.[49] The decree *Promulgato Codice*[50] refers to the specific discipline for the Eastern Churches. The 1993 *Ecumenical Directory* treats the problem from both sides, providing direction and norms for universal application, bearing in mind that:

> It is the task of the local Ordinary and of the Episcopal Conferences and Synods of Eastern Catholic Churches to see to it that the principles and norms contained in the Ecumenical Directory are faithfully applied, and with pastoral concern to take care that all possible deviations from them are avoided. (ED 6)

Certainly the communion between the Catholic Church and the Orthodox Church is closer than that of the Catholic Church with other non-Catholic ecclesial communions: one can admit an Orthodox sponsor along with a Catholic sponsor, as long as one provides for the Catholic education of the person to be baptized and the person is suitable to be a sponsor (cf. CCEO c. 618; CIC c. 874 §2). One can admit a baptized person of another ecclesial community as a wit-

---

47   CIC-17 c. 765, 2°: "In order to be a sponsor, one must belong to no heretical or schismatic sect [...]"; I. Řezáč, *Institutiones Iuris Canonici Orientalis* (Rome, 1958) 363.
48   *Comm.* 15 (1983) 182: "Notatur insuper Ecclesias Orientales Orthodoxas in schemata sub nomine communitatis ecclesialis non venire."
49   *I prænotanda dei nuovi testi liturgici*, ed. A. Donghi (Milan, 1989) 32.
50   Sacred Congregation for Divine Worship and Discipline of the Sacraments, *Promulgato Codice*, 12 September 1983: *Notitiæ* 19 (1983) 540-555.

ness of the baptism, but only with a Catholic sponsor.[51] A Catholic can carry out the same function in the case of a person who must be baptized in an Eastern Orthodox Church or in another ecclesial community. In such a case, the obligation to see to the Christian education belongs in the first place to the sponsor who is a member of the Church or ecclesial community in which the person is baptized.

Regarding the impediment of spiritual relationship that arises from baptism, but only between the Catholic sponsor and the baptized person, we refer to the matrimonial norm treated in the following chapter. It should be kept in mind that when there are several sponsors, the minister must designate one as the true sponsor; only that person assumes the obligation and contracts a spiritual relationship.

After the baptism, the local pastor must record in the proper register the name of the baptized person, the minister, the parents and sponsors, the witnesses (if there are any), the place and the date, the place of birth (CIC c. 877 §1; CCEO c. 689 §1); the CCEO adds also the Church *sui iuris* to which the baptized is ascribed, especially in those territories in which there are various jurisdictions.

IV.4. Chrismation with Holy Myron or Confirmation

Chrismation with holy Myron (CCEO) or confirmation (CIC) is designated in the Eastern and Latin tradition with different names that indicate the same reality: *manus impositio, Divini chrismatis unctio, cheirothesias* (=imposition of hands), *misticum unguentum, Sacramentum chrismatis, Chrisma salutis, mystikon chrisma, unguenti mysterium, aghion chrisma, spiritualis unguenti chrisma, phraghis, consignatio* (=sealing), *Signaculum frontium, Signaculum dominicum, Signaculum spiritale, Signaculum vitæ æternæ, perfectio baptismatis, complementum baptismatis, baptisma spiritalis*.

With the seal of the gift of the Holy Spirit, the baptized is anointed in the chrismation of holy Myron, to be comforted and strengthened in life. In the first place, the confirmation strengthens the bond of the faithful with the Church; one who receives the sacrament receives the special strength of the Holy Spirit to spread and defend the faith through word and deed as a true witness of Christ (LG 11). Undoubtedly, baptism is already a gift of the Holy Spirit on the believer, but what occurs with chrismation is comparable to that of Pentecost,[52] a strengthening to witness to Christ before the world. For Eastern faithful, this is the primary reason for the immediate conferral of this sacrament on a baptized person, which

---

51   ED 98; cf. *Comm.* 15 (1983) 182; *Nuntia* 4 (1977) 26. The function of the witness (CCEO c. 688 and CIC c. 875) is to prove the conferral of the baptism.
52   Cf. Paul VI, Apcon *Divinæ consortium naturæ*, 15 August 1971: CLD 7:604-611.

together with the Eucharist "constitute 'the sacraments of initiation,' whose unity must be safeguarded."[53]

Among the Eastern Churches of the Byzantine rite, the anointing is not performed with the imposition of hands, as in the Latin liturgy (CIC c. 880 §1), but on the most important parts of the body: the forehead, the eyes, the nose, the ears, the lips, the chest, the back, the hands and feet; the formula of the Latin Church is similar to that of the Churches of the Byzantine rite: *Accipe signaculum doni Spiritus Sancti—Signaculum doni Spiritus Sancti*.[54] For the non-Byzantine Eastern Churches, we have:

1. Syrians: *Chrismate sancto, quod est suavitas odoris Christi Dei, sigillum et signaculum fidei veritatis et consummatio donorum Spiritus Sancti, signatur N. in nomine Patris et Filii et Spiritus Sancti in vitam æternam.*[55]

2. Maronites: Beyond the Latin form, they also have *Chrismate Christi Dei, suavi odore veræ fidei, signaculo et plenitudine gratiæ Spiritus Sancti, signatur servus Dei, N. in nomine Patris et Filii et Spiritus Sancti.*[56]

3. Copts: *In nomine Patris et Filii et Spiritus Sancti unius Dei. Unctio gratiæ Spiritus Sancti, Amen,* and after other anointings, *Benedictus sis benedictione cœlesti et benedictione angelorum, benedicat tibi Dominus Iesus Christus et in eius nomine accipe Spiritum Sanctum, et esto vas sanctum, per eundem I. C. D. N. [...].*[57]

4. Ethiopians: *In unctionem gratiæ Spiritus Sancti, Amen,* and after other anointings, *Benedicti sitis benedictione cœlestium angelorum: Benedicat vobis Dominus Noster Iesus Christus. Accipe Spiritum Sanctum per virtutem Dei Patris, per virtutem Filii Iesu Christi, et per virtutem Spiritus Sancti. Sitis vasa electa et munda Domini nostri Iesu Christi [...].*[58]

5. Armenians: *Oleum suave effusum in nomine Iesu Christi super te, signaculum cœlestium donorum.*[59]

6. Chaldeans: Latin formula.[60]

---

53   CCC 1285.
54   Cf. CCC 1300.
55   *Synodus Sciarfensis Syrorum in Monte Libano celebrata anno MDCCCLXXXVIII* (Rome, 1896) ch. 5, art. 3, n. 3.
56   *Synodus provincialis Libanensis in Monte Libano celebrata anno MDCCXXXVI* (Rome, 1820) II, ch. 3, n. 5.
57   H. Denzinger, *Ritus Orientalium* (Wurzburg, 1863) 1:220.
58   *Ibid.*, 231.
59   *Ibid.*, 389.
60   A. Raes, *Introductio in liturgiam orientalem* (Rome, 1947) 145.

7. Malabars: Latin formula.[61]

8. Malankars: *Chrismate sancto, suavitate odoris Christi Dei, signo et sigillo fidei rectæ et perfectione donorum Spiritus Sancti signatur N. in nomine Patris et Filii et Spiritus Sancti in vitam æternam. Amen.*

CCEO	CIC
693. Holy Myron, which is made from the oil of olives or other plants and from aromatics, is confected only by a Bishop, without prejudice to particular law which reserves this power to the Patriarch.	880 §1. The sacrament of confirmation is conferred by anointing with chrism on the forehead, which is done by the imposition of the hand and through the words prescribed in the approved liturgical books.
694. According to the tradition of the Eastern Churches, chrismation with holy Myron is administered by a presbyter either in conjunction with baptism or separately.	§2. The chrism to be used in the sacrament of confirmation must have been consecrated by a bishop even if a presbyter administers the sacrament.
	882. The ordinary minister of confirmation is a bishop; a presbyter provided with this faculty in virtue of universal law or the special grant of the competent authority also confers this sacrament validly.

The consecration of chrism is reserved to the Bishop, but through particular law, according to the CCEO, it can be reserved to the Patriarch / Major Archbishop (Cf. CCEO c. 152; OE 13): "it manifests the bond of communion between the Bishops of a patriarchal Church or major archiepiscopal Church with the respective Patriarch or Major Archbishop."[62] Myron is composed of olive oil mixed with balsam and, according to the various traditions of each Church, many other ingredients.[63]

---

61   *Synodus Diamper. Syro-Malabarensium a. 1599*, act. IV, Mansi, v. 35.
62   D. Salachas, *L'iniziazione...*, 110; CS c. 285.
63   Cf. *Nuntia* 2 (1976) 14.

CCEO	CIC
695 §1. Chrismation with holy Myron must be administered in conjunction with baptism, except in a case of true necessity, in which case, however, care is to be taken to have it administered as soon as possible.	890. The faithful are obliged to receive this sacrament at the proper time. Parents and pastors of souls, especially pastors of parishes, are to take care that the faithful are properly instructed to receive the sacrament and come to it at the appropriate time.
§2. If the celebration of chrismation with holy Myron is not done together with baptism, the minister is obliged to notify the local pastor where the baptism was administered.	891. The sacrament of confirmation is to be conferred on the faithful at about the age of discretion unless the conference of bishops has determined another age, or there is a danger of death, or in the judgment of the minister a grave cause suggests otherwise.

The CCEO indicates that, if possible, chrismation must be administered immediately and together with baptism; only necessity dispenses from the obligation, and when it was not conferred together with baptism, it must be administered as soon as possible. If the chrismation was not administered together with baptism, either because urgency did not permit it or because the one who conferred baptism did not have the faculty, one is obliged to inform the local pastor where the chrismated person was baptized, in order to record it in the baptismal register.

IV.4.1. Minister

CCEO	CIC
696 §1. All presbyters of the Eastern Churches can validly administer this sacrament either along with baptism or separately to all the Christian faithful of any Church *sui iuris*, including the Latin Church.	883. The following possess the faculty of administering confirmation by the law itself:

1° within the boundaries of their jurisdiction, those who are equivalent in law to a diocesan bishop; |
| §2. The Christian faithful of Eastern Churches validly receive this sacrament even from presbyters of the Latin Church, according to the faculties they have. | |

CCEO (continued)	CIC (continued)
§3. Any presbyter licitly administers this sacrament only to the Christian faithful of his own Church *sui iuris*; but when it is a case of the Christian faithful of other Churches *sui iuris*, he acts licitly if they are his subjects, or those whom he licitly baptizes in virtue of another title, or those who are in danger of death, and always with due regard for the agreements entered between Churches *sui iuris* in this matter.	883. The following possess the faculty of 2° as regards the person in question, the presbyter who by virtue of office or mandate of the diocesan bishop baptizes one who is no longer an adult or admits one already baptized into the full communion of the Catholic Church; 3° as regards those in danger of death, the pastor or indeed any presbyter. 887. A presbyter who possesses the faculty of administering confirmation also confers this sacrament licitly on externs in the territory assigned to him unless their proper ordinary prohibits it; he cannot confer it validly on anyone in another territory, without prejudice to the prescript of can. 883, n. 3.

Regarding the minister of chrismation, there are divergences in the codes because of the different traditions. The CCEO confirms the ancient tradition of the Eastern Churches, according to which the minister of the sacrament of holy Myron, administered with or apart from baptism, is either the Bishop or the presbyter (OE 13). For the CIC, the administration of the sacrament is reserved to the Bishop as the ordinary minister;[64] other than the Bishop there are:[65]

1. *Ex iure* (c. 883)

- Those equivalent to the diocesan Bishop, in the respective circumscription and during their tenure in office (prelate and territorial abbot, vicar and apostolic prefect, apostolic administrator of an apostolic administration stably erected, diocesan administrator, military Ordinary); outside the territory of their competence they need *ad validitatem* a special faculty, except for those with episcopal dignity or if there is a danger of death;

---

64   In LG 26, we have the term "original" minister. The term "ordinary" is more juridical; the term "original" is more theological: *Comm.* 3 (1971) 204.
65   Cf. Sacred Congregation for the Discipline of the Sacraments, Decr *Spiritus Sancti munera*, 14 September 1946: *AAS* 38 (1946) 349-358. Surprisingly, CIC c. 882 does not apply to the presbyter endowed with the faculty to administer this sacrament the opposite term, "extraordinary," but he is designated as such: F. D'Ostilio, *Prontuario del Codice di Diritto Canonico*, 2nd ed. (Vatican City, 1996) 357.

- The priest who, in virtue of his office[66] or by mandate of the diocesan Bishop, baptizes an adult or admits him / her into full communion with the Catholic Church;[67]

- In danger of death, the pastor or any priest, even one under censure and canonical penalty.

2. A minister *through special concession* is the priest who has received the faculty to confirm from a competent authority (CIC c. 884 §1).[68]

3. A minister *through association* can be any priest who for a grave reason and in individual cases is invited by the principal celebrant to share in the conferral of the sacrament (CIC c. 884 §2): *odia restringi et favores convenit ampliari*.[69]

The *Cærimoniale Episcoporum* and the *Ritual of Confirmation* of the Latin Church counsel that the priests who can possibly be invited are the pastors of the *confirmandi* or of the place in which the confirmation is conferred, or the priests who have a particular responsibility or office in the diocese (vicars general, episcopal vicars, vicars forane).[70] Treating the extension of a mandate or concession, in the case of error or doubt, one applies the principle *supplet Ecclesia* of CIC c. 144 (CCEO c. 994).

The Bishop in his diocese legitimately administers the sacrament of confirmation to all his subjects and to those faithful who are not his subjects, at least if there is not an express prohibition by their Ordinary (CIC c. 886 §1). In another diocese, the Bishop lawfully administers confirmation to his subjects; however, for those who are not his subjects, the permission—even reasonably presumed—of the diocesan Bishop is necessary (CIC c. 886 §2).[71]

Likewise, a priest who enjoys the faculty to administer confirmation can exercise it on behalf of foreigners inside the territory for which he is designated,

---

66   Which office is treated? Only the diocesan administrator?
67   Cf. ED 101; if it is a case of a person baptized in the Catholic Church who had lost the faith from infancy and then returns to full communion with the Church, the disposition is not applied: *Comm.* 12 (1980) 23.
68   It is not necessary that the faculty be conferred in writing: cf. *Comm* 15 (1983) 186. According to CIC-17 c. 782 §§2 and 4, the concession was reserved to the Apostolic See and was only for Latin faithful, with due regard for contrary dispositions indicated in the indult.
69   Cf. M. De Pinho Ferrera, "A confirmação nas legislações da Igreja Latina e das Igrejas Orientais," *Forum Canonicum* 5 (1995) 3-17, especially 10.
70   Cf. *Cærimoniale Episcoporum ex decreto Sancrosancti Œcumenici Concilii Vaticani II instauratum auctoritate Ioannis Pauli PP. II promulgatum*, editio typica (Vatican City, 1985) 124, n. 456.
71   In danger of death, it is always administered validly and licitly.

even in exempt places (CIC c. 888), at least if there is no prohibition on the part of their own Ordinary, in which case it would be unlawful but valid. It would be invalid if it had been administered outside the designated territory, except in danger of death.

The Eastern priest administers chrismation of holy Myron to the faithful of his own Church *sui iuris* and those of another Church *sui iuris* only if they are his subjects or he is baptizing them in virtue of another lawful title, or in the case of danger of death. If these exceptions do not exist, the confirmation is unlawful (CCEO c. 696 §3).

Eastern priests always administer chrismation validly; Latin priests, except in the cases indicated above, do not validly administer confirmation.

The former practice provided the possibility that an Eastern priest could administer holy Myron to a member of the Eastern faithful of another rite, if in this rite administration was not reserved to the Bishop;[72] if the member of the faithful was a Latin, he could not receive the sacrament from an Eastern minister.[73] The CIC-17 codified it as follows: "It is nefarious for priests of the oriental rites who enjoy the privilege or faculty of confirming infants of their own rite at the time of their baptism to administer [confirmation] to latin rite infants" (c. 782 §5).[74]

The Sacred Congregation for the Eastern Church, after an agreement with the Sacred Congregation for the Discipline of the Sacraments, issued a decree regarding Eastern faithful in territories under the jurisdiction of a Latin rite Ordinary,[75] which permitted Latin priests who had the privilege to confer the sacrament of chrismation on their own faithful to confer it also on Eastern faithful entrusted to their pastoral care according to the norm of the apostolic letter *Orientalium dignitas* of 30 November 1894, art. 9. The logical consequence: Latin faithful, residing in Eastern regions and lacking their own priest, received chrismation of the Eastern priest.

Under the current legislation, the Eastern priest lawfully administers confirmation to the Latin faithful if they are his subjects, if he lawfully baptizes them

---

72   Cf. Sacred Congregation of the Holy Office, 22 April 1896: CollPF II:329, n. 1926; J. Kowalczyk, *De extraordinario confirmationis ministro. Comparatio inter disciplinam Ecclesiæ Latinæ et Ecclesiarum Orientalium* (Rome, 1969).
73   Benedict XIV, Apcon *Etsi pastoralis*, 26 May 1742, §3; Sacred Congregation of the Propagation of the Faith, 5 July 1886: CollPF, II:216, n. 1660.
74   Confirmed by the document *De Confirmatione administranda iis, qui gravi morbo in mortis periculo sunt constiututi*, 14 September 1946: *AAS* 38 (1946) 349-354. This prohibition made it unlawful for an Eastern priest to use their faculty to confirm the Latin child *in actu administrationis baptismi*, but it does not seem, in consideration of the text itself of the canon, to affect validity.
75   *AAS* 40 (1948) 422-423.

in virtue of another role or if they are in danger of death; "naturally, if a Bishop participates in the baptism, even in an unofficial way, he is the one who must confer the anointing with holy Myron, while the priest recites the other prayers."[76] In the same way, the Latin priest, endowed with the faculty to chrismate, validly and lawfully confers the sacrament together with baptism whenever he lawfully baptizes a child of Eastern parents; if he does not have this faculty, he cannot validly chrismate the Eastern child whom he baptized in virtue of another role (cf. OE 14). He can, however, validly and lawfully chrismate if the person is found to be in danger of death, even if he is not endowed with the faculty (CIC c. 883, 3°; CCEO c. 696 §2).

If, for example, the faithful of an Eastern Church *sui iuris* were lawfully entrusted to the care of a Latin pastor and he has the faculty to administer this sacrament, he administers it validly and licitly to these faithful together with baptism. If the Latin faithful of a given territory were entrusted to an Eastern pastor, he licitly administers this sacrament together with baptism to these faithful if the agreements regarding this matter between the various Churches *sui iuris* permit it, precisely to avoid every prejudice to the rite (cf. OE 14).[77] Excluding the danger of death (cf. CIC c. 889 §2), the Eastern priest does not licitly confirm even his Latin subject to whom he has administered baptism by virtue of a legitimate role (cf. CCEO c. 696 §3), if they do not fulfill the requirements of age,[78] preparation and disposition as provided in the law (cf. CIC c. 889 §2 and 891).[79] Therefore, the Eastern priest cannot licitly confirm a Latin child (who has not completed seven years of age)[80] just baptized by himself, except in danger of death, because

---

76   Cf. *Nuntia* 2 (1976) 15-16.

77   Cf. *Nuntia* 2 (1976) 19; for example, in the agreement between the Latin and Eastern Catholics of Poland, we read: "But Ruthenian Catholic priests, administering the sacrament [of baptism] to offspring pertaining to the Latin rite in the same aforementioned cases (unless necessity due to danger of death of the infant, or inclement weather, the distance between places or the difficulty of the journey is present), are in no way to dare [to administer] the sacrament of confirmation as well, under penalty of incurring *ipso facto* suspension *a divinis*, with due regard for other penalties to be inflicted according to the judgment of the Bishop": (Sacred Congregation for the Propagation of the Faith, Decr *Ad graves*, 6 October 1863: CollLac 2:563). In 1988, the Hungarian Episcopal Conference unanimously determined: "If the Greek Catholic pastor baptizes a Roman Catholic baby, he is not permitted to administer the sacrament of confirmation conjointly with the baptism," cited in P. Erdö, "Questioni interrituali (interecclesiali) del diritto dei sacramenti (Battesimo e Cresima)," *Folia Canonica* 1 (1998) 9-35, especially 33.

78   The Italian Episcopal Conference, in its Resolution n. 8 of 23 December 1983, established the age of around 12 years: ECEI 3:1596; for a commentary on this Resolution, see M. Calvi, "Commenti...," 390-399. For other episcopal conferences, see J. Martin de Agar, *Legislazione*....

79   D. Salachas has a contrary position: *L'iniziazione*..., 120.

80   This is with due regard for the possibility that the local episcopal conference did not permit confirmation at a lower age (CIC c. 891) or had established otherwise. Cf. J. Martin de Agar, *Legislazione*....

to chrismate Latin faithful who have not received an adequate formation "risks damaging the organic system of Christian Initiation in use in the Latin Church."[81] In the case of a conflict between a private right (of an individual or a family) and that of a Church, without the possibility of reconciliation, the law of the community must be respected. Further, in the case of common error, the principles of CIC c. 144 and CCEO cc. 994-995 apply.

A record is to be made in the proper parish books (mentioning the name of the chrismated, of the parents, of the sponsor, of the place and day); further, the pastor of the place where the baptism was performed must be informed. Note that in the Eastern parishes, generally there are baptismal registers in which the chrismation is also recorded, while in the Latin Church, the book of baptism is distinct from that of confirmation. It can happen that on the certificate of baptism of a member of the Eastern Christian faithful, there is no mention of chrismation. This does not authorize in any way a Catholic pastor, Latin or Eastern, to raise a doubt that chrismation was confirmed,[82] but "in order not to create misunderstandings, one would hope that the sacraments of Christian initiation would be conferred at the same time by an Eastern priest."[83]

IV.4.2. Sponsor

There is in the Church the custom of giving a sponsor (male or female) to the candidate for chrismation, whose role is that see that the confirmed person behaves as a true witness of Christ and faithfully fulfills the obligations inherent in that sacrament (CIC c. 892).

CIC c. 893 states simply that the requirements for the sponsor are the same as those established for the sponsor of baptism, recommending that it be the same sponsor as for the baptism. The prohibition against the parents acting as sponsors can create confusion because the Introduction of the *Rite of Confirmation* in the Latin Church (n. 5) states: "It may happen that the parents themselves present their child." The Congregation for Divine Worship has clarified this matter, ensuring that the parents cannot be sponsors.[84] The CCEO is silent regarding sponsors because ordinarily chrismation with holy Myron is administered conjointly with baptism; hence, the sponsor for baptism and confirmation are the same.

IV.5. Eucharist

Through the power of the Holy Spirit in the Divine Liturgy, what the Lord Jesus Christ did in the Last Supper is perpetuated (CCEO c. 698): "In the wedding

---

81   Instr. 50.
82   Cf. ED 99a.
83   A. Celeghin, "L'iniziazione cristiana nel CIC 1983. Seconda parte: alcune questioni particolari," *Periodica* 84 (1995) 297.
84   Cf. *Notitiæ* 20 (1984) 86.

Feast of the Eucharist, the Spouse (Christ) offers her (the Church) his Body and Blood, the beginning of the promised and invoked kingdom, rendered ardent by the fire of the Spirit."[85] The Eucharist is the center and the summit of all the sacraments, and through it the Church, the Mystical Body of Christ, lives and grows; from the Eucharist, the Church receives life, growth and unity. From the text of LG 26 one finds that:[86]

1. The Church of Christ is present in all the lawful local assemblies of Christians, which are also called Churches in the New Testament;

2. These local Churches are gathered with the preaching of the Gospel, and in them, under the ministry of the Bishop, the Eucharist is celebrated;

3. In such Eucharistic celebrations, through the sharing of the Body and Blood of Christ, these local Churches become the Body of Christ, which is the one holy, catholic and apostolic Church.

IV.5.1. Obligations of the Faithful

CCEO	CIC
881 §1. The Christian faithful are bound by the obligation to participate on Sundays and feast days in the Divine Liturgy, or according to the prescripts or legitimate custom of their own Church *sui iuris*, in the celebration of the divine praises.	1247. On Sundays and other holydays of obligation, the faithful are obliged to participate in the Mass. Moreover, they are to abstain from those works and affairs which hinder the worship to be rendered to God, the joy proper to the Lord's Day, or the suitable relaxation of mind and body.

---

85 Instr. 1.
86 "The Bishop, invested with the fullness of the sacrament of Orders, is the 'steward of grace of the supreme priesthood,' above all in the Eucharist, which he himself offers, or ensures that it is offered, from which the Church ever derives its life and on which it thrives. This Church of Christ is really present in all legitimately organized local groups of the faithful, which, in so far as they are united to their pastors, are also quite appropriately called Churches in the New Testament. For these are in fact, in their own localities, the new people called by God, in the power of the Holy Spirit and as the result of full conviction (cf. 1 Thess. 1:5). In them the faithful are gathered together through the preaching of the Gospel of Christ, and the mystery of the Lord's Supper is celebrated 'so that, by means of the flesh and blood of the Lord the whole brotherhood of the Body may be welded together.' In each altar community, under the sacred ministry of the bishop, a manifest symbol is to be seen of that charity and 'unity of the mystical body, without which there can be no salvation.' In these communities, though they may often be small and poor, or existing in the diaspora, Christ is present through whose power and influence the One, Holy, Catholic and Apostolic Church is constituted. For 'the sharing in the body and blood of Christ has no other effect than to accomplish our transformation into that which we receive.'"

The obligation of satisfying the festive precept, common to all the Catholic faithful of any Church *sui iuris*, can also be fulfilled by Eastern Catholics with the celebration of the Divine Praises (OE 15). The possible time for this fulfillment begins with the vespers of the vigil, a norm which takes into account the conditions and demands of modern times and which is based on the Eastern concept that the feast begins with the vespers of the vigil. Certainly, one is not dealing with a substitution (when it is not possible to participate in the Divine Liturgy), but with an alternative form.[87] Whenever Catholics participate in ecumenical services and services of other Churches and ecclesial communities on days of precept, they still have the obligation to participate in the Mass or Divine Praises (cf. ED 115). The Ordinary and Latin pastor to whom Eastern faithful are entrusted will keep these prescriptions and customs in mind, arranging for the best way that these faithful can express their faith according to their traditions.

IV.5.2. Participation

CIC c. 923 states: "The Christian faithful can participate in the eucharistic sacrifice and receive holy communion in any Catholic rite, without prejudice to the prescript of can. 844."

The possibility for Latin faithful to participate and receive the Eucharist in any rite applies *ex ipsa rei natura* also to Eastern faithful, bearing in mind the requirements of CCEO c. 403 §1: "With due regard for the right and obligation to observe everywhere their own rite, lay persons have the right to participate actively in the liturgical celebrations of any Church *sui iuris* whatsoever, according to the prescripts of the liturgical books."[88] The CIC-17 was more explicit: "To all the faithful of whatever rite, the faculty is given, for the sake of piety, to take communion in whatever rite it is confected" (c. 866 §1).[89]

---

[87] "In some regions, all the Eastern faithful consider participation in the Divine Liturgy obligatory on Sundays and feast days. Also, Eastern non-Catholics admit this same in practice. To mention in the Code that there is an alternative between the Divine Liturgy and the Divine Office would create grave confusion and would possibly induce the faithful to take the most easy path. Participation in the Divine Liturgy would be abandoned in a great measure"; the *Cœtus de expensione observationum* responded that "there is provided the clause 'according to the prescriptions and legitimate custom of the proper Church *sui iuris*'": *Nuntia* 28 (1989) 122.

[88] Pius X, Apcon *Tradita ab antiquis*, 14 September 1912: *AAS* 4 (1912) 616: "To all the faithful of whatever rite, the faculty is given, for the sake of piety, to receive the Eucharistic Sacrament in whatever rite it is confected"; cf. Sacred Congregation for the Eastern Church, Decr *Græci-rutheni ritus*, 24 May 1930, art. 37: *AAS* 22 (1930) 352.

[89] See also CIC-17 c. 1249: "The law of hearing the Sacred [rites] is satisfied wherever Mass is celebrated in a Catholic rite […]."

CCEO	CIC
710. Regarding the participation of infants in the Divine Eucharist after baptism and chrismation with holy Myron, suitable precautions are to be taken and the prescripts of the liturgical books of the respective Church *sui iuris* are to be observed.	913 §1. The administration of the Most Holy Eucharist to children requires that they have sufficient knowledge and careful preparation so that they understand the mystery of Christ according to their capacity and are able to receive the body of Christ with faith and devotion. §2. The Most Holy Eucharist, however, can be administered to children in danger of death if they can distinguish the body of Christ from ordinary food and receive communion reverently. 914. It is primarily the duty of parents and those who take the place of parents, as well as the duty of pastors, to take care that children who have reached the use of reason are prepared properly and, after they have made sacramental confession, are refreshed with this divine food as soon as possible. It is for the pastor to exercise vigilance so that children who have not attained the use of reason or whom he judges are not sufficiently disposed do not approach holy communion.

According to the Eastern legislation, immediately after baptism and chrismation one can administer the Eucharist to children, under the species of wine, bearing in mind the prescriptions of particular law.[90] For Eastern Christians, it is difficult to understand how chrism could be administered after the Eucharist, although they respect other traditions regarding this matter. Therefore, in the case of a member of the faithful who is not yet chrismated and wants to participate for the first time in the Eucharist, one ordinarily proceeds first with the administration of chrism and then admits the person to the Eucharist.

The Latin legislation, referring to the 8 August 1910 decree *Quam singulari* of Pius X,[91] received in CIC-17 c. 854, provides that for children to participate in

---

[90] Often First Communion is deferred until school age, but the Apostolic See expects the return to early practice and to the elaboration of norms and conform to the tradition of each Church *sui iuris*: cf. Instr. 51. The opinion of A. Sara in favor of First Communion at school age is interesting: cf. *Le lien* 63 (1988) 69-71. According to the particular law of the Maronite Church, prepared in May 1993, the age of reason is required: *Particular...*, ed.,K. Bharanikulangara, 203, art. 70.

[91] Denz, 3530-3536.

the Eucharist they must have reached the age of reason (seven years) and be sufficiently prepared, after having made a sacramental confession. The *Catechism of the Catholic Church* states:

> The Eastern Churches maintain a lively awareness of the unity of Christian initiation by giving Holy Communion to all the newly baptized and confirmed, even little children, recalling the Lord's words: "Let the children come to me, do not hinder them" (Mk 10:14). The Latin Church, which reserves admission to Holy Communion to those who have attained the age of reason, expresses the orientation of Baptism to the Eucharist by having the newly baptized child brought to the altar for the praying of the Our Father.[92]

CCEO	CIC
713 §2. Concerning the preparation for participation in the Divine Eucharist through fast, prayers and other works, the Christian faithful are to observe faithfully the norms of the Church *sui iuris* in which they are ascribed, not only within the territorial boundaries of the same Church, but, inasmuch as it is possible, everywhere.	919 §1. A person who is to receive the Most Holy Eucharist is to abstain for at least one hour before holy communion from any food and drink, except for only water and medicine.
	§2. A priest who celebrates the Most Holy Eucharist two or three times on the same day can take something before the second or third celebration even if there is less than one hour between them.
	§3. The elderly, the infirm, and those who care for them can receive the Most Holy Eucharist even if they have eaten something within the preceding hour.
	917. A person who has already received the Most Holy Eucharist can receive it a second time on the same day only within the eucharistic celebration in which the person participates, without prejudice to the prescript of can. 921, §2.

Everything regarding the preparation of the faithful for the Divine Eucharist is relegated to the particular law of each Church *sui iuris*, which must be observed by the Eastern faithful wherever they are (cf. CCEO c. 40 §3), even in the Latin dioceses, except in particular situations (cf. CCEO c. 883). Regarding the possibility of Eastern Catholics receiving the Eucharist a second time in the same day, it was not deemed opportune to insert such a norm in the common law; however,

---

92   CCC 1244.

it does not seem to be *contra ius seu mentem* of the Eastern Churches, but rather *præter ius*.[93]

IV.5.3. Minister of Distribution

CCEO	CIC
709 §1. The priest distributes the Divine Eucharist or, if the particular law of his Church *sui iuris* provides for it, also the deacon.	910 §1. The ordinary minister of holy communion is a bishop, presbyter, or deacon.
§2. The synod of Bishops of the patriarchal Church or the council of hierarchs is free to establish suitable norms according to which other Christian faithful, too, may distribute the Divine Eucharist.	§2. The extraordinary minister of holy communion is an acolyte or another member of the Christian faithful designated according to the norm of can. 230, §3
	230 §3. When the need of the Church warrants it and ministers are lacking, lay persons, even if they are not lectors or acolytes, can also supply certain of their duties, namely, to exercise the ministry of the word, to preside over liturgical prayers, to confer baptism, and to distribute Holy Communion, according to the prescripts of the law.

For the Eastern tradition, the principle remains firms that it is the role of priest celebrant to distribute the Eucharist,

> but it was agreed to maintain the present practice, which has now spread in some Eastern Churches and which should be maintained in due consideration of current pastoral needs. Therefore, it is appropriate that in both paragraphs (CCEO c. 709), it be left to the particular law of the Churches *sui iuris* to regulate this matter without giving in the canon itself specific directions in this matter.[94]

Hence, the Eastern Code is more cautious in admitting either the deacon or other faithful as ministers of the distribution of communion, emphasizing the exceptional character of collaboration on the part of the laity, as was also provided

---

93   Commission for the Interpretation of the CIC, *Response* of 11 July 1984: *AAS* 76 (1984) 746; it was prohibited by CIC-17 c. 857; CCC 1388; *Nuntia* 28 (1989) 90: "It is not appropriate to introduce such a norm (to be more specific) in common law."

94   *Nuntia* 15 (1982) 31; cf. V. J. Pospishil, *Eastern Catholic Church Law*, 2nd ed. (New York, 1996) 294-295.

in CIC c. 845, leaving this norm to particular law. "Even if this excludes enhancing the value of other criteria, also legitimate, and implies renouncing some convenience, a change of the traditional practice risks incurring a non-organic intrusion with respect to the spiritual framework to which it refers."[95] When a layperson distributes the Eucharist or performs other tasks in the function of sanctification, their exercise

> does not make Pastors of the lay faithful; in fact, a person is not a minister simply in performing a task, but through sacramental ordination. Only the Sacrament of Orders gives the ordained minister a particular participation in the office of Christ, the Shepherd and Head in his Eternal Priesthood. The task exercised in virtue of supply takes its legitimacy formally and immediately from the official deputation given by Pastors, as well as from its concrete exercise under the guidance of ecclesiastical authority.[96]

The legitimization of the substitution entrusted to the laity derives immediately and formally from the official deputation given by the pastors; its concrete realization is directed by ecclesiastical authority. "Temporary deputation for liturgical purposes, mentioned in canon 230 §2, does not confer any special or permanent title on the non-ordained faithful."[97] Further, the extraordinary minister of the Eucharist cannot exercise his supplementary position "when there are present in the Church, though not participating in the Eucharistic celebration, ordinary ministers who are not in any way impeded."[98] None of this confers on the lay faithful any right to remuneration or support on the part of the Church.

IV.5.4. Concelebration

"Concelebration" is the simultaneous participation of several presbyters in the same Eucharist under the presidency of a principal celebrant: "In this manner of celebrating Mass, several priests act together with one will and one voice, by the power of the same priesthood and in the place of the high priest; together they consecrate and offer the one sacrifice in one sacramental act, and together participate in it."[99] It was prohibited by CIC-17 c. 803, except on the occasion

---

95   Cf. Instr. 58; according to the particular law of the Maronite Church, prepared in May, 1993, the authorization of the Bishop is required to permit the deacon and the subdeacon to distribute the Eucharist: *Particular...*, ed. K. Bharanikulangara, 204, art. 73.
96   CL 23: *AAS* 81 (1989) 430.
97   Congregation for Clergy et al., *Istruzione su alcune questioni circa la collaborazione dei laici al ministero dei sacerdoti*, 15 August 1997, art. 1 §3: Suppl. to *L'Osservatore Romano*, 14 November 1997.
98   Authentic Response of 20 February 1987: *AAS* 80 (1988) 1373.
99   Sacred Congregation for Rites, Decr *Ecclesiæ semper*, 7 March 1965:*AAS* 57 (1965) 411: "In hac ratione Missam celebrandi plures sacerdotes, in virtute eiusdem Sacerdotii et in persona Summi Sacerdotis simul una voluntate et una voce agunt, atque

of presbyteral ordination, on the part of the newly-ordained, and on the occasion of episcopal ordination, on the part of the assisting Bishops. St. Thomas Aquinas, speaking about the concelebration of the newly-ordained, affirms: "The priest does not consecrate except in the person of Christ and they (the celebrants), though many, are only one in Christ"; so "it is of little importance that this sacrament is consecrated by one or many, as long as the rite of the Church is respected."[100]

The current legislations permit concelebration with great liberality. Furthermore, the CCEO legislates on inter-ecclesial concelebration:

> For a just cause and with the permission of the eparchial Bishop, Bishops and presbyters of different Churches *sui iuris* can concelebrate, especially to foster love and to manifest the unity of the Churches. All follow the prescripts of the liturgical books of the principal celebrant, avoiding any liturgical syncretism whatever, and preferably with all wearing the liturgical vestments and insignia of their own Church *sui iuris*. (CCEO c. 701)

Concelebration manifests the unity of the priesthood and the fullness of the profession of faith and of ecclesial communion (cf. SC 57), but when it occurs among priests belonging to different Churches *sui iuris*, liturgical syncretism is to be avoided: it is necessary to observe the liturgical prescriptions of the Church of the principal celebrant and to use the liturgical vestments and insignia proper to each concelebrant.

> It is a most eloquent way of showing the variety of the ecclesial traditions and their coming together in the unity of the Church. This is a meaningful symbol of the future unity in multiformity and an instrument to protect the Eastern Churches and their specificity against every assimilation, especially in places where they are in the minority.[101]

Because concelebration is a sacramental act, all the concelebrants must pronounce the consecratory words, as affirmed by Pius XII[102] as well as the response of the Sacred Congregation of the Holy Office to the doubt:

> Whether several priests validly concelebrate the sacrifice of the Mass, if only one of them pronounce the words "Hoc est corpus meum" and "Hic est sanguis meus" over the bread and wine, while the others

---

unicum Sacrificium unico actu sacramentali simul conficiunt et offerunt, idem simul participant."
100   S. Th. III, q. 82, art. 2, ad 2.
101   Instr. 57; cf. *Nuntia* 4 (1977) 32-33.
102   *AAS* 46 (1954) 666.

do not pronounce the words of the Lord, but, with the knowledge and consent of the celebrant, have the intention and manifest the intention to make his words and actions their own. Reply: In the negative, because, by the institution of Christ, he alone celebrates validly who pronounces the words of consecration.[103]

Concelebration among ministers of different Churches *sui iuris*, though not considered explicitly by the CIC (*lacuna legis*), is also applicable for Latin ministers, respecting certain principles:[104]

> The particular law of each Church *sui iuris* must establish accurately norms regarding the preparation of the eucharistic bread, the prayers to be recited by the priests before the Divine Liturgy, the observance of the eucharistic fast, the liturgical vestments, the time and place of the celebration and other similar matters.

> Without causing astonishment to the Christian faithful, it is permitted to use the liturgical vestments and bread of another Church *sui iuris*, if the liturgical vestments and bread of one's own Church *sui iuris* are not available. (CCEO c. 707)

Given the variety of the Eastern Churches, common law relegates the prescriptions of a rather liturgical character to the particular law of each Church *sui iuris*.[105] The provisions regarding concelebration do not affect the principle that to celebrate in a rite different than one's own requires a special indult of the Apostolic See; further, CCEO c. 40 §2 directs that all clerics must faithfully observe their own rite[106] and also the liturgical prescriptions of their own Church *sui iuris* (CCEO c. 674; CIC c. 846).[107]

---

103   *AAS* 49 (1957) 370: CLD 4:256-257.
104   The *Ritus servandus in concelebratione Missæ* (Vatican City, 1965) 15, n. 17, states than any Latin priest can concelebrate with other priests of the Latin rite, even if the Mass is celebrated in a rite different that his. However, the manner of thinking of the Church (the *mens*) appears clear in CCEO c. 701; for a history of concelebration, see B. Neunhauser, "La concelebrazione nella tradizione della Chiesa occidentale," in B. Neunhauser et al., *Concelebrazione, dottrina e pastorale* (Brescia, 1965) 1-17; E. Lanne, "La concelebrazione nella tradizione delle Chiese orientali," *ibid.*, 18-36.
105   Cf. C. Pujol, "Vinum 'cui modica aqua miscenda est,'" *Periodica* 81 (1992) 303-318; CIC-17 c. 816 states: "A priest in the celebration of the Mass according to his own rite, must use unleavened or leavened bread whenever he says the Holy [Mass]"; Pius X, Apcon *Tradita ab antiquis*, 14 September 1912: *AAS* 4 (1912) 609-617; Sacred Congregation for the Eastern Church, Decr *Græci-rutheni ritus*, 24 May 1930, art. 37: *AAS* 22 (1930) 352.
106   Cf. CS c. 2 §1.
107   Cf. Pius X, Apcon *Tradita ab antiquis*, 14 September 1912: *AAS* 4 (1912) 615: "Priests are not permitted to co-mingle the sacred rite: therefore, each priest is to confect

IV.5.5. Offerings for the Divine Liturgy

> The priest receives money, not as the price for consecrating the Eucharist, or for singing the Mass (for this would be simoniacal), but as a provision for his livelihood, as stated above.[108]

On 15 July 1908, the Sacred Congregation for the Propagation for the Faith for Eastern Rite Affairs established that Bishops and priests who wish to send Mass intentions to Eastern priests could do so through the same congregation or the apostolic delegates, if there were any in the respective regions of the East. They could also send them directly to Eastern Hierarchs who had ordinary episcopal jurisdiction in the East, for the needs of the priests subject to them. It was prohibited, however, to send them directly to Eastern priests or to superiors of Eastern religious congregations, as well as to Eastern prelates who were only titular Bishops or simply patriarchal vicars.[109] On 7 January 1930, it was established by the Sacred Congregation for the Eastern Church that "in order that any collection, whether of money or of Mass stipends, be made in a Latin diocese by any Eastern cleric of whatsoever order or dignity, the permission of the Sacred Congregation for the Eastern Church is absolutely required."[110] The new Eastern legislation leaves the faithful free to give Mass intentions, but

> [i]f they accept offerings for the Divine Liturgy from the Christian faithful of another Church *sui iuris*, priests are bound by the grave obligation of observing the norms of that Church regarding those offerings, unless it is established otherwise by the donor. (CCEO c. 717)

The norm, not considered in the CIC (cf. c. 945 §1), is especially important for Latin faithful who freely give offerings to Eastern priests for the celebration of holy Masses, since these priests are bound to observe the norms of each Church *sui iuris*, including the Latin Church, to which the donors belong.[111] For this purpose, inter-ecclesial collaboration among those who exercise their power in the same territory is opportune in order to establish the same norms regarding taxes and offerings (CCEO c. 1013 §2; CIC c. 952).[112]

---

and administer the Sacrament of the Body of Christ according to the rite of his Church"; CIC-17 c. 733.

108 S. Th. II-II, q. 100, art. 2, ad 2.
109 *ASS* 41 (1908) 640-641.
110 Sacred Congregation for the Eastern Church, Decr *Sæpenumero Apostolica Sedes*, 7 January 1930, art. 1: *AAS* 22 (1930) 108-110, especially 109. See also the *Monitum de queritantibus stipem pro Orientalibus*: *AAS* 20 (1928) 106: CLD 1:27.
111 Cf. *Nuntia* 15 (1982) 34; Congregation for the Clergy, Decr *Mos iugitur* on collective intentions, 22 February 1991: *AAS* 83 (1991) 443-446; V. De Paolis, "Liturgia e denaro. Indicazioni del 'Codice di diritto canonico' e del 'Codice dei canoni delle Chiese orientali,'" *Revista liturgica* 84 (1997) 245-260.
112 See section III.18.

IV.6. Penance and Indulgences

The sacrament of penance produces a two-fold effect: it pardons the offense made to God because Christ has obtained the Father's mercy for us, but it also reconciles us with the Church that we have injured with our sins, while it strengthens us to be converted with charity, example and prayer.

CCEO c. 718 corresponds to CIC c. 969, but the former seems more complete.

CCEO	CIC
718. In the sacrament of penance the Christian faithful who, having committed sins after baptism, led by the Holy Spirit, turn to God in their hearts and, moved by sorrow for their sins, resolve to lead a new life. Through the ministry of the priest, to whom they make confession and from whom they accept a fitting penance, they obtain forgiveness from God and at the same time are reconciled with the Church, which they have wounded through sin. Thus this sacrament contributes greatly to the fostering of Christian life and disposes the Christian faithful for the reception of the Divine Eucharist.	959. In the sacrament of penance the faithful who confess their sins to a legitimate minister, are sorry for them, and intend to reform themselves obtain from God through the absolution imparted by the same minister forgiveness for the sins they have committed after baptism and, at the same time, are reconciled with the Church which they have wounded by sinning.

Along with the ecclesiological element present in the CIC, the CCEO also has a pneumatological element: the faithful, who are sinners "led by the Holy Spirit, turn to God in their hearts"; there is then an acceptance of an appropriate satisfaction; finally, there is the relationship with the Christian life and the Eucharist: *Thus this sacrament contributes greatly to the fostering of Christian life and disposes the Christian faithful for the reception of the Divine Eucharist.*

CIC c. 959, curiously, is the only introductory canon to the sacraments that is not accompanied by any sources, although there is an obvious reference to LG 11 and PO 5.[113] On the contrary, CCEO c. 718 not only has relatively recent sources, but also ancient and particular ones.[114]

Both codes (CCEO c. 720 and CIC cc. 960-961) emphasize the meaning and value of the individual confession as the only ordinary way in which the Christian

---

113   Cf. Pontificia Commissio Codici Iuris Canonici Authentice Interpretando, *Codex Iuris Canonici. Fontium annotatione et indice analytico-alphabetico auctus* (Vatican City, 1989) 269.
114   Cf. Pontificium Consilium de Legum Textibus Interpretandis, *Codex Canonum Ecclesiarum Orientalium. Fontium annotatione auctus* (Vatican City, 1995) 261.

faithful, conscious of grave sin, obtain remission of it.¹¹⁵ However, the codes also take into consideration an extraordinary manner of conferral of this sacrament: the sacramental absolution of several penitents together in a general manner, without prior individual confession; this is extraordinary and exceptional. This extraordinariness must be verified in particular circumstances: imminent danger of death and lack of sufficient time to hear the confessions individually; other grave necessity, which can be verified when, taking into account the number of penitents, there are not a sufficient number of priests available to administer the sacrament to the individual penitents within a convenient time:

> In this case, however, one should not confuse such a situation in Eastern rites wherein there is recited before communion by the priest celebrant an absolutory prayer. The Roman Rite also has similar formulas. These formulas, not preceded by individual confession, presume the state of grace, the absence of grave guilt on the part of the participants and are only praiseworthy acts of ordinary, daily metanoia of the soul towards God.[116]

The eparchial Bishop (CCEO) or diocesan Bishop (CIC) is solely competent to determine the existence of the circumstances. The diocesan Bishop must act *attentis criteriis* agreed upon with the other members of the episcopal conference,[117] while the eparchial Bishop *collatis consiliis* with the Patriarchs and other eparchial Bishops of the other Churches *sui iuris* who exercise their power in the same territory. The Bishop cannot establish criteria on his own and in no way has the power to modify, add or remove conditions already established in the code and the criteria agreed upon with other Bishops.[118] There is a pastoral need to avoid confusion among the faithful who reside in the same territory; but whether the Bishop must rule on an individual case by case basis or by a general prescription (*etiam generalibus præscriptis*) is clearly indicated in CCEO c. 720 §3 and clarifies CIC c. 961 §2:

---

115 Cf. John Paul II, Mp *Misericordia Dei* on certain aspects of the celebration of the sacrament of penance, 7 April 2002: *AAS* 94 (2002) 452-459.

116 *Nuntia* 6 (1978) 56-57.

117 The Italian Episcopal Conference declared that the conditions to admit extraordinary confession mentioned in c. 961 §1, 2° are not met in Italy: cf. Nota della Presidenza della CEI del 30 aprile 1975, in *Notizario CEI* 4/1975, 70-72. For the other episcopal conferences, see J. Martin de Agar, *Legislazione*....

118 For an explanation on the norm regarding general absolution without prior individual confession, see *Comm.* 28 (1996) 141-146, 177-181.

CCEO	CIC
720 §3. The eparchial Bishop is competent to decide whether such grave necessity exists. He can, after having held consultation with Patriarchs and eparchial Bishops of other Churches *sui iuris* who exercise their power in the same territory, determine the cases of such necessity even through general prescripts.	961 §2. It belongs to the diocesan bishop to judge whether the conditions required according to the norm of §1, n. 2 are present. He can determine the cases of such necessity, attentive to the criteria agreed upon with the other members of the conference of bishops.

The place of the celebration of the sacrament of penance is a church or oratory, that is, a sacred place, but there is the traditional Eastern custom to celebrate it outside of a confessional, as in the Latin Church, but in a sacred building and, according to some traditions, before an icon of Christ. "It will be the task of the authorities of the individual Churches *sui iuris* carefully to examine their liturgical books, even those of the past, to find the formulas which best express the richness of their own traditions in this specific field."[119] In virtue of CIC c. 964 §2, the Italian Episcopal Conference has agreed to other places, though the following conditions must be assured: the sites must be in a proper place (church, oratory, or their attached building), must be decent and allow for the correct celebration of the sacrament.[120]

CCEO	CIC
736 §1. The proper place for the celebration of the sacrament of penance is a Church, without prejudice to particular law.	964 §1. The proper place to hear sacramental confessions is a church or oratory.
§2. Because of sickness or another just cause, this sacrament can be celebrated also outside its proper place.	§2. The conference of bishops is to establish norms regarding the confessional; it is to take care, however, that there are always confessionals with a fixed grate between the penitent and the confessor in an open place so that the faithful who wish to can use them freely.
	§3. Confessions are not to be heard outside a confessional without a just cause.

---

119   Instr. 89.
120   Cf. *Notizario CEI* 11 (1985) 46. For the other episcopal conferences, see J. Martin de Agar, *Legislazione*.... With regard to the fixed screen, as found in CIC c. 964 §2, the minister "legitime decrenere valeat, etiamsi pœnitens forte aliud postulet, ut confessio sacramentalis excipiatur in sede confessionali crate fixa instructa": *Authentic Response*, 7 July 1998: *Comm.* 30 (1988) 27.

The norms regarding ministers and faculties are the same in both codes: priests who have the faculty to administer the sacrament of penance in virtue of office (local Hierarch / Ordinary, canon penitentiary for the CIC, pastor and the one who takes the place of the pastor, chaplains for the CIC) and during the time they hold office, or through concession on the part of the local Hierarch / Ordinary of the place where the priests are incardinated or where they have a domicile,[121] can administer it validly in the entire world to any of the Christian faithful, unless in a special case the local Hierarch / Ordinary had expressly prohibited it (cf. OE 16).[122] Let us now point out certain peculiarities of both codes.

CIC c. 967 §1 expressly mentions the Roman Pontiff, while for the CCEO it is implied, keeping in mind canon 43: "The Bishop of the Roman Church, in whom continues the office (*munus*) given by the Lord uniquely to Peter, the first of the Apostles, and to be transmitted to his successors, is the head of the college of Bishops, the Vicar of Christ and pastor of the entire Church on earth. By virtue of his office (*munus*) he possesses supreme, full, immediate and universal ordinary power in the Church which he is always able to exercise freely."

In the CIC, cardinals have by virtue of the law itself the faculty, to be exercised freely without limitations, to administer the sacrament of penance (c. 967 §1);[123] no one can prohibit or limit its exercise, except of course the Roman Pontiff, or some possible canonical penalty that would have such a limiting effect; in the CCEO, it is not so stated expressly, but it applies both in virtue of the episcopal character with which cardinals normally are endowed and in virtue of the law itself (CIC).

With regard to the Patriarchs of the Eastern Churches who are not created cardinals, the CCEO is silent, differing from CS c. 283, 1°, which granted to them *ubique terrarum* to hear confessions of Eastern faithful and to absolve them of

---

121 The faculty ceases with the loss of domicile also for religious. "This does not mean that a Bishop cannot grant to a religious who lacks a domicile in his diocese the faculty to confess in his own diocese, nor that a Bishop cannot establish that a religious who is departing to retain the faculty to confess in his own diocese. In these cases, the faculty is not extended automatically to the entire world": V. De Paolis, "Il sacramento della penitenza," in *La funzione di santifcare della Chiesa*, ed. Gruppo Italiano Docenti di Diritto Canonico (Milan, 1995) 137.

122 CIC-17 c. 881 §1: "All priests of either type of clergy who are approved for the hearing of confessions in a place, whether so enabled by ordinary or delegated jurisdiction, can also validly and licitly absolve wanderers and travelers from another diocese or parish coming to them, and likewise Catholics of any Eastern rite."

123 Beyond the faculty to hear confession everywhere in the world, cardinals enjoy the ordinary faculty, which they cannot delegate to others, to absolve everywhere all penitents in the internal sacramental forum of the censures of excommunication *latæ sententiæ* or non-declared interdict, even those reserved to the Apostolic See, without recourse to the proper Ordinary of the faithful, but not from the censures treated in cc. 1382 and 1388: *Rescritto della Segreteria di Stato, n. 10*, in *Comm.* 31 (1999) 13.

every sin or censure, even reserved, but not those reserved to the Apostolic See.[124] Canon 127 §1, 1° of the *Testi Iniziali* of 1958 stated: "Ordinaria iurisdictione ad confessiones excipiendas potiuntur: Pro universa Ecclesia, præter Romanum Pontificem, S.R.E. Cardinales et Patriarchæ ad normam iuris." [125] Strangely, it was never spoken of in the deliberations of the Pontifical Commission for the Revision of the Code of Eastern Canon Law (Pontificia Commissio Codici iuris Canonici Orientalis Recognoscendo: PCCICOR), even if the power of the Patriarch, according to the norm of CCEO c. 78, is ordinary and proper over all the Christian faithful of the Church over which he presides. [126] An eparchial Bishop could prohibit in his eparchy his or another Patriarch from administering to the sacrament of penance in a special case, in virtue of CCEO c. 722 §2.

CIC c. 968 §1 mentions the canon penitentiary, a non-existent figure in the CCEO. CCEO c. 723 §2 also mentions the superior of a religious institute or of a clerical society of the common life *ad instar religiosorum* of patriarchal / major archiepiscopal right. An institute or society is of patriarchal or major archiepiscopal right if it was erected by a Patriarch or Major Archbishop, or recognized as such by a decree from them.

A canon that brings to mind inter-ecclesial collaboration is CIC c. 971:

> The local ordinary is not to grant the faculty of hearing confessions habitually to a presbyter, even one having a domicile or quasi-domicile in his jurisdiction, unless he has first heard the ordinary of the same presbyter insofar as possible.

CIC c. 991 involves *ex ipsa natura rei* also Eastern faithful: "Every member of the Christian faithful is free to confess sins to a legitimately approved confessor

---

124 CS c. 283, 1°: "Besides other privileges of common law, granted or recognized by the Roman Pontiff, all Patriarchs enjoy, after the enthronement has been performed according to c. 235, the following faculties and privileges: 1° to hear everywhere the confessions of the faithful of Eastern rites, also of the religious of both sexes, and to absolve from all sins and censures, including reserved ones, with the exclusion of those excepted in c. 185 §1, 1°."
125 *Nuntia* 6 (1978) 67.
126 CCEO c. 78: "§1. The power that the Patriarch possesses, according to the norm of the canons and legitimate customs, over bishops and other Christian faithful of the Church over which he presides is ordinary and proper, but personal; therefore, the Patriarch cannot constitute a vicar for the entire patriarchal Church nor can he delegate his power to someone for all cases.

"§2. The power of the Patriarch is exercised validly only within the territorial boundaries of the patriarchal Church unless the nature of the matter or the common or particular law approved by the Roman Pontiff establishes otherwise."

of his or her choice, even to one of another rite" (cf. OE 16),[127] but it is necessary to take the following into account.

CCEO c. 727 permits the limitation of the faculty to absolve from sins through its reservation to a particular authority: "While the establishment of an authority inferior to the Holy See competent to reserve sins is, in the context of the current canon law, of little efficacy, it seems opportune to retain it."[128] The Holy Office, in the *Instructio super casuum conscientiæ reservationes* of 13 July 1916, after having noted that the reservation is *ad ædificationem* and not *ad destructionem* (n. 1), recommends that reserved sins be *pauci omnino, tres, vel, ad summum, quatuor, atque ex gravioribus [. . .] et atrocioribus criminibus specifice determinatis* (n. 2), and that the reservation not last longer than the necessary time (n. 2); that the reserved sins not concern merely internal matters (n. 3), and that they not have been reserved to the Holy See (n. 4); further, the reservation is to be made known to the faithful (n. 6), and is to determine some cases in which the reservation ceases in order to avoid grave inconvenience.[129] The purpose of the reservation, therefore, is the salvation of souls; "retaining it in substance is consonant with the most genuine Eastern traditions, and is also truly efficacious to assure for the Eastern faithful in the modern world that *deterrent* which one hopes to achieve for the Latin faithful with the reserved excommunications *latæ*

---

[127] CIC-17 c. 905: "It is fundamental to each member of the faithful [to be allowed] to confess his / her sins, if he / she wishes, to a legitimately approved confessor even of another rite"; Sacred Congregation for the Propagation of the Faith for Eastern Rite Affairs, 18 August 1913: *AAS* 5 (1913) 397; *Id.*, 17 August 1914: *AAS* 6 (1914) 462; Sacred Congregation for the Eastern Church, 1 March 1929: *AAS* 21 (1929) 152ff; *Id.*, Decr *Græci-rutheni ritus*, de administratione Ordinariatus Græco-rutheni in regione Canadensi, 24 May 1930, *AAS* 22 (1930) 346-354: "The faithful of the Latin rite, even if a priest of their own rite is available, can validly and licitly confess their sins to, and receive absolution from, a priest of the Greek-Ruthenian rite who is approved by his Ordinary. Likewise the faithful of the Greek-Ruthenian rite can go to confession to a priest of the Latin rite who is approved by his Bishop. But priests of the Latin rite cannot absolve the faithful of the Greek-Ruthenian rite from censures and cases which the Greek-Ruthenian Ordinary has reserved to himself, without the latter's permission. The same thing in turn is true of the Greek-Ruthenian priests as regards censures and reservations established by the Ordinary of the Latin rite. But to avoid difficulties which rather frequently occur in practice, let all Ordinaries inform each other of any reservations they may have made" (art. 36, p. 352). "The Holy See has always held the maxim that one must not bind in any way the freedom of Christians in a manner as delicate as sacramental confession, and has always desired that it would be licit to everyone to reveal his / her sins to any approved minister they prefer. Equally it has never prohibited an approved confessor from hearing the confessions of any Catholic who presents him/herself to the sacred tribunal [...]. This always was and is the maxim and the practice held by the Holy See. No distinction is made regarding rite, since the administration of this sacrament does not bring any change of rite; indeed, the same Holy See, many times removing any doubt on the particular matter, has declared that no limitation of this kind should be made": CollPF I, n. 839.
[128] *Nuntia* 28 (1989) 98.
[129] *AAS* 8 (1916) 313-315.

sententiæ."[130] However, the eparchial Bishop will be able to apply this norm only with the consent of the Synod of Bishops of the patriarchal / major archiepiscopal Church (in the patriarchal / major archiepiscopal Churches) or of the Council of Hierarchs (in the metropolitan Churches *sui iuris*) or of the Apostolic See (in all other cases).[131]

Since the reservation directly affects the jurisdiction of the priest, which is this case becomes limited, it and the consequent limitation of the faculty regard not the place where the sin was committed, but the place where the confession is made. Therefore, all the faithful are subject to the reservation, both those who belong to the territory where there is a reservation and those who are transients who have committed a sin reserved in the territory, even if the sin was committed outside the territory of the reservation. On the other hand, one is to not subject to the reservation if the sin was committed in the territory where the sin was reserved and confessed in another territory in which the sin is not reserved.[132] The reason is because the reservation and the limitation of the faculty is an act of jurisdiction which has an effect only within the territory of the one making the reservation (cf. CCEO c. 729, 3°).

If religious belonging to a clerical institute, whose superior has ordinary power which he can delegate to others, absolve in virtue of the faculty granted by that superior and do so for the subjects of the said superior, they are not bound to the reservation made by the eparchial Bishop. Religious who confess to others or who use the faculty received from the Bishop are subject to reservation of the Bishop.

In virtue of CCEO c. 727, there can be differences in the discipline of reserved sins among the various Churches *sui iuris*, but we shall deal with the relations with the Latin Church.

According to CCEO c. 728, it is reserved to the Apostolic See (Apostolic Penitentiary, PB arts. 58 §2 and 118) to absolve from sins of violation of the sacramental seal and absolution of an accomplice *contra sextum*; further, it is reserved to the Roman Pontiff to absolve from the crime of physical violence or grave injury against the Roman Pontiff himself (major excommunication, CCEO c. 1445 §1); finally, absolution for a procured abortion is reserved to the eparchial Bishop[133] if the effect follows (there is the major excommunication according to the norm of CCEO cc. 1450 §2, 1456 §2 and 1457). But "with the *reservatio peccati ratione sui* in cases envisioned in c. 728, in practice the same disciplinary effects are achieved

---

130   *Nuntia* 20 (1985) 58.
131   Cf. *Nuntia* 28 (1989) 98.
132   Cf. Sacred Congregation for the Propagation of the Faith, Instructio ad Archiepiscopum Allepensis, 2 June 1835.
133   The eparchial Bishop can be either that of the eparchy in which the abortion was committed or that of another. The Bishop can delegate another confessor.

in practice with the *reservatio ratione censuræ* (found in the CIC), given that one must make recourse to the Apostolic See or, in the case of abortion, to the eparchial Bishop. With the *reservatio peccati ratione sui*, however, one is not going contrary to the traditions of the Eastern Churches, because it fundamentally belongs to the ancient penitential discipline."[134]

The Latin Code does not have sins that are directly reserved,[135] but provides excommunication *latæ sententiæ* reserved to the Apostolic See[136] for the following crimes: profanation of the Eucharistic species (c. 1367); physical violence against the Roman Pontiff (c. 1370); absolution of an accomplice of a sin against the sixth commandment (c. 1378 §1); episcopal consecration without the pontifical mandate (c. 1382); violation of the sacrament seal on the part of a confessor (c. 1388 §1). The crime of abortion[137] is not reserved to the Apostolic See (c. 1398) even though one incurs the same penalty mentioned above, as also is the case for the crime of apostasy, heresy and schism (c. 1364 §1). As soon as the crime is committed, the penalty (generally excommunication) is incurred; the intervention of a judicial authority is not necessary. To this list we must add the norm of the Congregation for the Doctrine of the Faith, which threatens excommunication *latæ sententiæ* against anyone who records by means of technical instruments or who divulges by means of instruments of social communication that which is said by the confessor and the penitent.[138]

The Eastern Code does not recognize penalties inflicted in an automatic manner, "because they do not correspond to the genuine Eastern traditions, are unknown in the Orthodox Churches and do not seem necessary for an adaptation of the Eastern Code to the present needs of the discipline of the Eastern Catholic Churches."[139]

---

134   *Nuntia* 28 (1989) 97-98; also, "the *remissio* is not to be distinguished from the *absolutio*": *Nuntia* 20 (1985) 8.
135   With the *reservatio peccati ratione sui* of the CCEO, one achieves the same disciplinary effects which are achieved with the *reservatio ratione censuræ* of the CIC: *Nuntia* 28 (1989) 97-98.
136   Cf. Appendix XI.
137   One must understand by abortion not only the expulsion of an immature fetus, but also the killing of the same fetus carried in any way and at any time from the moment of conception: *AAS* 81 (1989) 1818. The cardinal vicar of Rome, by mandate of the Roman Pontiff, delegated the faculty to absolve from this censure in the internal sacramental forum to any priest who has the faculty to hear confessions in the Diocese of Rome: Decr of 22 April 1984, *Rivista diocesana di Roma* 25 (1984) fascicle 3, 637.
138   Congregation for the Doctrine of the Faith, Decr *Congregatio*, 23 September 1988: *AAS* 80 (1988) 1367: CLD 12:809.
139   *Nuntia* 3 (1976) 9; the penal law included in the projects of the Eastern Code approved in 1948 by Pius XII was never promulgated; it followed the Latin legislation and adopted the penalties *latæ sententiæ*: cf. *Nuntia* 4 (1977) 114-127.

The CCEO requires a sentence or penal decree for the infliction of a penalty (cc. 1402 and 1408); however, when there are serious reasons against the ordinary procedure and the proofs are certain, some penalties can be applied by means of an extrajudicial decree.[140] Reserved sins are punished with major excommunication by means of a penal trial (cc. 1468-1482).[141] One must take note of the clause in CCEO c. 1408:[142] "without prejudice to the right of the Roman Pontiff or an ecumenical council to establish otherwise." For example, according to the apostolic constitution *Universi Dominici Gregis*,[143] which regulates the election of the future pope, the penalty of excommunication *latæ sententiæ* is incurred by those who do not observe secrecy regarding the election: the Secretary of the College of Cardinals; the Master of Pontifical Liturgical Celebrations; the two masters of ceremony; the two religious attached to the Pontifical Sacristy; the ecclesiastic chosen by the Cardinal Dean or the Cardinal who substitutes for him to assist him in his office; the religious confessors; the two doctors; the appropriate number of persons attached for table service and cleaning (n. 58). The same penalty is established for all those (cardinals and those taking part in the preparation and the implementation of what is necessary for the election) who commit the crime of simony (n. 78) or receive the function of the *veto* or *exclusiva*[144] (n. 80), and also for the participation on the part of the cardinal electors in any bargaining, agreements, promises or other commitments of any kind, which can constrict them to give or deny the vote to one or several candidates (n. 81).[145]

The CIC, while not having sins that are directly reserved, appears to leave to the possibility of reservation to the diocesan Bishop or diocesan particular law, because to the diocesan Bishop belong "all ordinary, proper, and immediate

---

140   According to CIC c. 1342, just causes are sufficient.

141   Minor excommunication consists in the deprivation of Eucharistic communion (CCEO c. 1431); major excommunication prohibits the reception of all the sacraments, the exercise of ministries, offices or other ecclesiastical functions (CCEO c. 1434). With the reservation of a sin *ratione sui* in the cases referred to in CCEO c. 728, one obtains, in practice, the same disciplinary effects that are obtained with the reservation of the sin *ratione censuræ*, given that one must make recourse to the Apostolic See or, in the case of abortion, to the eparchial Bishop. But with the reservation of the sin *ratione sui*, one does not go against the traditions of the Eastern Churches; thus, the ancient penitential discipline is maintained: cf. *Nuntia* 28 (1989) 97-98.

142   In c. 9 of the first project of 1976, there was explicit mention of the *latæ sententiæ* penalty; now it is treated implicitly.

143   *AAS* 88 (1996) 305-343.

144   The *veto* or *exclusiva* consisted in the official opposition exercised by some emperors or Catholic kings against the election of a candidate, declared publicly to the entire college by a cardinal entrusted by them at the moment of the counting of the votes.

145   According to J. Miñambres, the legislation on the election of the Roman Pontiff remains, in cases in which the crime be committed by an Eastern faithful, difficult for interpretation and application: J. Miñambres, "Il governo della Chiesa durante la vacanza della Sede Romana e l'elezione del Romano Pontefice," *Ius Ecclesiæ* 8 (1996) 713-729, especially 726.

power which is required for the exercise of his pastoral function except for cases which the law or a decree of the Supreme Pontiff reserves to the supreme authority or to another ecclesiastical authority" (CIC c. 381 §1).

According to PB art. 52, for the entire Catholic Church, "[the Congregation for the Doctrine of the Faith] examines offenses against the faith and more serious ones both in behavior or in the celebration of the sacraments which have been reported to it and, if need be, proceeds to the declaration or imposition of canonical sanctions in accordance with the norms of common or proper law." The more serious crimes in the celebration of the sacraments and against morals reserved to it are: 1) the removal or retention of the consecrated species for a sacrilegious purpose or its desecration; 2) attempt by one lacking power of the liturgical action of the Eucharistic Sacrifice, or the simulation of the same; 3) the prohibited concelebration of the Eucharistic sacrifice with ministers of ecclesial communities which do not have apostolic succession nor acknowledge the sacramental dignity of priestly ordination; 4) the consecration for a sacrilegious purpose of one matter without the other in the Eucharistic celebration, or even both outside the Eucharistic celebration; 5) the absolution of an accomplice in the sin against the sixth commandment of the Decalogue; 6) solicitation, in the occasion or the pretext of confession, to sin against the sixth commandment of the Decalogue, if it is directed to sin with the confessor himself; 7) direct violation of the sacramental seal; 8) the delict against the sixth commandment of the Decalogue by a cleric with a minor under 18 years of age.[146]

Bearing in mind that every member of the Christian faithful has the right to confess to any confessor he or she prefers, there might be some special cases. Can a Latin confessor absolve an Eastern member of the faithful who has committed a reserved sin? I believe that a Latin confessor can absolve an Eastern member of the faithful who has committed a reserved sin. Can an Eastern confessor absolve a Latin member of the faithful who has incurred a *latæ sententiæ* censure (cf. CIC cc. 1364 § 1; 1367; 1370 §§1-2; 1382)? I believe that an Eastern confessor can absolve a Latin member of the faithful who has incurred a *latæ sententiæ* censure, but illicitly, except in circumstances of grave inconvenience or danger of violating the sacramental seal. But if none of these circumstances exist an Eastern confessor must make recourse to the Apostolic Penitentiary to obtain permission to absolve the penitent of the censure. Can an Eastern confessor absolve a Latin member of the faithful who has committed a reserved sin in an Eastern territory? I believe that an Eastern confessor cannot absolve a Latin member of the faithful in the territory of the reservation. In the case of common error in fact or in law and in positive and probable doubt, CIC c. 144 and CCEO c. 994 apply: the Church supplies executive power of governance. In summary: Eastern faithful

---

146   Congregation for the Doctrine of the Faith, *Epistula ad totius Catholicæ Ecclesiæ Episcopos aliosque Ordinarios et Hierarchas interesse habentes de delictis gravioribus eidem Congregationi pro Doctrina Fidei reservatis*, 18 May 2001: *AAS* 93 (2001) 785-788.

– Latin confessor: In principle, the Latin priest, not being prohibited from hearing the confession of a particular sin, can absolve from all sins, including those the CCEO reserved to the Apostolic See or the eparchial Bishop and, of course, those reserved by particular law of their own Church. If one does not have the faculty, CIC c. 1357 §§1-2 can be followed. Latin faithful – Eastern confessor: the Eastern priest outside the territory of his Church *sui iuris* is not bound to any reservation established by its special legislation. In principle, he should not absolve a penitent who has incurred a *latæ sententiæ* censure, not so much because the Latin law obliges him directly, but because the law that determines the juridic condition of a person in the ecclesial community has an indirect binding effect for the superiors or ministers the sacrament, who must respect the capacity, or in the case the incapacity, of the member of the faithful in his / her community. One can apply CCEO c. 729:

CCEO	CIC
729. Any reservation of the absolution from sin lacks all force:	1357 §1. Without prejudice to the prescripts of cann. 508 and 976, a confessor can remit in the internal sacramental forum an undeclared *latæ sententiæ* censure of excommunication or interdict if it is burdensome for the penitent to remain in the state of grave sin during the time necessary for the competent superior to make provision.
1° if a sick person who cannot leave the house makes a confession, or a spouse confesses in order to celebrate marriage;	
2° if, in the prudent judgment of the confessor, the faculty cannot be requested from the competent authority without grave inconvenience to the penitent or without danger of violation of the sacramental seal;	§2. In granting the remission, the confessor is to impose on the penitent, under the penalty of reincidence, the obligation of making recourse within a month to the competent superior or to a priest endowed with the faculty and the obligation of obeying his mandates; in the meantime he is to impose a suitable penance and, insofar as it is demanded, reparation of any scandal and damage; however, recourse can also be made through the confessor, without mention of the name.
3° outside the territorial boundaries in which the authority who makes the reservation exercises power.	
	§3. After they have recovered, those for whom an imposed or declared censure or one reserved to the Apostolic See has been remitted according to the norm of can. 976 are also obliged to make recourse.

When one considers the cases treated in CCEO c. 729, any reservation—pontifical, patriarchal and eparchial—loses all value. For the CIC, the faculty of the confessor in particular situations is limited by the *latæ sententiæ* censures, of excommunication or interdict, not yet declared. Excluded are expiatory penalties, the censures of suspension, the censures *ferendæ sententiæ* and *latæ sententiæ* already declared. The confessor can proceed with the remission of the penalty or the forgiveness of the sin. In such a case, the priest will act as a delegate of the competent superior in the remission of the penalty and as a confessor in the forgiveness of the sin. Further, it emerges from these canons that it that in an urgent case the confessor can absolve from the penalty; the principle holds that the sphere of penal law is the external forum, with the imposition of recourse within one month only for the CIC, under the penalty of relapse. The obligation of recourse is an ecclesiastical law. Ecclesiastical laws do not oblige observance if there is a grave inconvenience, external in the law as such. The necessary time in question is fifteen days; doctrine admits that it can be reduced to one day.[147]

Among the faculties granted to priests who offer spiritual assistance to migrants, sailors and seafarers, nomads, circus people and travelling merchants, those one work at airports or on planes, as well as pilots, tourists, pilgrims, there is the faculty to absolve, in the sacramental forum, the faithful entrusted to them from undeclared censures *latæ sententiæ* not reserved to the Apostolic See, observing the required canonical prescriptions. This faculty, granted by the Pontifical Commission for the Pastoral Care of Migrants and Tourism, should also include Eastern faithful, because not only were the dicasteries of the Roman Curia competent in this matter consulted, but it was also approved by the Roman Pontiff.[148]

Regarding indulgences (CIC cc. 992-997), defined as the remission before God of temporal punishment due for sins, already forgiven with regard to guilt, that the faithful, properly disposed and in specific conditions, acquire through the intervention of the Church, which, as a minister of redemption, authoritatively dispenses and applies the treasury of the satisfaction of Christ and the saints,[149]

---

147 Analogous to a decision of the Commission for Interpretation of the CIC-17 concerning dispensation in matrimonial matters: *AAS* 14 (1922) 622-623. Many authors commonly admit that one night is sufficient: G. Michiels, *De delictis et pœnis*, III, *De pœnis in specie. Canones 2314-2414* (Paris-Tournai-Rome-New York, 1961) 155; E. Jombart, "Des délits et des peines," in *Traité de droit canonique*, 2nd ed., ed. R. Naz, (Paris, 1954) 4:581-807, especially 644. The latter attaches a response of the Penitentiary dated 14 May 1904, according to which it is sufficient in an urgent case that the penitent feels a great repugnance to remain for one day in the state of mortal sin. E. Jombart states, "One is dealing with a subjective disposition that is beneficial, in that it permits the confessor to create or develop in the penitent the horror of sin, an appreciation of the state of grace, dread of hellfire and the love of God, etc."
148 Decr *Pro materna*, 19 March 1982: *AAS* 74 (1982) 742-745: CLD 10:34-38.
149 Apostolic Penitentiary, *Enchiridion Indulgentiarum* (Vatican City, 1999) Norm 1. For a history of indulgences, see W. H. Woestman, *Sacraments. Initiation, Penance, Anointing of the Sick* (Ottawa, 1996). A brief history is also found in J. Canosa,

there is no norm in the CCEO, but the Eastern faithful can gain them,[150] taking into account CCEO c. 1492:

> Laws issued by the supreme authority of the Church, which do not expressly indicate the passive subject, affect the Christian faithful of the Eastern Churches only insofar as they concern matters of faith or morals or declarations of divine law, explicitly decide questions regarding these Christian faithful, or concern favors which contain nothing contrary to the Eastern rites.[151]

In addition to the supreme authority of the Church, indulgences[152] can be granted by those to whom this power is recognized by law or is conceded by the Roman Pontiff. In practice, they are granted: by eparchial or diocesan Bishops or their equivalents, even those lacking episcopal dignity, from the beginning of their pastoral office (partial indulgence to all the faithful who are in their own territory and to their own faithful outside the territory; papal blessing with plenary indulgences three times a year on solemnities or feasts of their choice, at the end of the Holy Mass);[153] by Metropolitans (partial indulgences in the suffragan eparchies and dioceses as in their own territory); by Patriarchs (partial indulgences in individual places, even exempt, of their own Patriarchate, in the Churches of their own rite outside the Patriarchate and anywhere for the faithful of their own rite; papal blessing with plenary indulgences three times a year; whenever some particular circumstance or religious reason arises that requires a plenary indulgence for the spiritual benefit of the faithful); by the Major Archbishop (the same

---

"La competenza della Penitenzieria Apostolica sulle indulgenze," *Ius Ecclesiæ* 5 (1993) 396-401.

150   Sacred Apostolic Penitentiary, *Responsum*, De indulgentiis quoad fideles ritus orientalis: *AAS* 9 (1917) 399; *Id.*, *Responsum*, De mariani rosarii recitatione apud christifideles ritus rutheni: *AAS* 22 (1930) 292; Sacred Congregation for the Eastern Church, *Indulgentia ditatur precula quædam ad Russiæ salutem impetrandam*, 24 May 1923: *AAS* 15 (1923) 295; *Id.*, *Notificatio*, 21 July 1935: *AAS* 27 (1935) 379; *Nuntia* 10 (1980) 10. Further, "from the nature of the matter, indulgences granted through the devout recitation of prayers that follow on the list below can be acquired by the faithful of any rite, no matter the liturgical tradition to which the prayers *per se* belong": Apostolic Penitentiary, *Enchiridion...*, 47.

151   See G. Nedungatt, "Normæ indolis iuridicæ ad tenorem c. 1492 CCEO applicandæ," *Periodica* 86 (1997) 477-491.

152   An indulgence is partial or plenary according to whether it frees partially or fully from the temporal punishment due to sin.

153   "Bishops in those churches that had once been cathedrals, and today are co-cathedrals existing in their territory, without prejudice to the provision that allows for the Papal Blessing to be [imparted in the Cathedral] on three Solemnities in the year, as established in art. n. 7, 2 of the *Enchiridion Indulgentiarum*, have the faculty to impart the Papal Blessing along with a Plenary Indulgence once a year, on the celebration of a solemnity that the bishops themselves will designate": Apostolic Penitentiary, 29 June 2002.

faculty as that of the Patriarchs applies); by cardinals (partial indulgence everywhere, which can be acquired only by those present on each occasion).[154] Books, brochures and flyers, etc., which contain the concession of indulgences must not be published without the permission of the local Ordinary or Hierarch.[155] The express permission of the Apostolic See is needed in order to print in any language an authentic collection of the concession of indulgences made by the Apostolic See.[156] Regarding the language, an indulgence attached to a prayer can be acquired in any language in which it is recited, provided the version is approved by the competent ecclesiastical authority.[157] Local Ordinaries and Hierarchs have the faculty to grant to the faithful over which they exercise their authority according to the norm of law, who reside in places where it is impossible or only possible with great difficulty to receive the sacraments of confession or communion, the ability to acquire the plenary indulgence without actual confession or communion, provided that they are contrite and are determined to receive these sacraments as soon as it is possible for them to do so.[158]

Christian faithful of any rite, even Latin, can acquire a plenary indulgence by reciting the hymn *Akathistos* or the office *Paraclisis*; among the Eastern faithful where there is no such devotion, "another similar exercise established by the Patriarch in honor of the Blessed Virgin Mary enjoys the same indulgence."[159] Furthermore, a partial indulgence is granted to those who recite one of the following prayers: *Oratio pro gratiarum actione* (from the Armenian tradition); *Oratio vespertina*, *Oratio pro defunctis* (from Byzantine tradition); *Oratio Sanctuarii*, *Oratio "Lakhu Mara" seu "Ad te Domine"* (from the Chaldean tradition); *Oratio ad thurificationem*, *Oratio ad glorificandam Dei Matrem Mariam* (from the Coptic tradition); *Oratio pro remissione peccatorum*, *Oratio pro adipiscenda sequela Christi* (from the Ethiopian tradition); *Oratio pro Ecclesia*, *Oratio post expletam Liturgiam* (from the Maronite tradition); *Intercessiones pro defunctis ex Liturgia S. Iacobi* (from the Syro-Antiochene tradition).[160]

IV.7. Anointing of the Sick

The new legislation, taking into account SC 73, no longer speaks of "extreme unction," but "anointing of the sick," to emphasize that this sacrament is also for those who are beginning to be in danger of death because of illness or old age.

---

154 See Apostolic Penitentiary, *Enchiridion*..., Norms 5-10.
155 *Ibid.*, 11 §2.
156 *Ibid.*, 11 §1.
157 *Ibid.*, 22.
158 *Ibid.*, 25.
159 *Ibid.*, *Concessiones* n. 23 §1.
160 *Ibid.*, *Concessiones* n. 23 §2. In the Italian edition the texts of the prayers are shown in full.

CCEO	CIC
741. The oil for use in the sacrament of the anointing the sick is to be blessed, and, indeed, unless the particular law of his Church *sui iuris* warrants otherwise, by the priest who administers the sacrament himself.	999. In addition to a bishop, the following can bless the oil to be used in the anointing of the sick: 1° those equivalent to a diocesan bishop by law; 2° any presbyter in a case of necessity, but only in the actual celebration of the sacrament.

In the CIC, it is for the Bishop and those who are equivalent in law to the diocesan Bishop to bless the oil to be used to administer the sacrament; for any priest in the case of necessity and in the same celebration of the sacrament. CIC-17 c. 945 permitted the blessing of oil to be done also by the priest who had obtained the faculty from the Apostolic See: "The oil of olives, to be used in the sacrament of extreme unction, must be blessed for this purpose a Bishop, or by a priest who has obtained from the Apostolic See the faculty for blessing it." For CCEO c. 741, the same priest who administers the sacrament can bless the oil, but particular law can reserve the blessing of the oil to the Bishop or Patriarch. An Eastern priest can bless the oil even if the priest is subject to a Latin Bishop.[161] In the Eastern Churches that have the custom of anointing being administered by several priests (usually seven), it must be conserved (CCEO c. 737 §2).[162] For the Latin Church, when the sacrament is concelebrated by various priests, they can divide the various parts of the rite, but one and the same priest must perform the anointing while pronouncing the sacramental form. The only valid minister is the priest, because this sacrament is related to the forgiveness of sins and the worthy reception of the Eucharist. "No other person may act as ordinary or extraordinary minister of the sacrament, since such constitutes simulation of the sacrament."[163] The Congregation for the Doctrine of the Faith on 11 February 2005 published a *Note on the Minister of the Sacrament of the Anointing of the Sick* with a cover letter to the presidents of episcopal conferences.[164] The *Note* reiterates the doctrine, *definitive tenenda*, expressed by the Council of Trent[165] and re-

---

161   Benedict XIV, Apcon *Etsi pastoralis*, §4, n. 1.

162   *Ibid.*, §5 in Denz, 2524.

163   Congregation for Clergy et al., *Istruzione su alcune questioni circa la collaborazione dei laici al ministero dei sacerdoti*, 15 August 1997, art. 9 §2: Suppl. to *L'Osservatore Romano*, 14 November 1997.

164   *L'Osservatore Romano*, 21 October 2005, 5.

165   "If anyone says the presbyters of the church who, as blessed James enjoins, should be brought in to anoint the sick person, are not priests who have been ordained by a bishop, but the elders in any community; and that on that account the proper minister of the last anointing is not exclusively a priest: let him be anathema": Sess. XIV, *De Sacramento extremæ uncitonis*, c. 4: DEC, 2:713.

ferred to by CIC c. 1003[166] and CCEO c. 739 §1 and by CCC 1516,[167] according to which only priests (Bishops and presbyters) are ministers of the sacrament of the anointing of the sick. Neither deacons nor lay persons can exercise that ministry; any action in this regard constitutes a simulation of the sacrament. In the cover letter, the Congregation considered it appropriate to send to *all* the pastors of the Catholic Church[168] the above-mentioned *Note* to remove any doubt regarding the minister of the sacrament of anointing of the sick. Lately, there have been manifestations of theological tendencies that create doubt regarding the doctrine of the Church according to which the minister is *omnis et solus sacerdos*. These tendencies address the theme mainly from a pastoral point of view, especially considering those regions in which the scarcity of priests makes the timely administration of the sacrament difficult, while such difficulty could be resolved if permanent deacons and even qualified lay persons could be designated as ministers of the sacrament. The *Note* of the Congregation wants to draw attention to these tendencies, to prevent the dangers of that there be attempting to put them into practice, to the detriment of the faith and with grave spiritual harm to the sick whom one wants to help.

But can a priest of one Church *sui iuris*, including the Latin Church, administer the Anointing to a member of the faithful of another Church *sui iuris*? Outside the case of necessity, the priest administers the sacrament validly, but illicitly if he has not obtained the permission of the proper pastor or Bishop of a member of the faithful (cf. CIC-17 c. 938 §2). However, if a member of the faithful is his subject according to the norm of law (*ad normam iuris*), he acts licitly and validly, observing the rite of the minister and not of the member of the faithful, at least if he has not obtained a special faculty from the Apostolic See (CCEO c. 674 and CIC c. 846).

IV.8. Sacred Ordination[169]

Those who receive the sacrament of Ordination are members of the faithful committed to service of the community for its sanctification in the name of Christ, externally with the ministry of the Word, internally with grace.

---

166   CIC c. 1003 §1: "Every priest and a priest alone validly administers the anointing of the sick."
167   CCC 1516: "Only priests (Bishops and presbyters) are ministers of the Anointing of the Sick. It is the duty of pastors to instruct the faithful on the benefits of this sacrament. The faithful should encourage the sick to call for a priest to receive this sacrament. The sick should prepare themselves to receive it with good disposition, assisted by their pastor and the whole ecclesial community, which is invited to surround the sick in a special way through their prayers and fraternal attention."
168   The cover letter was addressed to the presidents of the episcopal conferences, but is directed to all the pastors of the Catholic Church.
169   This section should be read along with III.6.

CCEO	CIC
746 §1. A Bishop should be ordained by three Bishops, except in case of extreme necessity. §2. If Bishops of the same Church *sui iuris* as the first ordaining Bishop cannot be present, the second and the third Bishop can be of another Church *sui iuris*.	1014. Unless the Apostolic See has granted a dispensation, the principal bishop consecrator in an episcopal consecration is to be joined by at least two consecrating bishops; it is especially appropriate, however, that all the bishops present consecrate the elect together with the bishops mentioned.

For episcopal ordination, the ordaining Bishop must have a mandate; this mandate, which integrates the Bishop in hierarchical communion and in the College of Bishops, is left exclusively to the Roman Pontiff in the CIC (c. 1013), while in the CCEO, beyond the Roman Pontiff, it is also left to the Patriarch, the Major Archbishop or the Metropolitan of a Church *sui iuris* (c. 745). Ordination without the mandate constitutes a criminal offense: "Bishops who have conferred episcopal ordination upon someone without a mandate of the competent authority, and the one who has accepted ordination from them in this manner, are to be punished with a major excommunication" (CCEO c. 1459 §1); "A bishop who consecrates someone a bishop without a pontifical mandate and the person who receives the consecration from him incur a *latæ sententiæ* excommunication reserved to the Apostolic See" (CIC c. 1382). Both codes admit the possibility of co-consecrating Bishops from other Churches *sui iuris*, even if the CIC is not so explicit. Therefore, a Latin Bishop can be admitted as the second or third ordaining Bishop for the ordination of Eastern Bishops, and vice versa. The consecration by three Bishops manifests communion with the College of Bishops and, thus, with the catholicity of the Church of God. For a consecration to be done by only one Bishop, a dispensation from the Holy See is necessary for the CIC, while the CCEO is silent, but should be granted, in addition to the Roman Pontiff, by the Patriarch, the Major Archbishop or the Metropolitan.[170]

Canonical provision is required order to be promoted to the episcopate. The ordinand, having accepted the lawful election, makes the profession of faith, the promise of obedience to the Roman Pontiff and, in the patriarchal and major archiepiscopal Churches, the promise of obedience to the Patriarch and Major Archbishop (CCEO c. 187 §§1-2). According to the CCEO, these two acts take place before the episcopal ordination; according to the CIC, they take place before taking possession (c. 380). CCEO c. 187 §2 speaks of *promise of obedience to the Roman Pontiff*, while CIC c. 380 speaks of an *oath of fidelity to the Apostolic See*. The CCEO has deliberately adopted the term *promissio*, because this code, conforming to the ancient canonical tradition, reveals a certain reserve with re-

---

[170] The initial text, c. 192 §1, stated: "Episcopus ordinetur ab Episcopis tribus, nisi indultum Sedis Apostolicæ ferat ut a duobus vel ab uno tantum Episcopo ordinetur": *Nuntia* 7 (1978) 65.

gard to oaths. Further, the CCEO speaks of *promise of obedience*, while the CIC employs the term *oath of fidelity*; this difference would be justified by taking into account the persons or organs to which they refer: the Eastern Bishops to the Roman Pontiff; the Latin Bishops to the Apostolic See. The Apostolic See refers not only to the Roman Pontiff, but also to the Roman Curia (cf. CIC c. 361).[171]

To ordain one's own subject who is ascribed to another Church *sui iuris*, the proper Bishop must request permission (indult) from the Apostolic See (CCEO c. 748 §2 and CIC c. 1015 §2) and ordain according to his own rite;[172] if the candidate for ordination belongs to a patriarchal or major archiepiscopal Church and has a domicile or quasi-domicile in the territory of the same Church, the Patriarch or Major Archbishop can grant this permission.[173] The proper Bishop for those who are to be ascribed in the secular clergy is the Bishop of the diocese in which the candidate has a domicile or the diocese in whose service he intends to devote himself. In the case of presbyteral ordination of secular deacons, the proper Bishop is the one in whose diocese the candidate for ordination was already incardinated with the diaconate. But can the Latin Bishop ascribe in his diocese a married Eastern member of the faithful who is a candidate for sacred ordination, or a married Eastern presbyter destined for an Eastern personal parish? Our opinion is yes, with due regard for the special norms of the Apostolic See established for specific regions (cf. CCEO c. 758 §3).[174]

A dimissorial letter can be sent to any Bishop in communion with the Apostolic See.[175] To be able to send a dimissorial letter to a Bishop of a Church *sui iuris* different than that of the candidate for ordination, permission of the Apostolic See is necessary; if the candidate belongs to a patriarchal or major archiepiscopal Church and has a domicile or quasi-domicile within the territory of the same Church, the Patriarch or Major Archbishop can grant this permission. In order to act lawfully, a Bishop must obtain a dimissorial letter. One who acts contrary to this norm is to be punished: according to the CCEO, with an appropriate penalty (c. 1459 §2); according to the CIC, with the prohibition to confer the order for a year (c. 1383). Further, the CIC provides, on the part of the ordained person, the suspension of the received order for an indeterminate period of time. It is for the Congregation for the Doctrine of the Faith to proceed to declare or impose canonical sanctions for crimes committed in the celebration of sacraments (PB art. 52).

---

171   Cf. R. Metz, "La désignation des évêques dans le droit actuel: étude comparative entre le Code latin de 1983 e le Code oriental de 1990," *Studia Canonica* 27 (1993) 321-334, especially 332; L. Lorusso, "La designazione dei Vescovi nel CCEO," *Quaderni di Diritto Ecclesiale* 12 (1999) 46-57.
172   CIC-17 c. 961; cf. Appendix XIII.
173   CCEO c. 775 and CIC c. 1054 note that it is necessary to send notification of this ordination to the pastor of the place of baptism, where it is to be recorded.
174   Refer to section III.6.
175   See Appendix XII.

In the Latin Church, the authority competent to grant a dimissorial letter for the secular clergy is, beyond the proper diocesan Bishop, an apostolic administrator and, with the consent of the college of consultors, the diocesan administrator; further, an apostolic vicar, an apostolic prefect, an abbot or territorial prelate can grant a dimissorial letter, as can an apostolic pro-vicar or pro-prefect with the consent of the council mentioned in CIC c. 495 §2. In the Eastern Churches, the competent authority for the eparchial clergy is, beyond the proper eparchial Bishop, also an apostolic or patriarchal exarch, the administrator of the patriarchal Church and, with the consent of the college of consultors, an administrator of an eparchy.

The required age for the presbyterate is 24 years for the CCEO (c. 759 §1), as it was in CIC-17 c. 975, while for the Latin Church it is 25 years (c. 1031 §1); between the diaconate and the presbyterate there must be a lapse of time of at least six months according to the CIC, while the CCEO relegates the observance of the interstice to particular law. Regarding the diaconate, both the CCEO and the CIC require the age of 23 years; for the permanent diaconate, the CCEO makes no determination, so the age of 23 for the transitional diaconate is provided; the CIC determines the age of 25 for the celibate man and 35 years for the married man, with the consent of the wife. Particular law or the episcopal conference can require a more advanced age, but while the CCEO extends the possibility to both orders (CCEO c. 759 §1),[176] the CIC only extends the possibility to the presbyterate and permanent diaconate, and not to the transitional diaconate (CIC c. 1031 §3). The dispensation from the age requirement, if it exceeds more than a year, is granted by the Patriarch or the Major Archbishop if the candidate has a domicile or quasi-domicile in the territory of the same Church, otherwise by the Apostolic See; for the Latins, the dispensation is reserved to the Apostolic See.[177]

The years of the curriculum of philosophical-theological study differ in the two codes: for the CCEO, it is lawful to ordain a deacon after the successful completion of the fourth year (*post feliciter expletum quartum annum*) (c. 760 §1); for the CIC, one can be ordained to the diaconate after completing the fifth year (*post expletum quintum annum*) (c. 1032 §1). However, those preparing for the permanent diaconate can be ordained after the third year (*post expletum tertium annum*) according to CCEO c. 760 §2, after completing the time for formation

---

176 According to the particular law of the Maronite Church, prepared in May, 1993, the required age is 23 for the diaconate and 25 for the priesthood: *Particular...*, ed. K. Bharanikulangara, 204, art. 79.

177 The Congregation for Divine Worship and the Discipline of the Sacraments decided not to grant a dispensation from the defect of age beyond the 12 months for which the Bishops are competent to dispense (CIC c. 1031 §4), except for most rare, exceptional cases exclusively based on serious pastoral needs for the *salus animarum*, provided that it is done at least six months before the date foreseen for the eventual ordination. It will grant it only for most brief periods of time and *in forma commissoria onerata conscientia Episcopi* ["obliging the conscience of the Bishop"]: *Comm.* 29 (1997) 233-235.

(*post expletum formationis tempus*) according to CIC c. 1032 §2; but, taking into account CIC c. 236, formation for candidates to the permanent diaconate must last at least three years.

In the CCEO there is no distinction between irregularities and impediments regarding the reception or exercise of sacred orders as there is in the CIC, because the category of "irregularity" is unknown in Eastern traditions. Regarding the substance rather than the discipline of the CIC and what was proposed in the Draft, there is no difference.[178] An impediment is a simple temporary defect that, consequently, can cease to exist at a certain point with the disappearance of the cause that produced it; an irregularity is a perpetual impediment, which, consequently, can cease to exist only by means of a dispensation. Neither one nor the other is of the character of a penalty, even if they sometimes suppose a penalty, but only of an incapacitating character that binds even those who do not know it (CIC c. 1045 and CCEO c. 765). A dispensation is ordinarily granted by the Ordinary; it is reserved to the Apostolic See or to the Patriarch or Major Archbishop for candidates or clerics who have a domicile or quasi-domicile in the territory of the Church over which he presides, if the fact on which the impediment is based is referred to the judicial forum, ecclesiastical or civil; the same applies for the public crimes of apostasy, heresy or schism; for an attempted marriage, even if only civilly, of one who is prevented by another marriage bond, by a sacred order, by a public vow of perpetual chastity; for voluntary homicide or for a procured abortion; for a marriage bond (only for the Latin Church). In very urgent occult cases in which the competent authority cannot be reached and there is an imminent danger of grave harm or infamy according to CCEO c. 767 §3 (= CIC-17 c. 990 §2), the confessor can dispense, but only to permit the penitent to exercise lawfully orders already received, with due regard for the obligation to present himself as soon as possible to the competent authority. According to CIC c. 1048, the interested party can avail himself of the faculty which is already given in the law, but makes recourse through a confessor.

IV.9. Sacramentals

Sacramentals are sacred signs instituted by the Church, different than sacraments which are instituted by Christ. Through them, primarily spiritual effects are signified and obtained to enable to the faithful to receive the principal effect of the sacraments and to sanctify all the circumstances of their life *ex Ecclesiæ impetratione*. Sacramentals can generally fall into four categories: consecrations, dedications, blessings, exorcisms.

The Latin law regarding the authority over sacramentals is centralized: only the Apostolic See can institute, abolish or modify them (CIC c. 1167 §1). For the

---

[178] *Nuntia* 28 (1989) 102.

CCEO, the norms of the particular law of the proper Church *sui iuris* must be observed regarding the sacramentals (c. 867§2).

Latin Bishops who have been entrusted with the care of Eastern Catholic faithful must take into account the specific norms that differ from the Latin legislation.

The dedication of a church, "a building in which the Christian community is assembled to hear the word of God, to pray as one, to receive the sacraments and to celebrate the Eucharist,"[179] is reserved to the diocesan (eparchial) Bishop[180] and those equivalent to them in law, but the CIC admits, in exceptional cases, entrusting "the function of carrying out a dedication in their territory to any bishop or, in exceptional cases, to a presbyter" (CIC c. 1206; cf. c. 1169 §1).[181] Could a diocesan Bishop entrust to an Eastern priest the consecration of a church destined for Eastern divine worship? We believe yes, but it would be opportune for the diocesan Bishop to participate in the celebration, leaving the part of the consecration of the church to the priest, or better, to an Eastern Hierarch especially invited.

Other than churches, places destined for worship are classified as "oratories" and "private chapels." Differing from churches, oratories and private chapels are not by definition "sacred places," but become so only if they are blessed according to the norm of CIC c. 1229; otherwise, they are only places of worship. Different from the CIC, the CCEO does not provide for a classification other than the general classification of "church" for places of worship, distinguishing them as "cathedral," "parochial," "of a monastery," "attached to a religious institute" (cf. cc. 869-871).

With regard to days of penance and feast days, the Eastern legislation deals pastorally with faithful who are found outside the territory of their own Church *sui iuris*: they can conform themselves fully to the norms that are in force in the place where they live (CCEO c. 883 §1).[182] As we have seen, families comprising members belonging to different Churches *sui iuris* observe the prescriptions of one or the other Church *sui iuris* (CCEO c. 883 §2; OE 21).[183] The Latin pastor, for a just reason and conforming to the dispositions of the diocesan Bishop, can *singulis in casibus* ("in individual cases") grant a dispensation from observance of a feast day or day of penance, or substitute it with other pious works; this also applies for superiors of clerical religious institutes of pontifical right, with refer-

---

179   *Cæremoniale Episcoporum*, 198, n. 864.
180   In the East it is not acceptable for one not endowed with the episcopal order to be able to consecrate churches: *Nuntia* 28 (1989) 120.
181   It was prohibited by CIC-17 c. 1155 §2: "The Ordinary of the territory, even though he lacks episcopal character, can give permission to any Bishop of his own rite to perform consecrations in his own territory."
182   This is mentioned in the Roman Synod of 1960: cf. *Prima Romana Synodus*, Normæ Præviæ, tit. I *De synodalibus constitutionibus* (Rome, 1960) n. 10.
183   Cf. *Nuntia* 10 (1980) 63, c. 224.

ence to their own subjects and to others who reside day and night in their house (CIC c. 1245).

A vow is a deliberate and free promise, made to God, for a possible or better good. It can be public or private, according to whether it is received by the lawful (ecclesiastical or religious) authority in the name of the Church (cf. SC 80; LG 44-45). It can be solemn or simple: it is solemn if it is recognized as such by the Church, otherwise it is simple.[184] It can be personal, real or mixed, depending on whether the object promised is an action, a thing or a reality that involves both. From CIC c. 607 §2, one can draw a distinction between a perpetual and temporary vow in relation to the duration of the vow. The two legislations pose differences for the dispensation from private vows.[185] Beyond the Roman Pontiff, according to CIC c. 1196, the following can dispense: the local Ordinary and the pastor can dispense their own subjects anywhere and transients in their own territory; the superior of a religious institute or a society of apostolic life, if it is clerical and of pontifical right, can dispense members of the institute, novices and those who reside day and night in the house of the institute or society; anyone who has received *ad hoc* delegation from the Apostolic See or the local Hierarch can dispense.[186]

According to CCEO c. 893, the Hierarch and the pastor can dispense their own subjects; the local Hierarch and the local pastor can dispense all other Christian faithful of their own Church *sui iuris* actually residing in the territory of their own eparchy or parish; superiors of institutes of consecrated life who have the power of governance can dispense their own subjects and those who reside day and night in the house of the institute; the confessor, but only in the internal forum.

However, for commutation, while the CCEO is silent, the CIC establishes that it can be done by the same person who made the vow, if one is dealing with a commutation into an equal or greater good; otherwise, commutation into a lesser good can be done only by those who have the faculty to dispense (CIC c. 1197). The obligation of the vow can be suspended by one who has power over the substance of the vow, as long as its fulfillment would adversely affect him (CIC c.

---

184   In the CIC this distinction no longer has any relevance. However, this important difference can be retained in the particular law of the religious orders: *Comm.* 12 (1980) 376 and 15 (1983) 73.
185   In the current legislation there are no private vows reserved to the Apostolic See. In the former discipline, "the vow of perfect and perpetual chastity and the vow of entering a religious [institute] of solemn vows, which are given absolutely and after the completion of eighteen years of age" (CIC-17 c. 1309) were reserved.
186   From the tenor of CIC c. 1196, 3°, it seems that major superiors of religious institutes and societies of apostolic, if they are clerical and of pontifical right, can also delegate this power according to the general norms of law.

1195). Vows made before religious profession remain suspended as long as the one who made them remains in the religious institute (CIC c. 1198).

With regard to an oath, the invocation of the name of God in witness to the truth, we emphasize that Eastern faithful can provide it only in the cases determined by law in order to produce canonical effects.[187]

CCEO	CIC
895. An oath is the invocation of the divine Name as witness to the truth. It can be made before the Church only in cases determined by law; otherwise it produces no canonical effect.	1199 §1. An oath, that is, the invocation of the divine name in witness to the truth, cannot be taken unless in truth, in judgment, and in justice. §2. An oath which the canons require or permit cannot be taken validly through a proxy.

The CCEO establishes an oath for an engaged couple, in danger of death and if it is not possible to have other proofs, of being baptized and not bound by any impediment (cf. CCEO. c. 785 §2); whenever the nature of the cause or the proofs is such that divulgation of the acts and of the proof can endanger the reputation of others, or if it can give rise to disputes or cause scandal or similar difficulty, the judge can oblige the witnesses and their advocates or procurators to keep the secret under oath (CCEO c. 1113 §3); the judge can designate an interpreter under oath if any person to be interrogated uses a language that is unknown by the judge or the parties (cf. CCEO c. 1130); in cases which concern the public good the judge can put the parties to be interrogated as well as the witnesses under oath to tell the truth or at least to have told the truth (cf. CCEO cc. 1213; 1243).

The Congregation for the Doctrine of the Faith, on 9 January 1989, published the formula of the Profession of the Faith to be used in cases in which it is required by law, and that of the Oath of Fidelity[188] to be made by the faithful mentioned in CIC c. 833: the participants in an ecumenical or particular council, in the Synod of Bishops or a diocesan synod, Cardinals of the Holy Roman Church, all those promoted to the episcopate and those equivalent to a diocesan Bishop, the diocesan administrator, vicar general, episcopal vicar and judicial vicar, the pastor, seminary rector, rector of a Catholic university, rector of an ecclesiastical

---

187 *Nuntia* 10 (1980) 16: "Regarding an oath, only one canon (c. 236) is proposed where, according to the most ancient traditions of the East, it is declared that it can be presented before the Church only in cases required by law; otherwise, it produces no juridic effect."

188 Congregation for the Doctrine of the Faith, *Professio Fidei et Iusiurandum fidelitatis in suscipiendo offcio nomine Ecclesiæ exercendo*, 9 January 1989, *Nota di presentazione, I Professio Fidei, II Iusiurandum fidelitatis in suscipiendo officio nomine Ecclesiæ exercendo*: AAS 81 (1989) 104, 105, 106.

university and faculty, teachers in disciplines pertaining to faith and morals in Catholic universities and in other ecclesiastical institutes of higher studies, candidates to the diaconate, superiors of clerical institutes and moderators of clerical societies. Because it juridically binds the faithful involved, it cannot be made by means of a procurator. There is not a corresponding canon in the CCEO, but given that Eastern Christian faithful can also assume one of these positions, it should apply also to them, as is provided by law (CCEO c. 895). The CCEO, while it does not have a counterpart to CIC c. 833, states, in the respective places in the code, who must make the profession of faith (*fidei Professio*) and before whom it must be done (*coram quo*): the newly-elected Patriarch before the Synod of Bishops of the patriarchal Church according to the approved formula (c. 76 §1); the newly-elected Major Archbishop before the Synod of Bishops of the major archiepiscopal Church according to the approved formula (c. 153 §3); a candidate for the episcopate before episcopal ordination, as well as making the promise of obedience towards the Roman Pontiff and, in the patriarchal Churches, a promise of obedience toward the Patriarch in those matters in which he is subject to the Patriarch according to the norm of law (c. 187 §2); the administrator of a vacant or impeded eparchy before the Patriarch (c. 220, 4°).

Chapter V

The Sacrament of Marriage

V.1. Doctrine and Legislation
V.2. Laws that Regulate Marriage
V.3. Preparation
V.4. Impediments in General
    V.4.1. Competent Authority
    V.4.2. Temporary Prohibition
V.5. Dispensation
V.6. Specific Impediments
    V.6.1. Impediment of Age
    V.6.2. Impediment of Abduction
    V.6.3. Impediment of Affinity
    V.6.4. Impediment of Public Propriety
    V.6.5. Impediment of Disparity of Worship
    V.6.6. Impediment of Spiritual Relationship
    V.6.7. Impediment of a Vow
V.7. Mixed Marriages
V.8. Marriage under Condition
V.9. Canonical Form
V.10. Competent Minister
    V.10.1. Competence of the Minister by Reason of Office
    V.10.2. Competence of the Minister by Reason of Territory
    V.10.3. Competence of the minister in virtue of one of the parties belonging to his Church *sui iuris*
    V.10.4. Delegated Faculty
V.11. Personal Scope of Canonical Form
V.12. Secret Celebration of Marriage

V.1. Doctrine and Legislation

Christian marriage evokes the entire work of the creation of the universe, which finds its culmination in man, created in the image and likeness of his Creator; this also reveals a relational dimension: a person is not made to be alone.[1] Every person, called to work and rule the land, needs a similar helpmate, with whom to form one flesh. In virtue of the common priesthood of the faithful, marriage for the baptized is a true act of worship. This aspect is not found among the non-baptized; though their conjugal union also has a religious character, it

---

[1] For a history of the celebration of marriage in the West and East, see G. Kadzioch, *Il ministro del sacramento del matrimonio nella tradizione e nel diritto canonico latino e orientale*. Tesi Gregoriana Serie Diritto Canonico 22 (Rome, 1997) 7-95. For certain specific questions, see L. Örsy, *Marriage Canon Law. Texts and Comments; Reflections and questions* (Minnesota, 1990).

does not reach a sacramental dignity since it lacks the external sign of union with Christ.[2]

Vatican II provides a definition that is important also from the perspective of canonistics:

> The intimate partnership of life and the love which constitutes the married state has been established by the Creator and endowed by him with its own proper laws: it is rooted in the contract of its partners, that is, in their irrevocable personal consent. It is an institution confirmed by the divine law and receiving its stability, even in the eyes of society, from the human act by which the partners mutually surrender themselves to each other; for the good of the partners, of the children, and of society this sacred bond no longer depends on human decision alone. (GS 48 a)

Marriage discipline in the CCEO and CIC rightly present necessary distinctions not only in the different norms of East and West, but especially in the different theological perspectives,[3] in other words, in the proper character of the Easterners and Westerners in presenting the mystery, and in our case, the sacrament of marriage:

> In the study of revealed truth East and West have used different methods and approaches in understanding and confessing divine things. It is hardly surprising, then, if sometimes one tradition has come nearer to a full appreciation of some aspects of a mystery of revelation than the other, or has expressed them better. In such cases, these various theological formulations are often to be considered complementary rather than conflicting. (UR 17)

Applying the principle of UR 17 in the field of theology and canonical norms regarding the sacrament of marriage, we note that the Eastern tradition emphasizes certain aspects of the marriage *mysterion*[4] more than the Latin tradition, concentrating on the sacerdotal ministry of the Church in the celebration the sacrament of marriage, presupposing the exchange of consent of the spouses: "In

---

2   Some fundamental texts of Vatican II on Catholic marriage doctrine are, for example, LG, 11, 2; 35, 3 and 41, 4; AA 11 and 29; GS 12, 4; 61,2; 67,3; 87 and especially 47-52.

3   The specific aspects of Eastern theology on the sacrament of marriage are well synthesized by D. Salachas, *Il sacramento del matrimonio nel Nuovo Diritto Canonico delle Chiese orientali* (Rome-Bologna, 1994) 29-34.

4   The thought and dispositions of the Fathers of the Church on the reading of Paul on the theme of *mysterion* and the covenant form are interesting . See O. Bucci, "Per la storia del matrimonio cristiano fra eredità giuridica orientale e tradizione romanistica," in *Il matrimonio nel Codice dei Canoni delle Chiese Orientali*, Studi Giuridici 32, eds. U. Navarette and J. Prader (Vatican City, 1994) 27-33.

marriage, the Church unites herself to the Spouse in the fecundity of new children and in the commitment of witness and evangelization";[5] while Latin theology concentrates much more on the consent,[6] the act that constitutes the sacrament of marriage, even if not with the same intensity of the prior legislation: "Christ the Lord raised the marriage contract itself to the dignity of a sacrament among the baptized" (CIC-17 c. 1012 §1; CA c. 1). The contractual character is less prominent in Eastern theology. At the same time, it emerges from both theologies that through the institution of Christ, the valid marriage between baptized persons is, in virtue of the fact itself, a sacrament (cf. CIC c. 1055 §2; CCEO c. 776 §2).

The two codes of the Catholic Church received the conciliar doctrine on marriage, but in different ways:

CCEO	CIC
776. §1. By the marriage covenant, founded by the Creator and ordered by His laws, a man and a woman by irrevocable personal consent establish between themselves a partnership of the whole of life; this covenant is by its very nature ordered to the good of the spouses and to the procreation and education of children.	1055 §1. The matrimonial covenant, by which a man and a woman establish between themselves a partnership of the whole of life and which is ordered by its nature to the good of the spouses and the procreation and education of offspring, has been raised by Christ the Lord to the dignity of a sacrament between the baptized.
§2. By Christ's institution, a valid marriage between baptized persons is by that very fact a sacrament in which the spouses are united by God after the pattern of Christ's indefectible union with the Church, and are, as it were, consecrated and strengthened by sacramental grace.	§2. For this reason, a valid matrimonial contract cannot exist between the baptized without it being by that fact a sacrament.

In the CIC the term *contractus* of the prior legislation (CIC-17 c. 1012 §1) is replaced by *fœdus*; the hierarchical treatment of the ends of marriage has disappeared (CIC-17 c. 1013 §1); the distance between marriage *in fieri* and marriage *in facto esse* is reduced. The term *consortium* [*totius vitæ consortium*] is preferred

---

5   Instr. 1.
6   "Consent expressed in words of the present between persons who are lawfully qualified to contract makes a marriage, because these two conditions are essential to the sacrament; while all else belongs to the solemnization of the sacrament, done in order that the marriage may be more fittingly performed. Hence if these should be omitted it is a true marriage, although the contracting parties sin, unless they have a lawful motive for being excused": S. Th. Suppl., q. 45, art. 5. For Saint Thomas, the blessing of the priest does not belong to the essence of the sacrament, but he does not exclude the necessity of this act that is required "with regard to the propriety, but not with regard to the power of the sacrament."

over the conciliar phrase *communitas vitæ et amoris* and in the same c. 1055 §2, the term *contractus* is used again, drawing from the text of CIC-17 c. 1012 §2, but to designate only one aspect of the complexity that constitutes the marriage. Further, the phrase *quo vir et mulier [. . .] constituunt* risks giving the impression that it is the parties themselves that conclude the covenant, and not that God Himself is the author under the human signs of the exchange of consent.

In the CCEO, there is a more clear separation between the marriage covenant and the sacrament of marriage, treating them in two distinct paragraphs; moreover, the CCEO does not merely state that the marriage covenant validly concluded between baptized persons is a sacrament, but specifies that the operative factor with this sacrament is the indefectible union of Christ with the Church.

In consideration of these general principles, we must treat in a very specific way the marriage between Catholics belonging to different Churches *sui iuris*, and also marriage between Catholics and baptized non-Catholics where there is a need to examine the norms that regulate the form of the celebration and that determine the juridic capacity of persons.[7] Form cannot be simultaneously regulated by two different legislations, while there can be certain differences in the capacity of persons.

V.2. Laws that Regulate Marriage

The right to marriage is one of the rights inherent in man and woman from creation, which no human law can remove or limit to anyone. However, the exercise of the right can be regulated not only by divine law, but also by human law that determines and expresses the divine law in the actual situation. Therefore, human law, canonical or civil, can prohibit the marriage of persons in particular situations or in situations not favorable to the ends, demands and dignity of marriage.

---

7   The term "person" currently in juridic language indicates a subject legally capable of rights and obligations. "Legally capable" means that the juridic capacity arises out of a certain law, as a norm of subjective rights and obligations. For the origins of this usage, see S. Tafaro, "*Persona*: origini e prospettive. Oltre l'antropocentismo," in *Incontro*, 2:583-613.

CCEO	CIC
780 §1. Even if only one party is Catholic, the marriage of Catholics is governed not only by divine law but also by canon law, without prejudice to the competence of civil authority concerning the merely civil effects of marriage. §2. Marriage between a Catholic and a baptized non-Catholic is governed, with due regard for divine law, also by: 1° the law proper to the Church or ecclesial community to which the non-Catholic belongs, if that community has its own matrimonial law; 2° the law to which the non-Catholic is subject, if the ecclesial community to which the person belongs has no matrimonial law of its own.	1059. Even if only one party is Catholic, the marriage of Catholics is governed not only by divine law but also by canon law, without prejudice to the competence of civil authority concerning the merely civil effects of the same marriage.

Before any other laws, all marriages are always regulated by divine law, natural or positive, to which all, Catholics and others, are subject, of which the custodian and interpreter is the Church of Christ.[8] But not all marriages are regulated by the same human law.

Regarding a Catholic marriage between a Latin party and an Eastern Catholic party, it is necessary to observe both legislations to which the respective parties are bound. The matter becomes more complex for the marriage of Catholics with baptized non-Catholics and non-baptized persons.

In both prior legislations, Latin and Eastern, it was stated: "Marriage of the baptized is ruled not only by divine law, but also by canon [law], with due regard for the competence of civil power concerning the merely civil effects of said marriage" (CIC-17 c. 1016; CA c. 5). There was an explicit affirmation of the doctrinal principle that the marriage of baptized persons is the exclusive competence of the Church, a principle always and everywhere valid. Presupposing the existence of true jurisdiction in the Eastern non-Catholic Churches, it is obvious that this jurisdiction also extends to the marriage-sacrament; these Churches are bound to provide for their faithful in the same manner as the Churches that are

---

[8] CIC c. 748 §1 states: "All persons are bound to seek the truth in those things which regard God and his Church and by virtue of divine law are bound by the obligation and possess the right of embracing and observing the truth which they have come to know."

in full communion with the Church of Rome do for their Catholic faithful. The new legislation is limited to regulate the marriage only of Catholics, based on the doctrinal principle of the competency of the Church and applying the respective first canons of the Code as well as CCEO c. 1490 and CIC c. 11:

> Merely ecclesiastical laws bind those who have been baptized in the Catholic Church (*ecclesiological criterion*) or received into it, possess the sufficient use of reason (*psychological criterion*), and, unless the law expressly provides otherwise, have completed seven years of age (*chronological criterion*).[9]

The norm implicitly recognizes the legal regulations of other non-Catholic Churches as *ius legitimum* (legitimate law). While this was explicit in the CCEO, it was not so in the CIC, at least until the promulgation of *Dignitas Connubii* of 25 January 2005. CCEO c. 780 §1, when compared to CA c. 5, does not contain any change of the law regulating the marriage of baptized non-Catholics, because they already governed themselves (or at least after the promulgation of *Unitatis Redintegratio* of 21 November 1964) with their own marriage law, since their Churches possess true ecclesiastical jurisdiction;[10] hence, the CCEO does not change the juridic state of Eastern non-Catholics.

The problem arises when one deals with a marriage between a Catholic and a Western non-Catholic: can Eastern and Western non-Catholics be treated in the same way? Is there ecclesiastical jurisdiction among Western non-Catholics? CCEO c. 780 §2 treats them in the same way.

CIC c. 1059, compared with CIC-17 c. 1016, involves a change with regard to the marriage of baptized non-Catholics who, according to CIC-17, were bound to the same legislation of Catholics in marriage matters, excepting the impediment of the disparity of worship (CIC-17 c. 1070) and the obligation of canonical form (CIC-17 c. 1099). With the new CIC, non-Catholics are exempt from the legislation of the Code, even marriage legislation, but the uncertainty remains,

---

9   There are cases in which the law requires a more mature age.
10   There was a tendency to hold the position that CA also bound the Eastern non-Catholics, inasmuch as the Catholic Church recognized the power of orders of the Bishops and not the power of jurisdiction; UR 16 and OE 5 finally resolved the question, but not entirely, since the problem of the *missio canonica* remains. I. Žužek, "La giurisdizione dei vescovi ortodossi dopo il Concilio Vaticano II," *La Civiltà Cattolica* 122/2 (1971) 562: "All jurisdictional acts of Orthodox Bishops are to be considered as performed in hierarchical communion with the Catholic Church, and thus are juridically valid and licit, except those which would be contrary to Scripture, Catholic doctrine and natural law." Cf. L. Spinelli, "L'incidenza della comunione gerarchica nell'esercizio della potestà di giurisdizione dei vescovi ortodossi," in *Incontro*, 2:183-191.

not having been clarified despite the suggestions advanced both in doctrine and in the work of the revision of the CIC.[11]

The CIC indicates only the law that governs the marriage of Catholics, but does not offer a solution when a marriage is celebrated between a Catholic and a baptized non-Catholic. According to c. 1059, even if only one of the parties is Catholic, the marriage is governed only by canon law (presupposing perhaps at least respect for the discipline of the Eastern non-Catholic Churches according to UR 16, but not of those Western non-Catholic ecclesial communions). Is this not a contradiction between canons 1 and 11? "We hope as soon as possible that this would be in some way provided for, so that this lacuna can be filled and that there can be a certitude of law regarding a matter of great importance."[12] However, according to some authors, one should take into account the statement of DH 4: "Therefore, provided the just requirements of public order are not violated, these groups have a right to immunity so that they may organize themselves according to their own principles."

The CCEO provides for a solution to the problem with canons 780 §2 and 781, an implementation of UR 16 and DH 4, taken up by John Paul II: "This is not the result of privileges guaranteed by Rome, but of the law itself that the Churches have possessed since apostolic times."[13] These canons are of particular importance for tribunal praxis of Latin ecclesiastical tribunals in the marriage nullity processes. These canons, although they clarify the uncertainty of the marriage canonical order,[14] were ineffective in the Latin Church, at least on the normative

---

11   The Commission for the Revision of the CIC proposed: "Matrimonium eorum qui licet baptizati non ad plenam communionem Ecclesiæ catholicæ pertinent regitur iure divino nec non normis in communitate ecclesiali ad quam pertinent vigentibus," but the text was not accepted (*Comm.* 9 [1977] 127). The difficulty was perceived by Card. Parrecattil, president of the Commission for the Revision of the Eastern Code, in his observations on the 1980 CIC Draft: *Relatio complectens synthesim animadversionum ab Em.mis atque Exc.mis Patribus Commissionis ad novissimum Schema Codicis Iuris Canonici exhibitarum, cum responsionibus a Secreteria et Consultoribus datis* (Vatican City, 1981) 246.   See also U. Navarrete, "Competentia Ecclesiæ in matrimonium baptizatorum eiusque limites," *Periodica* 67 (1978) 101ff: "If in the future, a contrary principle should be established [to that of the CIC-17] that non-Catholics are not bound by laws enacted by the Catholic Church, unless it is expressly declared, a great *lacuna legis* will be created."

12   U. Navarrete, "Ius matrimoniale latinum et orientale. Collatio inter Codicem latinum et orientalem," *Periodica* 80 (1991) 617. He has also suggested that the Eastern norms (CCEO cc. 780-781) serve to supply the lacuna remaining in the CIC on this point; cf. *Id.*, "Il matrimonio in oriente e in occidente," *Orientalia Christiana Periodica* 58 (1992) 563-569, especially 568-569.

13   John Paul II, Aplet *Euntes in Mundum Universum*, 25 January 1988, n. 10: *AAS* 80 (1988) 950: EV 11:151. For the evolution of CCEO cc. 780 §2 and 781: *Nuntia* 5 (1977) 52-62; 8 (1979) 5-9; 10 (1980) 3-4; 15 (1982) 3-97; 29 (1989) 104-106.

14   *Nuntia* 28 (1989) 104-106.

level, until the promulgation of *Dignitas Connubii*, with due regard for the force of the arguments that justify them.

The application of the proper law of the non-Catholic Churches or Communities concerns only the impediments of ecclesiastical law, and do not concern the laws regarding the defects and error of consent, nor the dissolution of the bond and the convalidation and the radical sanation of the marriage; but "if, for example, the law of the Catholic party and the law of the non-Catholic party contain norms that are incompatible,"[15] what needs to be done?

The CCEO provides a solution with c. 780: the marriage between an Eastern Catholic and an Eastern non-Catholic is governed both by canon law and the law of the Eastern non-Catholic Churches. A difficulty arises when the other party is a Western non-Catholic. Western non-Catholics were bound to the marriage law of the CIC-17, but when the new CIC went into force, were they still bound to the observance of Catholic marriage law? From the tenor of CIC c. 1059, some canonists respond affirmatively;[16] but have they not lost sight of DH 4? CCEO c. 780 is much more respectful of the regulations of the other Churches. If it is true that CCEO c. 780 not only canonizes but also directly recognizes the lawful jurisdiction of the Eastern Churches over marriages of their faithful with Catholics, then one can perfectly hypothesize that CIC c. 1059 should be re-interpreted in light of CCEO c. 780. In fact, it would be a recognition required by justice: this came with the instruction *Dignitas Connubii*.

Synthesizing, we can affirm that the form of the celebration of a marriage between a Catholic party and a non-Catholic party is regulated by canon law, save for the exceptions that follow. Regarding impediments and the defects of consent governed by human law, there are different positions among canonists as to whether the non-Catholic should depend on his / her own law or is exempt from it.[17] We

---

15　　U. Navarrete, "Ius matrimoniale…," 617.

16　　For example, L. Chiappetta, *Il Codice di Diritto Canonico. Commento giuridico-pastorale*, 2nd ed. (Rome, 1996) 2:262, n. 3760; *Id.*, *Il matrimonio nella nuova legislazione canonica e concordataria* (Rome, 1990) 52, n. 14; *Commento al Codice di diritto canonico*, Studia Urbaniana 21, 1st ed., ed. P. V. Pinto (Rome, 1985) 620; G. Ghirlanda, *Il diritto nella Chiesa mistero di comunione*, 2nd ed. (Rome-Cinisello Balsamo, 1993) 340.

17　　According to the prevailing doctrine followed in practice, the non-baptized person who contracted marriage with a Catholic party would be exempt from the impediments and defects of consent established by human law, for the reason that these would cease through the communication of the liberty of the Catholic party to the non-baptized party: cf. A. Abate, *Il matrimonio nella nuova legislazione canonica* (Rome-Brescia, 1979) 28-29. Other authors hold that the non-baptized party is subject to his / her own law, not admitting that the Catholic party, free from the impediments and defects of consent of merely positive law, can communicate this freedom to the non-Catholic party, for the reason that such a principle is not established by any canonical norm: cf. P. Gasparri, *Tractatus canonicus de matrimonio* (Rome, 1932) nn. 256 and 842.

hold that at least the non-baptized party is not directly bound to the canonical legislation, but is bound at least indirectly through the Catholic party with whom a single act is posed, that is, the celebration of marriage. Further, according to an authentic response, the defect of consent treated in CIC c. 1103 (= CCEO c. 825) is applicable also in the marriage of non-Catholics.[18] Certainly, mixed marriage involves some difficulties, not only from the juridical point of view, but also

> for the couples themselves, and for the children born to them, in maintaining their Christian faith and commitment and for the harmony of family life. For all these reasons, marriage between persons of the same ecclesial Community remains the objective to be recommended and encouraged.[19]

Since in the CIC there was an uncertainty regarding the norm to be applied in a specific case, can could have made recourse to suppletory sources established by the Legislator in CIC c. 19, that is, recourse to laws given for similar cases. Moreover, one could have considered the suppletory rule of the Supreme Tribunal of the Apostolic Signatura given on 28 November 1970 that declares a marriage celebrated between two Orthodox of the Byzantine rite before a civil official null because of a defect of *ritus sacer*.[20] Another decision of 7 July 1971 approved the sentence of a metropolitan tribunal in the United States that had declared null, because of a lack of *ritus sacer*, a marriage between an Orthodox and a Presbyterian Protestant, celebrated before a Presbyterian minister;[21] the same decision was given on 23 November 1974 for a marriage between Armenian schismatics, null because of defect of *ritus sacer*.[22] There is a rotal decision of 24 October 1967 that declared a marriage null under canon 72 of the Council of Trullo.[23] The judges therein claimed that "non-Catholics are bound by the laws of their own church, and the validity of their marriage, either by virtue of form or by virtue of impediments, depends on their own competent legislation, to be duly considered in individual cases." They mean to say, with a certain tacit reference to the abrogating capacity of CA and with it write that the Romanian non-Catholics "although they

---

18   25 November 1986: *AAS* 79 (1987) 1132; *ex natura rei*, it also applies to the CCEO. From the Middle Ages, it has been a question disputed in doctrine, if consent vitiated through grave fear renders the marriage null through natural law or positive law. According to the prevalent opinion sustained in jurisprudence, the norm is of ecclesiastical law. According to this opinion, it follows that CIC c. 1103 / CIC c. 828 does not apply to baptized non-Catholics who have contracted marriage through grave fear after the new legislation entered into force, not being subject to ecclesiastical laws (CIC c. 11 / CCEO c. 1490).
19   ED 144.
20   X. Ochoa, *Leges Ecclesiæ*, 5:6394-6399; *Apollinaris* 48 (1975) 19-28.
21   X. Ochoa, *Leges Ecclesiæ*, 4:6135.
22   *Apollinaris* 49 (1976) 9-29; cf. "The Competence of a Latin Rite Tribunal Regarding the Form of Celebration of an Eastern Church Marriage," *Roman Replies and CLSA Advisory Opinions 1994*, 62-66.
23   *Coram* Palazzini, *Ephemerides Iuris Canonici* 23 (1967) 331ff.

follow their own patriarchate, [...] as pertains to matrimonial legislation, they observe the laws of the Byzantine Orthodox Patriarchate" that the law that was referenced was a norm proper to a separated Church.[24]

To conclude this argument, every marriage, even canonical, is governed first by divine law. Further, the marriage of two baptized non-Catholics will be governed by their own laws. This rule is provided expressly for the Eastern Churches (cf. UR 16) and implicitly for the Western Churches (cf. DH 4 and CIC c. 11). One should take into consideration the norms of the non-Catholic communities, especially regarding the form and the impediments. The marriage of two non-baptized is governed by divine law as well as civil law. When non-Catholics enter into a relationship with the Catholic Church, through a subsequent conversion or because they wish to marry a Catholic,[25] the Church judges the validity of prior marriages, taking into account the applicable law and, above all, its harmony with divine law, of which the Catholic Church is the authoritative interpreter.[26]

---

24   Cf. V. Parlato, "Ecumenismo e diritto canonico," *Ius Canonicum* 9 (1969) 263-280.

25   Cf. Supreme Tribunal of the Apostolic Signatura, *Dichiarazione sulla giurisdizione della Chiesa riguardo al matrimonio celebrato tra due acattolici*, 28 June 1993 (Prot. N. 23805/92 V. T.), in *Ius Ecclesiæ* 6 (1994) 366.

26   It might be difficult to apply CCEO c. 781, especially when the Catholic Church must judge the validity of marriages celebrated in the Assyrian and certain monophysite Oriental Orthodox Churches (Syrian, Armenian, Coptic and Ethiopian). In general, CCEO c. 781, with the requirements of public consent and sacred rite, corresponds to the proper law of these different Churches. But problems arise when the Church in question recognizes as valid, for example, marriages celebrated before lay persons, in case of the danger of death or in cases where, through the application of the principle of economy, the same civil or mixed marriages, celebrated in another Church or ecclesial community without a sacred rite, are recognized as valid. If the Catholic Church applies CCEO c. 781 in these cases, it can happen that certain marriages would be null, while for the Church to which the non-Catholic belongs, this same marriage is valid. Another problem is that for some of these Churches, a marriage concluded without a sacred rite is considered as valid, but not sacramental, contrary to Catholic doctrine that teaches the unity of the marriage-contract and the marriage-sacrament.

V.3. Preparation

CCEO	CIC
784. In the particular law of each Church *sui iuris*, after consultation with the eparchial bishops of other Churches *sui iuris* exercising their power in the same territory, norms are to be established concerning the examination of the couple and other means for inquiries that are to be carried out before the marriage, especially those that concern baptism and the freedom to marry, which are to be diligently observed so that the celebration of the marriage can proceed.	1065 §1. Catholics who have not yet received the sacrament of confirmation are to receive it before they are admitted to marriage if it can be done without grave inconvenience. 1067. The conference of bishops is to establish norms about the examination of spouses and about the marriage banns or other opportune means to accomplish the investigations necessary before marriage. After these norms have been diligently observed, the pastor can proceed to assist at the marriage.

CCEO c. 784 relegates to particular law of the Churches *sui iuris* norms regarding the examination of engaged couples, the investigations of their free state and their baptism, the absence of impediments and the integrity of their consent, while the CIC relegates these matters to the episcopal conferences.[27] It should be noted that the CCEO, unlike the CIC, uses only the term baptism and does not refer to chrismation with holy Myron because, as was seen, the latter must be administered, according to Eastern tradition, conjointly with baptism (CCEO c. 695). The pastor who is entrusted with all these requirements is that of the parish where either of the parties has a canonical domicile or quasi-domicile or has resided there for a month, but if he is not the one who is to celebrate the marriage, he is obliged to inform the pastor who will celebrate the marriage of the results of the examination by means of an authentic document (CIC c. 1070; CCEO c. 787). There is the case of CCEO c. 916 §4, whereby the Latin pastor is to observe the particular law of the Church *sui iuris* of Eastern faithful; there is also CCEO c. 916 §5, whereby the Eastern or Latin pastor is to observe the disposition of the episcopal conferences. The premarital inquiries are made in the diocese / eparchy of residence, presenting the certificate of free state issued by the parish of origin.

Another norm of the CCEO which is formally absent in the CIC is the following:[28] "If after a diligent investigation there persists any doubt concerning the existence of an impediment, the pastor is to defer the matter to the hierarch" (CCEO c. 788). Therefore, the local Ordinaries and Latin pastors, in determining

---

27 Cf. Italian Episcopal Conference, *Decreto generale sul matrimonio canonico*, Roma, dalla Sede della CEI, 5 November 1990: *Notizario CEI* 16 (1990) 259-279.
28 CIC-17 c. 1031 §1, 3°: "If doubt about the existence of any impediments arises: He will not assist at the marriage without consulting the Ordinary, if he judges the doubt to be still operative."

the free state of an Eastern party entrusted to their pastoral care, have the obligation to know that there are differences between the CIC and the CCEO and are bound to know the norms of the latter.

CCEO	CIC
789. Although the marriage can be entered validly with regard to other matters, the priest, beyond the other cases defined by law, is not to bless without the permission of the local hierarch:	1071 §1. Except in a case of necessity, a person is not to assist without the permission of the local ordinary at:
1° the marriage of transients;	1° a marriage of transients;
2° a marriage that cannot be recognized or entered into in accord with the norms of civil law;	2° a marriage which cannot be recognized or celebrated according to the norm of civil law;
3° the marriage of a person who is bound by natural obligations toward a third party or toward children arising from a prior union with that party;	3° a marriage of a person who is bound by natural obligations toward another party or children arising from a previous union;
4° the marriage of a minor child of a family whose parents are unaware of or opposed to the marriage;	4° a marriage of a person who has notoriously rejected the Catholic faith;
5° the marriage of one who is forbidden by an ecclesiastical sentence to enter into a new marriage unless the person fulfills certain conditions;	5° a marriage of a person who is under a censure;
	6° a marriage of a minor child when the parents are unaware or reasonably opposed;
6° the marriage of a person who has publicly rejected the Catholic faith, even if that person did not become a member of a non-Catholic Church or ecclesial communion; the local hierarch in this case will not grant permission unless the norms of can. 814 are observed, making any necessary adaptations.	7° a marriage to be entered into through a proxy as mentioned in can. 1105.
	§2. The local ordinary is not to grant permission to assist at the marriage of a person who has notoriously rejected the Catholic faith unless the norms mentioned in can. 1125 have been observed with necessary adaptation.

With regard to the liceity of the marriage, the priest must request the permission of the local Ordinary / Hierarch for the categories of persons indicated in the canons. The two canons are rather similar, but they do have slight differences that need to be taken into account: while the CIC (and the prior Eastern legislation, CA c. 24) specified that one cannot celebrate the marriage of minors without the knowledge or against the *reasonable* will of the parents, the CCEO is more restrictive for the priest, since it is not licit to celebrate the marriage of minors against the will of the parents.²⁹ While the CIC includes one who is under an imposed or declared censure that has not been lifted (according to cc. 1331 §1, 2°, 1332 and 1335),³⁰ the CCEO does not include such a prohibition, but includes one who is prohibited by an ecclesiastical sentence to enter a new marriage if certain conditions have not been fulfilled.

The CIC prohibits the celebration of marriage by means of a proxy without the permission of the local Ordinary;³¹ the CCEO affirms that "marriage cannot be validly celebrated by proxy unless the particular law of the respective Church *sui iuris* establishes otherwise, in which case it must provide the conditions under which such a marriage can be celebrated" (c. 837 §2). This provision, while not consonant with Eastern tradition, can serve those faithful in regions that are predominantly Latin; but, given the seriousness of the matter, it is for the particular law of each Church *sui iuris* to regulate the conditions³² (cf. CIC c. 1105). Furthermore, the CIC also admits the celebration of marriage by means of an interpreter (c. 1106). In the case of CCEO c. 916 §§4-5, the pastor must observe CCEO c. 789 and request the permission of the local Hierarch / Ordinary. If one party belongs to one Church *sui iuris* and the other to the Latin Church, the pastor must take both codes into account.

---

29   According to the Italian Civil Code, persons under the age of 18 years old cannot contract matrimony. A dispensation can be granted to those who have reached the age of 16 years by the tribunal for the minors with a decree issued in chambers, having heard the public ministry, the parents or guardian, once it has been ascertained the minor's psycho-physical maturity and there exist grave reasons (art. 84).
30   A censure is a penal sanction imposed not as a punishment, but for medicinal purposes: it is a case, for example, of excommunication that impedes the reception of the sacraments.
31   This is an improper representative, since the proxy is in this case a messenger who brings and expresses the personal will of the marrying party.
32   *Nuntia* 28 (1989) 117. According to the particular law of the Maronite Church, prepared in May, 1993, to be able to celebrate marriage by proxy it is necessary to have the permission of the local Hierarch of the celebration, or his vicar, for grave reasons and according to the following conditions: "Marriage cannot be validly celebrated by proxy except with written permission from the eparchial Bishop, or his vicar, of the place where the contract will take place, for grave reasons and with the following conditions: 1° the presence of a competent priest, at least two witnesses, the presence of the one mandated with the mandate if it is still in force, organized before the ordinary of the place of the one mandating or his vicar and the mandate not having been revoked by the one mandating before the marriage is contacted. 2° people present in a city, locality or eparchy may not contract marriage by mandate except for a reason known and recognized by the local ordinary": *Particular Law of the Eastern Catholic Churches*, ed. K. Bharanikulangara (New York, 1996) 205, art. 87.

V.4. Impediments in General

An *impediment* to the celebration of marriage is "[…] an external circumstance or personal relationship, of divine or human law, that renders a person incapable of contracting marriage, which, if celebrated, would be not only illicit, but also radically invalid *ipso iure*."[33] In other words, impediments are legal prohibitions to celebrate marriage imposed by divine or human law in virtue of the above circumstances. Impediments belong to incapacitating laws defined by CCEO c. 1495 and CIC c. 10, as laws that specifically determine that an act is null or a person is incapable. CCEO c. 1497 §1 and CIC c. 15 §1 determine that "ignorance or error about invalidating or disqualifying laws does not impede their effect unless it is expressly established otherwise." Impediments cannot be presumed. They must always be determined by the competent authority.

There are certain differences between the two codes and one should not lose sight of another norm absent in the CIC,[34] but very important: "An impediment, even if only one of the parties has it, still renders the marriage invalid" (CCEO c. 790 §2). This principle applies not only to the marriage between Catholics of different Churches *sui iuris*, but also between Catholics and baptized non-Catholics or between Catholics and non-baptized persons. In the latter case, when there is a conflict between canon law and civil law, canonists differ on the superiority or observance of the laws.[35]

V.4.1. Competent Authority

CCEO	CIC
792. Diriment impediments are not to be established by the particular law of a Church *sui iuris* except for a most grave cause, after having consulted with eparchial bishops of other Churches *sui iuris* who have an interest, and after consultation with the Apostolic See; however, no lower authority can establish new diriment impediments.	1075 §1. It is only for the supreme authority of the Church to declare authentically when divine law prohibits or nullifies marriage. §2. Only the supreme authority has the right to establish other impediments for the baptized.

---

33   L. Chiappetta, *Il Codice*…, 2:290, n. 3837.
34   The norm was in CIC-17 c. 1036 §3: "Even though just one party has an impediment, nevertheless, the [whole] marriage is rendered illicit or invalid." It was not received into the new legislation because it was considered obvious: *Comm.* 9 (1977) 135.
35   On the superiority of ecclesiastical laws, see A. Abate, *Il matrimonio*…, 28. On the observance of civil laws: P. Gasparri, *Tractatus* …, n. 256.

One is obviously dealing with impediments of ecclesiastical law, since "it is only for the supreme authority of the Church to declare authentically when divine law prohibits or nullifies marriage" (CIC c. 1075 §1). It should be noted that this is a case of *declarare* (declaring), not of establishing new impediments of divine law. This *declaratio* is denied to Latin Bishops, both by the CIC-17 and the new CIC; it is also denied to particular councils and to episcopal conferences.[36] It was accorded to the synods of the Eastern Churches *sui iuris* (cf. OE 9; LG 27) and to all the equivalent bodies that constitute the supreme instance in the Churches *sui iuris*, and was denied to every authority inferior to them.[37] This right is limited territorially to particular law, that is, it applies only to the faithful in the territory of the patriarchal Church, or in the territory of a Church *sui iuris* according to CCEO c. 150 §2. Eparchial Bishops constituted outside the territory of the patriarchal Church (CCEO c. 150 §3) cannot attribute juridic value in their own eparchies to these impediments, according to the clause of CCEO c. 792 ("no lower authority can establish new diriment impediments"); to do this, they must obtain the approval of the Apostolic See. The clause of CCEO c. 792 was added in order not to create difficulty and differences regarding marriage impediments of parties belonging to different Churches *sui iuris*.[38]

V.4.2. Temporary Prohibition

CCEO	CIC
794 §1. The local hierarch can prohibit the marriage of the Christian faithful subject to him wherever they are and also of other Christian faithful of his own Church *sui iuris* actually present within the territorial boundaries of his eparchy in a special case, but only for a time, for a grave cause and as long as that cause exists.	1077 §1. In a special case, the local ordinary can prohibit marriage for his own subjects residing anywhere and for all actually present in his own territory but only for a time, for a grave cause, and for as long as the cause continues.
§2. If the local hierarch is one who exercises his power within the territorial boundaries of the patriarchal Church, the patriarch can add an invalidating clause to the prohibition; in other cases only the Apostolic See can do so.	§2. Only the supreme authority of the Church can add a nullifying clause to a prohibition.

---

36   Cf. *Comm.* 10 (1978) 126.
37   Competent authorities: Synod of Bishops of the patriarchal Church (cc. 110 §1 and 150 §§2-3); Synod of Bishops of the major archiepiscopal Church *sui iuris* (cc. 150 §§2-3 and 152); Council of Hierarchs of the metropolitan Church *sui iuris* (c. 167); the Hierarch who presides over the Church *sui iuris* (c. 176).
38   Cf. *Nuntia* 28 (1989) 107; 15 (1982) 64.

The local Hierarch can prohibit (not establish diriment impediments), in special cases (limits of time, of subjects, of reasons and of place), the celebration of the marriage for his subjects (Eastern or Latin) wherever they reside and, in his own territory, for non-subjects residing in his eparchy, who do not have a domicile or quasi-domicile there, but who belong to his Church *sui iuris*.[39] The local Ordinary can also prohibit all the faithful residing in his territory: the reference to CIC c. 1 is implicit here, and thus the canon refers only the Latin faithful, unless the Eastern faithful are his subjects according to the norm of law.[40] The explicit reference to Ordinary / Hierarch excludes all those (for example, pastors) who are not equivalent to them; logically, if the marriage is celebrated all the same, it is valid, but illicit. The addition of the diriment clause is reserved in the CIC to the Apostolic See. In the CCEO, the Patriarch and the Major Archbishop can also add it, if the Bishop is acting within the boundaries of the patriarchal or major archiepiscopal Church; only in this case, as long as the prohibition remains in effect, would the celebrated marriage be invalid.

V.5. Dispensation

A *dispensation* is a *relaxatio legis*, the exoneration of the law in a special case granted by an administrative authority; in it is realized the fundamental principle of all ecclesial law, to seek the spiritual good of the person in the concrete situations in which the person is found. The faculty to dispense is exercised with regard to prescriptive or prohibitive laws, but not regarding constitutive laws.[41] The faithful for whose benefit the authority to dispense is exercised according to the norm of law are all those, Eastern or Latin, who because of domicile or another title[42] are subject to the Bishop.[43] It should be kept in mind that a dispensation from impediments is an administrative act that can be posited only by those who enjoy the executive power of governance (CCEO c. 1510; CIC c. 35); it can be delegated in either in an individual case or for the totality of cases (CCEO cc. 988-995; CIC cc. 137-144).

---

39   CA c. 29 §1 states: "omnibus in suo territorio actu commorantibus."
40   Cf. J. Prader, *Il matrimonio in Oriente e Occidente*, 1st ed., Kanonika 1 (Rome, 1992) 78.
41   Cf. Paul VI, Mp *Episcopalis potestatis*, 2 May 1967: *AAS* 59 (1967) 385-390: CLD 6:25-29; *Id.*, Mp *Episcoporum muneribus*, 15 June 1966: *AAS* 58 (1967) 467-472: CLD 6:394-400.
42   When a Hierarch / Ordinary is entrusted with a group of faithful of another Church *sui iuris* lacking their own Hierarch / Ordinary in that territory.
43   Cf. Paul VI, Mp *Episcopalis potestatis*: CLD 6:27.

CCEO	CIC
795 §1. The local hierarch can dispense the Christian faithful subject to him wherever they are as well as other Christian faithful ascribed to another Church *sui iuris* actually present within the territorial boundaries of his eparchy from impediments of ecclesiastical law except those that follow:	1078 §1. The local Ordinary can dispense his own subjects residing anywhere and all actually present in his own territory from all impediments of ecclesiastical law except those whose dispensation is reserved to the Apostolic See.
1º sacred orders;	§2. Impediments whose dispensation is reserved to the Apostolic See are:
2º public perpetual vows of chastity in a religious institute, unless it is a case of congregations of eparchial right;	1º the impediment arising from sacred orders or from a public perpetual vow of chastity in a religious institute of pontifical right;
3º conjugicide.	
§2. Dispensation from these impediments is reserved to the Apostolic See; however, the patriarch can dispense from the impediment of conjugicide as well as of the one of a public perpetual vow of chastity made in congregations of any juridical condition.	2º the impediment of crime mentioned in c. 1090.
	§3. A dispensation is never given from the impediment of consanguinity in the direct line or in the second degree of the collateral line.
§3. A dispensation is never given from the impediment of consanguinity in the direct line or in the second degree of the collateral line.	

While the local Hierarch can dispense his subjects everywhere and non-subjects of his own Church *sui iuris* residing in his territory, the local Ordinary can also dispense all those residing in his territory, meaning the Latin faithful or Eastern Catholics, as long as they are his subjects according to the norm of law.[44]

In danger of death, local Hierarchs and local Ordinaries can dispense from all impediments of ecclesiastical law, except that of the order of priesthood, and from canonical form all the Christian faithful: subjects everywhere and non-subjects residing in their territory (CCEO c. 796 §1; CIC c. 1079 §1).

CCEO c. 795 §2 provides that a Patriarch can dispense from the impediments of conjugicide and from a public perpetual vow of chastity made in a congregation of any juridic condition. Does this also apply for the faithful residing outside the territory? In consideration CCEO c. 78 §2, that is, that the power of the Patriarch can be exercised only in the territory of the patriarchal Church, at least when

---

44   Cf. J. Prader, *Il matrimonio...*, 80.

it is not established otherwise by the nature of the matter or by common law or particular law approved by the Roman Pontiff, we must respond negatively with regard to both impediments.[45]

CCEO	CIC
796 §2. In the same situation and only for those cases in which the local hierarch cannot be reached, the following have the same power: the pastor; another priest endowed with the faculty of blessing the marriage and the Catholic priest referred to in can. 832, §2; the confessor, if it is a question of an occult impediment for the internal forum, whether within or outside the act of sacramental confession.	1079 §2. In the same circumstances mentioned in §1, but only for cases in which the local ordinary cannot be reached, the pastor, the properly delegated sacred minister, and the priest or deacon who assists at marriage according to the norm of can. 1116, §2 possess the same power of dispensing.

Paragraph two of each canon presents a difference because of the different theological tradition regarding the minister of the sacrament of marriage; the faculty to dispense from any marriage impediment is not granted to the deacon as is the case in the CIC.

The same applies also for CCEO cc. 797 §1 and 798 and CIC cc. 1080 §1 and 1081. The "danger of death" is not necessarily "the hour of death," but exists in situations when the probability of survival or death are equal.

According to CCEO c. 302 §2, the parochial vicar, by reason of his office, is not provided with the faculty of blessing marriages; but if it is accorded to him, he then enjoys the faculty to dispense in danger of death.

In the case of doubt of fact or of law regarding the existence or not of just reasons or their sufficiency for the concession of the dispensation, the concession remains licit and valid in virtue of CCEO c. 1536 §3 and CIC c. 90 §2. However, in the case of doubt of whether or not the impediment exists, recourse is made to CCEO c. 1496 and CIC c. 14; hence, in the case of the doubt of fact one grants the dispensation. Finally, if the doubt regards the existence of the power of the authority in question, either in ordinary or extraordinary cases, CCEO c. 994 and CIC c. 144 §1 apply; they prescribe that in the positive or probable doubt of law or of fact, the Church supplies either for the external or internal forum.

---

45 For a contrary opinion, see P. Pellegrino *Gli impedimenti relativi alla dignità dell'uomo nel matrimonio canonico* (Turin, 2000) 119; H. Alwan, "Gli impedimenti," in *Il matrimonio nel Codice dei canoni delle Chiese orientali*, Studi Giuridici 32, eds. U. Navarette and J. Prader (Vatican City, 1994) 177.

V.6. Specific Impediments

During the process of codification of the canons on impediments, the point of departure was that it was more convenient to have the same marriage impediments for all the faithful (Eastern and Latin) without a difference of rite affecting the fundamental rights of the faithful. Eventually, this position could not be accepted because the Redaction Commission was obliged to prepare a Code faithful to genuine Eastern traditions.[46] We shall examine those impediments that are significantly different in the two Codes. The impediment of impotence, of prior bond (the CIC explicitly states that one invalidly attempts marriage, even though the previous marriage was not consummated), of sacred orders, of conjugicide (the dispensation is reserved to the Apostolic See; the Patriarch can also dispense from it in the territory of the patriarchal Church), of consanguinity (the CIC explicitly applies the impediment to both legal and natural ancestors and descendants) and of legal relationship are regulated in both codes equally.

V.6.1. Impediment of Age

The particular law of the Church *sui iuris* is free to establish a higher age for the licit celebration of marriage (cf. CCEO c. 800 §2). In the Latin Church, it is for the episcopal conference to do so (CIC c. 1083 §2). In the case foreseen in CCEO c. 916 §4, the Latin pastor will observe CCEO c. 800 §2; in the case foreseen in CCEO c. 916 §5, the pastor will observe CIC c. 1083. For the civil effects of marriage, local civil law is to be taken into account.

V.6.2. Impediment of Abduction

Abduction is considered not as taking away the freedom of consent, but as rendering the kidnapped person and the kidnapper incapable of celebrating a valid marriage between them.[47]

CCEO	CIC
806. Marriage cannot be celebrated validly with a person who has been abducted, or at least detained, with a view to marriage, unless such a person has first been separated from the one responsible for the abduction or detention, and having been set in a safe and free place then freely chooses marriage.	1089. No marriage can exist between a man and a woman who has been abducted or at least detained with a view of contracting a marriage with her unless the woman chooses marriage of her own accord after she has been separated from the captor and established in a safe and free place.

---

46   Cf. *Nuntia* 28 (1989) 108-109.
47   For the ancient and prior law, see E. Vivó Undabarrena, "El nuevo derecho matrimonial oriental (estudio comparativo): doctrina general e impedimentos," in *Incontro*, 2:362-364.

For the impediment to exist, there must be moral or physical violence, with the direct intention of celebrating marriage, and not for other motives (lust, extortion or vendetta). Abduction is equated to the violent detention of a person, made by another for the purpose of marriage, in a place where the person lives or freely went. It is of no importance that the person initially had acted for the purpose of lust or vendetta. Both the abduction and the detention must be violent, carried out with physical or moral force: threats, fraud or deceit. The marriage would be null for two reasons: for the defect of consent and for the juridic incapacity of the contracting persons, which arises from the fact that a party exercises his power over another and that this person is a victim and therefore constricted in liberty.

The Eastern Code provides that this victim of abduction for the purpose of marriage can be a man, because this frequently occurs.[48] During the revision project of the CIC, some proposed the suppression of c. 1089, considering that sufficient protection for the freedom of the woman is found in the canon treating *vis et metus*;[49] the extension of the impediment to include the case that the kidnapped person could be a man was also proposed, but the proposal did not please the consultors because, generally, the cases of kidnapping concern women.[50] In the CIC, the possible marriage of a kidnapped man would equally be null because of the defect of consent. Kidnapping supposes the removal of the person from the place where he / she lives or is found occasionally and the forced transfer into the place selected by the kidnapper. The detention, while it is forced, can occur also in the place where the person lives, if the person is impeded from movement and acting freely. The impediment, of ecclesiastical law, does not bind non-Catholics, with due regard for the prescriptions of civil law to which they are subject, but exists even if only one of the two parties is Catholic. Therefore, the local Hierarch / Ordinary can dispense from it. In practice, one treats the cessation more than the dispensation of the impediment. Thus it is required that the kidnapped, or at least retained, person be separated from the one who kidnapped or retained, and be established in a secure and free place; then the person freely chooses marriage. This does not oblige non-Catholics or non-baptized persons, if they are not marrying a Catholic and are either the kidnapped or the kidnapper.

V.6.3. Impediment of Affinity

Affinity is the legal relationship that arises from a valid marriage, even if not consummated, and exists between one of the spouses and the blood relatives of the other, that is, between the husband and the blood relatives of the wife and between the wife and the blood relatives of the husband (CIC c. 109 §1; CCEO c. 919 §1). It does not cease with the dissolution of a valid marriage nor after the death of one spouse, while it does cease with the declaration of the nullity of the marriage.

---

48 Cf. *Nuntia* 15 (1982) 70.
49 *Comm.* 9 (1977) 266, c. 289.
50 *Comm.* 9 (1977) 266, c. 289.

CCEO	CIC
809 §1. Affinity invalidates a marriage in the direct line in any degree whatsoever; in the collateral line, in the second degree.	1092. Affinity in the direct line in any degree invalidates a marriage.

In the Eastern Code, the impediment is extended to any degree in the direct line and to the second degree in the collateral line; in the Latin Code, it extends only to the direct line.[51] Beyond the impediment between a father-in-law and a daughter-in-law, between a mother-in-law and daughter-in-law, between a step-father and step-daughter, between a step-mother and step-son, present in both codes, an Eastern Catholic cannot marry his sister-in-law, the sister of his own wife, just as an Eastern woman cannot marry her brother-in-law, the brother of her husband. In the CIC this was suppressed, because "often the marriage between affines constitutes a better solution to provide in the case of children born of a prior marriage."[52] The impediment is of ecclesiastical law, so the local Hierarch Ordinary can dispense from it, and it is not applicable to non-Catholics, with due regard for CCEO c. 780; but if the marriage was consummated, it is not customary to dispense in the first degree.[53]

---

[51] For an exhaustive treatment of consanguinity and affinity, see D. Salachas, *Il sacramento...*, 122-128. The CIC-17 also included the collateral line *up to the second degree inclusive*, corresponding to the third and fourth degree in the current system. For the ancient and prior law, see E. Vivó Undabarrena, "El Nuevo...," in *Incontro*, 2:369-373. According to the Italian Civil Code, affines in a direct or collateral line of the second degree cannot contract marriage (art. 87, 4-5), with the possibility of a dispensation in the second case.

[52] *Comm.* 9 (1977) 368.

[53] The CEI established that dispensation from this impediment is given only for serious reasons, taking into consideration that the marriage in this case cannot obtain civil effects: *Decreto generale sul matrimonio canonico*, Roma, dalla Sede della CEI, 5 November 1990, n. 39: *Notizario CEI* 16 (1990) 269.

V.6.4. Impediment of Public Propriety

CCEO	CIC
810 §1. The impediment of public propriety arises: 1° from an invalid marriage after which the couple have lived together; 2° from notorious or public concubinage; 3° from the cohabitation of a couple who are bound to the form of marriage celebration prescribed by law but have attempted marriage before a civil official or a non-Catholic minister. §2. This impediment invalidates marriage in the first degree of the direct line between a man and the blood relatives of the woman and between a woman and the blood relatives of the man.	1093. The impediment of public propriety arises from an invalid marriage after the establishment of common life or from notorious or public concubinage. It nullifies marriage in the first degree of the direct line between the man and the blood relatives of the woman, and vice versa.

From an invalid marriage in which there had to have been established a common life, or from public and notorious concubinage,[54] a juridic bond is created that is almost affinity and is called the sin of public propriety. For the Latin discipline, the impediment arises when a couple lives together as husband and wife after an invalid marriage or from public and notorious concubinage; it does not arise from a marriage celebrated in a form different from that prescribed in CIC c. 1108.[55] After the *motu proprio Omnium in mentem*, this also applies to Latin Catholics who have abandoned the Catholic faith and are bound to canonical form.[56]

According to the Eastern norm, the impediment arises also "from the cohabitation of a couple who are bound to the form of marriage celebration prescribed by law, but have attempted marriage before a civil official or a non-Catholic minister," with due regard for the disposition of CCEO c. 834 §2.[57] Hence, it invali-

---

54   This is a stable union and includes sexual relations between a man and a woman without marriage bonds. This is distinct from simple fornication.
55   The 1975 Draft also included civil marriage: *Comm.* 9 (1977) 131; the 1980 Draft suppressed it because civil law was always considered as non-existent with regard to canonical effects: *Comm.* 15 (1983) 224.
56   See *Comm.* 41 (2009) 265 (art. 4).
57   For the ancient and prior law, see E. Vivó Undabarrena, "El Nuevo ...," in *Incontro*, 2:373.

dates marriage in the first degree of the direct line between the man and the blood relatives of the woman and between the woman and the blood relatives of the man; the man cannot marry the mother or daughter of the woman with whom he cohabitated, and the woman cannot marry the father or son of the man with whom she cohabitated. The impediment is an ecclesiastical law and is by its nature perpetual; it can be dispensed by the local Ordinary / Hierarch.

Let us pose a concrete case. An Eastern Catholic man marries a Latin widow in the presence of a civil official. Later they divorce civilly. The Eastern Catholic man then marries the Latin daughter of his ex-wife before a Latin rite minister; the marriage is invalid because of the impediment of public propriety on the part of the Eastern Catholic party.

V.6.5. Impediment of Disparity of Worship

CCEO	CIC
803 §1. Marriage with a non-baptized person cannot validly be celebrated.	1086 §1. A marriage between two persons, one of whom has been baptized in the Catholic Church or received into it [and has not defected from it by a formal act] and the other of whom is not baptized, is invalid.

The CIC freed from the impediment those faithful who are separated from the Church by a formal act. For the CCEO, the impediment applies even to those faithful who are separated from Church by a formal act. This applies also to the obligation of canonical form and to the permission required to celebrate a mixed marriage. With the *motu proprio Omnium in mentem* of 26 October 2009, the text of c. 1086 § 1 is amended as follows: "A marriage between two persons, one of whom has been baptized in the Catholic Church or received into it, and the other of whom is not baptized, is invalid."[58] So, from the entry into force of the *motu proprio Omnium in mentem*, there is no longer a difference between the two codes regarding the impediment of disparity of worship.

V.6.6. Impediment of Spiritual Relationship

The CIC abolished the impediment of spiritual relationship,[59] while the CCEO retained it in c. 811 §1: "From baptism there arises a spiritual relationship between a sponsor and the baptized person and the parents of the same that invali-

---

58   Benedict XVI, Mp *Omnium in mentem*, 26 October 2009, in *Comm.* 41 (2009) 260-262 (Latin); 263-265 (Italian), especially 265 (art. 3).
59   But spiritual relationship evidently has not ceased. It was present in CIC-17 cc. 737§2; 742; 759; 762 §2; 763; 768; 797 and 1079; for the elimination of the juridic

dates marriage." It responds to genuine Eastern traditions that are still very important for some Eastern Churches.[60] Therefore, marriage between the godfather and the goddaughter or her mother and between the godmother and the godson or his father is prohibited. But there is no impediment if the baptism is administered under condition, provided that the same godparent had not be admitted for the second time (CCEO c. 811 §2). Further, the impediment does not arise between the Orthodox godparent, admitted together with the Catholic godparent, and the baptized and his parents. If a Latin Catholic wants to celebrate marriage with an Eastern Catholic and they are connected through spiritual relationship, a dispensation is required for the Eastern party, which can be granted by the local Hierarch / Ordinary. This does not oblige non-Catholics.

V.6.7. Impediment of a Vow

The public and perpetual vow of chastity renders marriage invalid if it was made in a religious institute (CIC c. 1088; CCEO c. 805). This impediment does not apply in the same manner in the two codes regarding hermits. An Eastern hermit is a member of a monastery *sui iuris*, while for the CIC, the hermit depends directly on the diocesan Bishop, that is, the Bishop of the place where the hermit desires to live the eremitical life, and does not constitute an institute in the sense of a juridic person (CCEO c. 481; CIC c. 603). Thus, the Latin hermit, not belonging to a religious institute, is not bound by such an impediment, in contrast to the Eastern hermit who continues to belong to the monastery. Certainly, in the face of a concrete and specific case, one must examine to what degree the matter is regulated by the diocesan Bishop.

V.7. Mixed Marriages

An innovation of the current Latin and Eastern legislation regards mixed marriages,[61] that is, a marriage celebrated by a Catholic party and a non-Catholic

---

effects, see *Comm.* 3 (1971) 201 and 205. For the ancient and prior law, see E. Vivó Undabarrena, "El nuevo…," in *Incontro*, 2:374-376.

60   Cf. *Nuntia* 15 (1982) 73. "Whereas the spiritual relationship is greater than the natural relationship; and since it has come to our knowledge that in some places certain persons who become sponsors to children in holy salvation-bearing baptism, afterwards contract matrimony with their mothers who are widows, we decree that for the future nothing of this sort is to be done. But if any, after the present canon, shall be observed to do this, they must, in the first place, desist from this unlawful marriage, and then be subjected to the penalties inflicted on fornicators": Trullo c. 53, cited in D. Salachas, *Il Diritto Canonico delle Chiese orientali nel primo millennio* (Rome-Bologna, 1997) 203.

61   For notes on the history of mixed marriages and on the formation of the legislation, see V. De Paolis, "I matrimoni misti," in *Matrimonio*, 142-149; B. Milone, *I Matrimoni Misti e la Morale matrimoniale con speciale riferimento all'America del Nord* (Turin, 1996) 31-42; B. Gianesin, *Matrimoni misti* (Bologna, 1991) 45-70; P. Erdö, "I matrimoni misti nella loro evoluzione storica (La disparità di culto)," in *I matrimoni misti*, Studi Giuridici 47, ed. C. Gullo (Vatican City, 1998) 11-22.

party, making a clear distinction between these marriages and those with non-baptized persons, for which there is the impediment of disparity of worship.[62] After centuries of rigid refusal and of separation of a Catholic party from all non-Catholics,[63] we have an opening, a welcoming of *the other* truly worthy of being emphasized. Such an innovative norm was desired by the Council and prepared by the *motu proprio Pastorale Munus* of 30 November 1963, with which the faculty of dispensing from the impediments relative to mixed marriages passed to residential Bishops;[64] by the decree *Crescens matrimoniorum* of 22 February 1967, issued by the Sacred Congregation for the Eastern Church, which extended the scope of OE 18 also to Catholics of the Latin rite;[65] by the instruction *Matrimonii sacramentum* of the Sacred Congregation for the Doctrine of the Faith of 18 March 1966, which abolished excommunication for Catholics who celebrate their mixed marriage in the presence of a non-Catholic minister and mitigated the requirements of the promises on the part of the non-Catholic party;[66] by the *motu proprio Matrimonia mixta* of Paul VI of 31 March 1970, whose norms constitute the basis of those actually in force and identify three types of mixed marriages: (1) the marriage between Catholics and Eastern non-Catholics; (2) the marriage between a Catholic and non-Eastern Christians; (3) marriage between Catholics and non-baptized persons.[67]

Until Vatican II, it was affirmed that the Church of Christ *is* the Catholic Church. A direct consequence of this affirmation is the fact that only in the Catholic Church are present all the goods which form and animate the Church of Christ, e.g., truth, grace, revelation and the participation in divine life. Outside the Catholic Church there was no sign or means of salvation. Vatican II revised this ecclesiological position and did not deny that among the non-Catholic Churches or ecclesial communities there exist ecclesial elements that issue, from their source, out of the patrimony of truth and grace entrusted by Christ to the Church (Cf. LG 8; 15).[68] The Catholic Church is the true Church of Christ in a *conclusive* manner not an *exclusive* manner.

The respective codes of the Catholic Church no longer speak about the juridic impediment called mixed religion, but simply prohibit these marriages without

---

62   For subjects of Catholic marriage law, refer to section V.2.
63   For mixed marriages in the canons of the first centuries, see D. Ceccarelli-Morolli, "I matrimoni misti alla luce dei *Sacri Canones* del primo millennio," *Nicolaus* 22 (1995) 137-143.
64   *AAS* 56 (1964) 8: CLD 6:374, n. 20.
65   *AAS* 59 (1967) 165-166: CLD 6:605-606.
66   *AAS* 58 (1966) 235-238: CLD 6:592-597.
67   *AAS* 62 (1970) 257-263: CLD 7:711-718.
68   On this subject, see A. Abate, "La tutela della fede nei matrimoni misti secondo il nuovo Codice di Diritto Canonico," in *Portare Cristo all'uomo*, Atti del Congresso del ventennio del Concilio Vaticano II, ed. Pontificia Università Urbaniana (Rome, 1985) 194-196.

the prior permission of the competent authority who must expressly grant it.[69] While the CIC at first freed those who had formally abandoned[70] the Catholic Church from this prohibition, the CCEO never admitted such an exception, since the sacred rite is needed for the validity of the marriage. With the *motu proprio Omnium in mentem*, a Latin Catholic who has formally abandoned the Catholic Church is also bound to this prohibition.[71]

The conditions required[72] are identical in both codes and are contained in CCEO cc. 814-816 and CIC cc. 1125-1126, which directly oblige the Catholic party, but indirectly the non-Catholic party, even if no promise, neither written nor oral, is required from the latter (cf. DH 2 and 6).[73] Mixed marriages must be celebrated according to the ordinary canonical form, but if the Catholic celebrates marriage with an Eastern non-Catholic, this is required only for lawfulness, with due regard for the intervention of the sacred minister for the validity of the marriage.[74] In the case of a marriage between a Catholic party and a non-Catholic non-Eastern party, dispensation from canonical form is possible. The Latin local

---

69   For mixed marriages in *Crebræ allatæ*, see B. Gianesin, *I Matrimoni misti* (Bologna, 1991) 63-70.

70   The separation can be *material* and *formal*. It is material if the person, while not practicing or rejecting the Catholic faith, does not pose a public act, juridically provable, which indicates and manifests his / her conscious and free intention of wanting to separate from the Catholic Church as a social body and of not feeling to be a member in it in any way. On the other hand, the separation is *formal* if the person poses an act that indicates and manifests the above-mentioned intention. It is explicit if the decision is declared openly, for example, in a public assembly, in a newspaper or with the written request to competent persons or bodies that that his classification as Catholic be removed from the official and civil records. It is implicit if the same decision emerges from an act clearly connected with the former, for example, from the voluntary entrance into another religious confession, Christian or non-Christian, or into an association with purposes or activities contrary to the Catholic faith. There are authors who follow a broad interpretation (A. Abate, *Il matrimonio*…, 185), and others a more strict interpretation (Z. Grocholewski, "I matrimoni misti," in *Matrimonio canonico* [Bologna, 1991] 266-267), when a baptized person declares his departure from the Church orally and explicitly to his own pastor or Ordinary in the presence of two witnesses.

71   Cf. *Comm.* 41 (2009) 265 (art. 5).

72   See A. Abate, "La tutela…," 199-205.

73   It should noted that if, despite all efforts, the offspring are neither baptized nor educated in the Catholic Church, the Catholic parent does not incur a censure imposed by canon law (ED 151; CIC c. 1366; CCEO c. 1439). The Greek Orthodox Church imposes that before marriage the spouses sign, in the presence of a notary, a public act by which they promise to baptize and educate the children in the Orthodox Church.

74   L. G. Matamoro, "La forma canónica de la celebración del matrimonio en el código de 1983," *Ciencia Tomista* 122 (1995) 15: "It should be noted that the intervention of the sacred minister, required for the validity of marriage in the case of c. 1127 §1, is not part of the canonical form, but a requirement that the legislator imposed in this particular case; thus, his intervention is necessary." This applies to Latin Catholics, but for the Eastern Churches, the intervention of a sacred minister (Bishop and priest) is an integral

Ordinary will grant a dispensation whenever grave difficulties oppose its observance in individual cases, after having consulted the local Ordinary where the celebration will take place; it pertains to the conference of Bishops to establish norms for the dispensation to be granted for uniform reasons.

> The reasons that justify a dispensation are, particularly, those regarding respect for the personal needs of the non-Catholic party, e.g., family or personal relationship with the non-Catholic minister, opposition of the family, the fact that the marriage will be celebrated abroad, in a non-Catholic context, etc.[75]

However, according to the CCEO, dispensation from ordinary canonical form is reserved to the Apostolic See or to the Patriarch / Major Archbishop: "Dispensation from the form for the celebration of marriage required by law is reserved to the Apostolic See or the patriarch, who will not grant it except for a most grave cause" (CCEO c. 835).[76] This restriction is applied to mixed marriages with Western non-Catholics, because in those with Eastern non-Catholics there is always the celebration of the sacred rite and, thus, the Bishop who is to authorize these marriages also has the faculty to grant the licit celebration of the marriage.[77] For the validity of the celebration of the marriage, it is also required that the celebrant be a priest and not a deacon, because in the Orthodox Churches a marriage is valid only if it is celebrated with a sacred rite, meaning the intervention of the priest who asks for and receives in the name of the Church the manifestation of the consent of the spouses and blesses them.[78] During the process of codification, there was a discussion regarding the possibility of granting the faculty to dispense from canonical form also to local Hierarchs, as is the case in the CIC, but it was

---

and active part of canonical form; thus, he must always intervene: cf. J. Fornés, "La forma en el matrimonio de un católico con un no católico," *Ius Canonicum* 37 (1997) 13-31.

75   Conferenza Episcopale Italiana, *Decreto generale sul matrimonio canonico*, Roma, dalla Sede della CEI, 5 November 1990, n. 50; cf. ED 154. See also L. Lorusso, "I matrimoni misti tra cattolici e valdesi in Italia. Testo comune e testo applicativo," *O Odigos* 21 (2002/3) 3-9.

76   In the United States, the Apostolic Nuncio enjoys the faculty to dispense from canonical form when an Eastern Catholic member of the faithful celebrates marriage with a non-Catholic: cf. *Roman Replies and CLSA Advisory Opinions 1992*, 48-50.

77   A recent official agreement between the Catholic Church and the Syro-Malankara Orthodox Church recognizes a marriage celebrated by either a Catholic or Syro-Malankara Orthodox priest: "Agreement between the Catholic Church and the Malankara Syrian Orthodox Church on inter-church marriages," *Information Service* 84 (1993/3-4) 159-161.

78   It should be noted that the Orthodox Churches require the presence of their priest for the validity of the celebration of the marriage. Therefore, a mixed marriage between a Catholic party and an Orthodox party celebrated in the Catholic Church is considered invalid by almost all the Orthodox Churches: cf. Conferenza Episcopale Italiana, *Vademecum per la pastorale delle parrocchie cattoliche verso gli orientali non cattolici*, 23 February 2010 (Bologna, 2010) n. 37.

held not to conform to Eastern traditions.[79] Consequently, with due regard for the exceptions provided in CCEO c. 796 §1 (danger of death) and CCEO c. 852 (radical sanation),[80] the dispensation from canonical form is reserved to the Apostolic See, the Patriarch and the Major Archbishop.

A prerogative of the local hierarch not codified in the CIC is the following:

> The local hierarch can give to any Catholic priest the faculty of blessing the marriage of the Christian faithful of an Eastern non-Catholic Church if those faithful cannot approach a priest of their own Church without great difficulty and if they voluntarily ask for the blessing as long as nothing stands in the way of a valid and licit celebration. (CCEO c. 833 §1)

This blessing differs from canonical form, because the marriage of two Orthodox cannot be celebrated in the Catholic Church according to canonical form, since neither the Catholic Hierarch nor pastor is competent. The local Latin Ordinaries do not enjoy this faculty unless the Apostolic See had so provided.[81]

This *lacuna legis* of the CIC can be filled by means of the application of the Eastern norm, taking into consideration CIC c. 19, but also *a fortiori* CIC c. 844 §3, according to which, in circumstances similar to those provided in CCEO c. 833 §1, the Catholic priest is authorized to administer to Eastern non-Catholics the sacraments of penance, Eucharist and anointing of the sick.

Regarding witnesses, it is possible to admit also non-Catholics, as it is possible for Catholics to carry out the same office in marriages duly celebrated in other Churches or ecclesial communities (ED 128; 136), but they must have the use of reason and to be at least fourteen years old (CIC c. 1550; CCEO c. 1231).

The Orthodox Church, while disapproving of mixed marriages, tolerates them and permits them on the condition that the children be baptized and educated in the Orthodox faith.[82] In the Pan-Orthodox Conference of 1961 and subsequent

---

79   *Nuntia* 15 (1982) 85; 28 (1989) 116-117.
80   According to Pospishil, if one is dealing with a radical sanation of invalidity arising out of canonical form, the Patriarch and the eparchial Bishop have the same competence: V. Pospishil, *Eastern Catholic Church Law*, 2nd ed. (New York, 1996) 604; others hold the opposite position: J. Prader, *Il matrimonio...*, 243; in favor of the dispensation on the part of the eparchial Bishop, there is P. Szabó, "La competenza del Vescovo eparchiale per la sanazione in radice del matrimonio," *Folia Canonica* 1 (1998) 151-161.
81   Cf. Conferenza Episcopale Italiana, Vad*emecum per la pastorale delle parrocchie cattoliche verso gli orientali non cattolici*, 23 February 2010 (Bologna, 2010) n. 43.
82   For the Orthodox position, see B. Gianesin, *I Matrimoni misti* (Bologna, 1991) 91-111.

to it, positive opinions have been expressed regarding mixed marriages. These can be synthesized as follows:

In the first place, a marriage between an Orthodox and a non-Orthodox Christian is prohibited (impeded) according to the canons of the Church,[83] but can be blessed for humanitarian reasons, out of philanthropic benevolence and loving solicitude for those concerned, on the explicit condition that the children born of the marriage be baptized and educated in the Orthodox Church. The local autocephalous Orthodox Churches can decide how to apply this principle when necessary. The Ancient Eastern Churches[84] of the Copts and the Ethiopians exclude the possibility of mixed marriages[85] with the exception of a particular agreement.[86] A considerable group of Churches on the one hand do not exclude mixed marriages, but on the other hand do not recognize the validity of marriages of their own faithful before a Catholic priest. Therefore, the marriage of an Orthodox can be celebrated only by an Orthodox priest in his capacity of minister of the sacrament;[87] thus, the Orthodox Church "accepts as sacramental only those marriages sanctified by the blessing imparted by an Orthodox priest."[88] The Russian and Polish Orthodox Churches have recognized as valid and licit a mixed marriage celebrated before a Catholic priest, with the prior permission and consent of the Orthodox Bishop.[89] The Syro-Malankara Orthodox Church at

[83] See, for example, Chalcedon c. 14, Laodicea cc. 10 and 12; for classic Orthodox law, see N. Edelby, "Les mariages mixtes: les legislations, ancienne et moderne, des Églises orientales," in *Acta Symposii Internationalis circa Codicem Canonicum Ecclesiarum Orientalium, USEK, 24-29 aprilis 1995*, eds. A. Al-Ahmar, A. Khalife and D. Le Tourneau (Lebanon, 1996) 515-520.

[84] The "Ancient Eastern Churches" are those Churches that do not recognize the Council of Chalcedon (451) or the Council of Ephesus (431): the Coptic Orthodox Church, the Syrian Orthodox Church (Jacobite), the Armenian Apostolic Church, the Orthodox Church of Ethiopia, the Orthodox Church of Eritrea, the Syro-Malankara Orthodox Church, the Assyrian Church of the East. In these Churches there are true sacraments and apostolic succession.

[85] See G. Kochakian and J. Meno, "Oriental Orthodox Guidelines for Marriages with Roman Catholics," in *Oriental-Orthodox – Roman Catholic Interchurch Marriages and Other Pastoral Relationships*, ed. National Conference of Catholic Bishops - Standing Conference of Oriental Orthodox Churches (Washington, 1995) 12 and 19.

[86] See for example, the agreement of 9 April 2001 between the Coptic Orthodox Church and the Greek Orthodox Church of Alexandria: *Service Orthodoxe de Presse* n. 258 (2001) 8.

[87] Orthodox-Roman Catholic Joint Consultation of the United States, *Joint Declaration on Mixed Marriages*, 4 November 1971: http://www.usccb.org/beliefs-and-teachings/dialogue-with-others/ecumenical/orthodox/mixed-marriage.cfm

[88] E. Kilmartin, *Toward Reunion: the Roman Catholic and the Orthodox Churches* (New York: Paulist Press, 1979) 88-92. Published also Consulta Ortodossa – Cattolica Romana degli USA, *La santitá del matrimonio*, New York, 8 dicembre 1978, in *Enchiridion Oecumenicum* 2, 1631, n. 3046.

[89] *Decreto del S. Sinodo del Patriarcato di Mosca*, in *Diakonia* 2 (1967) 201-202; for the Polish Church, see the response of Stephen, Orthodox Metropolitan of all of

first did not permit its members to be able to live within the Church after having celebrated a marriage with a partner who did not live in its communion.[90] Later, it signed an agreement with the Catholic Church that follows the principles of Vatican II.[91] The validity of Catholic sacraments was recognized also by the Syrian Orthodox Church and the Armenian Apostolic Church.[92] These Churches have a flexible position on mixed marriage: the Catholic party remains as such, while confessional membership of the children follows the ceremony of the marriage, the free choice of which is left to the couple.[93] There is a doubt only with regard to the sacramental character of mixed marriages celebrated according to the Latin rite that considers the minister of the sacrament to be only the parties and not the priest celebrant.[94]

In Syria and Lebanon, arts. 66-69 of the *Législation du droit familial des Églises orthodoxes* declare that mixed marriages are tolerated. The non-Orthodox (Catholic) woman who desires to marry an Orthodox man must commit herself to educate the offspring in Orthodoxy, while the marriage is blessed by an Orthodox priest. The text of the *Législation* is silent regarding a mixed marriage between a Catholic groom and an Orthodox bride, because the woman follows the groom in all matters: the marriage is blessed by a Catholic priest and the children are baptized and educated in the Catholic Church. Therefore, the legislation on mixed marriages contained in the codes of the Catholic Church is practically impossible and the problem is particularly felt by pastors.

> I suggest that the assembly of the Catholic episcopate of Syria write to the Holy Father, requesting, for the Middle East, that there be an elaboration of a new legislation in conformity with our customs and traditions in force, or the revision of this legislation.[95]

On 14 October 1996, the Catholic and Orthodox Patriarchs of the Middle East signed at Charfeh (Lebanon) an agreement on three pastoral questions, the first

---

Poland to the letter of Cardinal Agostino Bea in *Cerkownyj Wiestnik*, 14/6 (1967) 2.
90   Commissione Mista di Dialogo tra la Chiesa Cattolica e la Chiesa Siro-Malankarese, *Rapporto provvisorio su Matrimonio e Comunione Eucaristica* (Manganam-Kottayam, 1990): EO 3, n. 2037.
91   *Agreement between the Catholic Church and the Malankara Syrian Orthodox Church on Inter-Church Marriage. Pastoral Guidelines on Marriages*, in *Information Service* 27 (1993) 84/III-IV 159-161.
92   *Common Declaration of John Paul II and H. H. Mar Ignatius Zakka I Iwas*, June 23, 1984: *Information Service* 18 (1984) 55/II-III, 61-63; *Comunicato congiunto firmato da S. S. Giovanni Paolo II e S. B. Karekin II, catholicos degli armeni*: *L'Osservatore Romano*, 11 November 2000, 9.
93   G. Kochakian and J. Meno, *Oriental Orthodox...*, 13.
94   *Ibid.*, 17-18.
95   N. Edelby, "Les mariages mixtes," *Le Lien* 59 (1994 fasc. 5-6) 34-37, especially 37.

of which treats mixed marriages. The Patriarchs committed themselves to promulgate the following:

1. The freedom of the spouses to remain a member of his / her Church if so desired;

2. The celebration of the rite of marriage in the Church of the groom; the priest who celebrates the marriage will invite the pastor of the other party and, if he is present, invite him to recite some prayers;

3. The baptism of the offspring in the Church of the father;

4. In order to solidify this position, the promulgation of the decisions will take place in the various synods.[96]

The Personal Statutes of Lebanon state:[97]

- For Catholics, mixed marriages are prohibited without the explicit permission of the competent authority. The permission is granted for a just and reasonable cause according to specific conditions that guarantee the commitments and obligations of the parties (CCEO cc. 813-816; CIC cc. 1124-1129).

- For the Greeks and Syrian Orthodox, when one of the two spouses is a non-Orthodox Christian, the party must present a written request for membership in the Orthodox Church, by which the party will promise to submit to all the relevant obligations, conforming to the civil and religious procedure in force, to be admitted to the Orthodox Church (Stat. Grec., 25/2; Stat. Syr., 23/2).

- For the Armenian Church, in the case of a mixed marriage, the authorization is given by the local Ordinary, if "the spouses sign a written commitment by which they agree to be a part of the Armenian Orthodox community and to submit themselves to its regulations" (Stat. Arm., 25). Further, the Armenian Orthodox party signs this commitment to confirm continued membership in the Armenian Orthodox community.

---

96   For the canonical context and observations on this agreement, see D. Salachas, "I Matrimoni misti nel Codice latino e in quello delle Chiese Orientali Cattoliche," in *I Matrimoni misti*, Studi Guiridici 47, ed. C. Gullo (Vatican City, 1998) 57-91, especially 86-91. The text is published in *Le Lien* (October-December, 1996) 30-34.

97   M. Basile, *Statu Personnel et compétence judiciaire des communautés confessionnelles au Liban*, Excerpta ex dissertatione ad Doctoratum in Utroque Iure, PUL (Rome, 1992).

- For the evangelical community, in the case of a mixed marriage, no restriction or authorization is imposed. Only the free state on the part of the non-Protestant is required (Stat. Ev., 25).

- The Holy Synod of the Orthodox Church of Greece, confirming a preceding encyclical (n. 2550/2086 of 29 October 1903), published a new encyclical (19 April 1977), according to which mixed marriages are celebrated according to the norms of the Orthodox Church on the inviolable condition that the children who are born of these marriages be baptized and educated according to the dogmas of the Orthodox Church; prior to the marriage both parties are to sign a declaration before a notary.[98] According to art. 17 of the Personal Statutes of Lebanon, the following will be punished: a priest who celebrates the marriage of two persons not belonging to his religious community; a priest who celebrates the marriage without being authorized by the competent religious authority; a priest who celebrates the marriage of a couple, one of whom does not belong to his community, without having an attestation by which the contracting party is free from a prior bond.[99] The Orthodox Archdiocese of Italy permits mixed marriages provided that the future spouses, in a written declaration, assume the moral responsibility of educating the children in the Orthodox Church.

V.8. Marriage under Condition

A "marriage under condition" is an act of the will affixed to the juridic act by one or both of the parties, upon which the validity of marriage depends;[100] CIC c. 1102 states that a marriage celebrated under a future (*de futuro*) condition is invalid, while conditions are valid when they regard the present (*de præsenti*) or the past (*de præterito*), that is, a circumstance already fulfilled before the wedding, or existent at the time of the celebration of the wedding.[101] However, for liceity (*ad liceitatem*) the parties need the written authorization of the local Ordinary (CIC c. 1102 §3), who is to judge the appropriateness and the seriousness of the conditions that they intend to pose. For example: *I intend that my marriage to be valid when your father will give the dowry*, renders the marriage invalid *ipso facto*

---

98   Cf. D. Salachas, "La legislazione sui matrimoni misti in vigore in Grecia. Dati storici e giuridici," *Nicolaus* 2 (1974) 335.
99   Cf. J. Prader, *Il matrimonio nel mondo* (Padua, 1986) 372.
100   The codes do not give a definition of the condition, but a commission of the Holy See had defined it as an explicit act of the will on the part of a party in the marriage who has subordinated his / her consent to the existence of a certain quality, in such a way that if the quality is lacking, the subordinated consent is also lacking: *Sententia Commissionis specialis patrum cardinalium*, 2 August 1918: *AAS* 10 (1918) 389.
101   Cf. G. Putrino, "Il consenso matrimoniale condizionato," in *Matrimonio*, 101-113.

whether or not the dowry is given. The CIC-17 instead bound the validity of the marriage on the occurrence of the condition; this is applicable for a marriage celebrated before the new CIC acquired the force of law (27 November 1983). On the other hand, the past or present condition, valid for the CIC, must be expressed also in the declaration of consent and recorded in the act of the marriage: *Our marriage is valid only if your parents gave you an apartment before the wedding* (past); *Our marriage is valid if now (at the moment of marriage) you do not suffer from a grave illness* (present).

In both the prior law (CA c. 83) and the present Eastern law, a marriage under condition is not admitted. CA c. 83 did not specify if the condition affected the liceity or the validity of the marriage: "Marriage cannot be contracted under condition."[102] CCEO c. 826 establishes that marriage cannot be celebrated validly under any condition, because "for the East it is difficult to understand the *ritus sacer* being celebrated when the very validity of the marriage is *sub condicione*, either *de præsenti, de futuro*, or *de præterito*."[103]

The problem arises for a Catholic marriage between a Latin party and an Eastern party, when the former celebrates under a past or present condition, and the presupposition of the condition does not exist: is the marriage valid? Canonists differ. For Prader, "if the Latin groom made the validity of the marriage depend on the condition that his Eastern Catholic wife be a virgin, in the judicial decision CIC c. 1102 §2 and not CCEO c. 826 must be applied."[104] For Salachas, one must apply CCEO c. 826, because, by analogy, the impediment, if it exists only in one party, in any case renders the marriage invalid (cf. CCEO c. 790 §2): "If a party cannot give his / her consent to a marriage under condition, this also has an effect on the other party."[105] Doleres García Hervás directly applies the Eastern norm on conditions to the Latin faithful.[106] She begins from the false hypothesis that one cannot conceive of a single juridic order with two codes; for this reason, the only universally valid code for all Catholics would be the Latin Code. The Eastern Code is only subsidiary and, therefore, not a true code but only a special law subordinate to the Latin Code. An individual norm of this special law can mean not simply a legislative particularity responding to the characteristics of a specific

---

102   According to interpretations of CA c. 83, it does not mean that any condition must be considered as unattached and therefore the marriage should be considered in any case as valid; cf. P. Fedele, "L'equità nel diritto penale canonico. Il matrimonio condizionato," in *Incontro*, 2:51-54.
103   *Nuntia* 15 (1982) 80; cf. 6 (1978) 34-41; 10 (1980) 50; 24-25 (1987) 148; 29 (1989) 70.
104   J. Prader, *La legislazione matrimoniale latina e orientale* (Rome, 1993) 44; Id., "Il consenso matrimoniale condizionato," in *Il matrimonio nel Codice...*, eds. U. Navarette and J. Prader, 271-282, especially 281.
105   D. Salachas, *Il sacramento...*, 117.
106   D García Hervás, "La significación para la Iglesia del nuevo Código Oriental," in *Incontro*, 2:41-47.

class, but can also constitute a true development in the *mens* of the one legislator regarding a common matter, such as that of a condition, which therefore would also authentically modify the universal law.

It is our opinion that here one cannot apply CCEO c. 790 §2, because condition regards consent and not impediments. For a marriage placed under condition by the Latin party in reference to the Eastern party, one should apply the law which protects the person more, that is to say, the Eastern party. CCEO c. 826 could be applied also to Latin Catholics only if the Legislator or consistently held rotal jurisprudence should arrive at the belief that the placement of conditions on marital consent would be contrary to the natural law on marriage.[107]

V.9. Canonical Form

The celebration of marriage constitutes not only a sacramental act, but also a juridic act of particular importance, that for reasons of a religious, moral and social character must involve, in the interest of the spouses themselves, particular formalities established by the law. In the two current legislations, there is a difference because of the respective sensibilities and traditions.

CCEO	CIC
828 §1. Only those marriages are valid that are celebrated with a sacred rite, in the presence of the local hierarch, local pastor, or a priest who has been given the faculty of blessing the marriage by either of them, and at least two witnesses, according, however, to the prescripts of the following canons, without prejudice to the exceptions referred to in cann. 832 and 834, §2. §2. The very intervention of a priest who assists and blesses is regarded as a sacred rite for the present purpose.	1108 §1. Only those marriages are valid which are contracted before the local ordinary, pastor, or a priest or deacon delegated by either of them, who assist, and before two witnesses according to the rules expressed in the following canons and without prejudice to the exceptions mentioned in cann. 144, 1112, §1, 1116, and 1127, §§1-2. §2. The person who assists at a marriage is understood to be only that person who is present, asks for the manifestation of the consent of the contracting parties, and receives it in the name of the Church.

---

107   "If we hold this opinion, we must conclude that the Latin norm of c. 1102 clearly accepts the conditions of the past and present; one is not dealing with filling legislative *lacunæ* by recourse to legal analogies (CIC c. 19) nor to making an interpretation on an unclear norm through recourse to parallel places (CIC c. 17). For this reason, until it is derogated, Latin faithful are governed according to the norm c. 1102": P. Gefaell, "Il matrimonio condizionato durante la codificazione pio-benedettina fonte del c. 826 CCEO," *Ius Ecclesiæ* 7 (1995) 581-625, especially 621.

For the CIC, the essential elements of canonical form are the active presence of a priest or a delegated deacon, or, in certain circumstances, the presence of lay person, and two witnesses. For the CCEO, the active presence of a priest who performs the sacred rite in the presence of two witnesses is required; the sacred rite of the celebration of marriage is a constitutive element of canonical form, and is understood to be a priest assisting and blessing.[108] It is precisely the priest who celebrates the sacrament of marriage of Eastern faithful, which establishes between them with irrevocable consent the marriage covenant.[109] The blessing of the Church renders the spouses equal in dignity, value and quality. Thus, it binds them with the bond of love and holiness, and helps them to enter into married life with a spirit of faith, peace and love.[110]

The consultors of the Pontifical Commission for the Revision of the Code of Eastern Canon Law, in the redaction of c. 828, "hold that this fundamental norm is to be retained, by which Eastern law requires as a necessary condition for validity of the ordinary form of the celebration of marriage, beyond the active presence of a priest, a sacred rite, that is, a priestly blessing."[111] Further, in the study group, "there was a discussion as to whether the deacon should also be given the faculty of blessing a marriage. The consultors, in consideration of Eastern tradition and taking into account ecumenical concerns, hold that the deacon is not to be admitted as a minister before whom marriage is entered into by canonical form."[112]

---

108   Canonists differ on the minister of the sacrament of marriage in the East: cf. U. Navarrete, "De ministro sacramenti matrimonii in Ecclesia latina et in Ecclesiis Orientalibus: Tentamen explicationis concordantis," *Periodica* 84 (1995) 711-733; J. Prader, *La legislazione*..., 38-41. According to the interpretation of the Pontifical Commission for the Redaction of the Eastern Code, given in its response of 3 May 1953, by the term *benedicentis* is intended a simple blessing, without requiring for validity a particular liturgical formula or a specific liturgical rite: *AAS* 45 (1953) 313.
109   According to the Dominican theologian Melchior Cano, if the priest does not bless, the marriage is invalid: M. Cano, *De locis theologicis*, lib. 8, c. 5: J. P. Migne, *Theologiæ cursus completus*, tom. 1, col. 409.
110   The nuptial blessing is an integral part of the liturgical ceremony also in the Latin Church. "In keeping with the provisions of the *Constitution on the Liturgy* (art. 63b), each conference of Bishops may draw up its own marriage rite suited to the usages of the place and the people and approved by the Apostolic See. A necessary condition, however, is that in the rite the assisting minister must ask for and receive the consent of the contracting parties, and the nuptial blessing should always be given": Congregation for Divine Worship and Discipline of the Sacraments, Prænotanda *Matrimoniale fœdus*, 19 March 1990, n. 42. Among the functions entrusted to the pastor, CIC c. 530, 4° explicitly states the assistance and marriages and the nuptial blessing.
111   J. Prader (Relator), "Labor consultorum Commissionis circa canones de Matrimonio," *Nuntia* 8 (1979) 21.
112   *Nuntia* 8 (1979) 21.

In Eastern Churches, the blessing of the priest constitutes a central and fundamental act in the creation of the marriage bond.[113] In these conditions, one can well understand that a priest could not be replaced by a deacon, much less a lay person, as is possible in the current Latin law.[114]

In the Latin Church, it is the contracting parties who carry out the essential rite of marriage, and, thus, the spouses are usually considered to be the ministers of the sacrament. However, they are not considered ministers in virtue of a power that one might call "absolute," and in the exercise of which the Church, strictly speaking, would have nothing to say. They are ministers inasmuch as they are living members of the Body of Christ in which they make their vows, without which their decision, which cannot be substituted, makes the sacrament a pure and unique emanation of their love. The sacrament as such belongs totally to the mystery of the Church, into which they are introduced in a privileged way by their conjugal love. Thus, no couple exchanges the sacrament of marriage without the consent of the Church itself and in a form different than that which the Church establishes as most expressive of the mystery into which the sacrament leads the spouses: they are ministers in and through the Church, never putting in second place the One whose mystery is the source of the love.

In the Eastern Churches, however, beyond the consent of the spouses, the priest must perform the *ritus sacer*, which through the will of the Church became an essential element of the rite of the sacrament;[115] therefore, in the Eastern Churches the ministers of the sacrament of marriage are the spouses and the priest, Bishop or presbyter, who gives the blessing.[116]

---

113   For an explanation of the profound meaning of the element *ritus sacer*, see U. Navarrete, "Questioni sulla forma canonica ordinaria nei Codici latino e orientale," *Periodica* 85 (1996) 489-514; D. Salachas, "Il 'Ritus Sacer' nella forma canonica di celebrazione del sacramento del matrimonio secondo la tradizione delle Chiese orientali," *Euntes Docete* 47 (1994) 15-40; for the liturgy of marriage in the West, see A. Caprioli, "La celebrazione liturgica del matrimonio," in *Il matrimonio canonico in Italia*, ed. E. Cappellini (Brescia, 1984) 227-249.

114   For the delegation of a lay person three requirements must be verified: the diocesan Bishop can grant such a delegation only in cases where there is no priest or deacon and only after having obtained a favorable opinion of the Bishops Conference and the necessary permission of the Holy See for his own diocese. In these cases, the canonical norm on the validity of delegation and on the suitability, capacity and aptitude of the non-ordained faithful must be observed.

115   A brief historical profile of the ritual of Christian marriage and its acceptance *ad liceitatem* (for the Latin Church) and *ad validitatem* (for the Eastern Churches) can be found in O. Bucci, "Per la storia...," 34-36; on the Eastern form of celebrating the marriage of Catholics of different rites, see A. Coussa, *Epitome Prælectionum. De Iure Ecclesiastico Orientale. III. De Matrimonio* (Rome, 1950) 220-233.

116   CCC 1623: "In the Latin Church, it is ordinarily understood that the spouses, as ministers of Christ's grace, mutually confer upon each other the sacrament of Matrimony by expressing their consent before the Church. In the Eastern liturgies the minister of this

The dispensation from this canonical form is reserved to the Apostolic See or the Patriarch / Major Archbishop: "Dispensation from the form for the celebration of marriage required by law is reserved to the Apostolic See or the patriarch, who will not grant it except for a most grave cause" (CCEO c. 835). In the CIC the dispensation is reserved to the local Ordinary, whenever there are grave difficulties that impede its observance:[117]

> If grave difficulties hinder the observance of canonical form, the local ordinary of the Catholic party has the right of dispensing from the form in individual cases, after having consulted the ordinary of the place in which the marriage is celebrated and with some public form of celebration for validity. It is for the conference of bishops to establish norms by which the aforementioned dispensation is to be granted in a uniform manner. (CIC c. 1127 §2)

It is personal law that obliges the Eastern faithful everywhere and with whomever they marry.[118]

If there are Eastern faithful lawfully entrusted to a Latin Ordinary according to CCEO c. 916 §5, can the Latin Ordinary dispense them from ordinary canonical form according to CIC c. 1127 §2? The Latin Ordinary would not be able to dispense since he must safeguard the rights of the faithful entrusted to his care. This

sacrament (which is called "Crowning") is the priest or Bishop who, after receiving the mutual consent of the spouses, successively crowns the bridegroom and the bride as a sign of the marriage covenant." The corrected text, after the publication of the Latin *typical* edition, expressly states: "According to the Latin tradition the spouses, as ministers of the grace of Christ, mutually confer the sacrament of marriage expressing their consent before the Church. In the traditions of the Eastern Churches, priests, whether Bishops or presbyters, are witnesses of the exchange of reciprocal consent between the spouses but for the validity of the sacrament their blessing is also necessary." In the *Instruction for the Application of Liturgical Prescriptions of the Code of Canons of the Eastern Churches* of 1996, it is stated: "To bless means to act as the true minister of the sacrament, in virtue of his priestly power to sanctify" (n. 82).

117   ED 155: "The obligation imposed by some Churches or ecclesial Communities for the observance of their own form of marriage is not a motive for automatic dispensation from the Catholic canonical form. Such particular situations should form the subject of dialogue between the Churches, at least at the local level."

118   The question arises if the parties are subjects of the Latin Ordinary according to CCEO c. 916 §5: can this Ordinary delegate a Latin deacon to bless the marriage of Eastern faithful? We view the matter as follows: "By what reason does the rite bind Eastern faithful who are outside their own territory? Do they remain subjected to the laws of their own rite or are they subject to Latin laws? Today it is quite certain that rite has personal power and follows the person wherever the person is": A. Herman, "De Ritu in Iure Canonico," *Orientalia Christiana* 32 (1933) 138. "Wherever they are, the faithful retain their own rite as well as the liturgical and disciplinary laws. Therefore, Eastern law for the Eastern faithful, like Latin law for the Latin faithful, is not only territorial but personal": H. Cicognani and D. Staffa, *Commentarium in I libr. CIC* (Rome, 1939) 31.

can also be deduced from an interpretation of the *Ecumenical Directory*.[119] The local Ordinary, outside a case of danger of imminent death, cannot dispense from the canonical form of the celebration of marriage between two Catholics, but it will be up to the Apostolic See; this applies also to the Latin Bishops.[120] During the codification process, it was discussed whether to grant the faculty to dispense from canonical form also to the local hierarchs, as is the case in the CIC, but it was held that this does not conform to Eastern traditions.[121] Consequently, with due regard for the exceptions foreseen in CCEO c. 796 §1 (danger of death) and CCEO c. 852 (radical sanation),[122] dispensation from canonical form is reserved to the Apostolic See, the Patriarch and the Major Archbishop.

For the CIC, the function of the priest or the deacon is only to be an official competent witness, and no sacred rite is required for the marriage to be valid.[123] The CCEO provides an extraordinary form of the celebration of marriage in the presence of witnesses alone, in the case of the danger of death, if one cannot have a competent priest (c. 832); the Church permits this "so as not to impinge too much on the right of the faithful because of a lack of adequate administrative or pastoral structures [...]. The inevitable consequence is that in such marriages, even according to the CCEO, the spouses are the only ministers of the sacrament."[124]

119   "The local Ordinary of the Catholic partner, after having consulted the Local Ordinary of the place where the marriage will be celebrated, may for grave reasons and without prejudice to the law of the Eastern Churches, dispense the Catholic partner from the observance of the canonical form of marriage" (ED 154). The note refers to CCEO c. 835: "Dispensation from the form for the celebration of marriage required by law is reserved to the Apostolic See or the patriarch, who will not grant it except for a most grave cause."
120   Response of the Pontifical Commission for the Interpretation of the Code of Canon Law: *AAS* 77 (1985) 771.
121   *Nuntia* 15 (1982) 85; 28 (1989) 116-117.
122   According to Pospishil, if one is dealing with a radical sanation of invalidity arising from canonical form, the Patriarch or eparchial Bishop have the same competence: V. Pospishil, *Eastern Catholic Church Law*, 2nd ed. (New York, 1996) 604; J. Prader holds the opposite opinion, *Il Matrimonio...*, 243; P. Szabó is also in favor of the dispensation on the part of the eparchial Bishop: "La competenza del Vescovo eparchiale per la sanazione in radice del matrimonio," *Folia Canonica* 1 (1998) 151-161.
123   It should be noted that his role of witness is not equal or comparable to that of the other witnesses. He exercises an active function in the celebration, different than that of the other witnesses present at the marriage: he asks for a manifestation of consent of the contractants and receives it in the name of the Church.
124   U. Navarrete, "Questioni...," 500. D. Salachas observes: "One might admit that CCEO c. 832 draws its theological justification from the fact that the Church [...], in certain exceptional circumstances supplies the lack of the power of orders, in such a way that even with the absence of the priestly blessing of the marriage, it would be a true sacrament": D. Salachas, *Il sacramento...*, 209. R. Metz is of the same opinion, in *Le nouveau droit des Églises orientales catholiques* (Paris, 1997) 216. G. Kadzioch observes that "such a solution does not appear to be correct, in the first place because the

The religious ceremony must not lose sight that the sacramentality of the marriage consists neither in the rite nor any action of the pastors, but rather in the marriage itself, in the conjugal covenant between the couple.

The impossibility of which the Code speaks can be either physical or moral,[125] on the part of the minister or the spouses: "The impossibility is one of the excusing causes for which *ab intrinseco* the obligation of the law ceases for the individual, who would be incapable of fulfilling it."[126] Nevertheless, in these cases the couples should not fail to receive as soon as possible a blessing of the marriage from the priest (CCEO c. 832 §3).[127]

Outside the case of the danger of death, both codes recognize a valid marriage without the presence of the sacred minister in other cases foreseen by the legislation. Ordinary canonical form is omitted for the convalidation in cases in which the form was observed earlier than the moment in which the marriage becomes valid. According to CIC c. 1158 §2 and CCEO c. 845 §2, a marriage that is invalid because of a hidden diriment impediment can be convalidated without renewing the prescribed form; renewal of the consent, privately or secretly, on the part of the spouse who knew of the impediment or of both spouses if they knew of the impediment, suffices. According to CIC c. 1159 §2 and CCEO c. 846 §2, for the convalidation of a marriage that is invalid because of a defect of consent that cannot be proven, it is enough that the one who did not consent make the consent privately or secretly, without renewing the prescribed form. According to CIC c. 1161 §§1-2 and CCEO c. 848 §§1-2, radical sanation includes dispensation from canonical form if this was not observed. Further, in the case of a non-sacramental marriage, that is, between two non-baptized or between a baptized and a non-baptized, it becomes a sacrament through the baptism of the spouse or of the spouses who were not baptized at the moment of the celebration of the marriage; "such a marriage becomes a sacrament *ipso facto* because the two spouses are baptized; the doctrine of the Church is applied in the practice of the Holy See regarding the dissolution of a conjugal bond that is not sacramental as

---

Church does not supply the power of orders, and also because the Eastern legislator has established this extraordinary form based on the doctrine of the Church, according to which the essential part of the celebration of the marriage is found both in the ordinary form and the extraordinary form": G. Kadzioch, *Il ministro…*, 206. In fact, according to CCEO c. 994 and CIC c. 144 §1, the Church supplies for the lack of the executive power of governance.

125   *AAS* 20 (1928) 120.

126   G. P. Montini, "Il diritto canonico dalla A alla Z," *Quaderni di Diritto Ecclesiale* 10 (1997) 456-477, especially 460; cf. *AAS* 37 (1945) 149: "Whether the grave inconvenience mentioned in c. 1098 is only that which threatens the pastor or the delegated priest or whether it is also that which threatens both or one of the contracting parties of the marriage. R. Negative to the first part; affirmative to the second part."

127   For the historical origins of the extraordinary form, see I. Martinez de Alegria, *La forma extraordinaria del matrimonio canonico. Origen historico y regimen vigente* (Madrid, 1994) 468-490.

a consummated sacrament."[128] In these cases the marriage is valid and therefore a sacrament, or becomes a sacrament if the marriage was celebrated earlier, and does not become a sacrament at the moment in which the priest intervenes.

Returning to the ordinary form, for the valid celebration of marriage between a Latin Catholic party and an Eastern Catholic party, it is required that at least one party belong to the Church *sui iuris* of the local Ordinary or the pastor; that the sacred minister, beyond asking for and receiving the consent, imparts the nuptial blessing.[129] If the marriage was celebrated by a Latin deacon, I think that such a marriage is to be considered valid because in doubt of law, a merely ecclesiastical law does not oblige (CIC c. 14; CCEO c. 1496) and, further, I hold that one could also apply the principle that *Ecclesia supplet* (CIC c. 144; CCEO cc. 994-995).

Before CA acquired the force of law (22 February 1949), Eastern Catholics, when they celebrated marriage with Latin Catholics, were obliged to the form prescribed in CIC-17 c. 1099 §1, 3°; when they married among themselves or with non-Catholics, they were considered exempt from canonical form in virtue of CIC-17 c. 1099 §1, except for those who through particular law were bound to the form prescribed by the decree *Tametsi* of the Council of Trent[130] or by the decree *Ne temere* (2 August 1907),[131] or to the Eastern form. Outside the proper territory, these faithful were bound, like other Easterns, to observance of the sacred rite. With the promulgation of CA, the sacred rite was prescribed for all the faithful of the Eastern Catholic Churches (CA c. 85 §2; CCEO c. 828 §2).

---

128 U. Navarrete, "Differenze essenziali nella legislazione matrimoniale del Codice latino e del Codice orientale," in *Acta...*, eds. A. Al-Ahmar, A. Khalife and D. Le Tourneau (Lebanon, 1996) 273-304, especially 294-295.

129 The Decree of the Armenians states that the exchange of consent and not the blessing of the priest is the effective cause of the sacrament: DEC, 1:550.

130 The Italo-Albanians; the Ruthenians in Poland and Lithuania; the Maronites, if marrying among themselves in the patriarchal territory (Syria, Lebanon, Palestine, Egypt and Cyprus); the Armenians of Transylvania and L'viv in Galicia: cf. A. Coussa, *Epitome...*, 212-215; E. Eid, "La celebrazione del matrimonio dei Maroniti fuori del territorio del patriarcato prima del Motu Proprio 'Crebræ Allatæ,'" in *Dilexit Iustitiam. Studia in honorem Aurelii card. Sabattani*, Studi Giuridici 5, eds. Z. Grocholewski and V. Carcel Orti (Vatican City, 1984) 63-75. Regarding the decree *Tametsi*, see N. Schöch, "La solennizzazione giuridica della 'forma canonica' nel decreto *Tametsi* del Concilio di Trento," *Antonianum* 72 (1997) 637-672.

131 The Ruthenians and the Ukrainians in Galicia and Eastern Europe were subjects from 1911 (*AAS* 3 [1911] 398), in the United States from 1914 (*AAS* 6 [1914] 105), in Canada from 1913 (*AAS* 5 [1913] 463), in South America from 1917 (*Archiv für katholisches Kirchenrecht* 92 [1917] 484), in Yugoslavia from 1937. For these Eastern Catholics, the decree *Ne temere* was territorial particular law, to which they were bound within their proper territory.

V.10. Competent Minister

As we have seen in the canons cited above, for the CCEO, only the priest who possesses the faculty can bless the marriage: the local Hierarch, the local pastor, the priest endowed with the faculty from either of these.[132] The CIC also admits the deacon and even the lay person in specific conditions. For ordinary competence:

CCEO	CIC
829 §1. From the day of taking canonical possession of office and as long as they legitimately hold office, everywhere within the boundaries of their territory, local hierarchs and local pastors validly bless the marriage of parties whether they are subjects or non-subjects, provided that at least one of the parties is ascribed in his Church *sui iuris*.	1109. Unless the local ordinary and pastor have been excommunicated, interdicted, or suspended from office or declared such through a sentence or decree, by virtue of their office and within the confines of their territory they assist validly at the marriages not only of their subjects but also of those who are not their subjects provided that one of them is of the Latin rite.
§2. A personal hierarch and a personal pastor, by virtue of their office, validly bless marriages within the limits of their jurisdiction only of those of whom at least one party is their subject.	
§3. By the law itself, the patriarch is endowed with the faculty personally to bless marriages everywhere, as long as at least one of the parties is ascribed to the Church over which he presides, observing the other requirements of law.	

Therefore, the general requirements are:

1. One of the parties must belong to the Church *sui iuris* of the local Hierarch / Ordinary or pastor.

---

132   We do not share the position of J. Prader, who affirms that the *Catechism of the Catholic Church* refers only to the Eastern non-Catholic Churches, while it does not mention the Eastern Catholic Churches: J. Prader, "Aspetti specifici nel Codice orientale rispetto al Codice latino in materia matrimoniale," in *Matrimonio*, 31-50, especially 48. Rightly, "the opinion is incorrect of those who assert that the affirmation of the *Catechism* in its reference to the ministry of the priest in the sacrament of marriage is referring only to the Eastern Orthodox Churches, but not to the Eastern Catholic Churches. Indeed, the *Catechism* does not intend to expound on the doctrine of non-Catholics. Therefore, it is evident that Eastern Catholics consider the priest to be the minister of the sacrament": U. Navarrete, "De ministro…," 711.

2. The sacred minister imparts the marriage blessing, reserved to the priest in the Eastern Churches, extended to the deacon in the Latin Church.

Further, we have three types of competence: (1) by reason of office; (2) by reason of territory; (3) by reason of membership of one of the parties in the Church *sui iuris* of the Hierarch of the local pastor.

V.10.1. Competence of the Minister by Reason of Office

The ordinary faculty to assist at marriages belongs to the local Ordinary or local Hierarch[133] and the pastor of the place, both for his subjects and non-subjects, provided one of the parties belongs to his Church *sui iuris* (including the Latin Church).[134] Equivalent to pastors in all matters, including marriage, are military chaplains and chaplains for migrants, according to the instruction *Nemo est* of the Sacred Congregation for Bishops of 22 August 1969.[135] Also equivalent to pastors are all priests who constitute the *cœtus* mentioned in CIC c. 517 and CCEO c. 287, the quasi-pastor and priests who substitute in the case of vacancy, absence and impediment (the parochial administrator, the parochial vicar in the case foreseen in CIC cc. 541 §1 and 549). Further, both codes affirm that the personal Ordinary or Hierarch and the personal pastor, in virtue of their office, assist and validly bless only the marriages where at least one of the parties is their subject in the scope of their jurisdiction (CIC c. 1110 and CCEO c. 829 §2)[136]. With regard to liceity, CCEO c. 831 §2 establishes as a rule that the marriage should be celebrated before the pastor of the groom, while CIC c. 1115 establishes that the marriage should be celebrated in the parish in which one or the other contracting

---

133 Diocesan / eparchial Bishop; territorial Prelate / Hierarch and abbot; Apostolic Vicar and Apostolic Prefect / Apostolic Exarch; Apostolic administrator and diocesan / eparchial administrator; coadjutor Bishop and auxiliary Bishop with special faculties; vicar general / protosyncellus; episcopal vicar / syncellus constituted for a specific territory within this territory; episcopal vicar / syncellus constituted for the faithful of a specific rite or class, within that group of faithful; episcopal vicar / syncellus constituted for the pastoral care of families or for pastoral care in general; episcopal vicar / syncellus constituted for other particular sectors, can assist validly for marriages only if the diocesan Bishop intended to include such a faculty in their function; the Patriarch / Major Archbishop in the eparchy that he governs; the Metropolitan in the eparchy that he governs.

134 Pastor in his own territory; the personal pastor on behalf of his own faithful; the quasi-pastor (unknown in the CCEO); the parochial administrator; the parochial vicar (but according to CCEO c. 302 §2, the faculty to bless marriages is not provided by virtue of office; this faculty can be conferred on him not only by the local Hierarch but also by the pastor within the boundaries of his parish); the priest who assumes the governance of a parish in case of a vacancy; individual priests on a parochial team; those to whom the care of one or more parishes is entrusted *in solidum*.

135 *AAS* 61 (1969) 614-643.

136 The scope of their jurisdiction is not defined in canon law in the same way as that of the territorial pastor; it can be derived from the decree of erection.

parties has a domicile or quasi-domicile.[137] In the case of the creation of personal parishes for the Eastern faithful in Latin dioceses, the marriage between an Eastern faithful and Latin faithful must be celebrated by the personal Latin or Eastern pastor of the Eastern spouse.

V.10.2. Competence of the Minister by Reason of Territory

Territorial competence is required of the local Ordinary or Hierarch and of the local pastor; this can be exercised on behalf of their subjects or non-subjects, provided one of the parties belongs to his Church *sui iuris*.

It should be kept in mind that when a Pontifical Legation[138] is located in the territory of a diocese, it is exempt from the jurisdiction of the local Ordinary, but the exemption does not extend to the celebration of marriage (CIC c. 366 §1) and, thus, the Apostolic Delegate[139] or Apostolic Nuncio,[140] in order to assist validly at a marriage in the seat of his Legation, must obtain delegation from the local Ordinary or local pastor. The same applies to cardinals, metropolitan Bishops in the suffragan dioceses, primates outside their own dioceses, coadjutor and auxiliary Bishops (a least if they are not vicars general) and non-territorial Abbots or Prelates.[141] Likewise, the following lack the ordinary faculty: coadjutors and vicars; rectors of non-parochial churches; chaplains of associations of the faithful; seminary rectors. However, Patriarchs, in virtue of CCEO c. 829 §3, have the faculty to bless personally marriages in any part of the world, provided that one of the two parties is ascribed to the Church in which they preside. This faculty is strictly personal and thus cannot be delegated; but does it apply also to the Major Archbishop? The Patriarch cannot delegate anyone else, but one is not dealing with a faculty *reserved* to him. Further, since common law does not dispose differently and the nature of the matter does not indicate otherwise, the Major Archbishop can bless such a marriage, observing all other requirements.

---

137   The preference that the prior code gave to the parish of the bride and, in the case of mixed rite, to the parish of the groom is suppressed: CIC-17 c. 1097 §2; cf. *Comm.* 8 (1976) 55-56.

138   Legates of the Roman Pontiff are ecclesiastics, ordinarily ordained Bishops, who receive from the Roman Pontiff the responsibility of representing him in a stable manner in various regions or nations of the world: cf. Paul VI, Mp *Sollicitudo Omnium Ecclesiarum*, 24 June 1969, n. 1: *AAS* 61 (1969) 478.

139   When the legation is only for the local Churches, the representatives of the Roman Pontiff are called Apostolic Delegates.

140   When the legation is also involved in diplomacy, the representatives of the Roman Pontiff take the name of Nuncio, Pro-Nuncio or Inter-Nuncio, depending on whether they have the level of ambassadors, attached to the right of being the dean in the diplomatic corps or without such a right, or have the status of Envoy Extraordinary or Minister Plenipotentiary.

141   A. Bernárdez Cantón, *Compendio de Derecho Matrimonial Canónico*, 7th ed. (Madrid, 1991) 215.

One should also note that in exempt places, that is, places entrusted to an Ordinary / Hierarch or pastor of another Church *sui iuris*, in order to celebrate lawfully the marriage of one's own subjects, permission of the competent authority is required (CCEO cc. 829 §1 and 831 §1, 3°).

V.10.3. Competence of the Minister in Virtue of One of the Parties Belonging to His Church *sui iuris*

The local Ordinary and the local Latin pastor in their own territory cannot validly assist at the marriage of two members of the Eastern faithful. The local Hierarch and the local Eastern pastor within their own territory cannot validly assist at the marriage of two members of the Latin faithful or those belonging to a Church *sui iuris* different than their own. They can do so when the faithful are their subjects according to the norm of CCEO c. 916 §§4-5 and CIC c. 383 §2.

The Spanish episcopal conference has given an instruction that reflects the difficulty in the interpretation of CIC c. 1109. In fact, the document *Orientaciones para la atención pastoral de los cátolicos orientales* of 21 November 2003, in n. 29, affirms that "to assist and bless the canonical marriage of two Eastern Catholics, the local Ordinary and the Latin pastor are *per se* incompetent, even if the contractants are their subjects."[142] Nevertheless, the Latin text of CCEO c. 829 is clear and affirms that the Hierarch and the pastor are incompetent only for those who are not their subjects.[143]

The following are some examples:[144]

1. An Eastern pastor, in virtue of his office, validly blesses the marriage, in his territory, of two members of the Christian faithful who are his parishioners and who both belong to his Church *sui iuris*.

---

142 "To assist and bless the canonical marriage of two Eastern Catholics, the Latin local Ordinary and Latin pastor are by themselves incompetent, even if the contractants are subjects": Conferencia Episcopal Española, *Orientaciones para la atención pastoral de los católicos orientales*, LXXXI Asamblea plenaria, 17-21 noviembre 2003, n. 29, in *Boletín Oficial de la Conferencia Episcopal Española*, anno 17, 71 (31 December 2003) 56-63.

143 Cf. P. Gefaell, "Nota ai documenti della Conferenza Episcopale Spagnola 'Orientaciones para la atención pastoral de los católicos orientales en España (17-21 de noviembre de 2003)' e 'Servicios pastorales a orientales no católicos. Orientaciones (27-31 de marzo de 2006),'" *Ius Ecclesiæ* 18 (2006) 861-876, especially 868-870; L. Lorusso, "Servizio pastorale agli orientali cattolici in Spagna," *Angelicum* 84 (2007) 423-436, especially 432-433.

144 These are treated by D. Salachas in *Il Sacramento*..., 196-198, with certain modifications.

2. A Latin pastor, in virtue of his office, validly blesses the marriage, in his territory, of two members of the Christian faithful who are his parishioners and who both belong to the Latin Church.

3. An Eastern pastor, in virtue of his office, validly blesses the marriage, in his territory, of two members of the Christian faithful who are his parishioners, although both belong to the Latin Church or to a Church *sui iuris* different than his.

4. A Latin pastor, in virtue of his office, validly blesses the marriage, in his territory, of two members of the Christian faithful who are his parishioners and who both belong to an Eastern Church *sui iuris*.

5. An Eastern pastor, in virtue of his office, validly blesses the marriage, in his territory, of two members of the Christian faithful who are non-parishioners but who both belong to his Church *sui iuris*.

6. A Latin pastor, in virtue of his office, validly blesses the marriage, in his territory, of two members of the Christian faithful who are non-parishioners but who both belong to the Latin Church.

7. An Eastern pastor, in virtue of his office, validly blesses the marriage, in his territory, of a member of the Christian faithful who is his parishioner and belongs to his Church *sui iuris*, with a member of the Christian faithful who belongs to the Latin Church or to a different Eastern Church *sui iuris*.

8. A Latin pastor, in virtue of his office, validly blesses the marriage, in his territory, of a member of the Christian faithful who is his parishioner and belongs to the Latin Church, with a member of the Christian faithful who belongs to the Latin Church or to an Eastern Church *sui iuris*.

9. An Eastern pastor, in virtue of his office, validly blesses the marriage, in his territory, of a member of the Christian faithful, who is a non-parishioner and belongs to his Church *sui iuris*, with a member of the faithful belonging to the Latin Church or to a Church *sui iuris* different than his.

10. A Latin pastor, in virtue of his office, validly blesses the marriage, in his territory, of a member of the Christian faithful who is a non-parishioner and belongs to the Latin Church, with a member of the Christian faithful belonging to an Eastern Church *sui iuris*.

11. An Eastern pastor, in virtue of his office, invalidly blesses the marriage, in his territory, of two members of the Christian faithful belonging to the Latin Church or to a Church *sui iuris* different than his own.

12. A Latin pastor, in virtue of his office, invalidly blesses the marriage, in his territory, of two members of the Christian faithful belonging to an Eastern Church *sui iuris*.

13. An Eastern pastor, in virtue of his office, invalidly blesses the marriage of members of the Christian faithful, parishioners or non-parishioners, outside his territory, even if they belong to his Church *sui iuris*.

14. A Latin pastor, in virtue of his office, blesses invalidly the marriage of members of the Christian faithful, parishioners or non-parishioners, outside his territory, even if they belong to the Latin Church.

15. An Eastern pastor validly blesses the marriage, in his territory, of two Latin Catholics or those who belong to a Church *sui iuris* different than his, if he is lawfully appointed the pastor for those who reside in his territory and lack their own pastor.

16. A Latin pastor validly blesses the marriage, in his territory, of two Eastern faithful, if he is lawfully appointed the pastor for those who reside in his territory and lack their own pastor.

17. An Eastern pastor in the territory of the Eastern Church *sui iuris*, where there is a proper hierarchy for the Latin faithful, but in the place of the celebration of the marriage there is no parish for the faithful belonging to the Latin Church, invalidly blesses the marriage of two Latin Catholics without delegation from their Ordinary.

18. A Latin pastor in the territory of the Latin Church, where there is a hierarchy for the faithful of a certain Eastern Church *sui iuris*, but in the place of the celebration of the marriage there is no parish for the faithful belonging to this Eastern Church, invalidly blesses the marriage of two Eastern Catholic faithful without delegation from their Hierarch.

19. An Eastern pastor in the territory of an Eastern Church *sui iuris*, where there is neither a Latin hierarchy nor a Latin parish, but only an Eastern hierarchy, validly blesses the marriage of two Latin Catholics who reside in his parish territory, if he was granted the faculty by the proper local Hierarch.

20. A Latin pastor in the territory of the Latin Church, where there neither an Eastern hierarchy nor an Eastern parish, but only a Latin hierarchy, validly blesses the marriage of two Eastern Catholics who reside in his parish territory, if he was granted the faculty by the proper local Ordinary.

21. An Eastern pastor, for example, Maronite, in a territory where, in addition to the Maronite hierarchy, there are other Eastern hierarchies, but there is no

Hierarchy of the parties who intend to celebrate marriage, invalidly blesses their marriage, if the local Maronite Hierarch is not designated as the proper Hierarch of these same faithful.

22. A Latin pastor in a territory where, beyond the Latin hierarchy, there are other Eastern hierarchies, but not a Hierarch of the parties who intend to celebrate the marriage, invalidly blesses their marriage, if the local Ordinary is not designated as the proper Ordinary of these same faithful.

23. An Eastern pastor in his parish territory validly and licitly blesses the marriage of two members of the Eastern faithful of his Church *sui iuris*, whether or not they are subjects, in a place of worship belonging exclusively to another Church *sui iuris* which is found in the same territory, at least if the Hierarch, who exercises his power in that place, had not refused him.

With regard to the marriage between an Eastern Catholic and a non-Catholic or non-baptized, the local Ordinary and the local Latin pastor cannot assist at the marriage within their own territory, because of a lack of ritual competency with respect to the Catholic faithful (CIC c. 1109). On the other hand, the Catholic party constitutes the foundation for which this marriage is subject to canonical form. The same applies to a Hierarch and Eastern pastor (CCEO c. 829 §1). If it is a marriage between two Eastern non-Catholic faithful who cannot approach their own priest without grave inconvenience, the local Hierarch can grant to any Catholic priest, even Latin, the faculty to bless this marriage (CCEO c. 833 §1).

V.10.4. Delegated Faculty

CCEO c. 830 §1 declares: "As long as they legitimately hold office, the local hierarch and the local pastor can give the faculty to bless a determined marriage within their own territorial boundaries to priests of any Church *sui iuris*, even the Latin Church."[145] This canon refers only to validity: "This is not apparent from the text, but from the general principles stated in c. 674 §2, according to which 'the minister should celebrate the sacraments according to the liturgical prescripts of his own Church *sui iuris*.'"[146] Therefore, if the priest is of another Church *sui iuris*, he must follow his own liturgical rite and not that of the spouses, at least if he has not received from the Apostolic See an indult of bi-ritualism. The corresponding CIC c. 1111 §1 is substantially the same. One finds here a contradiction between CCEO c. 674 §2 and Instr. 83: "It is always necessary to take into account that, with the exception of the case in which the Hierarch or the parish priest are of another Church *sui iuris*, with respect to the norm of c. 916 of the *Code of Canons of the Eastern Churches*, the celebration must occur, *ad liceitatem*, according to

---

145 The norm is only a clarification and a simplification of CA 87 c. §1, 1° and 3°.
146 M. Brogi, "Il nuovo Codice...," 53.

the rites of the spouses, or of one of them if it is an inter-ritual marriage." Given such a contradiction, one should apply the norm in the Code.

A problem arises if the marriage between two Catholic parties, one an Eastern and the other a Latin, is celebrated in the Latin Church by a deacon according to CIC cc. 1108 §1 and 1111 §1 or by a lay person according to CIC c. 1112 §1. Unlike other canonists, such as D. Salachas[147] and J. Abbass,[148] J. Prader and U. Navarrete[149] claim that the local Latin Ordinary, where there is no proper Hierarch or pastor of the Eastern faithful, can validly and licitly delegate a Latin deacon to bless the marriage of Eastern faithful, if they are subjects of the Latin Ordinary in conformity with CCEO c. 916 §5:

> In places where not even an exarchy has been erected for the Christian faithful of a certain Church *sui iuris*, the local hierarch of another Church *sui iuris*, even the Latin Church, is to be considered as the proper hierarch of these faithful, with due regard for c. 101. If, however, there are several local hierarchs, that one whom the Apostolic See has designated is to be considered as their proper hierarch or, if it concerns members of the Christian faithful of a certain patriarchal Church, the one whom the patriarch has designated with the assent of the Apostolic See.

With regard to the delegation to a lay person, Prader asserts:

> In the Eastern Churches, a lay member of the Christian faithful cannot be delegated for the celebration of marriage, since the faculty to bless marriages is reserved to the priest. Thus a marriage between an Eastern rite Catholic and a Latin rite Catholic celebrated before a lay member of the Christian faithful lawfully delegated by the Bishop for the celebration of marriage would be invalid.[150]

But would not the marriage between an Eastern Catholic and a Latin Catholic celebrated before a Latin deacon lawfully delegated by the Bishop also be invalid because of a defect of form?

---

147   D. Salachas, *Il sacramento...*," 55-56; *Id.*, "Il 'Ritus Sacer' nella forma canonica di celebrazione del sacramento del matrimonio secondo la tradizione delle Chiese orientali," *Euntes Docete* 47 (1994) 15-40.
148   J. Abbass, "Marriage in the Codes of Canon Law," *Apollinaris* 68 (1995) 521-565, especially 531-534; *Id.*, "Canonical Dispositions for the Care of Eastern Catholics Outside Their Territory," *Periodica* 86 (1997) 321-362, especially 354-359. See also F. Marini, "The Adjudication of Interritual Marriage Cases in the Tribunal," *Folia Canonica* 2 (1999) 231-266, especially 260-261.
149   U. Navarrete, "Questioni...," 503-506; J. Prader, *Il Matrimonio...*," 38, 201.
150   J. Prader, *Il matrimonio...*, 211; cf. *Id.*, *La legislazione...*, 39-40.

We are of the opinion that the ordinary form is always observed for validity, and if the principle applies that the form of the celebration of marriage is not governed by *locus regit actum*, but by the personal law that obliges the faithful even outside the territory of the proper Church *sui iuris* in which they are ascribed, then the Latin Ordinary ordinarily should not delegate a deacon for the celebration of the Eastern faithful entrusted to his pastoral care. On the contrary, J. D. Faris and V. Pospishil, supporting the axiom of *locus regit actum*, state:

> While much attention is given to this element of Eastern marriage form, the celebration of marriage either in an Eastern or Latin Church is not so different when celebrated by a priest, since all such liturgical rites include several blessings consonant with the celebration of marriage. Because of this requirement of a priestly blessing, Eastern Catholic deacons cannot bless marriages, but if the marriage was lawfully transferred to the Latin Church, a deacon or layperson could validly and lawfully celebrate it in virtue of the axiom that the place governs the act.[151]

In summary, in the two codes the ordinary faculty is attached to two offices: Local Ordinary / Hierarch and pastors, either territorial or personal. This faculty can be delegated in the CIC to a priest, deacon, and to a layperson in specific circumstances;[152] in the CCEO, only to a priest. In both Codes, the Ordinary / Hierarchy and pastors can give the faculty to bless a determined marriage. In the CCEO, only the local Hierarch can grant a general faculty; in the CIC, the local Ordinary and pastors can delegate priests and deacons, and the local Ordinary can delegate laypersons. Regarding the scope of qualification, we have six principles to take into account:

1. *Principle of territoriality*: in the proper territory (*jurisdiction* for personal jurisdictions) competence with regard to all the faithful, of which at least one is ascribed to one's Church sui iuris; outside the territory (jurisdiction for personal jurisdictions), there is no competence. The single exception is the case of the Patriarch / Major Archbishop.

2. *Principle of exclusivity*: in the proper territory (jurisdiction for personal jurisdictions), the competence of the local Ordinaries / Hierarchs and of

---

151   J. D. Faris, "Canonical Issues in the Pastoral Care of Eastern Catholics," *CLSA Proceedings* 53 (1991) 154-164, especially 163; D. J. Walkowiak, "Sacramental law and the Code of Canons of the Eastern Churches: an Inter-Ecclesial Perspective," *CLSA Proceedings* 55 (1993) 214-233, especially 222; G. D. Gallaro, "Marriage in the Eastern Code," *The Priest* 1993, 41-47 (only the deacon delegated by the Latin Ordinary); *Id.*, "Latin Deacon Assisting in the Marriage of two Eastern Catholics, Opinion," *Roman Replies and CLSA Advisory Opinions 1995*, 91-92; V. Pospishil, *Eastern...*, 574.

152   The Italian Episcopal Conference has not given a favorable opinion for Italy: cf. Atti 22a ass. gen. straord. 19-23 settembre 1983 (Rome, 1984) 109.

pastors is exclusive, also in the case of mixed marriages, with due regard for principles nn. 3, 4 and 5 below.

3. *Principle of ritual membership*: limits the territoriality and regulates the marriage between a member of the Latin faithful and a member of the Eastern faithful, celebrated in the presence of a Latin official, provided that at least one of them be of the Latin rite153 (CIC c. 1109); in this specific case, it is our opinion that the minister must be a priest.

4. *Principle of ascription to a Church* sui iuris: limits the territoriality in the CCEO with the clause "provided that at least one of the parties is ascribed in his Church sui iuris" (CCEO c. 829 §1),valid also for delimiting the faculty of the Patriarch / Major Archbishop (CCEO c. 830 §3).

5. *Principle of cumulative non-reciprocal competence with Hierarchs and personal pastors:* the Ordinary / Hierarch and the local pastor have competence also on behalf of faithful belonging to an eparchy, diocese or personal parish, with due regard for principle n. 1; however, not vice versa (CIC c. 1109-1110; CCEO c. 829 §§1-2).

6. *Principle of personal limitation*: temporal limits within which the Ordinary / Hierarch and territorial or personal parishes can be qualified witnesses. The CCEO uses the phrase "as long as they legitimately hold office" (c. 829 §1); the CIC states "as long as they hold office validly" (c. 1111 §1).

V.11. Personal Scope of Canonical Form

CCEO	CIC
834 §1. The form for the celebration of marriage prescribed by law is to be observed if at least one of the parties celebrating the marriage was baptized in the Catholic Church or was received into it.	1117. The form prescribed above must be observed if at least one of the parties contracting the marriage was baptized in the Catholic Church or received into it [and has not defected from it by a formal act], without prejudice to the prescripts of can. 1127, §2.

All those baptized in the Catholic Church or received into it are bound to canonical form. The CCEO obliges all Catholics "who want their marriages to be valid in the eyes of the Church, whether or not they are educated as Catholics,

---

153 This norm has been in force in the Latin Church since the publication of the authentic interpretation of 3 May 1953 regarding CA c. 85 §2, which affirmed that the word "blessing" indicated a simple blessing without requiring for validity a specific liturgical form: *AAS* 45 (1953) 313.

and whether or not they have formally left the Catholic Church."[154] Since the *motu proprio Omnium in mentem* acquired the force of law, a Latin Catholic who has abandoned the Catholic faith is still bound to canonical form.[155]

V.12. Secret Celebration of Marriage

The CIC dedicates an entire chapter to the institute of the secret celebration of marriage (CIC cc. 1130-1133), while the CCEO has only one canon, placing it after mixed marriages (CCEO c. 840). But, notwithstanding the brevity of the CCEO, we can consider CCEO c. 840 as an authentic interpretation of the CIC, particularly c. 1131. Both codes reserve permission of the secret celebration of marriage to the local Ordinary / Hierarch when one finds a grave and urgent need (CIC c. 1130; CCEO c. 840 §1).

CCEO	CIC
840 §1. Permission for a secret marriage can be granted by the local hierarch for a grave and urgent cause and also includes the grave obligation of observing secrecy on the part of the local hierarch, the pastor, the priest who was granted the faculty of blessing the marriage, witnesses, and the one spouse if the other does not consent to revealing it.	1131. Permission to celebrate a marriage secretly entails the following: 1° the investigations which must be conducted before the marriage are done secretly; 2° the local ordinary, the one assisting, the witnesses, and the spouses observe secrecy about the marriage celebrated.

The CCEO lacks the provision contained in CIC c. 1131, 1° regarding the secrecy to be observed in the pre-nuptial inquiry, but the provision could be implied, if one considers that CCEO c. 784 refers to the particular law of each Church *sui iuris* those matters concerning the pre-nuptial examinations. Regarding the possibility of the revelation of the secret celebration of the marriage where there is the mutual consent of the couple, admitted explicitly in the CIC-17 c. 1105,[156] the CIC is silent, suggesting that the secret celebration of a marriage must always remain secret forever, except "if grave scandal or grave harm to the holiness of marriage is imminent due to the observance of the secret" (CIC c. 1132).

---

154 J. Vadakumcherry, "Il diritto matrimoniale nei Codici orientale e latino," in *Il Diritto Canonico Orientale nell'ordinamento ecclesiale*, Studi Giuridici 34, ed. K. Bharakulangara (Vatican City, 1995) 159.
155 Cf. *Comm.* 41 (2009) 265 (art. 4).
156 "Permission for the celebration of a marriage of conscience includes the promise and grave obligation of observing secrecy on the part of the assisting priest, the witnesses, the Ordinary and his successors, and even both spouses, as long as one of [the parties] does not consent to divulging it."

The CCEO is more explicit: "if the other does not consent to revealing it" (CCEO c. 840 §1).[157]

---

[157] Cf. L. M. Bernardis, "Un caso di osmosi fra diritto canonico latino e orientale: il matrimonio segreto," *Ius Ecclesiæ* 4 (1992) 629-636.

Chapter VI

Consecrated Life

VI.1. Religious and Hierarchy
VI.2. Admission
VI.3. Transfer
VI.4. Inter-ecclesial Collaboration

This chapter will treat the rich norms on the consecrated life contained in both codes of the Catholic Church, i.e., CIC Book II, Part III (cc. 573-746) and CCEO Title XIII (cc. 410-572). We shall only highlight certain characteristics of both codes that might pose difficulties in interpretation and implementation;[1] additionally, we shall then point out those canons that involve inter-ecclesial collaboration.

VI.1. Religious and Hierarchy

Every religious and all institutes of consecrated life have the Roman Pontiff as their supreme superior. But every institute, without prejudice to their internal autonomy and the power of the lawful superiors, must belong to one of the following juridic categories: pontifical right, when it is erected directly or later recognized as such by the Apostolic See; patriarchal / major archiepiscopal right, when it is erected or later recognized as such by the Patriarch / Major Archbishop; eparchial or diocesan right, when it is erected by the eparchial or diocesan Bishop in his eparchy or diocese.[2] However, an Eastern Bishop cannot erect an Order, but only a monastery *sui iuris* or a Congregation (CCEO cc. 435 and 506 §1); this is different from the Latin Bishop, who can erect any religious institute (CIC cc. 579 and 615).

---

1   For a complete exposition, see R. M. McDermott, "Two Approaches to Consecrated Life: The *Code of Canons of the Eastern Churches* and the *Code of Canon Law*," Studia Canonica 29 (1995) 193-239; D. J. Andrés, "Observaciones introductorias al titulo *De Monachis Cæterisque Religiosis* del CCEO," *Apollinaris* 65 (1992) 137-147; J. Beyer, "De vita consecrata in iure utriusque Codicis orientalis et occidentalis," *Periodica* 81 (1992) 283-302; C. Pujol, *La vita religiosa orientale. Commento al Codice di Diritto Canonico Orientale (canoni 410-572)* (Rome, 1994); J. Abbass, *Two Codes in Comparison*, Kanonika 7 (Rome, 1997). For a comparative table, see N. Loda, "Il Titolo XII del *CCEO* (C. 410-572). Prospetto tavolare di comparazione ed evoluzione normativa," *Commentarium pro religiosis et missionariis* 79 (1998) 73-94.
2   "With a view to providing better for the needs of the whole of the Lord's flock and for the sake of the general good, the Pope, as primate over the entire Church, can exempt any institute of Christian perfection and its individual members from the jurisdiction of local ordinaries and subject them to himself alone. Similarly they can be left or entrusted to the care of the appropriate patriarchal authorities" (LG 45).

The aggregation of one institute to another is an institution that does not appear in the CCEO; rather, the CCEO treats only the aggregation of a monastery *sui iuris* to a confederation (cf. CCEO c. 440 §1). It is important not to confuse this arrangement with *fusion*. To *aggregate*, according to the etymological meaning, simply means *to join*, to unite to a group flock, thus, to put together, associate. The aggregation of an institute of consecrated life means that one institute is aggregated to another, but the aggregated institute retains its own canonical autonomy, something that does not happen in fusion. They remain two or more institutes, although aggregated. It is a juridic act by which an institute of consecrated life acquires purely spiritual bonds with another institute. Such purely spiritual bonds can be of various forms: participation in the same spirituality, sharing of spiritual goods, of special vows, indulgences, etc. The aggregation to the receiving institute opens the way to spiritual aids for the newly aggregated institute and determines its sharing in the spiritual goods with the latter.

According to CIC c. 580, aggregation belongs to the competent authority of the aggregating institute, but if it reduces even partially the autonomy of the aggregated institute, the authorization of the Apostolic See is necessary. One might hypothesize the aggregation of an Eastern institute with a Latin institute or vice versa, when, for example, there is an affinity of apostolates between the two institutes. The establishment a confederation, according to the Latin Code, pertains exclusively to the Apostolic See (CIC c. 582), while in the CCEO c. 439 we have:

1. Consent and approval of the statutes by the eparchial Bishop for several monasteries *sui iuris* subject to the eparchial Bishop in the same eparchy;

2. Consent and approval of the statutes by the Patriarch, after having consulted the Eparchial Bishops who are concerned, for several monasteries *sui iuris* of various eparchies or stauropegial institutions situated in the territory of the patriarchal Church;

3. The Apostolic See in all other cases.

Consecrated life, while not belonging to the hierarchical structure of the Church, belongs unquestionably to its life and its holiness (cf. LG 44) and is, therefore, regulated by the hierarchy. When a Congregation of eparchial right extends into a Latin diocese, it is necessary to take the following canons into consideration:

CCEO	CIC
414 §3. If a congregation of eparchial right has expanded to other eparchies, nothing in the statutes themselves can be changed validly except with the consent of the eparchial bishop of the eparchy in which the principal house is located, after having consulted, however, the eparchial bishops in whose eparchies the other houses are located.	595 §1. It is for the bishop of the principal seat to approve the constitutions and confirm changes legitimately introduced into them, without prejudice to those things which the Apostolic See has taken in hand, and also to treat affairs of greater importance affecting the whole institute which exceed the power of internal authority, after he has consulted the other diocesan bishops, however, if the institute has spread to several dioceses.

Both codes attribute a particular position to the Bishop of the eparchy (diocese) where the principal house or generalate of the institute of eparchial / diocesan right is located. When a matter concerns an entire institute that extends outside the eparchy of the principal house, the Bishop of this eparchy must first consult the other eparchial Bishops who have houses of the institute in their territory.

Both codes provide that, for the erection of a house, the written consent of local Bishop is needed (CIC c. 609 §1; CCEO c. 509 §1);[3] for the erection of an Eastern monastery in a Latin diocese "where the presence of Eastern monasteries would give greater stability to the Eastern Churches in those countries and would make a valuable contribution to the religious life of Western Christians,"[4] the diocesan Bishop must keep in mind that it is necessary to consult the Apostolic See (CCEO c. 435 §1) even if the monastery is for men. This is different than the case of Latin male monasteries that are erected by the authority established in the constitution, whereby only prior written consent of the diocesan Bishop is required, while the erection of Latin monasteries for women additionally requires the permission of the Apostolic See (CIC c. 609).

During the canonical or pastoral visit and in cases of necessity, the eparchial Bishop *has the right and obligation* to visit houses of religious institutes that have a certain pastoral activity in his eparchy (CCEO c. 415 §2); on the other hand, the diocesan Bishop *has only the possibility* of doing so (CIC c. 683).

For the suppression of a religious house, only consultation with the eparchial / diocesan Bishop is needed (CCEO c. 510 and CIC c. 616 §1). Hence, if the Bishop is opposed to the suppression, the competent superior can still proceed, except in the case of the suppression of the only house of an Order or Congregation, wherein the suppression is reserved to the Apostolic See or, for a Congregation

---

3   See Appendix XIV.
4   John Paul II, *Orientale Lumen*, 2 May 1995, n. 27: *AAS* 87 (1995) 773.

of patriarchal or eparchial right, also to the Patriarch inside the territory of the patriarchal Church, after having consulted the interested parties and with the consent of the permanent synod and the Apostolic See. For the Latin Church, suppression of an institute of any juridic grade is the exclusive competence of the Apostolic See (CIC c. 584).

VI.2. Admission

Regarding the valid admission to the novitiate, the two Codes present noteworthy differences:

CCEO	CIC
450. With due regard for the prescripts of the typicon that require more, the following cannot be admitted validly to the novitiate:	643 §1. The following are admitted to the novitiate invalidly:
1° non-Catholics;	1° one who has not yet completed seventeen years of age;
2° those who have been punished with canonical penalties, except those mentioned in can. 1426;	2° a spouse, while the marriage continues to exist;
3° those threatened by a grave penalty on account of a delict for which they have been legitimately accused;	3° one who is currently bound by a sacred bond to some institute of consecrated life or is incorporated in some society of apostolic life, without prejudice to the prescript of can. 684;
4° those who have not yet completed eighteen years of age, unless it concerns a monastery that has temporary profession, in which case seventeen years of age is sufficient;	4° one who enters the institute induced by force, grave fear, or malice, or the one whom a superior, induced in the same way, has received;
5° those who enter the monastery induced by force, grave fear, or fraud or those whom a superior, induced in the same way, has received;	5° one who has concealed his or her incorporation in some institute of consecrated life or in some society of apostolic life.
6° spouses during a marriage;	
7° those who are bound by the bond of religious profession or by another sacred bond in an institute of consecrated life, unless it is a question of legitimate transfer.	

According to the CCEO, a non-Catholic cannot be admitted validly to the novitiate;[5] this applies also in the CIC, taking into consideration CIC c. 597 §1: "Any Catholic endowed with a right intention who has the qualities required by universal and proper law and who is not prevented by any impediment can be admitted into an institute of consecrated life." CCEO c. 450, 2° also mentions one who is under a canonical penalty, except for the penalty considered in c. 1426 §1: to carry out "some serious work of religion or piety or charity to be performed, such as certain prayers, a pious pilgrimage, a special fast, alms, spiritual retreats." This is not found in the current or prior CIC, but could be considered by c. 643 §2: "Proper law can establish other impediments even for validity of admission or can attach conditions." The provisions of CCEO c. 450, 3° are also absent in the prior or current CIC.

Regarding the extension of the time of the novitiate, there is a difference between the two codes: CCEO c. 457 §3 states that it must not be extended beyond three years; according to CIC c. 648 §3, it must not be extended beyond two years.

Regarding the admission to the novitiate of a monastery or a religious institute of another Church *sui iuris*, in particular the Latin Church, it is necessary to take the following into account:[6] Leo XIII established that for the entrance of an Eastern Catholic into a Latin institute, the permission of the proper Ordinary was needed: "It is not lawful for any Latin rite Order or Religious institute for either gender to receive into their society anyone of an Eastern rite who will not have first presented testimonial letters of his own Ordinary."[7] Later,[8] the admission of an Eastern candidate into a Latin religious institute without the permission of the Sacred Congregation for the Eastern Church was declared illicit (CIC-17

---

5   PA c. 70 / CIC-17 c. 538: "Any Catholic who is not prevented by a legitimate impediment, and who is moved by the right intention, and who is suitable to bear the burdens of religious [life], may be admitted into a religious [institute]."
6   CCEO c. 40 §2: "Other clerics and members of institutes of consecrated life are bound to observe faithfully their own rite and to acquire always a greater knowledge and more complete practice of it."

Nuntia 28 (1989) 28: "For this paragraph to be effective, a truly sincere cooperation is necessary on the part of Latin religious congregations. In certain Eastern regions, the majority of them have a good number of Eastern members who are practically Latinized."
7   Leo XIII, Aplet *Orientalium Dignitas*, cited in Sacred Congregation of the Propagation of the Faith for Eastern Rite Affairs, Ep Circ *Per apostolicas Litteras*, Ad Superiores generales Institutorum religiosorum Latini ritus, de modo tenendo antequam Orientales in eorum sodalitates admittantur, 15 June 1912: *AAS* 4 (1912) 534-535.
8   For legislation prior to the CIC, see M. Brogi, "Amissione di candidati di rito orientale in Istituti religiosi Latini," *Antonianum* 54 (1979) 701-732; *Id.*, "La normativa del Codex Canonum Ecclesiarum Orientalium sulla vita consacrata," *Quaderni di diritto ecclesiale* 8 (1995) 127-137.

c. 542, 2°);[9] the superior of the Latin institute who acted unlawfully could be punished *non exclusa officii privatione* (CIC-17 c. 2411). The Congregation, in granting permission to candidates in the novitiate and making temporary vows, permitted them to conform to the Latin rite; but before perpetual vows, they had to apply anew to the Sacred Congregation and request definitive transfer to the above-mentioned rite. However, a question was raised: "Whether Eastern Catholics who, retaining their own rite, are prepared to constitute a religious house or province of the Eastern rite, can be lawfully admitted to the novitiate in religious institutes of the Latin rite without permission." The Pontifical Commission for Interpretation responded on 19 November 1925: Affirmative,[10] allowing for certain perplexities to arise.[11] PA c. 74 §2, 6° modified the prior disposition:

> Without prejudice to the prescriptions of the statutes of each institute, the following are unlawfully, though validly admitted: Latins in Eastern institutes or even Easterns in Latin institutes—with the exception of those mentioned in c. 5—or in Eastern institutes of a different rite, without the written permission of the Sacred Congregation for the Eastern Church.

Thus, Mp *Postquam Apostolicis* extended also to Eastern religious institutes the prohibition against the admission of Latin candidates or of a member of the Eastern faithful of a rite different than that of the institute.[12] It further restricted the scope of the exception conceded in 1925: it is not sufficient that the Eastern candidates be prepared to constitute houses or provinces of the Eastern rite; rather it is necessary that such houses already exist.[13]

---

9 *AAS* 4 (1912) 534-535; in the decree there is reference to the Sacred Congregation of the Propagation of the Faith for Eastern Rite Affairs, but this will be suppressed by Benedict XV with the Mp *Dei Providentis* of 1 May 1917, constituting in its place the Sacred Congregation for the Eastern Church: *AAS* 9 (1917) 529-531; CIC-17 c. 257. Immediately after World War I, it was not possible to send any religious into the territories of the Apostolic Delegations of Constantinople, Egypt, Mesopotamia, Persia and Syria, without the explicit written permission both of the Congregation of the Propagation of the Faith and the Congregation for the Eastern Church. The same permission was also needed to open a new mission, work or residence. See Notificatio *In attesa*, 15 November 1918: *AAS* 10 (1918) 508-509.

10 *AAS* 17 (1925) 583; for a brief commentary on this response, see A. Vermeersch, *Periodica* 14 (1926) 184ff. See also A. Petrani, *De relatione iuridica inter diversos ritus in Ecclesia catholica* (Turin-Rome, 1930) 41-42.

11 See M. Brogi, "Ammissione...," 719.

12 Pius VII (*Ea sunt ordinis*, 30 July 1822) had permitted to Latin faithful to be admitted freely in the Order of Saint Basil the Great of the Ruthenians; this faculty was confirmed by Leo XIII, Aplet *Singulare præsidium*, 12 May 1882: *ASS* 14 (1882) 484.

13 PA c. 5 §1: "Houses of institutes of the Latin Rite which, with the approval of the Apostolic See, are attached to an Eastern Rite, must observe the prescriptions established by this law, with due regard for the prescriptions of statutes which refer to the

CIC c. 643 indicates only the cases of invalid admission to the novitiate and says nothing on the requirements for lawfulness or on the admission into an institute of another Church *sui iuris*.

The CCEO includes a norm according to which no one can be lawfully admitted to the novitiate in a monastery, in a religious institute or in a society of common life in the manner of religious of another Church *sui iuris* without the permission of the Apostolic See (CCEO cc. 451; 517 §2; 559 §1). Therefore, a member of the Eastern faithful, without the permission of the Apostolic See, cannot be lawfully admitted to the novitiate in a Latin monastery or religious institute, except in the case of a candidate destined for a lawfully constituted dependent monastery, province or house of an Eastern rite, which is part of a Latin monastery or religious institute. Permission for admission does not include the change of rite, for which the permission of the Apostolic See is required *ad validitatem* (CCEO c. 32 §1), but only the permission to conform to it,[14] in a way that if the candidate, for whatever reason, should cease to belong to that institute, he / she returns absolutely to his / her rite and Church.[15] If the person is a candidate for the priesthood, he should receive orders in his own rite, but sometimes the rescript of admission can prohibit the reception of orders, at least initially.[16] If the admission occurred without the permission of the Apostolic See, it is possible to apply to the same for regularization.[17] This religious remains subject to the Congregation for the Eastern Churches in all that concerns the rite, while for everything concerning religious life, he / she is subject to the Congregation for Institutes of Consecrated Life and Societies of Apostolic Life. Certainly, permission to adapt to the Latin rite can promote Latinization; on the part of the Apostolic See, there should be very precise norms and conditions in order to safeguard the right of every member of the faithful to follow the form of spiritual life most consonant with his / her culture and traditions. It would furthermore be opportune to send Eastern members of a Latin institute to Eastern academic institutions for philosophical-theological studies and for specialization.

---

internal government of the institute, and save for the privileges granted to the institute by the Apostolic See."

14   Adaptation to a rite means to conform to the liturgical, theological, spiritual and disciplinary patrimony of a specific Church *sui iuris* while remaining ascribed to one's own Church.

15   The right to exercise duly divine worship according to the prescriptions of one's own Church *sui iuris* includes "the right and the obligation to live according to one's own ritual traditions, indeed more suited to one's culture than others, especially of the Latin rite celebrated in a language and according to a mentality quite far from one's own": Congregation for the Eastern Churches, *Lettera Prot. N. 135/87 del 3 settembre 1997 al Rev.mo Herbert Schneider, ofm, Delegato generale Pro Monialibus*.

16   Cf. *Nuntia* 16 (1983) 40; see Appendices XIV, XV, XVI, and XVII.

17   See Appendices XVIII, XIX and XX.

For the dependent monastery, province or house, one must refer to CCEO c. 432:

> A dependent monastery, a house or province of a religious institute of any Church *sui iuris*, also of the Latin Church, that with the consent of the Apostolic See is ascribed to another Church *sui iuris*, must observe the law of this latter Church, except for the prescripts of the typicon or statutes that regard the internal governance of the same institute or for the privileges granted by the Apostolic See.[18]

The source of this canon is OE 6. The conciliar provision aims to free missionary work from any shade of proselytism in favor of the Latin rite, for which the blame, sometimes rightly, falls on the evangelizers of the Orders and Congregations that work in the East.[19] A deeper understanding of the Eastern world and the creation of collateral branches within the same institute would foster a better mutual comprehension and will give greater efficacy to the apostolic work.

A dependent Eastern monastery, house or province of a Latin institute, legitimately established, is bound to observe the law of the Church *sui iuris* to which it is ascribed, but also the statutes regarding the governance and internal discipline of the Latin institute to which it belongs; it is an Eastern juridic person, bound to live its own liturgical, theological, spiritual and disciplinary patrimony and subject in this matter to the power of the Eastern Bishop. It is obvious that an Eastern province of a Latin institute can receive Eastern candidates, formed and destined for the Eastern community; but it can also receive Latin candidates, after having obtained permission from the Apostolic See, who are formed and destined for the Eastern community. Whenever it is necessary—but this is not ideal—the Apostolic See could grant a general indult of biritualism for the Latin rite for all the Eastern members in the province, and for the Eastern rite for all the Latin members who are lawfully in the province. The contrary is also possible, that is, that a religious house or province of an Eastern institute passes to the Latin Church.[20] The request for the erection of an Eastern house or province of a Latin institute is prepared by the superior general or the provincial with the approval of the superior general, and is presented to the Congregation for the Eastern Churches.

---

18   Cf. PA c. 5; OE 6; C. Pujol, "Regimen domus orientalis in religione latina," *Periodica* 50 (1961) 137-159.

19   The Latin missionaries must see to it: "that all the praiseworthy institutes of the Greek Church, coming from the ancient traditions of the Fathers and sealed with Apostolic approval, remain in force and that they be put entirely into action by the faithful of that nation; nor are [these missionaries] to dare to suggest or recommend anything to them which could induce their contempt or diminution, much less are they to presume to innovate anything regarding these institutes on their own authority, or even to concede or admit any dispensation regarding them": Benedict XIV, Enc *Demandatam*, 24 December 1743, §19.

20   Cf. *Nuntia* 16 (1983) 26.

Thus, as a result, the Eastern house or province remains under the jurisdiction of the Congregation for Institutes of Consecrated Life and Societies of Apostolic Life for that which concerns religious life and its organization, and under the Congregation for the Eastern Churches in matters regarding relations with the local hierarchy and pastoral activity.

VI.3. Transfer

For the transfer of a monk to a monastery belonging to another Church *sui iuris*, including the Latin Church, the permission of the Apostolic See is required for validity (CCEO c. 487 §4), without changing ascription in the Church *sui iuris*.[21] For the transfer of a religious member of an order or congregation to another religious institution, both of which belong to the territory of the same patriarchal / major archiepiscopal Church, the consent of the Patriarch / Major Archbishop is required (CCEO c. 544 §1). For the transfer of a religious belonging to a congregation of eparchial right to another religious institute of eparchial right, the consent of the eparchial Bishop is required (CCEO c. 544 §2). For the transfer of a member of an order or congregation to another religious institute belonging to a different Church *sui iuris*, the consent of the Apostolic See is required (CCEO c. 544 §4); other possible situations are provided for in CCEO c. 544 §3. For the transfer of a monk to an order or to a congregation, CCEO c. 488 §3 refers to CCEO cc. 544-545, which require *ad validitatem* the consent of the external authority of the religious institutes. For the transfer from a monastery *sui iuris* to another monastery *sui iuris* of the same confederation (CCEO c. 487 §1), the consent of the president of the confederation is required. If the monasteries do not belong to the same confederation, but are subject to the same ecclesiastical authority, the intervention of the same authority is required (CCEO c. 487 §2). If the monasteries neither belong to the same confederation nor are subject to the same authority, the consent of both ecclesiastical authorities to which the monasteries are subject is required (CCEO c. 487 §2). For the transfer from a society of common life in the manner of religious to a religious institute belonging to the same Church *sui iuris*, the consent of any authority external to the society itself is not required (CCEO c. 562 §1). For the transfer from a society of common life in the manner of religious to another society of common life in the manner of religious or to a religious institute, but not belonging to the same Church *sui iuris*, the consent of the Apostolic See is required (CCEO c. 562 §1).[22]

---

21   A divergent opinion is found in *Commento al Codice dei Canoni delle Chiese Orientali*, Studium Romanæ Rotæ: Corpus Iuris Canonici II, ed. P. V. Pinto (Vatican City, 2001) 402: "When it is a transfer from a monastery of a Church *sui iuris* to a monastery of another Church *sui iuris*, including the Latin, the consent of the Apostolic See is required for validity since it involves the transfer to another Church *sui iuris*, a competency of the Holy See."

22   Cf. C. Baleani, "I requisiti di attuabilità dell'istituo giuridico del passaggio: il principio generale e il consenso," *Commentarium pro religiosis et missionariis* 80 (1999) 127-154.

All this concerns the canonical status of the person and should be observed by all, notwithstanding that the CIC is limited solely to the transfer of a religious to another institute. In fact, CIC c. 684 regulates the transfer of a religious in temporary or permanent vows to another institute as follows:

1. The transfer of one who is temporarily or permanently professed[23] from a monastery *sui iuris* to another monastery of the same institute, federation or confederation;

2. The transfer from a religious institute to a secular institute or vice versa;

3. The transfer from a religious institute to a society of apostolic life or vice versa;

4. The transfer of one who is permanently professed from a religious institute to another religious institute.

Case n. 1 requires the consent of the major superiors of both monasteries and the chapter of the monastery receiving the person, in addition to the provisions of proper law; a new profession is not required. In cases nn. 2 and 3, the permission of the Apostolic See is needed. In case n. 4, the consent of the supreme moderators of both institutes and the deliberative vote of their respective councils are required. The transferred candidate need not make a second novitiate. There is a probationary period at the end of which the transferred person can be admitted to perpetual vows in the new institute; it pertains to the particular law of each institute to determine the length of the probationary period and how it must be completed, but the minimum period is three years. Nothing is said regarding difference in ritual membership.

The CCEO regulates the transfer of a religious, with no difference between perpetual and temporary vows, from one institute to another, with the permission of the competent authority according to the juridic status, that is, the Apostolic See, the Patriarch / Major Archbishop or eparchial Bishop. For the transfer from a monastery to another of the same confederation, the permission of the president of the confederation suffices. For the transfer from a non-confederated monastery to another monastery subject to the same authority, the consent of that authority is required; if the monastery to which the transfer is made is subject to another authority, the consent of that authority is also required.[24]

---

23 Authentic response of 29 April 1987: *AAS* 79 (1987) 1249.
24 For the effects of the transfer in the two legislations, see J. Abbass, "Transfer to Another Religious Institute in the Latin and Eastern Catholic Churches," *Commentarium pro religiosis et missionariis* 79 (1998) 121-151, esp. 132-137.

The same applies for an indult of exclaustration:

CCEO	CIC
489 §1. The indult of exclaustration can be granted only to a member of a monastery *sui iuris* who is in perpetual vows. When the member himself or herself petitions, the indult can be granted by the authority to whom the monastery is subject, after having heard the superior of the monastery *sui iuris* along with the council. §2. The eparchial bishop can grant this indult only for up to three years.	686 §1. With the consent of the council, the supreme moderator for a grave cause can grant an indult of exclaustration to a member professed by perpetual vows, but not for more than three years, and if it concerns a cleric, with the prior consent of the ordinary of the place in which he must reside. To extend an indult or to grant it for more than three years is reserved to the Holy See, or to the diocesan bishop if it concerns institutes of diocesan right. §2. It is only for the Apostolic See to grant an indult of exclaustration for nuns.
491. The exclaustrated member remains bound by the vows and the other obligations of monastic profession that can be reconciled with his or her state; the member must put off the monastic habit; during the time of the exclaustration he or she lacks active and passive voice and is subject to the eparchial bishop of the place where he or she resides, in place of the superior of his or her own monastery also in virtue of the vow of obedience.	687. An exclaustrated member is considered freed from the obligations which cannot be reconciled with the new condition of his or her life, yet remains dependent upon and under the care of superiors and also of the local ordinary, especially if the member is a cleric. The member can wear the habit of the institute unless the indult determines otherwise. Nevertheless, the member lacks active and passive voice.

For the CCEO, the indult of exclaustration is always reserved to the ecclesiastical authority to which the institute is subject (cf. CCEO c. 548) and the eparchial Bishop can grant it for up to three years. The CIC grants the faculty to superiors general for up to three years, leaving the concession of a period longer than three years to the Apostolic See, or to the diocesan Bishop when it concerns institutes of diocesan right. The CIC is more restrictive for nuns: the indult is reserved exclusively to the Apostolic See.

Regarding the effects of the exclaustration, according to the CIC, the exclaustrated individual can wear the religious habit (at least if the indult does not determine otherwise) and remains under the dependence and care of the superiors. In CIC-17 c. 639 and in the CCEO, the exclaustrated person is bound to set aside the religious habit and is subject to the local eparchial Bishop where the person lives, in place of the superior, even in virtue of the vow of obedience.

VI.4. Inter-Ecclesial Collaboration

For the ordination of religious clerics, both major superiors and Bishops must take into account both legislations:

CCEO	CIC
537 §2. The bishop, to whom the superior must send the dismissorial letters, is the eparchial bishop of the place where the candidate for ordination has a domicile; to another bishop, instead, if the eparchial bishop has given permission, or is of a different Church *sui iuris* than that of the candidate, or is absent or, finally, if the eparchial see is vacant and the one who governs it is not an ordained bishop. In individual cases, it is necessary that these matters be established for the ordaining bishop by an authentic document of the eparchial curia.	1021. Dimissorial letters can be sent to any bishop in communion with the Apostolic See except to a bishop of a rite different from the rite of the candidate unless there is an apostolic indult.

One notes in these canons that the list of Bishops who are recipients of the dimissorial letters in the CCEO is more restricted than in the CIC. The CCEO requires a priority to be respected: the letter is sent first of all to the local Bishop where the ordinand has a domicile; to another Bishop, if the eparchial Bishop has given permission, is of a Church *sui iuris* different than that of the ordinand or is absent, or if the eparchial see is vacant and the one who governs it is not an ordained Bishop.

One must take into account also that an Eastern hermit is a member of a monastery *sui iuris*, while for the CIC a hermit can depend directly on the diocesan Bishop and does not constitute an institute in the sense of a juridic person (CCEO c. 481; CIC c. 603).[25]

Regarding punishments inflicted on religious on the part of the Bishop, there is one in the CIC that is not found in the CCEO:

> When a most grave cause demands it, a diocesan bishop can prohibit a member of a religious institute from residing in the diocese if his or her major superior, after having been informed, has neglected to make provision; moreover, the matter is to be referred immediately to the Holy See. (CIC c. 679)

---

[25] Hermits treated in CIC c. 603 are not to be confused with those who are part of monastic orders or of other religious institutes and, as such, depend on their own superiors: *Comm.* 11 (1979) 330-331; 15 (1983) 66.

The eparchial Bishop can, after having notified their local superior in vain, punish religious who commit delicts outside the religious house (CCEO c. 415 §4); the CIC is more explicit: "The local ordinary can coerce religious with penalties in all those matters in which they are subject to him" (CIC c. 1320). Further, if the eparchial Bishop discovers abuses in religious houses, after having notified in vain the religious superior, he must notify without delay the authority to which the religious institute is subject (CCEO c. 417); however, the diocesan Bishop can provide for the matter on his own authority (CIC c. 683 §2).

An institute of the CIC not present in the CCEO is the conference of major superiors, an absolute innovation in respect to prior law (PC 23; CD 35; AG 33).[26] It can be on the diocesan, provincial, regional, national or international level. The conferences provided for in CIC c. 708 have a juridic character and function differently than the episcopal conferences: they have no true authority sanctioned by the Code over the individual institute, they are not an intermediary organ between the institutes and the Apostolic See, they do have deliberative power, with due regard for what is provided in the respective statutes. Their purpose is articulated in CIC c. 708:

> Major superiors can be associated usefully in conferences or councils so that by common efforts they work to achieve more fully the purpose of the individual institutes, always without prejudice to their autonomy, character, and proper spirit, or to transact common affairs, or to establish appropriate coordination and cooperation with the conferences of bishops and also with individual bishops.

They are optional, and their erection and the approval of their statues pertain exclusively to the Apostolic See, which can constitute them as juridic persons according to CIC c. 709. Superiors of societies of apostolic life also belong to and participate in these conferences. Secular institutes are also organized into national and sometimes regional conferences. There is also a world conference of secular institutes. The involvement of Eastern religious will be treated in the statutes.

The CCEO provides for the promotion, on the part of the Patriarchs and local Hierarchs, of non-institutionalized assemblies with religious superiors, to proceed in agreement and mutual accord in apostolic works carried out by the members (CCEO c. 416); this corresponds to CIC c. 678 §3: "In organizing the works of the apostolate of religious, diocesan bishops and religious superiors must proceed through mutual consultation."

---

26   Cf. R. Soullard, "Les unions des Supérieurs majeurs," *L'Année canonique* 18 (1974) 221-230; V. Fagiolo, "Le conferenze dei Superiori maggiori nel dibattito conciliare," *Informationes SCRIS* 14 (1988/1) 35-48.

Some patriarchal synods and episcopal conferences have instituted appropriate commissions for the religious within the conference or patriarchal synod. Participation of the major superiors or their delegates in the various commissions can be a great opportunity for pastoral action. Reciprocal presence is also recommended by means of an exchange of delegates of the episcopal conferences or the patriarchal synods and of the assemblies of major superiors at the meetings of one or the other.

Conclusion

With the promulgation of the CCEO, the entire *Corpus Iuris Canonici* of the Catholic Church is complete. However, for this *Corpus* to have life, promulgated norms are not enough, even as perfect as they are: their correct interpretation and application are necessary and, beyond that, the development of a true ecclesial awareness, ecclesiologically and pastorally enhanced by canon law.

We have seen that the CCEO often states that the faithful have the right and obligation to observe their own rite. Canon 40 §3 also prescribes that they are bound to observe it everywhere. CCEO c. 28 employs the term "rite" not simply in its liturgical sense, but describes it as the liturgical, theological, spiritual and disciplinary patrimony that is distinguished by cultural and the historical circumstances of peoples and that is manifested in each Church *sui iuris* in its own manner of living the faith. The rites to which the code refers are those arising from the Alexandrian, Antiochene, Armenian, Chaldean and Constantinopolitan or Byzantine traditions. Each Church *sui iuris* follows one of these rites. One can see that "rite" refers to the manner by which one expresses the faith, while "Church *sui iuris*" refers to the Christian community united to its lawful Hierarch. The CCEO affirms not only that the faithful must observe their own rite everywhere, but additionally prescribes that the Hierarchs who are the heads of their respective Churches *sui iuris*, as well as the other Hierarchs, must see to the faithful safeguard and precise observance of the proper rite (cf. CCEO c. 40 §1). The Code affirms that the rites of the Eastern Churches are "the patrimony of the whole Church of Christ in which shines forth the tradition coming down from the Apostles through the Fathers [...]" (CCEO c. 39). This affirms that the rites of the Eastern Churches are important not only for these Churches themselves—an importance that explains the insistence of the CCEO on the observance and protection of the rite—but also for the entire Church. If the rites of the Eastern Churches disappear, it is a loss for the entire Church. In this case, the tradition that comes from the Apostles and the variety that affirms the divine unity of the Catholic faith will suffer. To keep this tradition alive and to maintain this variety in unity, there is a need to preserve and promote the rites of the Eastern Churches; these rites are not only the concern of the Eastern Churches, but have an importance for the entire Church.

In our work we have attempted to emphasize what inter-ecclesial issues there might be – a manifestation and expression of the legitimate variety of the Catholic Church – arising from the temporary or permanent presence of Eastern Catholics in Latin dioceses, and sometimes the contrary situation, Latin faithful in Eastern eparchies.

In the context of the universal Catholic Church, the Eastern Catholic Churches are "ecclesial minorities." However, because the traditions of these minorities are the patrimony of the *Ecclesia universa*, they must be supported in their struggle for survival.

> [The holy council] solemnly declares that the churches of the East like those of the West have the right and duty to govern themselves according to their own special disciplines. For these are guaranteed by ancient tradition, and seem to be better suited to the customs of their faithful and the good of their souls. (OE 5)

Hence, the canonical inter-ecclesial norms serve the "Eastern minorities" so that an equitable relationship with the "Latin majority" is established.

They both enjoy equal dignity, so that neither of them can prevail over the other by virtue of rite, and enjoy the same rights and are bound by the same obligations, even with regard to the preaching of the Gospel in the whole world (cf. Mk 16:15) under the direction of the Roman Pontiff (OE 3).

This is so because if the "majority" always prevails over the "minority" in their inter-ecclesial relationships, the latter will eventually dissolve.

Eastern Catholics residing in the Latin dioceses are truly a part of the diocese, but distinct from the Latin rite and from the particular discipline of the local Church. It is for the pastors of each particular Church, in virtue of the *munus regendi*, to provide appropriately for the stable groups of Eastern faithful (CIC c. 383 §2; CCEO cc. 192 §1 and 916 §5). The Roman Pontiff expressed it as follows:

> Regarding the pastoral care of the faithful of Eastern rites who live in dioceses of the Latin rite, according to the spirits and letter of the conciliar decree *Christus Dominus* 23, 3 and *Orientalium Ecclesiarum* 4, Latin ordinaries of these dioceses must ensure as soon as possible appropriate pastoral care of the faithful of an Eastern rite, by means of the ministry of priests or pastors of the rite, or when it is opportune through the work of an episcopal vicar.[1]

To accomplish this, one must begin with an exact application of Vatican II and the CCEO:

1. Regarding the diversity of the rites of the Catholic Church (OE 2) and their equality (SC 4; OE 3);

---

[1] John Paul II, *Udienza alla Plenaria della Congregazione per le Chiese Orientali*, 1 October 1998: *L'Osservatore Romano*, 2 October 1998, 5.

2. Regarding the obligation of the Easterns to preserve their rites (OC 6, 12; UR 15; CCEO cc. 38 and 41);

3. Regarding the concern of Bishops for the faithful of a different rite (CD 23, 38);

4. Regarding the appointment and office of episcopal vicars for faithful of a different rite (CD 27; CIC cc. 383 §2 and 476);

5. Regarding the erection of personal parishes (CIC cc. 383 §2 and 518; CCEO cc. 192 §1 and 280) with the consequent appointment of Eastern pastors, the necessary pastoral and organizational structures including the use of parish registers;

6. Regarding the possibility of Eastern priests, religious and laity to participate in the presbyteral and pastoral councils of the diocese;

7. Regarding the possibility of devoting Latin diocesan and religious clerics of Eastern origins for the service of Eastern faithful, as well as Latin clerics qualified for the celebration of an Eastern rite by the Congregation for the Eastern Churches (bi-ritual priests);

8. The constitution of a proper hierarchy wherever there is a sufficient number of Eastern faithful belonging to a specific Church *sui iuris*.

We have not forgotten the ecumenical task of these Eastern communities, according to the principles and orientations of Vatican Council II and in the application of the current discipline; for intrinsic reasons, these communities are naturally involved in the ecumenical question (OE 24).

During the course of our work, we realized that the codes do not always resolve all the problems. There are *lacunæ* to be filled in both codes, especially regarding the proper administration of the sacraments, which can be brought to equitable solution only by practice and respect for reciprocal differences.

Bearing all this in mind, there are certain perspectives that should be pursued by both Latin and Eastern Catholics:[2]

1. A recovery of authenticity in order to be true witnesses of their own ecclesial tradition.

---

2   See A. Silvestrini, "Le Chiese d'Oriente: attualità e prospettive," *O Odigos* 13 (1994) 5.

2. Insertion with full awareness in the journey of the Church—especially wherever Easterns have been on occasion excluded by historical circumstances—so they can make their contribution to the development of catholicity.

3. Overcoming the dispersion of energy and planning in order to have a robust and orderly ecclesial growth.

4. For all this, a large-scale formation program, through a more widespread reciprocal understanding, and theological, pastoral and charitable collaboration is needed.

Pastors, being vested with the triple function of the power of Christ to teach, sanctify and govern, must execute with full fidelity the canonical norms, which are at the service of growth of ecclesial communion and promote it concretely, protecting the rights of the faithful entrusted to their care. A greater commitment to the observance of such norms is required, at all levels in the life of the Church; respect for canonical ordering, expressed in the observance for such norms, contributes to the growth of ecclesial communion. Canonical norms are a part of the patrimony of the Church: they assist and facilitate the exercise of charity and, preventing possible arbitrariness, guarantee justice in the protection of rights and in the determination of obligations, so that persons can live their vocations to salvation in the Church. Canon law, informed by grace, is the light for the human way, a restraining light that, at the same time, is beneficial in a negative way (interdiction) by making the person aware of sin, which risks being permanent, and in a positive way by opening the person to transcendent goals (participation in divine life), giving one the strength to achieve them. For a Christian, the law of Christ is not a law among other laws, it is the only way to fulfill completely every other law; the law of Christ must penetrate and vitalize, as a work to be realized personally, though love and with the help of grace.

> May this Code be received, therefore, in its entirety and in each of its canons by the whole Church, in a serene spirit, and with the trust that its observance will draw upon all the Eastern Churches those heavenly graces which will make them prosper ever more throughout the world. This is an appeal that concerns particularly those norms of the Code which have been repeatedly at the center of my attention and finally decided as they are now in the Code, since the Supreme Pontiff considers them necessary for the good of the universal Church and to safeguard its right order and the more fundamental and essential rights of man redeemed by Christ.[3]

Let us conclude with an ancient and a contemporary exhortation:

---

3   John Paul II, *Discourse on the Presentation of the Code of Canons of the Eastern Churches*, 25 October 1990: *Nuntia* 31 (1990) 21-22. English translation from *Guide*, 28.

[...] With reference to the canons, this is what we must order you, O Bishops. If you observe them, you will be saved and you will have peace; but if you disobey them you will be punished and you will continuously war, one against the other, undergoing the punishment that your disobedience warrants. God, the only uncreated and creator of all things through Christ, will unite all of you with the peace of the Holy Spirit, and "make you complete in everything good so that you may do his will" (Heb 13:21), exempt from deviations, censure and rebuke, will grant you eternal life with us, through his beloved Son Jesus Christ, our God and Savior, and through whom glory to him, God the Father above all, in the Holy Spirit, the Paraclete, now and always and in the ages of ages. Amen. (Can. 85 of the Apostles)[4]

Called to conversion so that communion in the Holy Spirit is fulfilled according to the desire of Christ, we must promote the synergy of the churches of East and West in the same Church which can only thus breathe with two lungs, according to an expression dear to the Supreme Pontiff John Paul II. This communion in the Holy Spirit will be possible only to the degree which the churches of the East and West will strive to apply completely the conciliar decree that recognizes "that the Churches of the East, like those of the West have the right and duty to govern themselves according to their own special disciplines," since all these are praiseworthy by reason of their venerable antiquity, "better suited to the customs of their faithful and more suited to the good of their souls" (OE 5).[5]

Increased fidelity to one's own Church and thus, to one's own culture. The increased fidelity to one's own rite involves an awareness of the power of the Holy Spirit, which performs marvels of the Word, an awareness of the grace that springs with infinite super-abundance from the mystery of the Risen Christ. The increased fidelity to one's own culture, which cannot be exchanged, contaminated, mystified—or worse—betrayed or abandoned. Christians must live as a whole where they live and as they live out the history of humanity, participating in their whole existence in order to bring their active contribution for benefit of humanity. The best Christian contribution to humanity is to approach them with the vitality of their own lived culture intact.[6]

---

4   Cited in D. Salachas, *Il Diritto Canonico delle Chiese orientali nel primo millennio* (Rome-Bologna, 1997) 28.
5   *Propositiones al Sinodo per l'America*, 16 novembre – 12 dicembre 1997, prop. 60: *Il Regno-documenti* 1/98, 21.
6   See Eparchia di Lungro degli Italo-Albanesi dell'Italia Meridionale, *Dichiarazione e decisioni della 1ª Assemblea Eparchiale 1995-1996* (Lungro, 1997) 212-213.

Appendices

The appendices that follow intend to make available to pastors useful tools needed to face various concrete situations. They come from different sources:

1. Appendices 1-4, 7-10, 12-13, and 15-20 contain examples of formularies currently in use at the Congregation for the Eastern Churches and the author is grateful to the Congregation officials for providing them.

2. Appendix 5 contains the *declaratio* of the Congregation for the Eastern Churches regarding the scope of authority of the Ordinary for the Eastern Faithful in France.

3. Appendix 6 contains a copy of the decree of erection of the personal parish of S. Giovanni Crisostomo in Bari, Italy; the author is grateful to Archbishop Emeritus Mariano Magrassi for making it available.

4. Appendix 11 is a formulary composed by the author for recourse to the Apostolic Penitentiary through a confessor.

5. Appendix 14 is a copy of the decree of erection of a religious house conserved in the archive of the Dominican province of the author

Appendix 1. Transfer of a Lay Person to a Church *sui iuris*..286

Appendix 2. Transfer of a Lay Person to a Church *sui iuris* with Prohibition to Receive Sacred Orders..288

Appendix 3. Admission of an Eastern Non-Catholic into the Latin Church (Latin version)..290

Appendix 4. Admission of an Eastern Non-Catholic into the Latin Church (Italian version)..292

Appendix 5. Ordinariate in France for Eastern Catholics..294

Appendix 6. Erection of a Personal Parish According to the Prior Legislation..298

Appendix 7. Transfer of a Cleric to a Church *sui iuris*..300

Appendix 8. Indult of Bi-ritualism..302

Appendix 9. Celebret with the Indult of Biritualism..304

Appendix 10. Latin Priests of the Carrying Out Priestly Functions in an Eastern Rite.....306

Appendix 11. Recourse to the Apostolic Penitentiary through a Confessor..308

Appendix 12. Dimissorial Letter..310

Appendix 13. Ordination in the Latin Rite with the Faculty of Biritualism..312

Appendix 14. Sample of the Decree of Erection of a New Religious House..314

Appendix 15. Admission to an Institute of Another Church *sui iuris* with a Prohibition against the Reception of Sacred Orders..316

Appendix 16. Admission to an Institute of Another Church *sui iuris*..318

Appendix 17. Admission to an Institute of Another Church *sui iuris* (Italian Version)....320

Appendix 18. Regularization of the Canonical Situation of Eastern Faithful Admitted to the Novitiate of Another Church *sui iuris*..322

Appendix 19. Regularization of the Canonical Situation of Eastern Faithful Admitted to Temporary Profession in the Institute of Another Church *sui iuris*..324

Appendix 20. Regularization of the Canonical Situation of Eastern Faithful Admitted to Perpetual Profession in the Institute of Another Church *sui iuris*..326

Appendix 1. Transfer of a Lay Person to a Church *sui iuris*[1]

Prot. N. _____

Beatissime Pater,

____ ob rationes expositas petit indultum transeundi ab Ecclesia ____ ad Ecclesiam ____.

Congregatio pro Ecclesiis Orientalibus, vigore facultatum a Summo Pontifice ____ sibi tributarum, attentis precibus ac omnibus mature perpensis, concedit orat__ indultum transitus ____ ad omnes iuris effectus.

Transitus ad novam Ecclesiam vim habebit a momento quo orat__ coram dictæ Ecclesiæ parocho vel Hierarcha intra eorundem territorii fines - vel coram presbytero ab alterutro delegato - et duobus testibus, suam voluntatem novum ritum assumendi declaraverit.

Parochus vel Ordinarius, de quibus supra, sedulo curet:

1. Ut in libro baptizatorum novæ parœciæ peractus transitus quam primum adnotetur;
2. Ut de peracto transitu nuntius mittatur ad baptismi parochum, cuius erit ritus mutationem in libro   baptizatorum adnotare et de peracta adnotatione mittentem certiorem facere.
3. Filii infra decimum quartum ætatis annum expletum ipso iure ascribuntur novæ Ecclesiæ sui iuris   patris vel matris, ad normam CCEO can. 34; singula tamen eorum nomina expresse adnotentur in libro baptizatorum parœciæ ritus "ad quem" una cum nomine patris vel, in mixtis nuptiis, matris.

Sex mensibus a die concessionis elapsis, præsens Rescriptum omnem vim amittit.

Datum Romæ, ex Ædibus Congregationis pro Ecclesiis Orientalibus,

die ____ mensis ____ anno ____.

____

a secretis

---

[1] From CCEO cc. 32 §1, 34, 36 and 37.

Unofficial Translation

Prot. No. ....

Most Holy Father,

____, for the reasons provided. petitions for an indult to transfer from the ____ Church to the ____ Church.

The Congregation for the Eastern Churches, in virtue of the faculties granted to it by the Roman Pontiff ____, having considered the request and taking into account all aspects of it, grants to the petitioner an indult for transfer ____ with all the effects of law.

The transfer to the new Church will go into effect at the time that the petitioner, in the presence of the pastor or Hierarch of the above-mentioned Church within their territory, or in the presence of a priest delegated by either of them, and two witnesses, declares his / her intention to assume the new rite.

The pastor or Ordinary mentioned above of is carefully to see that:

1. The executed transfer is recorded in the baptismal register of the new parish as soon as possible.
2. The parish priest where the baptism was celebrated is informed that the transfer was completed; he will record the change of rite in the baptism register and notify the new parish that the record has been made.
3. Offspring below the age of fourteen years are by virtue of the law itself ascribed in the new Church *sui iuris* of the father or mother according to the norm of CCEO c. 34; their individual names are to be recorded in the baptismal register of the parish of the rite *ad quem* along with the name of the father or, in mixed marriages, the mother.

With the elapse of six months from the date of the concession, this rescript loses all force.

Given in Rome, at the offices of the Congregation for the Eastern Churches, the ____ day of the month ____ year ____.

_____

Secretary

Appendix 2. Transfer of a Lay Person to a Church *sui iuris* with Prohibition to Receive Sacred Orders[2]

Prot. N. ____

Beastissime Pater,

____ ob rationes expositas petit indultum transeundi ab Ecclesia ____ ad Ecclesiam ____.

Congregatio pro Ecclesiis Orientalibus, vigore facultatum a Summo Pontifice ____ sibi tributarum, attentis precibus ac omnibus mature perpensis, concedit oratori indultum transitus ____ ad omnes iuris effectus.

Transitus ad novam Ecclesiam vim habebit a momento quo orator coram dictæ Ecclesiæ parocho vel Hierarcha intra eorundem territorii fines - vel coram presbytero ab alterutro delegato - et duobus testibus, suam voluntatem novum ritum assumendi declaraverit, vetita tamen sacrorum Ordinum receptione.

Parochus vel Ordinarius, de quibus supra, sedulo curet:

1. Ut in libro baptizatorum novæ parœciæ peractus transitus quam primum adnotetur;

2. Ut de peracto transitu nuntius mittatur ad baptismi parochum, cuius erit ritus mutationem in libro baptizatorum adnotare et de peracta adnotatione mittentem certiorem facere.

3. Filii infra decimum quartum ætatis annum expletum ipso iure ascribuntur novæ Ecclesiæ sui iuris patris vel matris, ad normam CCEO can. 34; singula tamen eorum nomina expresse adnotentur in libro baptizatorum parœciæ ritus "ad quem" una cum nomine patris vel, in mixtis nuptiis, matris.

Sex mensibus a die concessionis elapsis, præsens Rescriptum omnem vim amittit.

Datum Romæ, ex Ædibus Congregationis pro Ecclesiis Orientalibus,

die ____ mensis ____ anno ____.

____

a secretis

---

[2] From CCEO cc. 32 §1, 34, 36 and 37. In this case, the rescript prohibits the reception of orders.

Unofficial Translation

Prot. No. ____

Most Holy Father,

____, for the reasons provided, petitions for an indult to transfer from the ____ Church to the ____ Church.

The Congregation for the Eastern Churches, in virtue of the faculties granted to it by the Roman Pontiff ____, having considered the request and taking into account all aspects of it, grants to the petitioner an indult for transfer ____ with all the effects of law.

The transfer to the new Church will go into effect at the time that the petitioner, in the presence of the pastor or Hierarch of the above-mentioned Church within their territory, or in the presence of a priest delegated by either of them, and two witnesses, declares his intention to assume the new rite. The reception of sacred orders is prohibited.

The pastor or Ordinary mentioned above is carefully to see that:

1. The executed transfer is recorded in the baptismal register of the new parish as soon as possible.

2. The parish priest where the baptism was celebrated be informed that the transfer was completed; he will record the change of rite in the baptism register and notify the new that the record has been made.

3. Offspring below the age of fourteen years are by virtue of the law itself ascribed in the new Church *sui iuris* of the father or mother according to the norm of CCEO c. 34; their individual names are to be recorded in the baptismal register of the parish of the rite *ad quem* along with the name of the father or, in mixed marriages, the mother.

With the elapse of six months from the date of the concession, this rescript loses all force.

Given in Rome, at the offices of the Congregation for the Eastern Churches, the ____ day of the month ____ year ____.

____

Secretary

Appendix 3. Admission of an Eastern Non-Catholic into the Latin Church (Latin version)[3]

Prot. N. ____

Beatissime Pater,

____, fidelis Ecclesiæ orthodoxæ ____ cupiens ad plenam communionem cum Ecclesia catholica pervenire, petit - ad normam can. 35 CCEO - ut Ecclesiæ latinæ ascribi possit.

Ordinarius latinus preces commendat.

Congregatio pro Ecclesiis Orientalibus vigore facultatum a Summo Pontifice ____ sibi tributarum, attentis precibus ac omnibus mature perpensis, concedit orat__ ut emittens professionem fidei catholicæ Ecclesiæ latinæ ascribi valeat, ceterum servatis de iure servandis.

Contrariis quibuslibet minime obstantibus.

Datum Romæ, ex Ædibus Congregationis pro Ecclesiis Orientalibus,

die ____ mensis ____ anno ____.

____

a secretis

---

[3] From CCEO cc. 35-37 and 897.

Unofficial Translation

Prot. No. ____

Most Holy Father,

____, a member of the faithful of the ____ Orthodox Church, desiring to come into full communion with the Catholic Church, petitions, according to the norm of CCEO c. 35, to be ascribed to the Latin Church.

The Latin Ordinary recommends the petition.

The Congregation for the Eastern Churches, in virtue of the faculties granted to it by the Roman Pontiff ____, having considered the request and taking into account all aspects of it, grants to the petitioner that making the profession of faith, he or she can be ascribed in the Latin Catholic Church, the requirements of law being observed in other respects.

Anything to the contrary notwithstanding.

Given in Rome, at the offices of the Congregation for the Eastern Churches, the ____ day of the month ____ year ____.

_____

Secretary

Appendix 4. Admission of an Eastern Non-Catholic into the Latin Church (Italian version)[4]

Prot. N. ____.

Beatissimo Padre,

____, nat__ e battezzat__ nella Chiesa ____ Ortodossa, desidero__ di passare alla piena comunione con la Chiesa Cattolica, chiede, a norma del can. 35 del Codex Canonum Ecclesiarum Orientalium, di essere ascritt__ alla Chiesa Latina, in seno alla Diocesi di ____.

L'Ordinario latino appoggia la richiesta.

La Congregazione per le Chiese Orientali, in virtù delle facoltà ad essa delegate dal Santo Padre ____, tutto ben considerato, benevolmente concede che l'Orat__ nell'emettere la professione di fede cattolica, possa essere ascritt__ alla Chiesa Latina, "ceterum servatis de iure servandis".

"Contrariis quibuslibet minime obstantibus".

Dalla Sede della Congregazione per le Chiese Orientali,

Città del Vaticano, ____.

———
a secretis

---

4   From CCEO cc. 35-37 and 897.

Unofficial Translation

Prot. No. ____

Most Holy Father,

____, a member of the faithful of the ____ Orthodox Church, desiring to come into full communion with the Catholic Church, petitions, according to the norm of CCEO c. 35, to be ascribed to the Latin Church.

The Latin Ordinary recommends the petition.

The Congregation for the Eastern Churches, in virtue of the faculties granted to it by the Roman Pontiff ____, having considered the request and taking into account all aspects of it, grants to the petitioner that making the profession of faith, he or she can be ascribed in the Latin Catholic Church, the requirements of law being observed in other respects.

Anything to the contrary notwithstanding.

Given in Rome, at the offices of the Congregation for the Eastern Churches, the ____ day of the month ____ year ____.

____

Secretary

Appendix 5. Ordinariate in France for Eastern Catholics

Congregatio pro Ecclesiis Orientalibus
Gallia
Ordinariatus pro Fidelibus Orientalibus Ritus
Declaratio
qua ambitus canonicæ potestatis Ordinarii pro fidelibus orientalibus ecclesiasticum Superiorem proprii ritus non habentibus pressius determinatur.[5]

Declaration interpretative du Decret du 27 juillet 1954

Par Décret du 27 juillet 1954, le Saint-Siège érigeait l'Ordinariat pour les Catholiques de rite oriental résidant en France, institué par le Pape Pie XII en date du 16 juin de la même année (*AAS* 47, 1955, pp. 612-613).

Des motifs d'ordre pastoral, encore valables aujourd'hui, induisirent toutefois le Saint-Siège à ne pas totalement soustraire les fidèles de rite oriental à la juridiction individuelle des Ordinaires de France. C'est la raison pour laquelle, à l'instar de la juridiction exercée par le Vicariat aux Armées, fut établie une double juridiction à savoir, d'une part, celle de l'Ordinaire pour les Orientaux conçue comme principale et, d'autre part, celle des Ordinaires du lieu, de caractère plutôt subsidiaire.

Plus d'une trentaine d'années se sont déjà écoulées et la présence des Orientaux catholiques en France est devenue encore plus consistante. Aussi les rapports avec les Hiérarchies orientales intéressées sont-ils plus fréquents et plus délicats, tandis que les problèmes qui se posent aux curies diocésaines sont de plus en plus nombreux et complexes.

Assurément, les principes du Décret de 1954 s'avèrent encore adaptés aux circonstances actuelles. Cependant, en vue d'assurer une indispensable unité d'orientation et une meilleure coordination des mesures qui s'imposent dans chaque cas particulier, il convient de mieux expliciter ces même principes et de formuler de façon plus concrète les normes qui en découlent.

Aussi, après avoir mûrement considéré la question à la lumière des situations nouvelles, la Congrégation pour les Églises Orientales a estimé devoir donner une interprétation de ce même Décret en formulant la présente Déclaration.

I - Conformément au Décret du 27 juillet 1954, l'Ordinaire des Orientaux catholiques résidant en France, qui en l'occurrence est l'Archevêque de Paris, exercera sa juridiction cumulativement à celle des Ordinaires du lieu.

Cependant, la juridiction de l'Ordinaire des Orientaux et celle des Ordinaires du lieu ne sont pas situées sur le même plan, ces derniers exerçant leur juridiction de façon plutôt subsidiaire par rapport à celle de l'Ordinaire des Orientaux, conçue comme principale.

---

5   *AAS* 78 (1986) 784-786.

II - Toutefois, l'Ordinaire des Orientaux ne prendra aucune mesure sans avoir préalablement obtenu l'accord des ordinaires du lieu intéressés. Cet accord est requis «ad validitatem».

III - Aux termes de ce qui précède, il appartient à l'Ordinaire des Orientaux de prendre les dispositions suivantes:

1) Autoriser la constitution de nouvelles communautés rattachées à des Églises Orientales, après avis de l'autorité supérieure des Églises rituelles concernées.

2) Reconnaître, après avis de l'autorité supérieure de l'Église rituelle, les groupes et associations de fidèles latins qui entendent vivre selon les traditions d'une Église orientale, en célébrer la Liturgie et en vivre la spiritualité.

3) Edifier des églises ou lieux de culte, autoriser leur construction ou, selon les circonstances, leur adaptation en faveur des fidèles orientaux.

4) Eriger des paroisses orientales, nommer leurs curés ainsi que les prêtres chargés d'un ministère auprès de fidèles ou de communautés rattachées à une Église Orientale, après consultation ou proposition de l'autorité supérieure de cette Église.

5) Approuver, «ad normam iuris», les statuts des monastères et des instituts de vie consacrée et de tout autre association ou groupe rattaché à une Église Orientale.

C'est pourquoi, après consultation de l'Ordinaire des Catholiques de rite oriental, du Président de la Conférence des Evêques de France, des Ordinaires du lieu particulièrement concernés ainsi que du Nonce Apostolique, le soussigné Cardinal Préfet de la Congrégation pour les Églises Orientales, au cours de l'Audience que lui a concédée Sa Sainteté Jean Paul II en date 28 avril 1986, a soumis la présente Déclaration interprétative à la bienveillante attention du Saint-Père qui a bien voulu l'approuver et ordonner qu'elle soit rendue publique et obligatoire pour toutes les personnes concernées.

Fait à Rome, au siège de la Congrégation pour les Églises Orientales, le 30 avril 1986.

D. Simon Card. Lourdusamy,
Préfet
Miroslav S. Marusyn,
Secrétaire

Unofficial Translation

Congregation for the Eastern Churches

France

Ordinariate for the Faithful of Eastern Rites

Declaration by which the scope of canonical power of the Ordinary for the Eastern faithful lacking an ecclesiastical superior of their own rite is more precisely determined.

Interpretative declaration of the Decree of 27 July 1954.

By the decree of 27 July 1954, the Holy See erected the Ordinariate for Catholics of the Eastern rite residing in France, instituted by Pope Pius XII on 16 June of the same year (*AAS* 47 [1955], 612-613).

Certain reasons of a pastoral order, still valid today, induced the Holy See not to withdraw the faithful of Eastern rite totally from the individual jurisdiction of the Ordinaries of France. This is the reason why a double jurisdiction was established, in a manner like that of jurisdiction exercised by the Vicariate for the Armed Forces; that is, the jurisdiction of the Ordinary for the Eastern faithful is considered to be primary, and, on the other hand, that of the local Ordinaries is considered of a rather secondary character.

More than thirty years have already passed and the presence of Eastern Catholics in France has become more stable. Also, the relations with the concerned Eastern Hierarchies are more frequent and more delicate, so that the problems presented to the diocesan curias are more numerous and complex.

Assuredly, the principles of the decree of 1954 have proven to be appropriate for the current circumstances. However, in view of assuring an indispensable unity of direction and a better coordination of the measures necessary in each particular case, it is appropriate to make these same principles more explicit and to formulate more concretely the norms that flow from them.

Hence, after having maturely considered the question in light of the new situations, the Congregation for the Eastern Churches has decided that it must give an interpretation of this same decree in formulating this present Declaration.

I. Conforming to the Decree of 27 July 1954, the Ordinary of the Eastern Catholics residing in France, who in this case is the Archbishop of Paris, exercises his jurisdiction cumulatively with that of the local ordinaries.

However, the jurisdiction of the Ordinary of the Eastern faithful and that of the local ordinaries are not on the same level, in that the latter exercise their jurisdiction in a manner that is secondary in relation to that of the Ordinary of the Eastern faithful, which is conceived of as primary.

II. Nevertheless, the Ordinary of the Eastern faithful will not take any measure without having previously obtained the agreement of the concerned local ordinaries. This agreement is *ad validitatem*.

III. In consideration of the above, it pertains to the Ordinary of the Eastern Catholics to take the following actions:

1. To authorize the constitution of new communities attached to the Eastern Churches, after notifying the superior authority of the interested ritual Churches.

2. To recognize, after having notified the superior authority of the ritual Church, groups and associations of Latin faithful who intend to live according to the traditions of an Eastern Church, in celebrating the Liturgy and in living the spirituality.

3. To build churches or places of worship, to authorize their construction or, according to the circumstances, their adaption for the benefit of Eastern faithful.

4. To erect Eastern parishes, to appoint their pastors and the priests charged with the ministry of the faithful or communities attached to an Eastern Church, after consultation or proposal of the superior authority of this Church.

5. To approve *ad normam iuris* the statutes of monasteries and institutes of consecrated life and of any other association or group attached to an Eastern Church.

Hence, after consultation with the Ordinary of Catholics of the Eastern Rite, with the President of the Conference of Bishops of France, with the local ordinaries particularly interested and with the Apostolic Nuncio, the undersigned Cardinal Prefect of the Congregation for the Eastern Churches, during an audience conceded to him by His Holiness Pope John Paul II on 28 April 1986, submitted the present interpretative decree to the benevolent attention of the Holy Father, who kindly approved it and ordered that it be published and be made obligatory for all the persons concerned.

Given in Rome, at the Congregation for the Eastern Churches, 30 April 1986

D. Simon Card. Lourdusamy, Prefect

Miroslav S. Marusyn, Secretary

Appendix 6. Erection of a Personal Parish According to the Prior Legislation[6]

Bello novissimo exardescente ac multo magis post exitum ipsius, in hac Nostra Civitate atque Archidiœcesi domicilium collocarunt, orientalibus regionibus profugis complures fideles byzantini ritus, qui, etsi sacras celebrationes latinas obire possunt, tamen ecclesiam byzantinam adire a Nobis flagitant.

Quapropter, animarum illarum bono spirituali, meliori modo qua possumus, providere volentes ac earum desiderium satisfacere cupientes, ad normam canonis 216 § 4 C.J.C., ex facultate Nobis concessa a Sacra Congregatione "Pro Ecclesia Orientali" sub die 2 aprilis 1957, invocato Domini Nostri Jesu Christi nomine eiusque Matris Mariæ, tenore præsentium, Parœciam personalem sub titulo "S. Joannis Chrysostomi," in Ecclesia S. Sebastiani huius Nostræ Civitatis, pro omnibus fidelibus byzantini ritus in tota Nostra Archidiœcesi degentibus, constituimus.

Libenti potissimus animo Parœciam hanc erigimus, cum ad celebrationes decorandas, quæ Barii hisce diebus habentur in honorem Sancti Nicolai, eius ossa hodierna ipsa die Cardinalis Adeodatus Joannes Piazza, SS. Domini Nostri Pii Papæ XII Legatus a latere, in perantiquum sepulcrum, quod in nuper refecta Basilicæ crypta situm est, reponit, fere omnes orientales ritus in vetusta Nicolaiana Basilica nituerint, Ecclesiæ unitatem ostendentes mira varietate circumdatam.

Dotatio novæ Parœciæ consistit in titulo publici fenoris Lib. 1.120.000 quarum reditus annus 56.000 libellarum sic distribuendus est: pro Parocho Lib. 55.000, pro cultus impensis Lib. 1.000.

Enixe, ergo, Dominum rogamus, Divo Nicolao intercedente, ut orientales dissidentes ad unitatem Ecclesiæ revocare dignetur et fiat tandem unum ovile et unus Pastor.

Datum Barii, ex Nostra Archiepiscopali Palatio, die 7 maii 1957

Cancellarius Archiepiscopalis
Can. Dominicus Sportelli

+ Henricus, Archiepiscopus

---

6   This was obtained from the Archbishop of Bari-Bitonto

Unofficial Translation

During the conflagration of the last war and much more so after it, numerous members of the faithful of the Byzantine rite, fleeing Eastern regions, established domicile in our city and archdiocese. Although they can avail themselves of Latin sacred celebrations, they nevertheless ask us to establish a Byzantine church.

For this reason, for the spiritual good of their souls, desiring to provide and respond to their request in the best way that we can, according to the norm of CIC c. 216 §4, by the faculty granted to us by the Sacred Congregation "for the Eastern Church" on 2 April 1957, invoking the name of Our Lord Jesus Christ and His Mother Mary, we constitute the personal parish under the title of "Saint John Chrysostom" in the Church of Saint Sebastian in our city for the benefit of all the faithful of the Byzantine rite found in our entire Archdiocese.

We erect this parish in most happy spirits, when almost all the Eastern rites will shine forth at the ancient Nicolan basilica, manifesting the unity of the Church encompassed with wonderful diversity, for the sake of honoring those celebrations that will take place at this time in Bari in honor of Saint Nicholas, whose bones Cardinal Adeodatus Joannes Piazza, Legate *a latere* of Pope Pius XII, will place in the very ancient tomb located in the crypt of the newly-restored basilica.

This endowment of the new parish consists of a public trust of L. 1,120,000 , with an annual income of L. 56,000, to be distributed as follows: to the pastor L. 55,000, for the expenses of worship L. 1,000.

We thus earnestly ask the Lord, through the intercession of Saint Nicholas, that the dissident Eastern Churches deign to recall the unity of the Church, and that there be finally one flock and one pastor.

Given in Bari at our Archiepiscopal Palace on 7 May 1957.

Archiepiscopal Chancellor
Can. Dominicus Sportelli

+ Henricus, Archbishop

Appendix 7. Transfer of a Cleric to a Church *sui iuris*[7]

Prot. N. ____

Beatissime Pater,

____, Sacerdos Ecclesiæ ____ Eparchiæ ____, ob rationes expositas petit indultum transeundi ab Ecclesia ____ ad Ecclesiam ____.

Congregatio pro Ecclesiis Orientalibus, vigore facultatum a Summo Pontifice ____ sibi tributarum, attentis precibus ac omnibus mature perpensis, concedit Oratori indultum transitus ab Ecclesia ____ ad Ecclesiam ____ ad omnes iuris effectus.

Transitus ad novam Ecclesiam vim habebit a momento quo Orator coram dictæ Ecclesiæ parocho vel Hierarcha intra eorundem territorii fines - vel coram presbytero ab alterutro delegato - et duobus testibus, suam voluntatem novum ritum assumendi declaraverit.

Parochus vel Ordinarius, de quibus supra, sedulo curet:

I. Ut in libro baptizatorum novæ parœciæ peractus transitus quam primum adnotetur;

II. Ut de peracto transitu nuntius mittatur ad baptismi parochum, cuius erit ritus mutationem in libro baptizatorum adnotare et de peracta adnotatione mittentem certiorem facere.

Sex mensibus a die concessionis elapsis, præsens Rescriptum omnem vim amittit.

Datum Romæ, ex Ædibus Congregationis pro Ecclesiis Orientalibus,

die ____ mensis ____ anno ____.

____

a secretis

---

[7] From CCEO cc. 32 §1; 36 and 37

Unofficial Translation

Prot. No. ____

Most Holy Father,

____, a priest of the ____ Church in the Eparchy of ____, for the reasons presented requests an indult to transfer from the ____ Church to the ____ Church.

The Congregation for the Eastern Churches, in virtue of the faculties granted to it by the Roman Pontiff ____, having considered the request and taking into account all aspects of it, grants to the petitioner an indult for transfer ____ with all the effects of law.

The transfer to the new Church will go into effect at the time that the petitioner, in the presence of the pastor or Hierarch of the above-mentioned Church within their territory, or in the presence of a priest delegated by them, and two witnesses, declares his intention to assume the new rite.

The pastor or Ordinary mentioned above is carefully to see that:

1. The executed transfer is recorded in the baptismal register of the new parish as soon as possible.

2. The parish priest where the baptism was celebrated be informed that the transfer was completed; he will record the change of rite in the baptism register and notify the new parish that the record has been made.

With the elapse of six months from the date of the concession, this rescript loses all force.

Given in Rome, at the offices of the Congregation for the Eastern Churches, the ____ day of the month ____ year ____.

                                                                                    Secretary

Appendix 8. Indult of Bi-ritualism[8]

Prot. N. ____

Beatissime Pater,

____, sacerdos Ecclesiæ ____ diœcesis vel eparchiæ ____, humiliter postulat, ut facultas sibi fiat Sacrum litandi atque cetera sacerdotalia munera ritu quoque ____ obeundi.

Causa est: bonum spirituale fidelium Ecclesiæ ____ inter quos versatur.

Congregatio pro Ecclesiis Orientalibus, vigore facultatum quibus pollet ex concessione Summi Pontificis ____, omnibus mature perpensis, gratiam petitam benigne largitur, iuxta preces, cauto tamen ut Orator de Hierarchæ seu Ordinarii loci sententia, ritum ____ scite didicerit; remoto quovis vel admirationis periculo et excluso omni illegitimo syncretismo liturgico, ceterum servatis iure servandis.

Præsentibus ad ____ valituris.

Contrariis quibuslibet non obstantibus.

Datum Romæ, ex Ædibus Congregationis pro Ecclesiis Orientalibus,

die ____ mensis ____ anno ____.

_____

a secretis

---

[8] From CCEO c. 674 §2.

Unofficial Translation

Prot. No. ____

Most Holy Father,

____, a priest of the ____ Church in the diocese or eparchy of ____, humbly requests that the faculty be given to him for celebrating the Holy Sacrifice and performing other priestly functions also according to the ____ rite.

The reason is the spiritual good of the faithful of the ____ Church among whom he lives.

The Congregation for the Eastern Churches, in virtue of the faculties it enjoys from the concession of the Roman Pontiff ____, taking into account all aspects of the matter, kindly grants the requested favor according to the petition, provided nevertheless that the petitioner, according to the opinion of the Hierarch or local Ordinary of the place, has learned in a practical way the ____ Rite; every danger of bewilderment is to be removed, and all unlawful liturgical syncretism is to be excluded; the requirements of law in other respects are to be observed.

This is valid for ____.

Anything to the contrary notwithstanding.

Given in Rome, at the offices of the Congregation for the Eastern Churches, the ____ day of the month ____ year ____.

                                                                ____

                                                               Secretary

Appendix 9. *Celebret* with the Indult of Biritualism[9]

Prot. N. ____

Presentibus litteris fidem facimus atque testamur Rev. ____ bonis moribus præditum esse, nullaque - quod sciamus - ecclesiastica censura irretitum.

Quapropter eum enixe in Domino commendamus omnibus Ordinariis locorum ad quæ divertere contigerit ut illum ad Sacrosanctum Missæ Sacrificium celebrandum admittant ritu quoque latino.

Præsentibus valituris ad ____

Datum Romæ, ex Ædibus Congregationis pro Ecclesiis Orientalibus,

Die ____ mensis ____ anno ____.

————
a secretis

---

[9] From CCEO cc. 674 §2 and 703 §1

Unofficial Translation

Prot. No. ____

With this letter we verify and attest Rev. ____ to be of good character, and, to the best of our knowledge, not to be impeded by any ecclesiastical censure. For this reason, we strongly recommend him in the Lord to all Local Ordinaries to which he might come, that they admit him to celebrate the Holy Sacrifice of the Mass also in the Latin Rite.

This is valid until ____.

Given in Rome, at the offices of the Congregation for the Eastern Churches, the ____ day of the month ____ year ____.

                                                                 Secretary

Appendix 10. Latin Priests Carrying Out Priestly Functions in an Eastern Rite[10]

Prot. N. ____

Beatissime Pater,

Sacerdos ____, ritus Latini, humiliter postulat ut ipsi, ad bonum animarum promovendum, facultas quævis sacerdotalia munera ritu latino implendi, tamquam sacerdos Eparchiæ ____ adscriptus, sub iurisdictione Hierarchæ loci, proprio tamen ritu retento, concedatur.

Congregatio pro Ecclesiis Orientalibus, vigore facultatum a Summo Pontifice ____ sibi tributarum, benigne indulget ut Orator, iuxta preces, in omnibus tamquam sacerdos ritus ____ Eparchiæ ____ adscriptus se gerat, proprio tamen ritu retento, quo, si casus ferat, uti valebit in eadem vel alia Eparchia in bonum fidelium ritus latini, ac vel etiam devotionis causa, dummodo ne pastoralia munera impediantur; ea tamen lege ut ritu latino uti debeat, si supradictam Eparchiam, quacumque ex causa, relinquerit.

Contrariis quibuscumque minime obstantibus.

Datum Romæ, ex Ædibus Congregationis pro Ecclesiis Orientalibus,

Die ____ mensis ____ anno ____.

____

a secretis

---

10   From CCEO c. 674 §1.

Unofficial Translation

Prot. No. ____

Most Holy Father,

_____, a priest of the Latin rite, humbly asks that, for the promotion of the good of souls, the faculty of fulfilling certain priestly ministries in the Latin rite be granted to him, as a priest ascribed to the Eparchy of _____, but with his own rite retained.

The Congregation for Eastern Churches, in virtue of the faculties granted to it by the Supreme Pontiff ___, graciously grants that the petitioner, according to his request, may act in all things as a priest ascribed to Eparchy of ___ of the _____ rite, nevertheless retaining his own rite, which, if the situation demands it, he will be able to use in the same or another Eparchy for the good of the faithful of the Latin rite, or even for reason of devotion, as long as pastoral duties are not impeded. Nevertheless he must by the same law use the Latin rite, if he should leave the aforementioned Eparchy for whatever reason. Anything else to the contrary notwithstanding.

Given in Rome, at the offices of the Congregation for the Eastern Churches, the ____ day of the month ____ year ____.

____

Secretary

Appendix 11. Recourse to the Apostolic Penitentiary through a Confessor

Eminenza Revma,

Caio sacerdote (*indicare l'ufficio, per esempio parroco o viceparroco, se ha cura di anime*) ha assolto una volta il complice nel peccato turpe (*indicare il sesso e, se i complici sono più di uno, anche il numero e il sesso di ciascuno; se ha assolto più volte, indicare quante volte ha assolto ciascuno*).

Dopo, mosso da pentimento è venuto da me confessore a chiedere l'assoluzione della censura e del peccato. Io l'ho assolto a tenore del can. 1357 §1 CIC, essendogli duro rimanere in stato di peccato grave per il tempo necessario a ricorrere al superiore competente.

Ora, per obbedire ai comandi della Chiesa, egli ricorre per il mio tramite, quale confessore, alla Sede Apostolica per ricevere i mandati, disposto a fare la penitenza che in pena del suo delitto Vostra Eminenza vorrà imporgli.

    Giorno ___ mese ___ anno ___

    N. N. (*Cognome e nome del confessore e suo indirizzo per la risposta*)

    (*sulla busta*)
    Em.mo Signor Cardinale ___
    Penitenziere Maggiore
    Piazza della Cancelleria, 1
    00120 CITTÀ DEL VATICANO

Unofficial Translation

Your Eminence,

Caius, a priest, (indicate his office, for example, pastor or parochial vicar if he has the care of souls) absolved one time his accomplice of a sin against chastity (indicate the gender or, if the accomplices are more than one, the number and the gender of each; if he absolved more than one time, indicate how many times he absolved each.)

Afterwards, moved by a penitent spirit he approached me, his confessor, to ask for absolution from the censure and the sin. I absolved him in conformity with CIC c. 1357 §1, since it would have been difficult for him to remain in a state of grave for the time necessary to make recourse to the competent superior.

Now, in obedience to the commandments of the Church, he is making recourse through me, his confessor, to the Apostolic See to receive its mandates. He is disposed to do the penance that your Eminence wishes to impose on him.

    Date

    Name of Confessor and return address

    On the envelope:
    Em.mo Signor Cardinale ____
    Penitenziere Maggiore
    Piazza della Cancelleria, 1
    00120 Città del Vaticano

Appendix 12. Dimissorial Letter[11]

Prot. N.____

Cum ____ Ecclesiæ ____ alumnus, nullo canonico impedimento irretitus, postulaverit ut ad ordinem ____ admittatur; cumque ex eiusdem alumni Moderatoris testimonio constet ipsum religione, pietate ac morum integritate commendabilem, litterarum ac S. Doctrinæ studiis operam laudabiliter navasse, nec non divinæ vocationis ad ecclesiastica munia obeunda haud levia præbuisse argumenta;

Congregatio pro Ecclesiis Orientalibus, vigore facultatum a Summo Pontifice ____ concessarum, alumnum, de quo supra, per præsentes litteras ad ____ dimittit, ut per Episcopum Ecclesiæ ____ aut per alium quempiam Antistitem, cum Romana Ecclesia Catholica communionem habentem, ad enunciat____ ordine ____ promoveri valeat, dummodo, prævio legitimo examine, idoneus habeatur.

Datum Romæ, ex Ædibus Congregationis pro Ecclesiis Orientalibus,

die ____ mensis ____ anno ____

_____
a secretis

---

11   From CCEO cc. 747, 748 §2 and 752.

Unofficial Translation

Prot. No. ____

Since ____, a student of the _____ Church, under no canonical penalty, requested to be admitted to the order of ____, and since it is shown from the testimony of the same Moderator that the student is commendable in religion, piety and integrity of morals, has laudably completed his studies of Sacred Doctrine and letters, and has offered strong arguments of a divine vocation for assuming ecclesiastical duties

The Congregation for the Eastern Churches, in virtue of the faculties granted to it by the Roman Pontiff ___, hereby releases the above-mentioned student to ____, so that he can be promoted to the said order of _____ by a Bishop of the ____ Church or any other Bishop having full communion with the Roman Catholic Church, provided that after legitimate examination he is deemed worthy

Given in Rome, at the offices of the Congregation for the Eastern Churches, the ____ day of the month ____ year ____.

_____

Secretary

Appendix 13. Ordination in the Latin Rite with the Faculty of Biritualism[12]

Prot. N. ____

Beastissime Pater,

____, scholasticus (alumnus) in ____ fidelis Ecclesiæ ____ diœceseos vel eparchiæ ____ humiliter petit ut ad sacrum Diaconatus et Presbyteratus Ordinem ritu latino admittit possit ob causas allatas; insuper, aliquando ordinatus, facultas fiat sibi Sacrum litandi atque cetera diaconalia, deinde sacerdotalia munera utroque ritu, ____, obeundi, iusta bonum spirituale fidelium cuiuscumque ritus adstantium, inter quos versatur.

Præpositi, tum Provincialis tum Generalis, preces commendant.

Congregatio pro Ecclesiis Orientalibus, vigore facultatum a Summo Pontifice ____ sibi tributarum, benigne concedit gratiam, iuxta preces, servatis de iure servandis, ea tamen lege ut Orator Ecclesiæ ____ adscriptus maneat.

Contrariis quibuslibet non obstantibus.

Datum Romæ, ex Ædibus Congregationis pro Ecclesiis Orientalibus,

die ____ mensis ____ anno____.

____

a secretis

---

12   From CCEO cc. 748 §2 and 752.

Unofficial Translation

Prot. No. ____

Most Holy Father,

____, a seminarian (student) in _____, a member of the faithful of the _____ Church in the diocese or eparchy of _____, humbly requests to be able to be admitted to the Order of Deacon and Presbyter in the Latin rite for the reasons provided. Further, whenever he is ordained, he asks to be given the faculty of celebrating the Holy Sacrifice and carrying out diaconal and later priestly functions in both rites, _____, for the spiritual good of the faithful of each rite present where he lives.

Both the provincial and general superiors recommend the request.

The Congregation for the Eastern Churches, in virtue of the faculties granted to it by the Roman Pontiff _____, kindly concedes the favor, according to his request, with the requirements of law being observed, but with the rule that the petitioner remain ascribed to the ____ Church.

Anything else to the contrary notwithstanding.

Given in Rome, at the offices of the Congregation for the Eastern Churches, the ____ day of the month ____ year ____.

                                                                          Secretary

Appendix 14. Sample of the Decree of Erection of a New Religious House[13]

Autorizzo la costituzione della Comunità religiosa dei Frati Predicatori in Lecce, affidando ad essa il compito della evangelizzazione della cultura, in particolare nell'ambiente universitario, nonché la rettoria della antica Chiesa Domenicana di S. Giovanni Battista, perché divenga centro fecondo di spiritualità e di inculturazione evangelica, sotto la protezione della B. V. Maria del S. Rosario, la cui devozione è ivi degnamente promossa dalla omonima Confraternita di S. Domenico di Guzman e di S. Tommaso d'Aquino.

---

[13] Decree of Msgr. Cosmo Francesco Ruppi, Archbishop Lecce, 8 December 1996: *Per noi frati* 1 (1997) 1.

Unofficial Translation

I authorize the constitution of the religious community of the Friar Preachers of Lecce, entrusting to it the task of evangelizing culture, especially in the context of the university, as well as the rectory of the ancient Dominican church of S. Giovanni Battista, that it become a fruitful center of spirituality and inculturation of the Gospel under the protection of the Blessed Virgin Mary of the Rosary, whose devotion is worthily promoted there by the Confraternity of S. Domenico di Guzman and of St. Thomas Aquinas.

Appendix 15. Admission to an Institute of Another Church *sui iuris* with a Prohibition against the Reception of Sacred Orders[14]

Prot. N. ____

Beatissime Pater,

____ fidelis Ecclesiæ ____ humiliter petit ut in Ordine ____ ad novitiatum admitti possit et, præscripto tempore, in eodem Instituto religiosam professionem emittere valeat, ritui ____ sese conformando.

Congregatio pro Ecclesiis Orientalibus, vigore facultatum a Summo Pontifice ____ sibi tributarum, benigne concedit ut Orat___ in Instituto de quo in precibus ad novitiatum et ad religiosam professionem admitti possit, exclusa ss. Ordinum receptione.

Eidem Oratori fit insuper facultas sese in omnibus conformandi ritui ____, ea tamen lege ut propriæ Ecclesiæ sui iuris adscriptus maneat, eundemque sequi debeat, si, quacumque de causa, ad nuper dictum Institutum pertinere desierit.

Contrariis quibuslibet non obstantibus.

Datum Romæ, ex Ædibus Congregationis pro Ecclesiis Orientalibus,

die ____ mensis ____ anno ____.

———
a secretis

---

14 From CCEO cc. 451; 517 §2; and 559 §1. In this case, the rescript prohibits the reception of Orders.

Unofficial Translation

Prot. No. ____

Most Holy Father,

____, a member of the Christian faithful of the ____ Church, humbly petitions to be able to be admitted into the novitiate of ____ and, after the prescribed time, to be able to make religious profession in the same Institute, conforming him/herself to the ____ rite.

The Congregation for the Eastern Churches, in virtue of the faculties granted to it by the Roman Pontiff ____, kindly grants that the petitioner be able to enter and make religious profession in the Institute mentioned in the request, excluding the reception of Sacred Orders.

Further, the petitioner is given the faculty to conform to the ____ rite, while nevertheless remaining ascribed to his / her own Church *sui iuris*; he / she must follow the same, if for any reason, he / she ceases to belong to the above-mentioned Institute.

Anything to the contrary notwithstanding.

Given in Rome, at the offices of the Congregation for the Eastern Churches, the ____ day of the month ____ year ____.

____

Secretary

Appendix 16. Admission to an Institute of Another Church *sui iuris*[15]

Prot. N. ____

Beatissime Pater,

____, fidelis Ecclesiæ ____, diœceseos vel eparchiæ ____ humiliter petit ut in ____ad novitiatum admitti possit et, præscripto tempore, in eodem Instituto religiosam professionem emittere valeat, ritui ____ sese conformando.

Congregatio pro Ecclesiis Orientalibus, vigore facultatum a Summo Pontifice ____ sibi tributarum, benigne concedit ut Orat__ in Instituto de quo in precibus ad novitiatum et ad religiosam professionem admitti possit.

Eidem Orat__ fit insuper facultas sese in omnibus conformandi ritui ____, ea tamen lege ut propriæ Ecclesiæ sui iuris adscript__ maneat, eundemque sequi debeat, si, quacumque de causa, ad nuper dictum Institutum pertinere desierit.

Contrariis quibuslibet non obstantibus.

Datum Romæ, ex Ædibus Congregationis pro Ecclesiis Orientalibus,

die ____ mensis ____ anno ____.

____

a secretis

---

15   CCEO cc. 451, 517 §2 and 559 §1.

Unofficial Translation

Prot. No. ____

Most Holy Father,

____, a member of the Christian faithful of the ____ Church, in the diocese or eparchy of ____, humbly petitions to be able to be admitted into the novitiate of ____ and, after the prescribed time, to be able to make religious profession in the same Institute, conforming him/herself to the ____ rite.

The Congregation for the Eastern Churches, in virtue of the faculties granted to it by the Roman Pontiff ____, kindly grants that the petitioner be able to enter and make religious profession in the Institute mentioned in the request.

Further, the petitioner is given the faculty to conform to the ____ rite, while nevertheless remaining ascribed to his / her own Church *sui iuris*; he / she must follow the same, if for any reason, he / she ceases to belong to the above-mentioned Institute.

Anything to the contrary notwithstanding.

Given in Rome, at the offices of the Congregation for the Eastern Churches, the ____ day of the month ____ year ____.

____

Secretary

Appendix 17. Admission to an Institute of Another Church *sui iuris* (Italian Version)[16]

Prot. N. ____

Beatissimo Padre,

____, della Chiesa ____ umilmente chiede di poter essere ammess__ nel noviziato ____ e conformarsi al rito latino.

La Congregazione per le Chiese Orientali, in virtù delle facoltà concesse dal Pontefice Romano ____, con la presente concede all'orat__ di poter essere ammess__ al noviziato del sopramenzionat__ e di conformarsi in tutto al rito latino, comunque rimanendo ascritt__ alla propria Chiesa, di modo che, se dovesse, per qualsiasi ragione, cessare di appartenere a codest__ ____, ess__ ritornerà in assoluto alla propria Chiesa.

Contrariis quibuslibet minime obstantibus.

Roma, dalla Sede della Congregazione per le Chiese Orientali,

lì, ____

____
a secretis

---

16 CCEO cc. 451, 517 §2 and 559 §1.

Unofficial Translation

Most Holy Father,

____, of the ____ Church, humbly asks to be able to be admitted in the ____ novitiate and to conform to the Latin Rite.

The Congregation for the Eastern Churches, in virtue of the faculties granted to it by the Roman Pontiff ____, hereby grants that the petitioner be able to be admitted to the novitiate of the above-mentioned Institute and to conform to the Latin Rite, while remaining ascribed to his / her own Church in such a way that, if he / she should for any reason cease to belong to the above-mentioned Institute, he / she will return in an absolute manner to his / her own Church.

Anything to the contrary notwithstanding.

Rome, at the Congregation for the Eastern Churches, [date].

                                                                             Secretary

Appendix 18. Regularization of the Canonical Situation of Eastern Faithful Admitted to the Novitiate of Another Church *sui iuris*

Prot. N. ____

Beatissimo Padre,

____, fedele della Chiesa ____, essendo stata ammessa nel noviziato ____ senza il previo permesso della Sede Apostolica, come richiesto dal Diritto Canonico (CCEO can. 517 §2), umilmente chiede la regolarizzazione della sua posizione canonica.

La Congregazione per le Chiese Orientali, avendo preso atto dell'avvenuta ammissione nel noviziato, tutto ben considerato, in virtù delle facoltà ad essa concesse dal Pontefice Romano ____, con la presente regolarizza la posizione canonica della sopra nominata ____ e le concede di conformarsi in tutto al rito latino, comunque rimanendo ascritta alla propria Chiesa ____ di modo che, se dovesse, per qualsiasi ragione, cessare di appartenere all'istituto di cui sopra, essa ritornerà in assoluto alla propria Chiesa ____.

Contrariis quibuslibet minime obstantibus.

Roma, dalla Sede della Congregazione per le Chiese Orientali,

lì, ____.

____
a secretis

Unofficial Translation

Most Holy Father,

____, a member of the Christian faithful of the ____ Church, having been admitted in the ____ novitiate without the prior permission of the Apostolic See as required by Canon Law (CCEO c. 517 §2), humbly asks for the regularization of his / her canonical position.

The Congregation for the Eastern Churches, informed of the admission into the novitiate, all things duly considered, in virtue of the faculty granted to it by the Roman Pontiff ____, hereby regularizes the canonical position of the above named ____ and grants to him / her permission to conform to the Latin rite in all matters, while remaining ascribed to his / her own ____ Church, in such a way that if he /she should for any reason cease to belong to the above-mentioned Institute, he / she will return in an absolute manner to his / her own Church.

Anything to the contrary notwithstanding.

Rome, at the Congregation for the Eastern Churches, [date].

                                                                                    Secretary

Appendix 19. Regularization of the Canonical Situation of Eastern Faithful Admitted to Temporary Profession in the Institute of Another Church *sui iuris*

Prot. N. ____

Beatissimo Padre,

____, fedele della Chiesa ____, essendo stata ammessa nel noviziato ____ e già professa di voti temporanei senza il previo permesso della Sede Apostolica, come richiesto dal Diritto Canonico (CCEO can. 517 §2), umilmente chiede la regolarizzazione della sua posizione canonica.

La Congregazione per le Chiese Orientali, avendo preso atto dell'avvenuta ammissione nel noviziato e della professione dei voti temporanei, tutto ben considerato, in virtù delle facoltà ad essa concesse dal Pontefice Romano ____, con la presente regolarizza la posizione canonica della sopra nominata ____ e le concede di conformarsi in tutto al rito latino, comunque rimanendo ascritta alla propria Chiesa ____ di modo che, se dovesse, per qualsiasi ragione, cessare di appartenere a quel monastero, essa ritornerà in assoluto alla propria Chiesa ____.

Contrariis quibuslibet minime obstantibus.

Roma, dalla Sede della Congregazione per le Chiese Orientali,

lì, ____.

a secretis

Unofficial Translation

Most Holy Father,

____, a member of the Christian faithful of the ____ Church, having been admitted in the ____ novitiate and having already made temporary vows without the prior permission of the Apostolic See as required by Canon Law (CCEO c. 517 §2), humbly asks for the regularization of his / her canonical position.

The Congregation for the Eastern Churches, informed of the admission into the novitiate and profession of temporary vows, all things duly considered, in virtue of the faculty granted to it by the Roman Pontiff ____, hereby regularizes the canonical position of the above named ____ and grants to him / her permission to conform to the Latin rite in all matters, while remaining ascribed to his / her own ____ Church, in such a way that if he /she should for any reason cease to belong to the above-mentioned Institute, he / she will return in an absolute manner to his / her own Church.

Anything to the contrary notwithstanding.

Rome, at the Congregation for the Eastern Churches, [date].

_____
Secretary

Appendix 20. Regularization of the Canonical Situation of Eastern Faithful Admitted to Perpetual Profession in the Institute of Another Church *sui iuris*

Prot. N. ____

Beatissimo Padre,

____, fedele della Chiesa ____, essendo stata ammessa nel noviziato ____, e già professa di voti perpetui senza il previo permesso della Sede Apostolica, come richiesto dal Diritto Canonico (CCEO can. 517 §2), umilmente chiede la regolarizzazione della sua posizione canonica.

La Congregazione per le Chiese Orientali, avendo preso atto dell'avvenuta ammissione nel noviziato e della professione dei voti temporanei e poi perpetui, tutto ben considerato, in virtù delle facoltà ad essa concesse dal Pontefice Romano ____, con la presente regolarizza la posizione canonica della sopra nominata ____ e le concede di conformarsi in tutto al rito latino, comunque rimanendo ascritta alla propria Chiesa ____, di modo che, se dovesse, per qualsiasi ragione, cessare di appartenere a quel monastero, essa ritornerà in assoluto alla propria Chiesa ____.

Contrariis quibuslibet minime obstantibus.

Roma, dalla Sede della Congregazione per le Chiese Orientali,

lì, ____.

____

a secretis

Unofficial Translation

Most Holy Father,

____, a member of Christian faithful of the ____ Church, having been admitted in the ____ novitiate and having already made perpetual vows without the prior permission of the Apostolic See as required by Canon Law (CCEO c. 517 §2), humbly asks for the regularization of his / her canonical position.

The Congregation for the Eastern Churches, noting the admission into the novitiate and of the profession of temporary and perpetual vows, all things duly considered, in virtue of the faculty granted to it by the Roman Pontiff ____, hereby regularizes the canonical position of the above named ____ and grants to him / her permission to conform to the Latin rite in all matters, while remaining ascribed to his / her own ____ Church, in such a way that if he /she should for any reason cease to belong to that monastery, he / she will return in an absolute manner to his / her own Church.

Anything to the contrary notwithstanding.

Rome, at the offices of the Congregation for the Eastern Churches, [date].

———
Secretary

Select Bibliography

1. Sources
    1.1 Conciliar Sources
    1.2 Papal Documents
    1.3 Documents of the Holy See
    1.4 Particular Documents
2. Studies

1. Sources

1.1 Conciliar Sources (by Date)

Lateran Council IV. Const. 9, *De diversis ritibus in eadem fide*: DEC, 239.

Council of Florence. Sess. VIII, Bull of Union with the Armenians, *Exsultate Deo*, 22 November 1439: DEC, 534-559.

_____. Sess. XI, Bull of Union with the Copts, *Cantate Domino*, 4 February 1442: DEC, 567-583.

Vatican Council II. *Acta Synodalia*. Vatican City, 1970-1978.

_____. Const. on the Sacred Liturgy, *Sacrosanctum Concilium*, 4 December 1963: Flannery, 1-36.

_____. Dogmatic Const. on the Church, *Lumen gentium*, 21 November 1964: Flannery, 350-426.

_____. Decr on the Eastern Catholic Churches, *Orientalium Ecclesiarum*, 21 November 1964: Flannery, 441-451.

_____. Decr on Ecumenism, *Unitatis redintegratio*, 21 November 1964: Flannery, 452-473.

_____. Decr on the Pastoral Office of Bishops, *Christus Dominus*, 28 October 1965: Flannery, 564-590.

_____. Declaration on Religious Liberty, *Dignitatis humanæ*, 7 December 1965: Flannery, 799-812.

1.2 Papal Documents (by Date)

Benedict XIV. Apcon *Etsi Pastoralis*, 26 May 1742: Gasparri, *CICFontes*, I:734-755, n. 328.

_____. Ep Enc *Demandatam*, 24 December 1743: Gasparri, *CICFontes*, I:795-803, n. 338.

Leo XIII. Aplet *Singulare præsidium*, de Ordine s. Basilii M. Ruthenæ Nationis in Gallicia reformando, 12 May 1882: *ASS* 14 (1882) 481-487.

_____. Aplet *Orientalium dignitas*, de disciplina orientalium conservanda et tuenda, 30 November 1894: *ASS* 27 (1894-95) 257-264.

Pius X. Aplet *Ea semper*, quibus ritus ruthenus constituitur in Statibus fœderatis Americæ Septemtrionalis, 14 June 1907: *ASS* 41 (1907) 3-12.

———. Aplet *Officium supremi*, committitur episcopo ritus rutheni adsistentia spiritualis Ruthenorum in Canadensi regione commorantium, 15 July 1912: *AAS* 4 (1912) 555-556.

———. Apcon *Tradita ab antiquis*, de sanctissima Eucharistia promiscuo ritu sumenda, 14 September 1912: *AAS* 4 (1912) 609-617.

Benedict XV. Apcon *Catholici fideles*, erectio novæ diœcesis græci ritus "Lungrensis" nuncupatæ, 13 February 1919: *AAS* 11 (1919) 222-226.

Pius XI. Apcon *Pervetustum Cryptæferratæ Cœnobium*, 26 September 1937: *AAS* 30 (1938) 183-186.

———. Apcon *Apostolica Sedes*, erectio novæ diœcesis græci ritus, 26 October 1937: *AAS* 30 (1938) 213-216.

Pius XII. Mp *Crebræ Allatæ*, de disciplina sacramenti matrimonii pro Ecclesia Orientali, 22 February 1949: *AAS* 41 (1949) 89-117.

———. Mp *Sollicitudinem nostram*, de iudiciis pro Ecclesia Orientali, 6 January 1950: *AAS* 42 (1950) 5-120.

———. Mp *Postquam Apostolicis Litteris*, de religiosis, de bonis Ecclesiæ temporalibus et de verborum significatione pro Ecclesiis orientalibus, 9 February 1952: *AAS* 44 (1952) 65-152.

———. Apcon *Exul familia*, de spirituali emigrantium cura, id est, de materna Ecclesiæ in emigrantes sollicitudine, et de normis pro spirituali emigrantium curæ gerendæ, 1 August 1952: *AAS* 44 (1952) 649-704.

———. Mp *Cleri Sanctitati*, de Ritibus Orientalibus, de personis pro Ecclesiis orientalibus, 2 June 1957: *AAS* 59 (1957) 433-603.

John XXIII. Apcon *Cum ob immane bellum*, in natione germanica exarchia constituitur pro fidelibus ruthenis byzantini ritus ibidem commorantibus, 17 April 1959: *AAS* 51 (1959) 789-791.

———. Apcon *Æterni Pastoris*, Novus in Gallia conditur Exarchatus Apostolicus pro christifidelibus Ucrainis byzantini ritus ibidem commorantibus, 22 July 1960: *AAS* 53 (1961) 341-342.

———. Apcon *Sacratissima*, Armenorum cœtus in Gallia commorantium ab Ordinariatu pro fidelibus ritus orientalis separatur et in Exarchatus formam redigitur, 22 July 1960: *AAS* 53 (1961) 343-344.

Paul VI. Mp *Pastorale munus*, Facultates et privilegia quædam Episcopis conceduntur, 30 November 1963: *AAS* 56 (1964) 5-12.

_____. Apcon *Byzantini Melkitarum*, In Fœderatis Americæ Septemtrionalis Civitatibus exarchatus apostolicus constituitur pro fidelibus byzantini Melkitarum ritus,10 January 1966: *AAS* 58 (1966) 563-564.

_____. Apcon *Cum supremi*, In Fœderatis Americæ Septemtrionalis Civitatibus exarchatus apostolicus constituitur pro fidelibus ritus Antiocheni Maronitarum, 10 January 1966: *AAS* 59 (1967) 529-530.

_____. Mp *De Episcoporum muneribus*, Normæ Episcopis impertiuntur ad facultatem dispensandi spectantes, 15 June 1966: *AAS* 58 (1966) 467-472.

_____. Mp *Ecclesiæ sanctæ*, normæ ad quædam exsequenda Concilii Vaticani Secundi decreta, 6 August 1966: *AAS* 58 (1966) 757-787.

_____. Mp *Episcopalis potestatis*, Normæ Episcopis Ecclesiarum Orientalium, ad facultatem dispensandi spectantes, impertiuntur, 2 May 1967: *AAS* 59 (1967) 385-390.

_____. Mp *Sollicitudo Omnium Ecclesiarum*, de muneribus Legatorum Romani Pontificis, 24 June 1969: *AAS* 61 (1969) 473-484.

_____. Mp *Matrimonia mixta*, normæ de matrimoniis mixtis statuuntur, 31 March 1970: *AAS* 62 (1970) 257-263.

_____. Apcon *Vicariæ potestatis*, qua Vicariatus Urbis nova ratione ordinatur, 6 January 1977: *AAS* 69 (1977) 5-18.

John Paul II. Apcon *Qui benignissimo*, In Canada Exarchatus Apostolicus conditur pro omnibus fidelibus catholicis Byzantini Ritus Melkitarum ibi commorantibus, 13 October 1980: *AAS* 72 (1980) 1075-1076.

_____. *Omelia alla Divina Liturgia in Rito Armeno*, Rome, 21 November 1987: *S.I.C.O.* Suppl. to nn. 485-556, 4-7.

_____. Aplet *Euntes in mundum universum*, ob expletum Millennium a Baptismo Regionis Rus' Kioviensis, 25 January 1988: *AAS* 80 (1988) 935-956.

_____. Apcon *Pastor Bonus*, de Romana Curia, 28 June 1988: *AAS* 80 (1988) 841-930.

_____. *Omelia alla Preghiera dell'Incenso in Rito Alessandrino-Copto*, Rome, 14 August 1988: *S.I.C.O.* Suppl. to nn. 485-556, 22-24.

_____. Aplet *Vicesimus quintus annus*, quinto iam lustro expleto conciliari ab promulgata de Sacra Liturgia constitutione, 4 December 1988: *AAS* 81 (1989) 897-918.

_____. *Ai partecipanti al Sinodo del Patriarcato Cattolico Armeno*, 26 August 1989: *S.I.C.O.* Suppl. to nn. 485-556, 41-44.

_____. *Discourse on the Presentation of the Code of Canons of the Eastern Churches*, 25 October 1990: *Nuntia* 31 (1990) 17-23.

_____. *Catechism of the Catholic Church.* Vatican City, 1992.

_____. *Ai Vescovi della Chiesa Armena Cattolica*, 19 November 1992: *S.I.C.O.* Suppl. to nn. 485-556, 51-54.

_____. *Discorso ai partecipanti alla riunione sui problemi pastorali della Chiesa cattolica di rito bizantino in Romania*, 22 January 1994: *L'Osservatore Romano*, 22 January 1994.

_____. Ep Ap *Orientale lumen*, centesimo expleto anno ab editis Litteris "Orientalium dignitas," 2 May 1995: *AAS* 87 (1995) 745-774.

_____. Litt Enc *Ut unum sint*, de œcumenico officio, 25 May 1995: *AAS* 87 (1995) 921-982.

_____. Apcon *Universi Dominici Gregis*, de Sede Apostolica vacante deque Romani Pontificis electione, 22 February 1996: *AAS* 88 (1996) 305-343.

_____. *Discorso ai membri della Conferenza inter-rituale dei Vescovi della Romania*, 7 December 1996: *L'Osservatore Romano*, 8 December 1996.

_____. Ap Exh *Una speranza nuova per il Libano*, 10 May 1997: Suppl. to *L'Osservatore Romano*, 12-13 May 1997.

_____. Aplet *È una grande gioia*, al Sinodo dei Vescovi della Chiesa siro-malabarese, 14 March 1998: *Il Regno-documenti* 9/1998, 269-270.

_____. Mp *Apostolos Suos*, de theologica et iuridica natura conferentiarum episcoporum, 21 May 1998: Suppl. to *L'Osservatore Romano*, 24 July 1998.

_____. *Udienza ai Patriarchi delle Chiese Orientali Cattoliche*, 29 September 1998: *L'Osservatore Romano*, 30 September 1998.

_____. *Udienza alla Plenaria della Congregazione per le Chiese Orientali*, 1 October 1998: *L'Osservatore Romano*, 2 October 1998.

Benedict XVI. Mp *Omnium in mentem*, 26 October 2009: *Communicationes* 41 (2009) 260-262 (Latin); 263-265 (Italian).

1.3 Documents of the Holy See (by the Order of *Pastor bonus* and date)

Secretariat of State. Rescriptum ex Audientia Ss.mi *Ad normam can. 112*, quo fit facultas licentiam de qua in can. 112 §1, 1° CIC legitime, in casu, præsumendi, 26 November 1992: *AAS* 85 (1993) 81.

Sacred Congregation for the Doctrine of the Faith. *Matrimonium sacramentum*, Instructio de matrimoniis mixtis, 18 March 1966: *AAS* 58 (1966) 235-239.

Congregation for the Doctrine of the Faith. Instructio *Pastoralis actio*, De baptismo parvulorum, 20 October 1980: *AAS* 72 (1980) 1137-1153.

_____. *Professio Fidei et Iusiurandum fidelitatis in suscipiendo officio nomine Ecclesiæ exercendo*, 9 January 1989: *AAS* 81 (1989) 104-106.

_____. *Litteræ ad Catholicæ Ecclesiæ episcopos de aliquibus aspectibus Ecclesiæ prout est communio*, 28 May 1992: AAS 85 (1993) 838-850.

_____. *Adnotatio de Ministro Sacramenti Unctionis Infirmorum*, 11 February 2005: Communicationes 37 (2005) 175-179.

_____. *Responsa ad quaestiones de aliquibus sententiis ad doctrinam de Ecclesia pertinentibus*, 29 June 2007: AAS 99 (2007) 604-608.

Sacred Congregation for the Propagation of the Faith for Eastern Rite Matters. Ep circ *Ad locorum Ordinarios latini ritus, de non permittendis Orientalibus eleemosynarum emendicationibus absque venia eiusdem S. Congregationis*, 1 January 1912: AAS 4 (1912) 532-533.

_____. Ep Circ *Per apostolicas Litteras*, Ad Superiores generales Institutorum religiosorum latini ritus, de modo tenendo antequam Orientales in eorum Sodalitates admittantur, 15 June 1912: AAS 4 (1912) 534-535.

_____. Decr *Fidelibus ruthenis*, quo statuuntur mutuæ relationes disciplinares inter episcopos latinos Canadenses et episcopum ruthenum illius regionis, nec non inter clerum et fideles utriusque ritus, 18 August 1913: AAS 5 (1913) 393-399.

_____. Decr *Cum Episcopo*, de spirituali administratione ecclesiæ græco-ruthenæ in Fœderatis Civitatibus Americæ septemtrionalis, 17 August 1914: AAS 6 (1914) 458-463.

Sacred Congregation for the Eastern Church. Notificatio *In attesa*, circa missiones ad Delegationes Apostolicas Constantinopolis, Ægypti, Mesopotamiæ, Persiæ et Syriæ pertinentes, 15 November 1918: AAS 10 (1918) 508-509.

_____. *Indulgentia ditatur precula quædam ad Russiæ salutem impetrandam*, 24 May 1923: AAS 15 (1923) 295.

_____. Decr *Nemini licere*, de venia apostolica transitus ad alium ritum a Romani Pontificis Legatis concedenda, 6 December 1928: AAS 20 (1928) 416-417.

_____. Decr *Cum data*, de spirituali administratione Ordinariatum Græco-Ruthenorum in Fœderatis Civitatibus Americæ Septemtrionalis, 1 March 1929: AAS 21 (1929) 152-159.

_____. Decr *Qua sollerti alacritate*, de clericis orientalibus, sive sæcularibus, sive religiosis, qui e territoriis aut diœcesibus orientalibus in septemtrionalem vel mediam, vel meridionalem Americam, vel in Australiæ regiones demigrant, ut spiritualem inibi curam præstent fidelibus proprii ritus, 23 December 1929: AAS 22 (1930) 99-105.

_____. Decr *Græci-rutheni ritus*, de administratione ordinariatus græco-rutheni in regione Canadensi, 24 May 1930: AAS 22 (1930) 346-354.

_____. Decr *Sæpenumero Apostolica Sedes*, de clericis orientalibus eleemosynas, pecuniam vel Missarum stipendia colligentibus seu corrogantibus extra orientales regiones et diœceses, 7 January 1930: *AAS* 22 (1930) 108-110.

_____. *Notificatio*, fideles orientales adeant pro indulgentiis S. Pænitentiariam, 21 July 1935: *AAS* 27 (1935) 379.

_____. Decr *Quo firmior*, facultas concedendi transitum ad alium ritum deinceps uni S. Sedi reservatur, 23 November 1940: *AAS* 33 (1941) 28.

_____. Decr *Cum fidelium*, Ordinariatus in Brasilia constituitur pro fidelibus ritum orientalium, 14 November 1951: *AAS* 44 (1952) 382-383.

_____. Decr *Nobilis Galliæ*, ordinariatus pro omnibus christifidelibus ritus orientalis in Gallia degentibus instituitur, 27 July 1954: *AAS* 47 (1955) 612-613.

_____. Decr *Annis præteritis*, ordinariatus pro fidelibus ritus orientalis in Argentina erigitur, 19 February 1959: *AAS* 54 (1962) 49-50.

_____. Decr *Crescens matrimoniorum*, De matrimoniis mixtis inter catholicos et orientales baptizatos acatholicos, 22 February 1967: *AAS* 59 (1967) 165-166.

Sacred Congregation for the Eastern Churches. Declaratio *Apostolica Sedes*, de Hierarchis extra fines territorii Patriarchalis constitutis, 25 March 1970: *AAS* 62 (1970) 179.

_____, ed. *Oriente cattolico. Cenni storici e statistiche.* 4th ed. Vatican City, 1974.

_____. Decr *Gallia: ordinariatus pro fidelibus orientalibus ritus* [*Déclaration interpretative du décret du 27 juillet 1954*], 30 April 1986: *AAS* 78 (1986) 784-786.

Congregation for the Eastern Churches. *Istruzione per l'applicazione delle prescrizioni liturgiche del Codice dei Canoni delle Chiese Orientali*. Vatican City, 1996.

_____. *Orientamenti fondamentali concernenti la liturgia siro-malabarese*, 16 March 1998: *Il Regno-documenti* 9/1998, 270-271.

Sacred Congregation for the Discipline of the Sacraments. Decr *Spiritus Sancti munera*, de Confirmatione administranda iis, qui ex gravi morbo in mortis periculo sunt constituti, 14 September 1946: *AAS* 38 (1946) 349-358.

Sacred Congregation for Rites. Decr *Ecclesiæ semper*, Ritus concelebrationis et communionis sub utraque specie promulgantur, 7 March 1965: *AAS* 57 (1965) 410-412.

Sacred Congregation for Divine Worship. Decr *Ordinis baptismi adultorum*, 6 January 1972: *AAS* 64 (1972) 252.

Sacred Congregation for Divine Worship and Discipline of the Sacraments. *Promulgato Codice*, variationes in novas editiones librorum liturgicorum introducendæ, 12 September 1983: *EV* 9:394-408.

Congregation for Divine Worship and Discipline of the Sacraments. Prænotanda *Matrimoniale fœdus*, ordo celebrandi matrimonium, 19 March 1990: *EV* 12:182-225.

Sacred Congregation for Bishops. Instructio *Nemo est*, de pastorali migratorum cura, 22 August 1969: *AAS* 61 (1969) 614-643.

_____. Directorium *Ecclesiæ imago*, de pastorali ministerio Episcoporum, 22 February 1973: Cf. CLD 8:244-245.

Congregation for Bishops. *Formulary for the Quinquennial Report*. Vatican City, 1997.

Sacred Congregation for Clergy. Notæ directivæ *Postquam Apostoli*, de mutua Ecclesiarum particularium cooperatione promovenda, 25 March 1980: *AAS* 72 (1980) 343-364.

Congregation for Clergy. *Dives Ecclesiæ*, Directory for the Life and Ministry of Priests, 31 March 1994. Vatican City, 1994.

Congregation for Clergy et al. *Istruzione su alcune questioni circa la collaborazione dei laici al ministero dei sacerdoti*, 15 August 1997: Suppl. to *L'Osservatore Romano*, 14 November 1997.

Sacred Congregation for Seminaries and Universities. Litt. *Quod catholicis hominibus*, de studiis orientalium rerum et de catechesi in seminariis impensius excolendis, 28 August 1929: *AAS* 22 (1930) 146-148.

Congregation for Catholic Education. *Circular Letter concerning Studies of the Oriental Churches*, 6 January 1987: CLD 12:130-134.

Sacred Apostolic Penitentiary. *Responsum*, De indulgentiis quoad fideles ritus orientalis: *AAS* 9 (1917) 399.

_____. *Responsum*, De mariani rosarii recitatione apud christifideles ritus rutheni: *AAS* 22 (1930) 292.

Apostolic Penitentiary. Decr *Mater Christi*, conceditur plenaria Indulgentia christifidelibus devote recitantibus hymnum *Acathistos* in ecclesia, aut oratorio vel in familia, in religiosa communitate vel in pia Consociatione, 31 May 1991: *AAS* 83 (1991) 627-628.

_____. *Enchiridion Indulgentiarum*. Vatican City, 1999.

Pontifical Council for Promoting Christian Unity. *Directoire pour l'application des principes et des norms sur l'œcumenisme*, 25 March 1993: *AAS* 85 (1993) 1039-1119; *Directory for the Application of Principles and Norms on Ecumenism*. Washington, 1993.

Pontifical Council for the Pastoral Care of Migrants and Itinerant People. Decr *Pro materna*, de facultatibus et privilegiis pro hominibus sedem mutantibus, 19 March 1982: *AAS* 74 (1982) 742-745; CLD 10:34-38.

_____. Instructio *Erga migrantes caritas Christi*, 3 May 2004: *AAS* 96 (2004) 762-822.

Pontifical Council for Legislative Texts. *Dignitas Connubii*, Instruction to be observed by diocesan and interdiocesan tribunals in handling causes of the nullity of marriage, 25 January 2005. Vatican City, 2005.

Pontifical Work for Ecclesiastical Vocations. *Nuove vocazioni per una nuova Europa*, Documento finale del Congresso sulle Vocazioni al Sacerdozio e alla Vita Consacrata in Europa (Rome, 5-10 May 1997): Suppl. to *L'Osservatore Romano*, 28 January 1998.

1.4. Particular Documents

Annuario Pontificio 2010. Vatican City, 2010.

Archidiocesis de Valencia. "Decreto por el que se nombra Vicario Episcopal personal para los sacerdotes diocesanos residentes en Roma y se determinan las competencias de su oficio, 22 enero 1995." *Ius Ecclesiæ* 8 (1996) 383-384.

Conferencia Episcopal Española. *Orientacion es para la atención pastoral de los católicos orientales*, LXXXI Asamblea plenaria, 17-21 noviembre 2003, n. 29. In *Boletín Oficial de la Conferencia Episcopal Española*, anno 17, n. 71 (31 December 2003) 56-63.

Conferenza Episcopale Italiana. *Decreto generale sul matrimonio canonico*, Roma, dalla Sede della CEI, 5 November 1990. In *Notiziario CEI* 16 (1990) 258-279.

_____. *Rito dell'Iniziazione Cristiana degli Adulti*. Vatican City, 1989.

_____. *Vademecum per la pastorale delle parrocchie cattoliche verso gli orientali non cattolici*, 23 February 2010. Bologna, 2010.

Eparchia di Lungro degli Italo-Albanesi dell'Italia Meridionale. *Dichiarazioni e decisioni della 1ª Assemblea Eparchiale 1995-1996*. Lungro, 1997.

Synod of Bishops. Relatio *"Principia quæ,"* regarding the Principles of Revision of the CIC, 7 October 1967: *Comm.* 1 (1969) 77-85.

2. Studies

Abate, A. *Il matrimonio nell'attuale legislazione canonica*, Studia Urbaniana 6. Rome-Brescia, 1979.

_____. *I ministeri nella missione e nel governo della Chiesa*. Rome, 1976.

_____. "La tutela della fede nei matrimoni misti secondo il nuovo Codice di Diritto Canonico." In *Portare Cristo all'Uomo*, Atti del Congresso del Ventennio dal Concilio Vaticano II, ed. Pontificia Università Urbaniana, 193-205.

Abbass, J. "Canonical Dispositions for the Care of Eastern Catholics Outside Their Territory." *Periodica* 86 (1997) 321-362.

———. "Canonical Interpretation by Recourse to 'Parallel Passages': A Comparative Study of the Latin and Eastern Codes." *The Jurist* 51 (1991) 293-310.

———. "The Historical Basis for the Unqualified Use of *Apostolic See* in the Oriental Legislation." In *The Code of Canons of the Eastern Churches*, eds. J. Chiramel and K. Bharanikulangara, 230-257.

———. "The Interrelationship of the Latin and Eastern Codes." *The Jurist* 58 (1998) 1-40.

———. "Marriage in the Codes of Canon Law." *Apollinaris* 68 (1995) 521-565.

———. "Transfer to another Religious Institute in the Latin and Eastern Catholic Churches." *Commentarium pro religiosis et missionariis* 79 (1998) 121-151.

———. "Trials in General: A Comparative Study of the Eastern and Latin Codes." *The Jurist* 55 (1995) 834-874.

———. *Two Codes in Comparison*, Kanonika 7. Rome, 1997.

Acebal Luján, J. L., et al. *Código de cánones de las Iglesias orientales*, edición bilingüe comentada, B.A.C. 542. Madrid, 1994.

Al-Ahmar, A., A. Khalife and D. Le Tourneau, eds. *Acta Symposii Internationalis circa Codicem Canonum Ecclesiarum Orientalium, USEK, 24-29 aprilis 1995*. Kaslik, 1996.

Andrés D. J. "Observaciones introductorias al titulo *De Monachis Cœterisque Religiosis* del CCEO." *Apollinaris* 65 (1992) 137-147.

Arrieta, J. I., and G. P. Milan, eds. *Metodo, Fonti e Soggetti del Diritto canonico*, Atti del Convegno Internazionale di Studi, "La Scienza Canonistica nella seconda metà del '900. Fondamenti, metodi, prospettive in D'Avack, Lombardia, Gismondi e Corecco," Roma 13-16 novembre 1996, Pontificia Università della Santa Croce, Università di Roma Tor Vergata, Vatican City, 1999.

Arruty, J. A. F. "La visita ad limina de los obispos de rito latino y de rito oriental." In *Incontro fra canoni d'oriente e d'occidente*, Atti del Congresso internazionale, ed. R. Coppola, 2:229-237.

Baleani, C. "I requisiti di attuabilità dell'istituto giuridico del passaggio: il principio generale e il consenso." *Commentarium pro religiosis et missionariis* 80 (1999) 127-154.

Barral, I., and J. Escrivá Ivars. *Table de concordance entre le Code de 1983 et le Code de 1917*. In *Code de Droit Canonique*, eds. E. Caparros, M. Thériault and J. Thorn, 1387-1406.

Basile, M. *Statut personnel et compétence judiciaire des communautés confessionnelles au Liban*, Excerpta ex dissertatione ad doctoratum, PUL. Rome, 1992.

Benlloch Poueda, A., ed. *Código de Derecho Canónico. Edición bilingüe, fuentes y comentarios de todos los cánones.* Valencia, 1993.

Benz, M. "Nota al c. 111." In *Código de Derecho Canónico. Edición bilingüe, fuentes y comentarios de todos los cánones,* ed. A. Benlloch Poueda, 73.

Bernández Cantón, A. *Compendio de Derecho Matrimonial Canónico.* 7th ed. Madrid, 1991.

Betti, U. *La dottrina sull'episcopato nel capitolo II della costituzione dommatica Lumen Gentium.* Rome, 1968.

Beyer, J. "Commento a un canone. Il primo canone del Codice." *Quaderni di diritto ecclesiale* 6 (1993) 298-306.

———. "De synodo diœcesana." *Periodica* 81 (1992) 381-423.

———. "De vita consecrata in iure utriusque Codicis orientalis et occidentalis." *Periodica* 81 (1992) 283-302.

Bharanikulangara, K., ed. *Il Diritto Canonico Orientale nell'ordinamento ecclesiale,* Studi Giuridici 34. Vatican City, 1995.

———, ed. *Particular Law of the Eastern Catholic Churches.* New York, 1996.

Bianchi, P. "Gli statuti del Consiglio presbiterale." *Quaderni di diritto ecclesiale* 8 (1995) 72-93.

Bianco, L. *Nuovo Dizionario di Diritto Canonico,* eds. C. C. Salvador, V. De Paolis and G. Ghirlanda, s.v. "Conferenza Episcopale Italiana." Cinisello Balsamo, 1993.

Biffi, F., ed. *I diritti fondamentali della Persona Umana e la libertà religiosa.* Atti del V Colloquio Giuridico (8-10 marzo 1984). Rome, 1985.

Borras, A. *Les sanctions dans l'Église.* Paris, 1990.

Borrmans, M. "Osservazioni e suggerimenti a proposito dei matrimoni misti tra parte cattolica e parte musulmana." *Quaderni di diritto ecclesiale* 4 (1992) 321-332.

Brogi, M. "Ammissione di candidati di rito orientale in Istituti religiosi latini." *Antonianum* 54 (1979) 701-732.

———. "I Cattolici orientali nel Codex Iuris Canonici." *Antonianum* 58 (1983) 218-243.

———. "Le Chiese *sui iuris* nel Codex Canonum Ecclesiarum Orientalium." In *Il Diritto Canonico Orientale nell'ordinamento ecclesiale,* Studi Giuridici 34, ed. K. Bharanikulangara, 49-75.

———. "Le Chiese *sui iuris* nel Codex Canonum Ecclesiarum Orientalium." *Revista Española de Derecho Canónico* 48 (1991) 517-544.

———. "Commento agli Statuti dell'Assemblea degli Ordinari cattolici di Terra Santa." *Ius Ecclesiæ* 6 (1994) 836-842.

———. "Cura pastorale di fedeli di altra Chiesa 'sui iuris.'" *Revista Española de Derecho Canónico* 53 (1996) 119-131.

———. "Il diritto all'osservanza del proprio rito (CIC c. 214)." *Antonianum* 68 (1993) 108-119.

———. "Licenza presunta della Santa Sede per il cambiamento di Chiesa 'sui iuris.'" *Revista Española de Derecho Canónico* 50 (1993) 661-668.

———. "La normativa del Codex Canonum Ecclesiarum Orientalium sulla vita consacrata." *Quaderni di diritto ecclesiale* 8 (1995) 127-137.

———. "Il nuovo Codice orientale e la Chiesa latina." *Antonianum* 66 (1991) 35-61.

———. "Sinodi patriarcali, Assemblee e Conferenze Episcopali di rito orientale." *Antonianum* 51 (1976) 256-265.

Bucci, O. "Il Codice di Diritto Canonico Orientale nella storia della Chiesa." In *Miscellanea in onore dei Professori Anastasio Gutierrez e Pietro Tocanel*, ed. Pontificium Institutum Utriusque Iuris Apollinaris, 122-200.

———. "Per la storia del matrimonio cristiano fra eredità giuridica orientale e tradizione romanistica." In *Il matrimonio nel Codice dei Canoni delle Chiese Orientali*, Studi Giuridici 32, eds. U. Navarette and J. Prader, 7-92.

Bux, N. *La liturgia degli orientali.* Bari, 1996.

Calvi, M. "Commenti alle Delibere della CEI: Forma del Battesimo ed età della Cresima." *Quaderni di diritto ecclesiale* 4 (1991) 390-399.

Canosa, J. "La competenza della Penitenzieria Apostolica sulle indulgenze." *Ius Ecclesiæ* 5 (1993) 396-401.

———. "La presunzione della licenza di cui al can. 112 §1, 1° del Codice di Diritto Canonico." *Ius Ecclesiæ* 5 (1993) 613-631.

Caparros, E., M. Thériault and J. Thorn, eds. *Code de Droit Canonique.* Montréal, 1990.

Cappellini, E., ed. *Il matrimonio canonico in Italia.* Brescia, 1984.

———, ed. *La normativa del nuovo Codice.* 2nd ed. Brescia, 1985.

Cappello, F. *De administrativa amotione parochorum.* Rome, 1911.

Caprioli, A. "La celebrazione liturgica del matrimonio." In *Il matrimonio canonico in Italia*, ed. E. Cappellini, 227-249.

Carcione, F. *Le Chiese d'Oriente. Identità, patrimonio e quadro storico generale 1997.* Cinisello Balsamo, 1998.

Ceccarelli-Morolli, D. *Il Codex Canonum Ecclesiarum Orientalium e l'Ecumenismo*, Quaderni di "Oriente Cristiano," Studi 9. Palermo, 1998.

———. "I matrimoni misti alla luce dei *Sacri Canones* del primo millennio." *Nicolaus* 22 (1995) 137-143.

Celeghin A. "L'iniziazione cristiana nel CIC 1983. Prima parte: alcuni aspetti generali." *Periodica* 84 (1995) 31-75.

_____. "L'iniziazione cristiana nel CIC 1983. Seconda parte: alcune questioni particolari." *Periodica* 84 (1995) 267-314.

Cereti, G. *Per un'ecclesiologia ecumenica.* Bologna, 1996.

Che Chen-Tao, V. "Aspetti giuridici della visita 'ad limina.'" In *Ius in vita et in missione Ecclesiæ*, ed. Pontificium Consilium de Legum Textibus Interpretandis, 325-336.

Chiappetta, L. *Il Codice di Diritto Canonico. Commento giuridico-pastorale.* 2nd ed. Rome, 1996.

_____. *Dizionario del nuovo Codice di Diritto Canonico.* Naples, 1986.

_____. *Il matrimonio nella nuova legislazione canonica e concordataria.* Rome, 1990.

_____. *Prontuario di Diritto Canonico e Concordatario.* Rome, 1994.

Chiramel, J. "Hierarchical Structuring in the Oriental Legislation." In *The Code of Canons of the Eastern Churches*, eds. J. Chiramel and K. Bharanikulangara, 91-107.

Chiramel, J., and K. Bharanikulangara, eds. *The Code of Canons of the Eastern Churches.* Alwaye, 1992.

Cholij, R. "Celibacy, Married Clergy, and the Oriental Code." In *Acta Symposii Internationalis circa Codicem Canonum Ecclesiarum Orientalium, USEK, 24-29 aprilis 1995*, eds. A. Al-Ahmar, A. Khalife, and D. Le Tourneau, 179-202.

_____. "An Eastern Catholic Married Clergy in North America: Recent Changes in Legal Status and Ecclesiological Perspective." *Studia Canonica* 31 (1997) 331-339.

"Chronique des Églises: Hongrie." *Irénikon* 70 (1997) 287-292.

Cicognani, H., and D. Staffa. *Commentarium in I libr. CIC.* Rome, 1939.

Ciprotti, P. *Lezioni di diritto canonico. Parte generale.* Padua, 1943.

Cito, D. "La remissione della pena canonica." In *Le sanzioni nella Chiesa*, XXIII Incontro Studio Abbazia di Maguzzano - Lonato (Brescia) 1 luglio-5 luglio 1996, ed. Gruppo Italiano Docenti di Diritto Canonico, 113-132.

Congar, Y. *Diversités et communion*, Cogitatio Fidei 112. Paris, 1982.

_____. *Église et papauté*, Cogitatio Fidei 184. Paris, 1994.

Congregazione per le Chiese Orientali, ed. *Ius Ecclesiarum vehiculum caritatis.* Vatican City, 2004

Coppola, R. "Carattere della pena nel 'Codex Iuris Canonici' e nel 'Codex Canonum Ecclesiarum Orientalium.'" In *Ius in vita et in missione Ecclesiæ*, ed. Pontificium Consilium de Legum Textibus Interpretandis. Vatican City, 1994.

_____, ed. *Incontro fra canoni d'oriente e d'occidente*, Atti del Congresso internazionale. 3 vols. Bari, 1994.

Corecco, E. "Il Catalogo dei doveri-diritti nel CIC." In *I diritti fondamentali della Persona Umana e la libertà religiosa*, Atti del V Colloquio Giuridico (8-10 marzo 1984), ed. F. Biffi, 101-125.

Corecco, E., and L. Gerosa. *Il diritto della Chiesa*, Amateca 12. Milan, 1995.

Coussa, A. *Epitome Prælectionum. De Iure Ecclesiastico Orientale. III. De Matrimonio.* Rome, 1950.

Dalmais, H. I. "Signification de la diversité des rites au regard de l'unité chrétienne." *Istina* 7 (1960) 311-318.

De Bernardis, L. M. "Un caso di osmosi fra diritto canonico latino e orientale: il matrimonio segreto." *Ius Ecclesiæ* 4 (1992) 629-636.

_____. "Possibilità e limiti dell'osmosi fra CIC e CCEO." In *Ius in vita et in missione Ecclesiæ*, ed. Pontificium Consilium de Legum Textibus Interpretandis, 785-790.

De Clercq, C. "De ritu et adscriptione ritui apud Orientales Catholicos." *Ephemerides Liturgicæ* 46 (1932) 473-480.

_____. "Decretum. Ordinariatus pro fidelibus ritus orientalis in Argentina erigitur. Adnotationes." *Apollinaris* 35 (1962) 24.

Denzinger, H. *Ritus Orientalium*. Wurzburg, 1863.

De Paolis, V. "Liturgia e denaro. Indicazioni del 'Codice di diritto canonico' e del 'Codice dei canoni delle Chiese orientali.'" *Rivista liturgica* 84 (1997) 245-260.

_____. "I matrimoni misti." In *Matrimonio e disciplina ecclesiastica*, XXI Incontro Studio Passo della Mendola - Trento 4 luglio-8 luglio 1994, ed. Gruppo Italiano Docenti di Diritto Canonico, 142-149.

De Pinho Ferreira, M. "A Confirmação nas legislações da Igreja Latina e das Igrejas Orientais." *Forum Canonicum* 5 (1995) 3-17.

De Vries, G. *Oriente cristiano ieri e oggi*. Rome, 1949.

_____. "La S. Sede ed i patriarcati cattolici d'Oriente." *Orientalia Christiana Periodica* 27 (1961) 313-361.

Di Mattia, G. "I Consigli presbiterali: qualificazione e collocazione ecclesiologico-giuridica." In *Ius in vita et in missione Ecclesiæ*, ed. Pontificium Consilium de Legum Textibus Interpretandis, 407-426.

_____. "La normativa di diritto penale nel Codex iuris Canonici e nel Codex canonum Ecclesiarum Orientalium." In *Incontro fra canoni d'oriente e d'occidente*, Atti del Congresso internazionale, ed. R. Coppola, 2:511-534.

Donghi, A., ed. *I Prænotanda dei nuovi testi liturgici*. Milan, 1989.

D'Ostilio, F. *Prontuario del Codice di Diritto Canonico*. 2nd ed. Vatican City, 1996.

Edelby, N. "Les mariages mixtes." *Le lien* 59 (1994/5-6) 34-37.

_____. "Les mariages mixtes: les legislations, ancienne et moderne, des Églises orientales." In *Acta Symposii Internationalis circa Codicem Canonum Ecclesiarum Orientalium, USEK, 24-29 aprilis 1995*, eds. A. Al-Ahmar, A. Khalife and D. Le Tourneau, 515-520.

Edelby, N., and I. Dick. *Les Églises Orientales Catholiques. Décret Orientalium Ecclesiarum*, Unam Sanctam 76. Paris, 1970.

Editorial. *Irénikon* 63 (1990) 449-450.

Eid, E. "Authority and Autonomy (critical report in francese)." In *Incontro fra canoni d'oriente e d'occidente*, Atti del Congresso internazionale, ed. R. Coppola, 1:428-447.

_____. "La celebrazione del matrimonio dei Maroniti fuori del territorio del patriarcato prima del Motu Proprio 'Crebræ Allatæ.'" In *Dilexit Iustitiam. Studia in honorem Aurelii card. Sabattani*, Studi Giuridici 5, eds. Z. Grocholewski and V. Carcel Orti, 63-75.

_____. "La révision du Code de droit canonique oriental: histoire et principes." *L'Année Canonique* 33 (1990) 11-27.

_____. "Rite – Église de droit propre – Juridiction." *L'Année Canonique* 40 (1998) 7-18.

Erdö, P. "I matrimoni misti nella loro evoluzione storica (La disparità di culto)." In *I matrimoni misti*, Studi Giuridici 47, ed. C. Gullo, 11-22.

_____. "La participation des Évêques orientaux à la Conférence épiscopale." *Apollinaris* 64 (1991) 295-308.

_____. "Questioni interrituali del diritto dei sacramenti (Battesimo e Cresima)." *Periodica* 84 (1995) 315-353.

_____. "Questioni interrituali (interecclesiali) del diritto dei sacramenti (Battesimo e Cresima)." *Folia Canonica* 1 (1998) 9-35.

Esposito, B., ed. *Attuali problemi di interpretazione del Codice di Diritto Canonico*, Atti del Simposio Internazionale in occasione del I Centenario della Facoltà di Diritto Canonico della PUST (Roma, 24-26 ottobre 1996). Rome, 1997.

Fagiolo, V. "Le conferenze dei Superiori maggiori nel dibattito conciliare." *Informationes SCRIS* 14 (1988/I) 35-48.

Faltin, D. "Adnotationes ad Constitutiones Apostolicas de Exarchatibus Orientalibus." *Apollinaris* 34 (1961) 278-279.

Faris, J. "Canonical Issues in the Pastoral Care of Eastern Catholics." *CLSA Proceedings* 53 (1991) 154-164.

_____. *Eastern Catholic Churches, Constitution and Governance, According to the Code of Canons of the Eastern Churches*. New York, 1992.

_____. "La storia della codificazione orientale." In *Il Diritto Canonico Orientale nell'ordinamento ecclesiale*, Studi Giuridici 34, ed. K. Bharanikulangara, 255-268.

Fedele, P. "L'equità nel diritto penale canonico. Il matrimonio condizionato." In *Incontro fra canoni d'oriente e d'occidente*, Atti del Congresso internazionale, ed. R. Coppola, 2:51-54.

Fornés, J. "La forma en el matrimonio de un católico con un no católico." *Ius Canonicum* 37 (1997) 13-31.

Fürst, C. G. *Canones Synopse zum Codex Iuris Canonici und Codex Canonum Ecclesiarum Orientalium*. Freiburg-Basel-Wien, 1992.

_____. "Interdipendenza del diritto canonico latino ed orientale." In *Il Diritto Canonico Orientale nell'ordinamento ecclesiale*, Studi Giuridici 34, ed. K. Bharanikulangara, 13-33.

Gaeta, S. "Cronologia della CEI (1952-1996)." *Communio* 149 (1996) 85-94.

Gallaro, G. D. "Marriage in the Eastern Code." *The Priest* 1993, 41-47.

García Hervás, D. "La significación para la Iglesia del nuevo Código Oriental." In *Incontro fra canoni d'oriente e d'occidente*, Atti del Congresso internazionale, ed. R. Coppola, 2:41-47.

García Martín, J. *Le norme generali del Codex Iuris Canonici*. Rome, 1996.

Gasparri, P. *Tractatus canonicus de matrimonio*. Rome, 1932.

Gauthier, A. *Principi generali dell'attività giuridica nella Chiesa (Commentario dei canoni 96-203 del Libro I del Codice di Diritto Canonico)*. Rome, 1993.

Gefaell, P. "Il matrimonio condizionato durante la codificazione pio-benedettina fonte del c. 826 CCEO." *Ius Ecclesiæ* 7 (1995) 581-625.

_____. "Nota ai documenti della Conferenza Episcopale Spagnola 'Orientaciones para la atención pastoral de los católicos orientales en España (17-21 de noviembre de 2003)' e 'Servicios pastorales a orientales no católicos. Orientaciones (27-31 de marzo de 2006).'" *Ius Ecclesiæ* 18 (2006) 861-876.

_____. "Rapporti tra i due 'Codici' dell'unico 'Corpus iuris canonici.'" In *Metodo, Fonti e Soggetti del Diritto canonico*, Atti del Convegno Internazionale di Studi, "La Scienza Canonistica nella seconda metà del '900. Fondamenti, metodi, prospettive in D'Avack, Lombardia, Gismondi e Corecco," Roma 13-16 novembre 1996, Pontificia Università della Santa Croce, Università di Roma Tor Vergata, eds. J. I. Arrieta and G. P. Milan, 654-669.

Gelsi, D. *Nuovo Dizionario di Liturgia*, eds. D. Sartore and A. M. Triacca, s.v. "Orientali, Liturgie." Cinisello Balsamo, 1988.

Gherro, S., ed. *Studi sul Codex Canonum Ecclesiarum Orientalium*. Padua, 1994.

Ghirlanda, G. *Il diritto nella Chiesa mistero di comunione*. 2nd ed. Rome-Cinisello Balsamo, 1993.

_____. *Nuovo Dizionario di Diritto Canonico*, eds. C. C. Salvador, V. De Paolis and G. Ghirlanda, s.v. "Conferenza dei Vescovi." Cinisello Balsamo, 1993.

Gianesin, B. *Matrimoni misti*. Bologna, 1991.

Green, T. J. "Penal Law in the *Code of Canon Law* and in the *Code of Canons of the Eastern Churches*: Some Comparative Reflections." *Studia Canonica* 28 (1994) 407-451.

_____. "Reflections on the Eastern Code Revision Process." *The Jurist* 51 (1991) 18-37.

_____. "The Teaching Function of the Church: A Comparison of Selected Canons in the Latin and Eastern Codes." *The Jurist* 55 (1995) 93-140.

Grocholewski, Z. "I matrimoni misti." In *Il matrimonio canonico fra tradizione e rinnovamento*, 2nd ed., ed. A. Longhitano et al., 237-256.

Grocholewski, Z., and V. Carcel Orti, eds. *Dilexit Iustitiam. Studia in honorem Aurelii card. Sabattani*, Studi Giuridici 5. Vatican City, 1984.

Gruppo Italiano Docenti di Diritto Canonico, ed. *Il diritto nel mistero della Chiesa*. 2nd ed. 2 vol. Rome, 1990.

_____, ed. *La funzione di santificare della Chiesa*, XX Incontro di Studio Passo della Mendola - Trento 5 luglio-9 luglio 1993. Milan, 1995.

_____, ed. *Matrimonio e disciplina ecclesiastica*, XXI Incontro Studio Passo della Mendola - Trento 4 luglio-8 luglio 1994. Milan, 1996.

_____, ed. *Le sanzioni nella Chiesa*, XXIII Incontro Studio Abbazia di Maguzzano - Lonato (Brescia) 1 luglio-5 luglio 1996. Milan, 1997.

Guillemette, F. *Théologie des conférences épiscopales. Une herméneutique de Vatican II*, Collection Brèches théologiques 21. Montréal-Paris, 1994.

Gullo, C., ed. *I matrimoni misti*, Studi Giuridici 47. Vatican City, 1998.

Halligan, N. "Some Inter-Ritual Norms." *The Jurist* 42 (1982) 164-169.

Herman, A. "De Ritu in Iure Canonico." *Orientalia Christiana* 32 (1933) 96-158.

_____. "Decretum. Ordinariatus pro omnibus christifidelibus ritus orientalis in Gallia degentibus instituitur. Adnotationes." *Monitor Ecclesiasticus* 81 (1956) 27-30.

Hervada, J. "Significado actual del principio de territorialidad." *Fidelium Iura* 2 (1992) 221-239.

Hoffman, H. L. *De Benedicti XIV latinizationibus.* 2nd ed. Rome, 1958.

Jiménez Urresti, T. I. "Nota al c. 32." In J. L. Acebal Luján et al., *Código de cánones de las Iglesias orientales,* edición bilingüe comentada, B.A.C. 542, 37.

Jombart, E. "Des délits et des peines." In *Traité de droit canonique,* IV, 2nd ed., ed. R. Naz, 581-807.

Kochakian, G., and J. Meno. "Oriental Orthodox Guidelines for Marriages with Roman Catholics." In *Oriental-Orthodox Roman Catholic Interchurch Marriages and other Pastoral Relationships,* ed. National Conference of Catholic Bishops – Standing Conference of Oriental Orthodox Churches, 10-25.

Kowalczyk, J. *De extraordinario confirmationis ministro. Comparatio inter disciplinam Ecclesiæ latinæ et Ecclesiarum orientalium.* Rome, 1969.

Labandeira, E. *Trattato di Diritto Amministrativo Canonico.* Milan, 1994.

Lanne, E. "Les Catholiques orientaux: liberté religieuse et Oecuménisme." *Irénikon* 63 (1990) 20-46.

———. "L'Oriente cristiano nella prospettiva del Vaticano II." In *Orientalium Dignitas,* Atti del Simposio commemorativo della ricorrenza centenaria della Lettera Apostolica di papa Leone XIII, 2-4 November 1994, ed. L. Orosz, 131-145.

Lefebre, C. "De orientalis codificationis auctoritate ad CIC interpretationem." *Apollinaris* 32 (1959) 87-104.

Le Tourneau, D. "Le soin pastoral des catholiques orientaux en dehors de leur Église de rite propre. Le cas de l'Ordinariat français." *Ius Ecclesiæ* 13 (2001) 391-419.

Loda, N. "Il Titolo XII del *CCEO* (C. 410-572). Prospetto tavolare di comparazione ed evoluzione normativa." *Commentarium pro religiosis et missionariis* 79 (1998) 73-94.

Longhitano A., et al. eds. *Il matrimonio canonico fra tradizione e rinnovamento.* 2nd ed. Bologna, 1991

Lorusso, L. "Alcuni aspetti circa la dottrina sulla Chiesa utili al dialogo ecumenico." *O Odigos* 26 (2007/3) 22-28.

———. "L'ambito d'applicazione del Codice dei canoni delle Chiese Orientali. Commento sistematico al can. 1 del CCEO." *Angelicum* 82 (2005) 451-478.

———. *Il culto divino nel Codex Canonum Ecclesiarum Orientalium,* Analecta Nicolaiana 5. Bari, 2008.

———. "La designazione dei Vescovi nel CCEO." *Quaderni di diritto ecclesiale* 12 (1999) 46-57.

———. "I matrimoni misti tra cattolici e valdesi in Italia. Testo comune e testo applicativo." *O Odigos* 21 (2002/3) 3-9.

———. "Le pene nei singoli delitti." *O Odigos* 19 (2000/unico) 23-28.

———. "Servizio pastorale agli orientali cattolici in Spagna." *Angelicum* 84 (2007) 423-436.

Lynch, J. E. "The Eastern Churches: Historical Background." *The Jurist* 51 (1991) 1-17.

Mailleux, R. G. "Domicile légal et domicile des religieux dans l'histoire de la doctrine canonique." *Antonianum* 66 (1991) 62-139.

Manna, S. *Chiesa latina e Chiese orientali all'epoca del Patriarca Giuseppe Valerga (1813-72)*, Excerpta e dissertatione ad Lauream. Naples, 1972.

Manna, S., and G. Distante. *Orientalium Ecclesiarum - Decreto sulle Chiese Orientali cattoliche*. Casale Monferrato, 1986.

Marchesi, M. "Il Consiglio presbiterale: gruppo di sacerdoti, rappresentante di un presbiterio." *Quaderni di diritto ecclesiale* 8 (1995) 61-71.

Marcuzzi, P. G. "Il Consiglio pastorale parrocchiale." In *Ius in vita et in missione Ecclesiæ*, ed. Pontificium Consilium de Legum Textibus Interpretandis, 437-464.

Marini, F. "The Adjudication of Interritual Marriage Cases in the Tribunal." *Folia Canonica* 2 (1999) 231-266.

Martín De Agar, J. T. *Elementi di Diritto Canonico*. Rome, 1996.

_____. *Legislazione delle Conferenze Episcopali complementare al CIC*. Milan, 1990.

Martinez de Alegria, I. *La forma extraordinaria del matrimonio canonico. Origen historico y regimen vigente*. Madrid, 1994.

Marzoa, A., et al., eds. *Comentario exegético al Código de Derecho Canónico*. 5 vol. Pamplona, 1996.

Matamoro, L. G. "La forma canónica de la celebración del matrimonio en el código de 1983." *Ciencia Tomista* 122 (1995) 367-401.

Mazzoni, G. "Le norme generali." In *La normativa del nuovo Codice*, 2nd ed., ed. E. Cappellini, 27-66.

McDermott, R. M. "Two Approaches to Consecrated Life: The *Code of Canons of the Eastern Churches* and the *Code of Canon Law*." *Studia Canonica* 29 (1995) 193-239.

McManus, F. "The Code of Canons of the Eastern Catholic Churches." *The Jurist* 53 (1993) 22-61.

_____. "The Possibility of New Rites in the Church." *The Jurist* 50 (1990) 435-458.

Metz, R. "La désignation des évêques dans le droit actuel: étude comparative entre le Code latin de 1983 et le Code oriental de 1990." *Studia Canonica* 27 (1993) 321-334.

_____. "Le nouveau code de droit canonique des Église orientales catholique." *Revue de droit canonique* 42 (1992) 99-117.

_____. *Le nouveau droit des Églises orientales catholiques*. Paris, 1997.

_____. "Quel est le droit pour les Églises orientales unies à Rome?" *L'Année Canonique* 30 (1987) 393-409.

Michiels, G. *De delictis et pœnis*, III, *De pœnis in specie. Canones 2314-2414*. Paris-Tournai-Rome-New York, 1961.

Miele, M. "I Patriarchi orientali nel collegio cardinalizio." In *Incontro fra canoni d'oriente e d'occidente*, Atti del Congresso internazionale, ed. R. Coppola, 2:253-271.

Milone, B. *I Matrimoni Misti e la Morale Matrimoniale con speciale riferimento all'America del Nord*. Turin, 1996.

Miñambres, J. "Il governo della Chiesa durante la vacanza della Sede Romana e l'elezione del Romano Pontefice." *Ius Ecclesiæ* 8 (1996) 713-729.

Mistò, L. "Il libro IV: la funzione di santificare della Chiesa." *La Scuola Cattolica* 112 (1984) 297-307.

Montini, G. P. "Le Conferenze episcopali e i Sinodi delle Chiese orientali." *Quaderni di diritto ecclesiale* 9 (1996) 433-448.

_____. "Il diritto canonico dalla A alla Z." *Quaderni di diritto ecclesiale* 10 (1997) 456-477.

Mogavero, D. "I ministri sacri o chierici." In *Il diritto nel mistero della Chiesa*, 2nd ed., ed. Gruppo Italiano Docenti di Diritto Canonico, 2:75-141.

Mörsdorf, K. "L'autonomia della Chiesa locale." In *Atti del congresso internazionale di Diritto Canonico: la Chiesa dopo il Concilio*, ed. Università di Roma, 1:163-185.

National Conference of Catholic Bishops – Standing Conference of Oriental Orthodox Churches. *Oriental-Orthodox Roman Catholic Interchurch Marriages and other Pastoral Relationships*. Washington, 1995

Navarrete, U. "Competentia Ecclesiæ in matrimonium baptizatorum eiusque limites." *Periodica* 67 (1978) 95-115.

_____. "De ministro sacramenti matrimonii in Ecclesia latina et in Ecclesiis Orientalibus: Tentamen explicationis concordantis." *Periodica* 84 (1995) 711-733.

_____. "Differenze essenziali nella legislazione matrimoniale del Codice latino e del Codice orientale." In *Acta Symposii Internationalis circa Codicem Canonum Ecclesiarum Orientalium, USEK, 24-29 aprilis 1995*, eds. A. Al-Ahmar, A. Khalife, and D. Le Tourneau, 273-304.

_____. *Indicazioni metodologiche per gli studenti di Diritto Canonico*. Rome, 1996.

_____. "Ius matrimoniale latinum et orientale. Collatio Codicem latinum inter et orientalem." *Periodica* 80 (1991) 609-639.

_____. "Il matrimonio in oriente e in occidente." *Orientalia Christiana Periodica* 58 (1992) 563-569.

_____. "Questioni sulla forma canonica ordinaria nei Codici latino e orientale." *Periodica* 85 (1996) 489-514.

Navarette, U., and J. Prader, eds. *Il matrimonio nel Codice dei Canoni delle Chiese Orientali*, Studi Giuridici 32. Vatican City, 1994.

Navarro Marfá, L. *Table de concordance entre le Code de 1917 et le Code de 1983*. In *Code de Droit Canonique*, eds. E. Caparros, M. Thériault and J. Thorn, 1357-1385.

Naz, R., ed. *Traité de droit canonique*. 2nd ed. 4 Vol. Paris, 1954.

Nedungatt, G. *A Companion to the Eastern Code*, Kanonika 5. Rome, 1994.

_____, ed. *A Guide to the Eastern Code: A Commentary on the Code of Canons of the Eastern Churches*, Kanonika 10. Rome, 2002.

_____. "Normæ indolis iuridicæ ad tenorem c. 1492 CCEO applicandæ." *Periodica* 86 (1997) 477-491.

_____. "Presentazione del CCEO." EV 12:889-894.

_____. *The Spirit of the Eastern Code*. Rome-Bangalore, 1993.

Neunheuser, B., et al. *Concelebrazione, dottrina e pastorale*. Brescia, 1965.

Ochoa, X. *Index verborum ac locutionum Codicis Iuris Canonici*. Rome, 1983.

Okulik, L. *La condición jurídica del fiel cristiano. Contribución al estudio comparado del Codex Iuris Canonici y del Codex Canonum Ecclesiarum Orientalium*. Buenos Aires, 1995.

Orosz, L. *Orientalium Dignitas*, Atti del Simposio commemorativo della ricorrenza centenaria della Lettera Apostolica di papa Leo XIII, 2-4 November 1994. Nyíregyháza, 1995.

Örsy, L. "Interpretation in View of Action: A Quest for Clarity and Simplicity (Canon 96)." *The Jurist* 52 (1992) 587-597.

_____. *Marriage in Canon Law. Texts and Comments; Reflections and Questions*. Minnesota, 1990.

Otaduy, J. "Comentario al canon 19." In *Comentario exegético al Código de Derecho Canónico*, eds. A. Marzoa et al., 1:382-384.

_____. "Los medios interpretativos de la ley canónica y su relación con las distintas doctrinas de la interpretación." *Ius Canonicum* 35 (1995) 447-500.

Parlato, V. "Ecumenismo e diritto canonico." *Ius Canonicum* 9 (1969) 263-280.

Passicos, J. "L'Ordinariat des catholiques de rite oriental résidant en France." *L'Année Canonique* 40 (1998) 151-163.

Pedone, F. S., and J. I. Donlon, eds. *Roman Replies and CLSA Advisory Opinions 2000*. Washington, 2000.

Pellegrino, P. *Gli impedimenti relativi alla dignità dell'uomo nel matrimonio canonico*. Turin, 2000.

Petrani, A. "An adsit ritus præstantior." *Apollinaris* 6 (1933) 74-82.

_____. *De relatione iuridica inter diversos ritus in Ecclesia catholica*. Turin-Rome, 1930.

Philips, G. *La Chiesa e il suo mistero*. Milan, 1989.

Pinto, P. V., ed. *Commento al Codice dei Canoni delle Chiese Orientali*, Studium Romanæ Rotæ: Corpus Iuris Canonici II. Vatican City, 2001.

_____. *Commento al Codice di diritto canonico*, Studia Urbaniana 21. 1st ed. Rome, 1985; 2nd ed. Studium Romanæ Rotæ: Corpus Iuris Canonici I. Vatican City, 2001.

Pontificia Università S. Tommaso d'Aquino. *Questioni canoniche*, Studia Universitatis S. Thomæ in Urbe 22. Milan, 1984.

Pontificia Università Urbaniana, ed. *Portare Cristo all'Uomo*, Atti del Congresso del Ventennio dal Concilio Vaticano II. Rome, 1985.

Pontificium Consilium de Legum Textibus Interpretandis, ed. *Ius in vita et in missione Ecclesiæ*. Vatican City, 1994.

Pontificium Institutum Utriusque Iuris Apollinaris, ed. *Miscellanea in onore dei Professori Anastasio Gutierrez e Pietro Tocanel*. Rome, 1982.

Pospishil, V. J. *Eastern Catholic Church Law*. 2nd ed. New York, 1996.

_____. *Eastern Catholic Marriage Law*. Brooklyn, 1991.

Prader, J. "Aspetti specifici nel Codice orientale rispetto al Codice latino in materia matrimoniale." In *Matrimonio e disciplina ecclesiastica*, XXI Incontro Studio Passo della Mendola - Trento 4 luglio-8 luglio 1994, ed. Gruppo Italiano Docenti di Diritto Canonico, 31-50.

_____. "Il consenso matrimoniale condizionato." In *Il matrimonio nel Codice dei Canoni delle Chiese Orientali*, Studi Giuridici 32, eds. U. Navarette and J. Prader, 271-282.

_____. *La legislazione matrimoniale latina e orientale*. Rome. 1993.

_____. *Il matrimonio in Oriente e Occidente*, Kanonika 1. 1st. ed. Rome, 1992; 2nd ed. Rome, 2003.

Pujol, C. "Condicio fidelis orientalis ritus extra suum territorium." *Periodica* 73 (1984) 489-504.

_____. "Regimen domus orientalis ritus in religione latina." *Periodica* 50 (1961) 137-159.

_____. "O recente Código das Igrejas de rito oriental." *Brotéria* 135 (1992) 178-200.

_____. *I santi sacramenti nel Codice dei Canoni delle Chiese Orientali*, dispense ad uso dei studenti. Rome, no date.

_____. *La vita religiosa orientale. Commento al Codice di Diritto Canonico Orientale (canoni 410-572)*. Rome, 1994.

Putrino, G. "Il consenso matrimoniale condizionato." In *Matrimonio e disciplina ecclesiastica*, XXI Incontro Studio Passo della Mendola - Trento 4 luglio-8 luglio 1994, ed. Gruppo Italiano Docenti di Diritto Canonico, 101-113.

Rachford, N. R. A. "Norms of Particular Law for the Byzantine Metroplitan Church *sui iuris* of Pittsburgh, USA." *CLSA Proceedings* 62 (2000) 233-243.

_____. "Two Lungs, two Ventricles: the Eastern Canons as Suppletory Law." *CLSA Proceedings* 56 (1994) 153-170.

Raes, A. *Introductio in liturgiam orientalem*. Rome, 1947.

Redaelli, C. "Il vescovo di fronte alle associazioni." *Quaderni di diritto ecclesiale* 8 (1995) 349-371.

"Règlement intérieur du Conseil des Patriarches catholiques d'Orient." *Le lien* 61 (1996/2) 44-48.

Řezáč, I. *Institutiones Iuris Canonici Orientalis*. Rome, 1958.

Ricciardi A. "La CEI nel postconcilio." *Communio* 149 (1996) 15-29.

Rivella, M. "Commento a un canone. Il rapporto fra Codice di diritto canonico e diritto liturgico (can. 2)." *Quaderni di diritto ecclesiale* 8 (1995) 193-200.

———. "Le funzioni del Consiglio presbiterale." *Quaderni di diritto ecclesiale* 8 (1995) 48-60.

Rizzi, M. "Decretum. Ordinariatus pro omnibus christifidelibus ritus orientalis in Gallia degentibus instituitur. Adnotationes." *Apollinaris* 28 (1955) 211-216.

Rohban, L. "Codification du droit canonique oriental." *Apollinaris* 65 (1992) 241-251.

Sabbarese, L. "Cultura, lingua e rito: aspetti canonici." *Euntes Docete* 56 (2003) 91-116.

———. *Girovaghi, migranti, forestieri e naviganti nella legislazione ecclesiastica*. Vatican City, 2006.

Saïd, E. *Les Églises orientales et leurs droits, hier, aujourd'hui... demain.* Paris 1989.

Salachas, D. "L'appartenenza giuridica dei fedeli a una Chiesa orientale 'sui iuris' o alla Chiesa latina." *Periodica* 83 (1994) 19-55.

———. "Autocephalie ou autonomie des Églises orthodoxes et status 'sui iuris' des Églises orientales catholiques." In *Incontro fra canoni d'oriente e d'occidente*, Atti del Congresso internazionale, ed. R. Coppola, 1:372-380.

———. "Il concetto ecclesiologico e canonico di 'Chiese orientali' (*Ecclesia sui iuris*)." *Oriente Cristiano* nn. 1-2 (1990) 45-53.

———. *Il dialogo teologico ufficiale tra la chiesa cattolico-romana e la chiesa ortodossa.* Bari, 1994.

———. *Il Diritto Canonico delle Chiese orientali nel primo millennio.* Rome-Bologna 1997.

———. "The Ecumenical significance of the New Code." in *The Code of Canons of the Eastern Churches*, ed. J. Chiramel and K. Bharanikulangara, 258-275.

———. *L'iniziazione cristiana nei Codici orientale e latino.* Rome-Bologna, 1991.

———. "L'istituzione ecclesiale dell'assemblea eparchiale' nel diritto delle Chiese orientali." *Apollinaris* 61 (1988) 861-877.

———. *Istituzioni di diritto canonico delle Chiese cattoliche orientali.* Rome-Bologna, 1993.

———. *Il magistero e l'evangelizzazione dei popoli nei codici latino e orientale.* Bologna, 2001.

———. "I matrimoni misti nel Codice latino e in quello delle Chiese Orientali Cattoliche." In *I Matrimoni misti*, Studi Giuridici 47, ed. C. Gullo, 57-91.

———. "Il nuovo Codice dei Canoni delle Chiese Orientali. Prospettive ecumeniche e limiti." *Euntes Docete* 49 (1996) 229-265.

———. "Le prescrizioni liturgiche del '*Codice dei Canoni delle Chiese Orientali*' alla luce dell'Istruzione della Congregazione per le Chiese Orientali (6 gennaio 1996)." *Ecclesia Orans* 15 (1998) 239-273.

———. "Principi di interpretazione del Codex Canonum Ecclesiarum Orientalium." In *Attuali problemi di interpretazione del Codice di Diritto Canonico*, Atti del Simposio Internazionale in occasione del I Centenario della Facoltà di Diritto Canonico della PUST (Roma, 24-26 ottobre 1996), ed. B. Esposito, 245-268.

———. "Problematiche interrituali nei due Codici orientale e latino." *Apollinaris* 67 (1994) 635-690.

———. "Il 'Ritus Sacer' nella forma canonica di celebrazione del sacramento del matrimonio secondo la tradizione delle Chiese orientali." *Euntes Docete* 47 (1994) 15-40.

———. *Il sacramento del matrimonio nel Nuovo Diritto Canonico delle Chiese orientali*. Rome-Bologna, 1994.

———. "Lo stato giuridico delle minoranze di fedeli cattolici orientali nei territori della Chiesa latina." Seminario di storia delle istituzioni religiose e relazioni tra Stato e Chiesa, Università degli Studi di Firenze, Facoltà di Scienze Politiche "C. Alfieri." Reprint series No. 23. Florence, 1997.

———. "Le status d'autonomie des Églises catholiques orientales et leur communion avec le Siège Apostolique de Rome." *L'Année Canonique* 38 (1996) 75-90.

———. "Le 'status' ecclésiologique et canonique des Églises catholique orientales '*sui iuris*' et des Églises orthodoxes autocéphales." *L'Année Canonique* 33 (1990) 29-56.

———. "Lo 'status *sui iuris*' delle Chiese patriarcali nel diritto canonico orientale." *Periodica* 83 (1994) 569-609.

———. "Teologia e nomotecnica del 'Codex Canonum Ecclesiarum Orientalium.'" *Periodica* 82 (1993) 317-338; 511-528.

Salachas, D., and K. Nitkiewicz. *Rapporti interecclesiali tra cattolici orientali e latini*. Rome, 2007.

Salachas, D., and L. Sabbarese. *Chierici e ministero sacro nel Codice latino e orientale. Prospettive interecclesiali*. Vatican City, 2004.

Sarzi Sartori, G. "Presbiterio e Consiglio presbiterale nelle fonti conciliari della disciplina canonica." *Quaderni di diritto ecclesiale* 8 (1995) 6-47.

Silvestrini, A. "Assemblea Speciale per l'America del Sinodo dei Vescovi," XVI Congregazione Generale. *L'Osservatore Romano*, 29 November 1997, 4.

———. "Le Chiese d'Oriente: attualità e prospettive." *O Odigos* 13 (1994) 2-5, 16.

Sleman, É. "De 'Ritus' à 'Ecclesia sui iuris' dans le Code des Canons des Églises Orientales." *L'Année Canonique* 41 (1999) 253-276.

Sollazzo, F. "I Patriarchi nel diritto canonico orientale e occidentale." In *Incontro fra canoni d'oriente e d'occidente*, Atti del Congresso internazionale, ed. R. Coppola, 2:239-252.

Soullard, R. "Les unions des Supérieurs majeurs." *L'Année Canonique* 18 (1974) 221-230.

Spinelli, L. "L'incidenza della comunione gerarchica nell'esercizio della potestà di giurisdizione dei vescovi ortodossi." In *Incontro fra canoni d'oriente e d'occidente*, Atti del Congresso internazionale, ed. R. Coppola, 2:183-191.

Szabó, P. "La competenza del Vescovo eparchiale per la sanazione in radice del matrimonio." *Folia Canonica* 1 (1998) 151-161.

———. "Diritto particolare e coordinazione interordinamentale. Osservazioni alla luce di un caso concreto." *Folia Canonica* 10 (2007) 167-178.

———. "I libri liturgici orientali e la Sede Apostolica. Sviluppo della prassi e dello stato attuale." *Folia Canonica* 7 (2004) 261-278.

———. "Opinioni sulla natura delle Chiese '*sui iuris*' nella canonistica odierna." *Folia Canonica* 7 (1996) 235-247.

Tafaro, S. "Persona: origini e prospettive. Oltre l'antropocentrismo." In *Incontro fra canoni d'oriente e d'occidente*, Atti del Congresso internazionale, ed. R. Coppola, 2:583-613.

Terzian, M. *L'Institut Patriarcal de Bzommar*, Collection Bzommarienne n. 1. Bzommar, 1983.

Theriault, M. "Canonical Questions Brought about by the Presence of Eastern Catholics in Latin Areas in the Light of the 'Codex Canonum Ecclesiarum Orientalium.'" *Ius Ecclesiæ* 3 (1991) 201-232.

Tocanel, P. "Constitutio Apostolica. In natione germanica Exarchia constituitur pro fidelibus ruthenis byzantini ritus ibidem commorantibus. Adnotationes." *Apollinaris* 34 (1961) 15-16.

Triacca, A. M. *Nuovo Dizionario di Liturgia*, eds. D. Sartore and A. M. Triacca, s.v. "Ambrosiana, Liturgia." Cinisello Balsamo, 1988.

———. "Tradiciones sacramentarias Occidental y Oriental: originalidad y reciprocidad." *Phase* (1994) 265-296.

Università di Roma, ed. *Atti del congresso internazionale di Diritto Canonico: la Chiesa dopo il Concilio*. 3 vol. Milan, 1972.

Urru, A. "Ministro straordinario del battesimo: fondamento di tale potestà." In *Questioni canoniche*, Studia Universitatis S. Thomæ in Urbe 22, ed. Pontificia Università S. Tommaso d'Aquino.

———. *Sanzioni penali nella Chiesa*. 4th ed. Rome, 1996.

Urrutia, F. J. "Canones præliminares codicis (CIC). Comparatio cum canonibus præliminaribus Codicis Canonum Ecclesiarum Orientalium (CC)." *Periodica* 81 (1992) 153-177.

———. *Les normes générales*. Paris, 1994.

Vadakumcherry, J. "Il diritto matrimoniale nei Codici orientale e latino." In *Il Diritto Canonico Orientale nell'ordinamento ecclesiale*, Studi Giuridici 34, ed. K. Bharanikulangara, 142-163.

Vasil', C. "Norme riguardanti l'edizione dei libri liturgici." In *Ius Ecclesiarum vehiculum caritatis*, ed. Congregazione per le Chiese Orientali, 363-391.

Ventura, M. "Spunti di comparazione in diritto penale canonico dopo la promulgazione del Codice delle Chiese Orientali." *Il Diritto Ecclesiastico* 107 (1996) 637-666.

Vere, P. J. "Non-Baptized Person as Minister of Baptism." In *Roman Replies and CLSA Advisory Opinions 2000*, eds. F. S. Pedone and J. I. Donlon, 163-164.

Vivó Undabarrena, E. "El nuevo derecho matrimonial oriental (estudio comparativo): doctrina general e impedimentos." In *Incontro fra canoni d'oriente e d'occidente*, Atti del Congresso internazionale, ed. R. Coppola, 2:315-379.

Walkowiak, D. J. "Sacramental Law and the Code of Canons of the Eastern Churches: an Inter-Ecclesial Perspective." *CLSA Proceedings* 55 (1993) 214-233.

Woestman, W. H. *Sacraments. Initiation, Penance, Anointing of the Sick*. Ottawa, 1996.

Wuyts, A. "Le droit des personnes dans l'Église orientale." *Nouvelle Revue Théologique* 80 (1958) 359-383.

Zuzek, I. "Che cosa è una Chiesa, un Rito Orientale?" *Seminarium* 27 (1975) 263-277.

———. "Un Codice per una *Varietas Ecclesiarum*." In *Studi sul Codex Canonum Ecclesiarum Orientalium*, ed. S. Gherro, 1-32.

———. "Common Canons and Ecclesial Experience in the Oriental Catholic Churches." In *Incontro fra canoni d'oriente e d'occidente*, Atti del Congresso internazionale, ed. R. Coppola, 1:21-56.

———. "La giurisdizione dei vescovi ortodossi dopo il Concilio Vaticano II." *La Civiltà Cattolica* 122/2 (1971) 550-562.

———. "Incidenza del 'Codex Canonum Ecclesiarum Orientalium' nella storia moderna della Chiesa universale." In *Ius in vita et in missione Ecclesiæ*, ed. Pontificium Consilium de Legum Textibus Interpretandis, 677-735.

———. *Index analyticus Codicis Canonum Ecclesiarum Orientalium* (Kanonika 2). Rome, 1992.

———. "La 'Lex Ecclesiæ Fundamentalis' et les deux Codes." *L'Année Canonique* 40 (1998) 19-48.

———. "Presentazione del 'Codex Canonum Ecclesiarum Orientalium.'" *Monitor Ecclesiasticus* 95 (1990) 591-612.

———. "Riflessioni circa la Costituzione Apostolica 'Sacri Canones' (18 ottobre 1990)." *Apollinaris* 65 (1992) 53-64.

———. *Understanding the Eastern Code*, Kanonika 8. Rome, 1997.